Praise for

Shakespeare Was a Woman

and Other Heresies

"Elizabeth Winkler's *Shakespeare Was a Woman and Other Heresies* is one of the most engaging, riveting, scholarly, and challenging whodunits anyone with an interest in theater, human psychology, literature, and history can hope to read. Following in the footsteps of Henry James, Mark Twain, Mark Rylance, and innumerable other skeptics, Winkler writes about what has been essentially a centuries-old theological dispute about the origins of Shakespeare's astounding body of work like a Shakespearean drama itself: full of complex characters with false reputations and deceptive appearances."

—Bessel van der Kolk, MD, *New York Times* bestselling author of *The Body Keeps the Score*

"A fascinating detective story . . . whose irreverence is part of its appeal."

—*The Guardian*

"Lively. . . . Winkler is a crackerjack researcher, deftly laying out the myriad questions, arguments, and mysteries swirling around Shakespeare."

—*The Washington Post*

"No, Elizabeth Winkler doesn't reveal the true identity of the writer Ruth Bader Ginsburg termed 'the literary genius known by the name William Shakespeare.' But she does explain how we've wound up with, among an army of others, a republican Shakespeare and a monarchist Shakespeare, a Shakespeare who hated his wife and one who loved his, a Shakespeare who wrote all the plays and a Shakespeare who could not write at all. Along her intrepid way, Winkler charts, with refreshing clarity, the much-contested ground underfoot, studded with flinty convictions, gnarled fictions, and a surprising number of land mines."

—Stacy Schiff, Pulitzer Prize–winning author of *The Revolutionary*

"Elizabeth Winkler is blessed with the clear-eyed wit of a heroine in a Shakespearean comedy. Her undoing of the fools in the forest of the authorship question is iconoclasm *As You Like It*—joy to behold, lesson for us all."

—Lewis Lapham, founder of *Lapham's Quarterly*

"An extraordinarily brilliant and scholarly work, written with an unyielding sleuthing instinct and sparkling with pleasurably naughty moments. This page-turner is mesmerizing."

—André Aciman, PhD, *New York Times* bestselling author of *Call Me by Your Name*

"As a literary-investigative reporter, Elizabeth Winkler . . . pursues her quarry with tenacity and grips it like a dog with a bone."

—*The Wall Street Journal*

"A fascinating read. Winkler boldly pushes against traditional boundaries of gender and identity to show that meaning can be constructed in many different ways."

—Amanda Foreman, PhD, internationally bestselling author of *Georgiana*

"A perfect introduction to a world of unbridled passion, retribution, and intrigue—I refer of course to the Shakespeare authorship question. Brilliant and mind-blowing."

—Karen Joy Fowler, *New York Times* bestselling author of *Booth*

"The book has the pull of detective fiction. . . . [Winkler] is an Alice in Wonderland pursuing a Cheshire Cat who maddeningly disappears."

—*The Village Voice*

"[An] entertaining survey of the history of the authorship debate."

—*The Telegraph* (UK)

"Winkler's prose is smooth, her jokes land, her synthesis of the considerable amounts of research she's done is gracefully rendered, and she has a keen eye for the foibles of Shakespeare biographers."

—*Slate*

"Winkler's book is eye-opening: she clearly shows the increasing schism between English literature departments, who accept Shakespeare's authorship without question or discussion, and other departments who may also claim to have expertise in the area."

—*Sydney Morning Herald*

"A fascinating indictment of incurious scholars."

—*The Irish Times*

"Enormously entertaining as a comedy of manners about academic scholarship . . . [with] characters straight out of a Philip Roth campus novel."

—*Washington Free Beacon*

"Deeply researched and fearlessly reported, this book takes on what Winkler terms the 'literary malpractice' and mob mentality of elite Shakespeare scholars invested in maintaining comfortable yet deeply problematic narratives. *Shakespeare Was a Woman and Other Heresies* is, at heart, an impassioned call to reexamine history and evidence (and lack thereof)—and to pursue scholarly truth even in the face of vicious opposition."

—Lesley Blume, *New York Times* bestselling author of *Everybody Behaves Badly*

"Probing and smart, this is sure to stir up lively debate. . . . [Winkler] uses the controversy to serve up thoughtful meditations on the role of the author, the objectivity of biography, and the limits of scholarly study."

—*Publishers Weekly* (starred review)

"A shrewd, entertaining journey into a literary quagmire."

—*Kirkus Reviews*

"Fun to read. Here, dusty, scholarly disputes seem scandalous, high-stakes, and thrilling."

—*The New Statesman* (UK)

"Brilliantly combines literary criticism and journalism to expose the social, cultural, and institutional dimensions of the taboo against questioning Shakespeare's identity . . . *Shakespeare Was a Woman and Other Heresies* may represent something of an 'emperor's-no-clothes' moment for academia, for it reveals a startling absence at the center of western literary culture which few of its professed leaders seem willing to confront."

—*Winnipeg Free Press*

"Witty, illuminating . . . [and] enthralling."

—*New Zealand Listener*

"A must-read for those obsessed with the bard."

—*Booklist*

"Winkler's splendid book offers hours of absolutely fascinating reading on the subject of what is essentially academic censorship."

—*Critical Stages*

"Engaging. . . . Winkler's prose is readable and often witty, landing some good blows."

—*The Spectator* (UK)

"So erudite and learned about British culture and history that you wonder how an American managed to parse it all."

—*Broadway Direct*

"Tremendously exciting."

—*Strong Words* (UK)

"Delightful! *Shakespeare Was a Woman and Other Heresies* charms from beginning to end."

—Anonymous, author of *Becoming Duchess Goldblatt*

"Blending interviews with those on both sides of the question with a concise history of the debate, Winkler's book is engaging and stimulating from its first chapter . . . and often humorous."

—*The Age* (Australia)

How Doubting the Bard Became the Biggest Taboo in Literature

Shakespeare Was a Woman

and Other Heresies

Elizabeth Winkler

SIMON & SCHUSTER PAPERBACKS
New York London Toronto Sydney New Delhi

An Imprint of Simon and Schuster, LLC
1230 Avenue of the Americas
New York, NY 10020

First Simon & Schuster trade paperback edition April 2024

SIMON & SCHUSTER PAPERBACKS and colophon are registered trademarks of Simon & Schuster, LLC

Simon & Schuster: Celebrating 100 Years of Publishing in 2024

For information about special discounts for bulk purchases, please contact Simon & Schuster Special Sales at 1-866-506-1949 or business@simonandschuster.com.

The Simon & Schuster Speakers Bureau can bring authors to your live event. For more information or to book an event, contact the Simon & Schuster Speakers Bureau at 1-866-248-3049 or visit our website at www.simonspeakers.com.

Interior design by Lewelin Polanco

Manufactured in the United States of America

1 3 5 7 9 10 8 6 4 2

Library of Congress Cataloging-in-Publication Data has been applied for.

ISBN 978-1-9821-7126-1
ISBN 978-1-9821-7127-8 (pbk)
ISBN 978-1-9821-7128-5 (ebook)

"I have come to think of history as a game—
a game that we play with the past."

—Beverley Southgate

Contents

Shakespeare Was a Woman

and Other Heresies

Prologue

In England in the summer of 1964, an unusual case came before the courts. It involved a squabble over the will of Miss Evelyn May Hopkins and the authorship of the works of William Shakespeare. Miss Hopkins had died, leaving a third of her inheritance to the Francis Bacon Society for the purpose of finding the original manuscripts of Shakespeare's plays. She referred to them as the "Bacon-Shakespeare manuscripts," believing the true author of the works to have been Francis Bacon, the Elizabethan philosopher and statesman. The aim of finding the manuscripts was to prove that Bacon was, in fact, the author of the works attributed to Shakespeare. Her heirs were not pleased. Naturally, they preferred that the money go to themselves. Seeking to reclaim their inheritance, the heirs brought a suit against the society, arguing that Miss Hopkins's provision should be set aside on the grounds that the search would be a "wild goose chase." To support their case, they solicited the testimony of scholarly experts. The Right Honorable Richard Wilberforce, a justice of Her Majesty's High Court, presided.

Counsel for the next of kin "described it as a wild goose chase; but wild geese can, with good fortune, be apprehended," observed the justice. Many discoveries are unlikely until they are made, he pointed out: "one may think of the Codex Sinaiticus, or the Tomb of Tutankhamen, or the Dead Sea Scrolls." Wilberforce was a stolid Englishman, a former classics scholar at Oxford University who rose through Britain's legal ranks to become a senior Law Lord in the House of Lords and a member of the Queen's Privy Council. Having reviewed the evidence submitted to the court, he summarized it as follows:

"The orthodox opinion, which at the present time is unanimous, or nearly so, among scholars and experts in sixteenth and seventeenth century literature and history, is that the plays were written by William Shakespeare of Stratford-upon-Avon, actor." However, Justice Wilberforce continued, "The evidence in favour of Shakespeare's authorship is quantitatively slight. It rests positively, in the main, on the explicit statements in the First Folio of 1623, and on continuous tradition; negatively on the lack of any challenge to this ascription at the time" of the First Folio's publication. Furthermore, the justice found, "There are a number of difficulties in the way of the traditional ascription . . . a number of known facts which are difficult to reconcile. . . . [S]o far from these difficulties tending to diminish with time, the intensive search of the nineteenth century has widened the evidentiary gulf between William Shakespeare the man, and the author of the plays."

The justice went on to consider the testimony of the scholarly experts. Kenneth Muir, King Alfred Professor of English literature at the University of Liverpool, supported the plaintiffs, Miss Hopkins's aggrieved heirs. He considered it "certain" that Bacon could not have written the works of Shakespeare. Hugh Trevor-Roper, Regius Professor of Modern History at the University of Oxford, departed slightly from his English literature colleagues, taking what the justice deemed "a more cautious line." Though Professor Trevor-Roper "definitely does not believe that the works of 'Shakespeare' could have been written by Francis Bacon, he also considers that the case for Shakespeare rests on a narrow balance of evidence and that new material could upset it; that though almost all professional scholars accept 'Shakespeare's' authorship, a settled scholarly tradition can inhibit free thought, that heretics are not necessarily wrong. His conclusion is that the question of authorship cannot be considered as closed."

Justice Wilberforce agreed. The question was not closed. The evidence for Shakespeare was too slim, the problems too many. The scholars might be wrong. Even if Francis Bacon was unlikely, new material might show someone other than Shakespeare to have been the author. Whoever wrote them, the manuscripts of Shakespeare's plays had never been found. Their discovery would be "of the highest value to history and to literature," Wilberforce proclaimed. Indeed, he added, to the consternation of the plaintiffs and the Shakespeare scholars, "the revelation of a manuscript would contribute, probably decisively, to a solution to the authorship problem, and this alone is benefit enough."

Miss Hopkins's bequest to the Francis Bacon Society was upheld.

ONE

The Question That Does Not Exist

WHO HAS THE AUTHORITY TO determine the truth about the past? Usually the answer is historians. In the case of Shakespeare, it is Shakespeare scholars, a small but highly prestigious subset of English literature professors concentrated mostly in Britain and America. Their prestige derives from their specialty. They are priests not of one of the lesser gods of the English literary pantheon but of the highest god—the god who gives English literature as a discipline its very raison d'être. They act as his representatives, interpreting and mediating for the masses the meaning of Shakespeare, and so, like the priests of the sun god Apollo, they glow with the radiance cast by his rays.

Among Shakespeare scholars, the Shakespeare authorship question—the theory that William Shakespeare might not have written the works published under his name—does not exist; that is, it is not permitted. As a consequence, it has become the most horrible, vexed, unspeakable subject in the history of English literature. In literary circles, even the phrase "Shakespeare authorship question" elicits contempt—eye-rolling, name-calling, mudslinging. If you raise it casually in a social setting, someone might chastise you as though you've uttered a deeply offensive profanity. Someone else might get up and leave the room. Tears may be shed. A whip may be produced. You will be punished, which is to say, educated. Because it is obscene to suggest that the god of English literature might be a false god. It is heresy.

The heresy persists because the "difficulties in the way of the traditional ascription," as Justice Wilberforce termed them, have not been resolved. The longer scholars have tried to resolve them—the more they've learned about the man from Stratford-upon-Avon and about the plays and poems—the wider the "evidentiary gulf" has grown between the man and the works. For instance, William of Stratford had no recorded education; at most, he may have attended his local grammar school, which taught Latin grammar and arithmetic. But the works published under the name "William Shakespeare" are dazzling in their erudition, steeped in the learning of Renaissance humanism. "He was at home in the Aristotelian cosmology of his time. He had learned the new Platonic philosophy," marveled Hugh Trevor-Roper, the Oxford historian who testified in the 1964 lawsuit. "He was familiar with foreign countries, foreign affairs, foreign languages."

Another difficulty: Scholars have turned up a mass of personal records from the man's lifetime—more, it is often said, than exist for other writers of the period. They show his theatrical activities, his financial and property transactions, his lawsuits. They show that he was a businessman, an actor, a shareholder in an acting company, and a property investor. But they don't show that he wrote. As the Oxford historian Blair Worden laments, "the extent and loudness of the documentary silence are startling." This silence aggravates scholars in the extreme. "I would love to find a contemporary document that said William Shakespeare was the dramatist of Stratford-upon-Avon, written during his lifetime," Sir Stanley Wells told *Newsweek*. "That would shut the buggers up!"

Why don't the plays and poems bear any connection to the man's life? "The relationship between an artist's biography and his writing is always a difficult subject," concedes Worden, "but there can be no other important writer since the invention of printing for whom we are unable to demonstrate any relationship at all."

Why didn't Shakespeare bother to educate his children? His daughters couldn't write. One signed with what Sir Edward Maunde Thompson, paleographer and director of the British Museum, called a "painfully formed signature, which was probably the most that she was capable of doing with the pen." The other, he concluded, "could not write at all, for she signed with a mark." How could a writer—any writer, let alone the greatest writer in the English language—be indifferent to the literacy of his children?

Why didn't he mention his writing in his will? When he died, he left detailed instructions for the distribution of his assets but mentioned no books, poems, or manuscripts of any kind. At his death, only half of his plays had been published. Did he have no concern for their preservation? Why didn't he say anything about his poems—several major narrative poems, 154 sonnets? What about his library? Other men of letters passed down their books and left detailed instructions for the preservation of their works. His will bore no trace of literary interests, let alone a literary life.

And at his death in 1616, the literary world was silent. Though it was an age of effusive eulogies, there were no tributes at his passing, no mourning of his death in poems or letters. When the playwright Francis Beaumont died just seven weeks earlier, he was honored for his service to the nation with a resting place among the poets at Westminster Abbey. When the playwright Ben Jonson died in 1637, his funeral was attended by "all or the greatest part of the nobility then in town." But when Shakespeare died—crickets.

"It is exasperating and almost incredible," Hugh Trevor-Roper wrote in an essay. Shakespeare lived "in the full daylight of the English Renaissance, in the well-documented reigns of Queen Elizabeth and King James I," he emphasized. "He was connected with some of the best-known public figures in the most conspicuous court in English history. Since his death, and particularly in the last century, he has been subjected to the greatest battery of organized research that has ever been directed upon a single person. And yet the greatest of all Englishmen, after this tremendous inquisition, still remains so close a mystery that even his identity can still be doubted."

Like Juliet pining for Romeo, Trevor-Roper titled the essay, "What's in a Name?" *A rose by any other name would smell as sweet.* The authorship debate often looks like a comedy. To those who believe the author's true name has been lost, it is also a tragedy. Mostly, though, it is a romance—a love affair and a quest to uncover Shakespeare's identity.

The 1964 trial did not rule directly on the authorship question—Did he or didn't he?—but it raised the problem of authority. Were the

Shakespeare scholars called to testify to the traditional attribution, in support of Miss Hopkins's irritated heirs, infallible? Was it possible that heretics—nonspecialists—might be right? Behind the observations that "a settled scholarly tradition can inhibit free thought" and "heretics are not necessarily wrong" lay the whole history of knowledge: of truth perverted by confirmation bias and groupthink; of scholars clinging to outdated theories, contemptuous of ideas that threaten their authority; of long-held certainties rendered quaint by new knowledge; of entire fields revolutionized by heresy. The trial had the effect of displacing the authority of the scholars, making them mere witnesses—biased, partial—and putting the truth in the hands of the court, which concluded, in fact, that the truth was not certain.

Outside the civilizing order of the courtroom, the authorship question takes on the dimensions—and the absurdities—of a religious war. All sides fight in the name of God, but what is His name? After the Bible, the works of Shakespeare are the most-quoted texts in the English-speaking world. The full breadth and depth of their influence is impossible to measure, except perhaps to say that the course of history in the alternate world in which they were never written must look very different from the one we know. Like God, he is omnipresent. "Shakespeare one gets acquainted with without knowing how," observes a character in Jane Austen's 1814 novel *Mansfield Park*. "His thoughts and beauties are so spread abroad that one touches them everywhere; one is intimate with him by instinct." Another character agrees, noting that Shakespeare's passages are "quoted by everybody; they are in half the books we open, and we all talk Shakespeare, use his similes, and describe with his descriptions."

For Britons, he is a national hero, the singular representation of the English tradition. "Since England bore thee, master of human song, / Thy folk are we, children of thee," the poet laureate Robert Bridges declared in 1916, making Shakespeare at once father of the nation and Britain's favored son.

He is also Britain's greatest export, his works a "world-conquering speech, / Which surg'd as a river high-descended," Bridges continued. "And floateth the ships deep-laden with merchandise / Out on the windy seas to traffic in foreign climes." It is sometimes said that if Little England had not attained the global reach of empire to become Great Britain, Shakespeare would never have become our "universal poet." But the case might equally be made that Little England could never have become Great Britain without Shakespeare: his "world-conquering speech" floated the ships; having made the language, the literature, the culture, and even, through his history plays, the history, he helped make the empire. Today children in India study Shakespeare's plays. When China's authoritarian leader, Xi Jinping, issued a list of recommended books for his citizens to read, he devoted an entire category to Shakespeare. *Macbeth* was adapted to Zulu and *Love's Labour's Lost* staged in Kabul in the face of Taliban threats. A dozen replicas of the Globe Theatre have been built around the world, and the Globe's *Hamlet* toured to 197 countries. In 2011 a poll commissioned by the think tank Demos found that Shakespeare is the cultural symbol of which Britons are most proud—ahead of the monarchy, the armed forces, the Beatles, and the Union Jack. When Volodymyr Zelensky appealed to the UK Parliament for aid in the midst of the Russian invasion, he astutely invoked this pillar of British nationalism. "The question for us now is to be or not to be," the Ukrainian president observed, "this Shakespearean question."

Americans have in many ways adopted Shakespeare as one of their own—a representation of the American dream; a boy who came from nothing and made himself immortal. When Thomas Jefferson made a pilgrimage to Shakespeare's birthplace in Stratford-upon-Avon in 1786, he "fell upon the ground and kissed it." John Adams, who accompanied Jefferson, sliced a "relic" from the armchair said to have belonged to the playwright. "Let me search for the clue which led great Shakespeare into the labyrinth of human nature," he wrote in his diary. In 1787 George Washington escaped political haggling over the new constitution to watch a production of *The Tempest.* Touring America in the 1830s, the French writer Alexis de Tocqueville noted: "There is hardly a pioneer's hut which does not contain a few odd volumes of Shakespeare." Abraham Lincoln kept three tomes on his desk at the White House: the Bible, a copy of the US statutes, and Shakespeare. While Lincoln turned to Shakespeare for wisdom and direction, his assassin used Shakespeare to justify murder. John Wilkes Booth, a Shakespearean actor, fancied himself a Brutus and saw Lincoln as Caesar—a tyrant to be overthrown. "But alas!" he wrote in a letter before the assassination, "Caesar must bleed for it," summoning *Julius Caesar* to rationalize his shooting of the president. Shakespeare had become a moral authority to be invoked, like God, on opposing sides of any conflict.

"The hold which Shakespeare has acquired and maintained upon minds so many and so various . . . is one of the most noteworthy phenomena in the history of literature," observed the nineteenth-century poet James Russell Lowell. He suspected it had something to do with the feeling that Shakespeare understands us better than we understand ourselves. For "the more we have familiarized ourselves with the operations of our own consciousness, the more do we find, reading [Shakespeare], that he has been beforehand with us, and that, while we have been vainly endeavoring to find the door of his being, he has searched every nook and cranny of our own," he wrote. Shakespeare *knows* us as only an omniscient being—as only God—could know us. It followed, then, that when the directors of the Great Texas Fair of 1936 sought to erect their Shakespeare Theatre, a replica of the Globe, they sent a cable to Stratford requesting earth from Shakespeare's garden and water from the Avon River with which to consecrate it. A group of Stratford citizens dutifully fulfilled the request, gathering the sacred dirt and holy water and sending them to Dallas, where they were ritually sprinkled on the faux Globe.

Like other theological disputes, the authorship dispute is over origins: Where did these works come from? What circumstances, influences, and qualities of mind made them possible? What was this genius from which they emanated? Seeing the origin of the works in the man from Stratford, traditionalists are, in the terminology of the dispute, Stratfordians—defenders of the faith; orthodox believers in the one true church. The heretics banging their ninety-five theses against the church door are anti-Stratfordians—against Stratford as the origin—but their quest for truth has splintered them into sects, sometimes warring but loosely affiliated under the sign of their dissent from orthodoxy: Baconians, Marlovians,

Oxfordians, Sidneyans, Nevillians, and others, each named according to their god. Like the Protestant Reformers, they seek a purer form of faith; a return to the true religion, before it was corrupted by the creeds and dogmas and vanities of men.

The authorship question is, in the fashion of religious wars, a messy, ugly dispute. No one takes kindly to the denial of his god. Shakespeare scholars—which is to say the Shakespearean priesthood; the ordained and professionalized ranks of Stratfordians—decry the snobbery in the view that a glover's son could not have written the works of Shakespeare. (Was not a carpenter's son the savior of mankind?) In the same breath, they resent the affront to their apostolic authority by what they see as a rabble of amateurs and cranks. Those meddling kids! Anti-Stratfordians resent the injustice of such characterizations. To the charge of snobbery, they respond that no one is claiming a glover's son could not write the works—only that no one, however genius, is born with knowledge. It must be acquired through education and access to books. Other writers of humble origins left records of how they acquired their knowledge—tracks by which we can follow, however faintly, the course of their development. How did the glover's son do it *without leaving a trace*?

Stratfordians and anti-Stratfordians alike agree that Shakespeare is a mystery. "Shakespeare's knowledge of classics and philosophy has always puzzled his biographers," admitted the scholar E. K. Chambers. "A few years at the Stratford Grammar School do not explain it." Others have tried to resolve the puzzle by downplaying Shakespeare's erudition. The plays merely "*looked* learned," especially "to the less literate public," insisted Harvard's Alfred Harbage. But the plays have sent scholars writing whole books on the law in Shakespeare, medicine in Shakespeare, theology in Shakespeare. Shakespeare and astronomy. Shakespeare and music. Shakespeare and the classics. Shakespeare and the Italian novella. Shakespeare and the French language. "The creative artist absorbs information from the surrounding air," Harbage assured his readers, floating a theory of education by osmosis. Throwing up his hands, Samuel Schoenbaum, one of the twentieth century's leading Shakespeare scholars, resolved the conundrum by explaining that "Shakespeare was superhuman," an explanation that is, of course, no explanation at all. Shakespeare is, it would seem, a miracle that must be accepted on faith. "How this particular man produced the works that dominate the cultures of much of the world almost four hundred years after his death remains one of life's mysteries," reads the introduction to the Folger Shakespeare Library's edition of the plays, "and one that will continue to tease our imaginations as we continue to delight in his plays and poems." The suspicion arises that Shakespeare's godlike status owes something to this mystery, this perfect unknowability. For if he knows us as only God knows us, we know him about as well as we know God.

"It is a great comfort, to my way of thinking, that so little is known concerning the poet," Charles Dickens wrote in 1847. "The life of Shakespeare is a fine mystery, and I tremble everyday lest something turn up." The mystery inspires our awe, is part of what we love about Shakespeare, is part of what, in fact, *makes* Shakespeare Shakespeare. "Others abide our question. Thou art free"—eternally eluding us—wrote the poet Matthew Arnold. "We ask and ask—Thou smilest and art still, / Out-topping knowledge." Shakespeare is inscrutable, a sphinx, a Mona Lisa, smirking at our efforts to know him, smirking at all he knows that we do not. Yet we do not begrudge him his secrecy. "Thou, who didst the stars and sunbeams know, / Self-school'd, self-scann'd, self-honour'd, self-secure, / Didst tread on earth unguess'd at.—Better so!"

Shakespeare satisfies our need for the sacred, for something that surpasses our ability to understand. Henry James suggested that the unknowability comforts us even, writing of moments "in this age of sound and fury, of connections in every sense, too maddeningly multiplied, when we are willing to let it pass as a mystery, the most soothing, cooling, consoling too perhaps, that ever was." And yet, he added, there are others "when, speaking for myself, its power to torment us intellectually seems scarcely to be borne."

Anti-Stratfordians have not been willing to let the mystery pass. They want to know the man who so completely and entirely knows us, to touch the face of God. What they cannot stand is the possibility that we have been kneeling at the wrong altar, paying homage to a false idol.

⁂

Was it Francis Bacon, as Miss Hopkins suspected? In 1603, Bacon wrote a mysterious letter to a lawyer who was riding to meet the new king, James I. Bacon asked the lawyer to speak well of him to the king and defend his name "if there be any biting or nibbling at it in that place." Then he signed off with this wish: "So desiring you to be good to concealed poets."

Who was the concealed poet? Was it Christopher Marlowe, a playwright and government agent who disappeared in 1593—reportedly murdered—just weeks before "Shakespeare" emerged? What about William Stanley, the 6th Earl of Derby? A Jesuit spy sent in 1599 to probe whether the earl might help advance the Roman Catholic cause in England reported back that Stanley was "busied only in penning comedies for the common players." But no comedies under the Earl of Derby's name have ever been found. Or was it Edward de Vere—far and away the favorite candidate today—the eccentric 17th Earl of Oxford, who traveled through the precise areas of northern Italy with which Shakespeare seems most familiar? A theory of group authorship has arisen, too, with a woman tossed in to account for the plays' "feminine intuition": Mary Sidney Herbert, the Countess of Pembroke, a celebrated patron of writers who turned her country estate into a literary salon—a "paradise for poets."

The authorship question is a massive game of Clue played out over the centuries. The weapon is a pen. The crime is the composition of the greatest works of literature in the English language. The suspects are numerous. The game is played in back rooms and basements, beyond the purview of the authorities. Now and then, reports of the game surface in the press, and the authorities (by which I mean the Shakespeare scholars) are incensed. They come in blowing their whistles and stomping their feet, waving their batons wildly. They denounce the game in the strongest terms, attacking not only the legitimacy of the question but also the sanity of those pursuing it. Shrieking that there is no game to be played, the authorities overturn the board and send the pieces flying. Their protest is too much. It is so excessive, so disproportionate to its object, that it only confirms for the players the worthiness of their pursuit, bestowing on it a sense of sacred purpose. When the authorities finally retreat, red faced and sweaty, exhausted by too much baton waving, the players quietly set the board straight and continue playing, fortified by their oppression like some persecuted religious sect.

Like any infamous, unsolved crime, the authorship mystery has attracted a certain class of cranks who sometimes call in claiming to have arrived, irrefutably, at the elusive solution. The authorities seize on these figures, painting all skeptics with the same brush. Those who doubt Shakespeare suffer from an "intellectual aberration," Sir Sidney Lee declared in the early twentieth century; it was "madhouse chatter," a "foolish craze," "morbid psychology." But the ranks of skeptics have included many formidable minds: novelists, poets, statesmen, Supreme Court justices, scientists, and professors of history, philosophy, theater, anthropology, psychology, and, only occasionally, English. To ask Shakespeare scholars to research the authorship is "like asking the College of Cardinals to honestly research the Resurrection," wrote Robin Fox, professor of social theory at Rutgers University. At York University in Canada, a professor of theater named Don Rubin created a course on the authorship question. His colleagues in English scoffed, assuring him that no one would sign up, but there was a waiting list every year. By 2018, the University of London was offering an online course called Introduction to Who Wrote Shakespeare.

The renegades have the thrilling sense of being detectives in a real-life literary mystery. They are Sherlock Holmes and Dr. Watson, working to outsmart the bumbling professionals of Scotland Yard. The game is its own reward; the pursuit of truth an intrinsic virtue. One can get postmodern about The Truth; one can argue that The Author is merely the creation of various cultural discourses, that texts are continuously remade by the actors that perform them and the readers that consume them. But one cannot get around the fact that some person or persons set those words down on paper. Whodunit?

In 2019 I published a long essay in the *Atlantic*, "Was Shakespeare a Woman?," exploring the case for a newly proposed candidate, Emilia Bassano. Like others, I was intrigued by the plays' "feminine intuition."

Shakespeare's women are rebellious and clever, critical of women's subordinate status, quick to point out the folly of men, and adept at outwitting patriarchal controls. "Why should their liberty than ours be more?" Adriana exclaims in *The Comedy of Errors*, bemoaning the limitations of her life. Instructed that "a wife's will must be bridled by her husband's," she retorts, "There's none but asses will be bridled so!" When Beatrice's uncle suggests she find a husband in *Much Ado About Nothing*, she laughs and says, "Not till God make men of some other metal than earth. Would it not grieve a woman to be overmastered with a piece of valiant dust? To make an account of her life to a clod of wayward marl? No, Uncle, I'll none." Shakespeare's women follow their own consciences, refusing to be subdued into feminine silence, and they use language itself as a tool of liberation. "My tongue will tell the anger of my heart, / Or else my heart, concealing it, will break," Kate insists, denouncing her abusive husband, Petruchio, in *The Taming of the Shrew*. "And, rather that it shall, I will be free / Even to the uttermost, as I please, in words."

When I was a student, these voices formed a kind of chorus in my head, informing and molding my own incipient womanhood. It struck me that Shakespeare understood what it was to be female—better than most men writing today. He saw the misogyny of his time—there are plenty of misogynists in his plays—but he held that misogyny up for critical appraisal. And he created women who resist it. In *All's Well That Ends Well*, Helena, exhausted by the prospect of guarding her virginity—her only value in the world—against men whose chief policy is to "blow you up" (impregnate you) wonders, "Is there no military policy how virgins might blow up men?" "To whom should I complain?" Isabella asks in *Measure for Measure* when the judge, Angelo, threatens to rape her, "Did I tell this, who would believe me?" Women are human, like men, Emilia argues in *Othello*, just before Iago kills her:

Let husbands know
Their wives have sense like them: they see and smell
And have their palates both for sweet and sour,
As husbands have. . . .

And have not we affections?
Desires for sport, and frailty, as men have?
Then let them use us well: else let them know,
The ills we do, their ills instruct us so.

In the comedies, women often subvert the masculine order by disguising themselves as men. Portia, dressed as a lawyer, presides over Antonio's trial, outsmarting the men in *The Merchant of Venice*: "In such a habit . . . they shall think we are accomplished / With what we lack" (that is, a penis), she says with a laugh to her friend Nerissa, conscious that gender is a performance. Rosalind in *As You Like It* cross-dresses and affects the swagger of masculine confidence to escape rape and robbery on the road: "We'll have a swashing and a martial outside, / As many other mannish cowards have / That do outface it with their semblances," she tells her cousin Celia.

The female friendships in Shakespeare are remarkable: "If she be a traitor, / Why so am I," Celia declares, defying her father to join Rosalind in exile. "We still have slept together, / Rose at an instant, learn'd, play'd, eat together, / And wheresoever we went, like Juno's swans, / Still we went coupled and inseparable." Beatrice and Hero, Emilia and Desdemona, Paulina and Hermione in *The Winter's Tale*: all coupled and inseparable in their devotion, like Juno's swans. Mistresses Ford and Page in *The Merry Wives of Windsor* colluding to get their revenge on Falstaff: "Let's consult together against this greasy knight." Helena in *A Midsummer Night's Dream* recalling lovingly how she and Hermia grew together, like a double cherry, "as if our hands, our sides, voices, and minds, / Had been incorporate . . . two lovely berries moulded on one stem . . . with two seeming bodies, but one heart."

Hasn't the classic complaint against male writers been that they don't depict relationships between women, showing them only in relation to men? Though Shakespeare often drew on earlier tales and sources in writing his plays, these female friendships are often fresh inventions. In his history plays, too, he added female characters, giving powerful voices to women who were barely mentioned in the historical record. "Who intercepts me in my expedition?" Richard III demands. His mother responds:

"O, she that might have intercepted thee, / By strangling thee in her accursed womb, / From all the slaughters, wretch, that thou hast done!"

My admiration for Shakespeare's women was hardly novel. Back in 1975, as the women's movement was inching its way into the masculine halls of literary study, the Cambridge scholar Juliet Dusinberre argued that Shakespeare's drama "deserves the name feminist," for in his plays, "the struggle for women is to be human in a world which declares them only female." Another scholar, Anne Barton (the first female fellow at New College, Oxford), observed that "Shakespeare's sympathy with and almost uncanny understanding of women characters is one of the distinguishing features of his comedy, as opposed to that of most of his contemporaries. His heroines not only tend to overshadow their male counterparts, as Rosalind overshadows Orlando [in *As You Like It*], Julia Proteus [in *The Two Gentlemen of Verona*], or Viola Orsino [in *Twelfth Night*]: they adumbrate and urge throughout the play values which, with their help, will triumph in the more enlightened society of the end." In other words, when things end happily—in a more humane, understanding world—it is often because the heroines win.

At the time, these observations provoked fierce controversy. The dusty Shakespeare establishment—almost entirely male—was not pleased to have English literature's supreme genius co-opted by female scholars and declared a feminist. "I—and others—shed blood," Dusinberre reflected years later, looking back on the battle. "Shakespeare then, as now, had the status of the Bible in British culture. No one, and especially no woman . . . must make free with the sacred text." The rankled scholars were, she noted, "still immersed in preconceptions which Shakespeare discarded about the nature of women." What was the battle really about, Dusinberre wondered in retrospect.

"In the simplest terms, it was about the asking of questions. The educated world, with its cherished traditions of free speech, operates its own censors," she wrote. "Scholars can hide even from themselves their own inner censorship, a process familiar to all students of literature in the late sixteenth and early seventeenth centuries. What can and cannot be said."

Fifty years later, feminist readings have gone mainstream in Shakespeare studies, as they have in literary studies generally. It is now completely unremarkable for scholars to reflect on the moral authority of Shakespeare's heroines or the many ways in which they outwit his male characters. Like the heroines they studied, Dusinberre and her feminist comrades triumphed. But the censors—"sometimes overt . . . but more often closely concealed," Dusinberre observed—still operate in Shakespeare scholarship. The asking of certain questions remains intellectually dangerous.

For example, how did Shakespeare come to write feminist drama? Women's struggle to be human is not, historically, a subject that has held much interest for men except, perhaps, insofar as they have opposed it. What accounts for his "uncanny understanding" of women—an understanding apparently lacking in his fellow playwrights? And why, though Shakespeare wrote highly intelligent, even erudite women, did he neglect his own daughters' education? The women of the plays write letters, compose sonnets, and read Ovid. "It is striking how many of Shakespeare's women are shown reading," the Harvard scholar Stephen Greenblatt has remarked. It is striking because Shakespeare's daughters were, by all appearances, illiterate. The most dangerous question of all—the most censored, the most ridiculed—remains, of course, the one in which all of these smaller questions culminate: Did Shakespeare actually write the body of works we call Shakespeare?

I wondered if the two mysteries—how Shakespeare wrote the works and why he wrote feminist drama—might share the same answer: that the author was not an uneducated man but an educated woman, concealing herself beneath a male name, as the heroines of the plays so often disguise themselves in masculine garb. Literary history is strewn with women whose authorship was hidden, even into the nineteenth and twentieth centuries: George Eliot (Mary Ann Evans); Currer, Ellis, and Acton Bell (Charlotte, Emily, and Anne Brontë); George Sand (Amantine Lucile Aurore Dupin); Jane Austen, whose name appeared only after her death. In France, Colette's first four novels, which recount the semiautobiographical coming of age of a young woman, were published—absurdly—under her husband's name. Women have used pen names for the obvious reasons—to be taken seriously, to improve their commercial marketability. In the Renaissance, they had an even greater incentive: appearing in print as a woman carried a moral stigma. The poet Richard Lovelace wrote, for example, of a woman who "Powders a Sonnet as she does her hair, / Then prostitutes them both to publick Aire." To publish as a woman—to sell your words in the marketplace—was immodest, a kind of prostitution.

⁂

I wrote the *Atlantic* article in a spirit of inquiry and open-minded skepticism, questioning the received wisdom about Shakespeare but not making any definitive claims about the woman's role. Never mind. I had cast doubt on Shakespeare, and that, to some, was unacceptable.

The article went online on a Friday morning in May, climbing quickly to the website's number one "most read" spot. It sat there all afternoon and evening and into Saturday, which was when the trouble began. My phone, which had been buzzing periodically with Twitter notifications, began buzzing constantly like the demonic device (it now became clear to me) it really was. The buzzing meant someone was tweeting at me. At first, they had been cheery tweets, enthusiastically sharing the article. Then, quite sharply, they turned sour. By Sunday, I was besieged by a (mostly male) army of Twitter trolls, and the sudden, jarring buzzing became a kind of Chinese water torture sending little jolts of dread through my fraying nerves. Shakespeare's defenders had arrived, many of them tweeting under pseudonymous names—an irony to which they seemed oblivious. I thought about silencing the notifications but did not, stupidly needing to know exactly what was being said.

As it turned out, I need not have stayed on Twitter to follow the discourse, for the outrage flowed fluently off the platform and into several attack articles. In the online magazine *Quillette* a British journalist named Oliver Kamm accused me of "conspiracism," associated me with Holocaust deniers (my crime being the "denial" of Shakespeare), and called for the *Atlantic* to retract my essay. *Shakespeare Magazine* suggested I suffered from "Shakespeare derangement syndrome." An article in the *Week* found that I was in the grip of "neurotic fantasies." The *Spectator* took a sarcastic, ridiculing tone: "'Was Shakespeare a Woman?,' Elizabeth Winkler asks in the new issue of the *Atlantic.* Of course he was." *The Federalist* began by dismissing the article as a "crazy-sounding" conspiracy theory before adding, oddly, that it was "well worth reading."

I was deranged! I was neurotic! I was denying Shakespeare! This was very serious indeed.

The *Atlantic* responded by commissioning a range of responses to my article—an unusual measure, provoked by the ferocity of the Internet reaction. Some of the responses were supportive. "I'm absolutely certain that women had a hand in the writing of many plays performed in his [Shakespeare's] theater," wrote Phyllis Rackin, a professor from the University of Pennsylvania and past president of the Shakespeare Association of America. Of course, their names, she cautioned, might be impossible to retrieve, explaining: "Numerous reasons, ranging from social propriety to commercial marketability, existed for concealing the fact that a woman had a hand in writing a play." David Kastan of Yale University acknowledged that Shakespeare did not work alone and that it was "not impossible" that Bassano had worked with him. And Mark Rylance, the former artistic director of Shakespeare's Globe, emphasized that "Shakespeare's women far surpass in their variety and humanity the writing of women characters by any other dramatist." He urged readers to continue questioning the authorship of the plays and called out the "literary thuggery" of Shakespeare's defenders—those "ad hominem attacks delivered in a condescending moan as a defense of what is presented as legitimate Shakespearean scholarship."

Some complaints in this register came from Professor James Shapiro of Columbia University. "To speculate about the authorship of Shakespeare's plays is to pursue conspiracy theories," he scolded in the *Atlantic*, equating me with Obama birthers and anti-vaxxers and linking to the *Quillette* article (penned by his friend Oliver Kamm) that had associated me with Holocaust deniers. He offered a few tendentious arguments in defense of Shakespeare's authorship and snidely challenged me to disprove them. ("Good luck with that.") Then he added that there was "no stigma attached to a woman writing or publishing a play," apparently unaware of the rich, centuries-long history of women writing under male names. To prove his point, he cited the only original play published by a woman in Renaissance England, *The Tragedy of Mariam*, which appeared in 1613—after Shakespeare had ceased writing—and only under her initials, E. C., a detail that itself suggested the existence of the stigma. He neglected to add that the play never saw the stage; it was relegated to private reading.

"I once found conspiracy theories like this mildly amusing. I no longer do," Shapiro wrote. "I hope Winkler abandons her authorship fantasies." In closing, he invited me to improve my understanding of Shakespeare by attending a performance of New York City's Shakespeare in the Park—where he sits as "Shakespeare scholar in residence"—as though I had never read or seen a Shakespeare play before.

On Twitter, Shakespeare's defenders gloated and high-fived. One observer noted the Shakespearean comedy of it all, writing, "Whoever he or she was, 'Shakespeare' would have enjoyed the debate." It was true. Shakespeare reveled in parodies of patronizing scholars, puffed up on their own authority; in fools who turn out to be fonts of wisdom; in disguises and mistaken identities and things not being what they seem. But I was too shocked at the time to enjoy the comedy. As a young journalist still building my reputation, it was mortifying and bewildering to be compared to Holocaust deniers and anti-vaxxers. If I had known in advance just how brutal the attacks would be, I would probably have pulled the article. I was *deranged*, *neurotic*, *a conspiracy theorist*, *a fantasist*.

There was nothing particularly new about the name-calling. It was the same language Sir Sidney Lee had used a century before ("madhouse chatter," "foolish craze," "morbid psychology"). The language betrayed a lack of confidence in their own position. Instead of arguing calmly from facts, they resorted to the old ad hominem attacks.

Later, when the initial shock had subsided, I realized that the responses had given me something extremely interesting. Shapiro and the others might as well have planted signs that said, "Dig here." Why were they so emotional? Why was a literary question being framed as a *moral* problem—on par with Holocaust denial and vaccine refusal? "You deny the reality of Shakespeare one moment, you can deny the reality of the

Holocaust the next," a Shakespeare professor named Jonathan Bate told PBS in 2002. It was a specious comparison. The historical evidence of the Holocaust and vast scientific data on vaccines are not equivalent to the paltry evidence for Shakespeare's authorship, nor does questioning Shakespeare hold the sort of dangerous consequences that come with denying genocide or lifesaving medicine. And yet in 2011 Sir Stanley Wells declared, "It is immoral to question history and to take credit away from William Shakespeare of Stratford-upon-Avon." *Immoral* to question history—when inquiry is the very basis of the historical discipline!

I recounted this detail to Carol Symes, a Harvard-educated, Shakespeare-doubting professor of history and theater at the University of Illinois, who shook her brunette bob and laughed before pointing out that the Latin *mores* means "the customs of the ancestors." "It is immoral in that very specific sense to question this received tradition," she said. It contravenes the customs of the ancestors. Symes was exasperated by her colleagues in English departments. "I think it's unethical for a group of scholars to be confronted with perfectly plausible questions and some plausible evidence and to refuse to consider it," she told me. "I'm hard-pressed to think of another realm of scholarly discussion in which real, interesting scholarship is being done by people outside the academy, which is threatening to people in the academy." When I asked why she thinks her colleagues feel threatened rather than intrigued or interested, she suggested it might have to do with their special position. "Shakespeare scholarship has tended to be a cult of genius in its own right, and the great Shakespeare scholars have a very unique profile and megaphone," she pointed out. "There's maybe a sense in which not only does questioning Shakespeare's authorship open up a can of worms about Shakespeare, but it opens up a can of worms about who gets to do Shakespeare scholarship. They are the high priests of the cult, so if there's no cult to be a high priest of, or if you're saying that we need other people involved, then that means they're no longer on top of the pyramid."

James Shapiro is certainly on top of the pyramid. The author of award-winning books on Shakespeare, the presenter of a BBC Shakespeare documentary, and a contributor to the *New Yorker*, the *New York Times*, and other publications, he has achieved the coveted status of "public intellectual." I liked his early book *Shakespeare and the Jews* (1996), which was original and subversive, examining Jewish identity and anti-Semitism in early modern England. But his later books—popular biographies such as *1599: A Year in the Life of William Shakespeare* and *The Year of Lear: Shakespeare in 1606*—were highly fictional imaginings of Shakespeare's life. Scholars have occasionally reprimanded him. ("He plays fast and loose with discovered 'facts' and the responsible interpretation thereof," wrote a critic in the journal *Medieval & Renaissance Drama in England.*) But the newspapers have mostly fawned: "It is to be hoped that Mr. Shapiro might be persuaded to write a book for every year of Shakespeare's life," a reviewer simpered in the *Wall Street Journal.*

Annoyed that readers kept asking him if Shakespeare really wrote Shakespeare, Shapiro sought to put an end to the authorship question once and for all. In 2010 he published *Contested Will: Who Wrote Shakespeare?* The authorship question is "walled off from serious study by Shakespeare scholars," he wrote, and "remains virtually taboo in academic circles." Courageously breaking the taboo, Shapiro took up the question only to shut it down again. "For more than two hundred years after William Shakespeare's death, no one doubted that he had written his plays," he insisted, maintaining that the authorship question was a "conspiracy theory" born in the mid-nineteenth century. To support this claim, he offered an anecdote—his discovery that a manuscript from 1805, which documented early doubts about Shakespeare, was a forgery. In fact, the forgery had been unmasked by an anti-Stratfordian, a physicist named John Rollett, but Shapiro gave the impression that he had unmasked it himself. Secure in the conviction that no one before the 1840s doubted Shakespeare, he wondered: "Why, after two centuries, did so many people start questioning whether Shakespeare wrote the plays?" (One might similarly ask: Why, after so many centuries, did people start questioning whether the sun revolved around the earth?) The rest of the book unfolds as a search for the motives that drive such deviant thinking. Shapiro argues from two premises. The first is his own belief: "I happen to believe that William Shakespeare wrote the plays and poems attributed to him."

The second is that those who don't believe are in some way disturbed; they have "turned against Shakespeare."

What is most striking about this position is not Shapiro's belief in Shakespeare but his refusal to admit any room at all for doubt. Skepticism is usually a virtue in the scholarly world, but when it comes to Shakespeare, skepticism is a sin. It constitutes treason: "turn[ing] against Shakespeare." There can be no recognition of ambiguities or uncertainties in our construction of the past. There is only adherence to the belief, which operates like a kind of religious fundamentalism. It cannot be challenged. It is the only legitimate belief. Anything else is a "conspiracy theory."

A chapter published in an academic volume called *Teaching and Learning Practices for Academic Freedom* would later examine the rhetoric used to suppress inquiries into the authorship question. Michael Dudley, a university librarian, observed that the charge of "conspiracy theory" is used as "a mechanism of exclusion by which critical questions and claims are symbolically delegitimized . . . a reframing device that neutralizes questions about power and motive while turning the force of challenges back onto their speakers, rendering them unfit public interlocutors." The intended purpose of the charge is thus "to pejoratively call the speaker's character into question, while mischaracterizing their claims and equating them with other, totally unrelated or clearly absurd claims." By branding doubts about Shakespeare "conspiracy theories" at a time when conspiracy theories were undermining democracies worldwide, Shapiro and his allies signaled that no rational, fact-loving person should pay them any attention. And in many ways, the tactic worked. An editor at the *Atlantic* confessed to me a desire never to touch the subject again.

⁂

Amid all the buzzing, I received a message—not a tweet this time but a private message.

"Without getting tangled up in the vitriolic threads of others, I wanted to say that I enjoyed yr piece," the sender began. I looked him up. He was a professor of Renaissance literature—of Shakespeare—at what is called an "elite university." Disagreeing politely with the case for Emilia

Bassano, he launched into a discussion of the authorship question in the course of which he wrote something that Shakespeare professors are not supposed to write. "Yes, of course 'Shakespeare' could be a pen name or a scam or a committee of Bacon/Marlowe/Oxford/Henry Neville/etc.," he conceded, listing some of the alternate authorship candidates.

I was surprised. But perhaps I shouldn't have been. A survey conducted in 2007 by the *New York Times* found that 17 percent of Shakespeare professors in the United States have some doubts about who wrote Shakespeare. Few dare to breathe a word, though, of the cracks in their faith. The professor, I understood, wasn't going to say anything publicly. The threat of humiliation is a powerful deterrent, and to question Shakespeare is to face public humiliation.

As we exchanged emails, it seemed this professor was perfectly fine with letting Shakespeare be seen as the author, even if he knew it might not be true. An agnostic. "I think we've got a big enough task in figuring out what the plays are doing in themselves," he explained, although I wondered if knowing more about their author wouldn't help with that. Knowing that the Irish playwright Samuel Beckett spent many years in France helps us understand the French influences in his work. Knowing that the English playwright Tom Stoppard comes from a Jewish immigrant family gives us a deeper appreciation for why he wrote about the Holocaust. If someone discovered that Arthur Miller's plays were really written by his wife, it wouldn't change *The Crucible*, but it would probably alter interpretations of the play. D. H. Lawrence explained his decision to offer a bit of biographical background to his own collection of poetry by lamenting the absence of biographical background for Shakespeare. "If we knew a little more of Shakespeare's self and circumstance," he wrote in 1928, "how much more complete the Sonnets would be to us, how their strange, torn edges would be softened and merged into the whole body!"

The professor seemed to have concluded that the task was hopeless, that the author could not be known, and that everyone should stop trying. He poured scorn on the "endless nonsense" of the biographies. "For my part, I just wish for an end to biographies of Shakespeare, 'Shakespeare,' or whatever!" he exclaimed. "Partisans of all sides (Stratfordians and everyone else) all yearn for a certainty that it seems to me the evidence denies."

I wondered about his desire to be rid of that troublesome authorial identity—"Shakespeare, 'Shakespeare,' or whatever!"—as though the bard haunted him, stalking English departments as the ghost of Hamlet's father stalks the battlements of Elsinore Castle. "'Shakespeare' is present as an absence—which is to say, as a ghost," the Harvard professor Marjorie Garber once wrote. What haunts is the very emptiness of the authorial identity, yet it is precisely this emptiness that has proven so fruitful for scholars. Since the 1998 film *Shakespeare in Love* alone, there have been twenty-five full-length biographies of Shakespeare. As long as the center remains empty, the biographies can proliferate, each scholar manufacturing his own Shakespeare. "A great deal seems invested in *not* finding the answer," Garber observed.

Was it really not possible to know the author, or did the professor simply not *want* to? Not knowing the author granted a certain freedom. The professor could analyze the plays however he wished, could find in them whatever meanings seemed good to him. That has been the "right" of literary criticism since at least the 1940s, when the New Critics, a school of American literary scholars, announced that authorial intent was irrelevant to understanding a literary text. The idea was given further credence by later French theorists: "The death of the author is the birth of the reader," Roland Barthes declared in 1967, liberating the text from the interpretative tyranny of the author. Shakespeare's works are the quintessentially liberated texts, limitless in their possible meanings, and Shakespeare is the deadest author—always already absent, as the theorists like to say. His death has meant, above all, the birth of the scholar.

⁂

And yet despite this freedom to think anything they like, most seem to end up thinking a certain way. Earlier that year, at the annual meeting of the Shakespeare Association of America, a psychiatrist named Richard Waugaman had circulated a paper arguing that Shakespeare professors are unconsciously influenced by groupthink, a phenomenon of social psychology in which a group maintains cohesion by agreeing not to question unproven core assumptions and excluding anyone who deviates from group doctrine. Brazenly, he delivered this diagnosis *to* Shakespeare scholars. A professor of clinical psychiatry at Georgetown University and an analyst emeritus of the Washington Baltimore Center for Psychoanalysis, Waugaman treated Shakespeareans as a case study deserving of the analytic lens. Their cognitive errors, he argued, were inadvertently undermining attempts to understand the truth about the author.

"There are many cognitive errors that ensue from overconfidence in one's beliefs," he noted in the paper. "First, we mistake beliefs for facts. As a result, we are likely to engage in unconscious circular reasoning." Confirmation bias, he added, further leads us to cherry-pick evidence that confirms our beliefs and to ignore evidence that contradicts those beliefs. And the dynamics of groupthink, to which academia is not immune, encourage conformity. Scholars seek approval from leaders in their fields: journal editors, peer reviewers, department chairs, colleagues, and mentors. They fear rejection. And though Shakespeare scholars may have interpretive differences, they adhere to a fundamental set of common beliefs—their core belief being the traditional theory of authorship. "Shakespeare has been revered so much by so many people for so long that it is deeply disconcerting to be told we may have been admiring the wrong man," Waugaman noted sympathetically.

The paper never appeared in any literary journal. It was published instead in the *International Journal of Applied Psychoanalytic Studies.* Waugaman's most provocative suggestion was that scholarly attacks on authorship skeptics are the result of projection—that scholars attribute to skeptics what they cannot face in themselves. He sees the claim that skeptics are elitist snobs, for example, as a projection of their own snobbish insistence that they alone—the literary elite—can speak about Shakespeare with any authority; their accusation that skeptics are asserting a conspiracy theory as a projection of the "concerted way that Stratfordians have muzzled those who challenge their assertions"; their charge that skeptics are "deniers" of Shakespeare as a projection of their own denial of evidence suggesting a concealed author.

I met Dr. Waugaman at one of Washington's private social clubs, a beaux arts mansion surrounded by embassies and diplomatic residences. A gregarious, energetic man of seventy, Waugaman greeted me warmly. He was joined by his wife, Elisabeth, an elegant woman with a PhD in medieval French literature and a slight southern twang. We sat in the club's dining room, where the Waugamans recounted their adventures in Shakespearean heresy. He had stumbled onto the authorship question by way of his interest in Sigmund Freud, he explained. The founder of psychoanalysis was one of the earliest twentieth-century intellectuals to support the theory that Edward de Vere, the 17th Earl of Oxford, wrote the works of Shakespeare. ("The man from Stratford seems to have nothing at all to justify his claim," Freud noted, "whereas Oxford has everything.") Initially, Waugaman thought little of it, he told me. Freud had lots of eccentric ideas.

Then, in 2002 Waugaman happened upon an article about the authorship question in the *New York Times*, which mentioned Freud again as one of the prominent intellectuals who supported Oxford's claim. The more Waugaman read into the authorship question—and into the Oxfordian theory—the more reasonable the question seemed. "Everything we think and do is shaped by prior life experiences," he explained. "Practicing clinical psychoanalysis has convinced me of that. So, I could not accept the Stratfordian premise that the author's biography has no connection to the works."

I'd asked Waugaman to meet because I wanted to better understand the reactions to my article. He explained projection as a defense mechanism. "Let's say you start having nagging doubts at the edge of your awareness, and you can't shake those doubts. It's as though you"—or rather, your subconscious brain—"then say, 'Oh, I've got it. This isn't about me. This is about them. They're the ones who are elitists, conspiracy theorists, who don't know how to evaluate evidence.' The best defense is a good offense, so they cope with the weakness of their case by saying these things about us."

"You think they have nagging doubts?"

"I would say that consciously they don't allow themselves to have doubt, but if you were to wake them up from a deep sleep, it might be different." I smiled at this image of Shakespeare scholars asleep on the psychoanalyst's couch. Shakespeare's penetrating portraits of human psychology—of love, jealousy, fear, greed—heavily influenced Freud's psychoanalytic theories.

("Freud is essentially prosified Shakespeare," wrote Harold Bloom. "Shakespeare is the inventor of psychoanalysis; Freud its codifier.") Shakespeare scholarship in turn drew heavily on the writings of Freud and his followers. No graduate student in English could complete coursework without encountering Freud's case histories or *The Interpretation of Dreams*—the interpretation of the unconscious being a kind of literary criticism; an analysis of images, words, symbols. Literary criticism can also be a kind of psychoanalytic practice: an analysis of the author's desires and neuroses. In this tangle of readings and texts, there was something fitting in turning psychoanalysis on the scholars themselves. What did *they* desire, fear, or envy?

"Stratfordians must be deeply conflicted about their wish for some relevant biographical data about their author," Waugaman continued. "So I suspect their envy toward us for having far more biographical material about our candidate drives some of their intemperate attacks." A new diagnosis! Were Stratfordians *jealous* of Oxfordians?

Another place Waugaman sees projection is in the claim that skeptics don't understand genius. This erects a "false binary" between genius and education, he explained. The two "work synergistically, so that innate genius can reach its fullest potential through the best possible education." He referenced the work of Dean Keith Simonton, distinguished professor of psychology at the University of California, Davis and the world's leading expert on genius. "Too often absurdities in the traditional [Shakespeare] attribution are dismissed with hand-waving references to the presumed power of 'genius,'" Simonton wrote. "After studying geniuses for more than three decades, I can say with confidence that even geniuses do not possess such supposed mysterious powers. The real author was a genuine human being rooted deeply in a biographical past. We will never understand his genius until we know the experiences that shaped his development."

"Whoever was writing the plays had an incredible knowledge of what was happening in France," Elisabeth piped in. She had been quiet and retiring as her husband held court, but now a flood of knowledge came pouring out. She had been reading French scholars who point to Shakespeare's knowledge of French politics, geography, and literature. "I don't know how scholarship like that can be ignored. It's not because Shakespeare scholars don't know French. I think it's because it's so devastating to the traditional narrative."

The Waugamans had been attending meetings of their club's Shakespeare Group. (The club has various intellectual groups—an American history group, an economics group, a legal affairs group, and so forth—formed according to the interests of its members.) In the Shakespeare Group, the authorship question is off-limits for discussion. When Waugaman asked the group chairs—who happen to be prominent Shakespeare scholars—if the taboo could be rescinded, he was advised to form his own group. "I said I'd have lunch by myself on the fifth Thursday of the month and think heretical thoughts," he said, laughing. But other members wanted to discuss the authorship issue, too. A schism ensued. The club became home to two rival Shakespeare societies: the Shakespeare Authorship Group, which inquired into the authorship, and the Shakespeare Group, which emphatically did not.

At one point, the chairs of the Shakespeare Group argued that the existence of two Shakespeare groups was confusing to club members. How were they to know the difference? They might wander unwittingly into a meeting of the Shakespeare Authorship Group and get indoctrinated into heresy. The Shakespeare Group requested that the Shakespeare Authorship Group change its name. The leaders of the respective groups sat down for a tense, confidential meeting.

"She kept saying, 'Shakespeare belongs to us! You can't use it,'" Elisabeth recalled of one of the scholars. "How can anyone say the name 'Shakespeare' belongs to them?"

"Why was she so upset?" I asked.

"Numbers, numbers!" said Waugaman. "We had more people than they were getting at their group."

The Shakespeare Authorship Group declined to remove "Shakespeare" from its name but agreed to amend it to Shakespeare Authorship Inquiries Group, so as to minimize confusion.

Waugaman has made the authorship question his primary focus in recent years, inching his way into literary journals such as the *Renaissance Quarterly* and *Notes & Queries.* Despite fierce opposition, he keeps at it. "I hate bullies," he explained. When I confessed that I've sometimes wondered whether it *is* crazy to question Shakespeare in the face of staunch scholarly opposition, he had another psychological explanation at hand: the Stratfordian insistence that there is no question "can play with our head," he said. "It's a mild form of gaslighting."

As we parted, I asked Waugaman if his paper on projection had elicited any responses from Shakespeare scholars. The *International Journal of Applied Psychoanalytic Studies* had, in fact, run several commentaries, including one from the professor who convened the seminar at which Waugaman originally delivered his analysis. He sent me the commentary, which I read with astonishment:

"Nothing, *nothing*, generates consensus among Shakespeareans like our collective alignment against the anti-Stratfordian position," wrote Paul Menzer, a professor at Mary Baldwin University, affirming the sense in which anti-Stratfordians provide the animus, the common enemy, against which the group—Shakespeareans—cohere. "Anti-Stratfordians aim quite literally to demystify Shakespeare. And Shakespeareans don't want him demystified," he continued. "The disparity between the origins and the accomplishment generates much of the torque that powers our tenacious interest in the 'Man from Stratford.' And just one of the things that this genius transcended was his humble origins, which Oxfordians would deprive us of. And so, the Oxfordian position doesn't just 'solve the mystery' of Shakespeare's accomplishment, doesn't just demystify the man, it deprives the Shakespeare community of its primary source of power. . . . In less hyperbolic terms, anti-Stratfordians spoil the fun. They provide an answer to a question that we don't want answered. They provide the final pieces to a puzzle we'd prefer to keep on solving. How did a young man from the depths of Warwickshire *scale* the heights of literary fame, armed with nothing more than a grammar school education? Well, he didn't. Instead, an extremely well-educated, well-off, well-traveled, and well-connected young aristocrat wrote the plays. His well-documented life explains *everything*, in fact, and in so doing leaves little room for speculation. And . . . the study of Shakespeare is a speculative act. By urging us to look not at the murky image of Shakespeare but the clearly defined one of Oxford, the anti-Stratfordians deprive us of the pleasure of looking altogether."

In closing, Menzer invoked the Hindu principle of darshan: the act of divine seeing. "This was what Hindus went to the temple for: to see their god. The more attention conferred on a god, the greater its power grows. We make our gods visible by looking at them. And Shakespeare might seem a bit like this, drawing his power from constant attention . . . But in a real way, Shakespeare is the anti-darshan. The more we try to see him, the harder we look, the more we fail to bring him clearly into focus. And it is that obscurity, that fuzziness, that blur where we seem to desire focus that keeps us peering. We don't actually want to see Shakespeare, we just want to keep on looking."

⁂

In England, William Leahy, a professor of Shakespeare at Brunel University, did the unthinkable: he defected from the faith. Those who are certain that the man from Stratford wrote the plays are "involved in a system of belief," he wrote in 2010. Given the paucity of evidence, it is "only possible for anyone to say, 'I *believe* Shakespeare of Stratford wrote the plays'; it is not possible—or at least not legitimate—to say, 'I *know* Shakespeare of Stratford wrote the plays.'" But the effects of this belief are profound, he emphasized. "They determine the very 'realms of truth' of this entire field of investigation; they define what is possible or not possible to say; they confer authority on some and deny authority to others; further, they enable individual researchers to be regarded as inspirational and others as idiotic. In short, this belief determines the truth."

Leahy is a mild-mannered man, with thick-framed glasses and tightly cut gray hair. For years, he was "just your normal, bog-standard scholar," he told me, publishing papers on Shakespeare's history plays. "Very orthodox publications in orthodox journals." In 2005 the *New Statesman*, a British weekly, asked him to respond to Mark Rylance's comments on the authorship. Rylance, then the artistic director of the Globe, is an open Shakespeare skeptic. The *Times Higher Education Supplement* asked him to write more on the subject, so Leahy attended one of Rylance's authorship conferences at the Globe. "I remember asking really skeptical questions. But I found some of the talks very engaging," he said. "I decided to do some proper research into the authorship question itself."

At Brunel, Leahy created the Shakespeare Authorship Studies program, he explained, because much of the research being done on the authorship question is of the highest quality. (Some of it is less so, he admitted, and the weaker research undermines the better research.) Also, because traditional Shakespeare scholarship is, to some extent, "indebted" to the ideas of authorship skeptics. He pointed to the new research on Shakespeare's coauthors. For most of the twentieth century, it was a kind of heresy to suggest that the Bard did not write the plays alone. Now it's accepted, and scholars of "stylometry," as the field is called, occupy themselves in teasing out different hands from different bits of the plays. To Leahy, that development is one effect of the authorship question, though one that remains unacknowledged by the academic establishment.

News of the new Authorship Studies program—the first of its kind—was reported around the world, prompting Sir Stanley Wells to write to Brunel's vice chancellor that Leahy was damaging the university's reputation. "They really, really went for it," said Leahy. "I'm fed up with posh people telling me I'm a snob. I come from a working-class background. And anyway, it's not a scholarly argument. It's refusing to engage with the argument by throwing out this abuse." He reflected on the ways people identify with Shakespeare, projecting themselves onto the vacuum of the author. At a conference, he recalled seeing a famous Shakespeare scholar dressed a bit like Shakespeare. "People find themselves in Shakespeare. Maybe I do as well," Leahy admitted. "Shakespeare as a kind of antiauthoritarian, a kind of renegade, a dissident, maybe. I've never thought that through," he added after a pause, "but I'm open to that analysis of myself as well."

⁂

Months later, in the midst of the coronavirus pandemic, the agnostic professor reached out again. He had "managed to get the plague thing after giving a lecture in Singapore," he wrote, but was now recovered. Did I want to come to campus for a socially distanced outdoor lunch? I was perplexed. I had been excommunicated from the church. I was an apostate to the faith. Why did he want to meet with me? Naturally, I went.

The train was almost entirely empty. I felt weirdly like a student again, traveling back to school after a holiday. I had, not so long ago, been a very dutiful English literature student at a university very much like the one toward which I was heading. I spent long evenings reading my professors' publications on *Hamlet* and spilled out of lectures on George Eliot breathless with the excitement of some epiphanic insight. I won department awards. I was earnest and probably intolerable.

Though I had heard, vaguely, that there was a question around Shakespeare's authorship, I didn't give the question much thought. It was never addressed in my lectures or seminars. There was no discussion of Shakespeare's education or influences. For all intents and purposes, there was no author. The plays were self-generated, like the universe itself, exploding out of nothing. The unspoken sentiment seemed to be that, while *of course* Shakespeare wrote Shakespeare, it also did not matter *too much* who wrote Shakespeare. What mattered were the works. It was trivial, tawdry even, to wonder about the artist—to concern yourself with the mundane details of biography—when we had the art.

Sometimes this sentiment finds open articulation. "Who wrote Shakespeare? I don't care," Gregory Doran, the artistic director of the Royal Shakespeare Company, told *The Guardian*. "Ultimately we've got this fantastic body of plays, and I don't care who he, she, or they were in a way because we've got them."

This show of indifference is a popular response to the authorship question—a way of side-stepping an unpleasant dispute, hiding cowardice beneath a claim of incuriosity, or perhaps merely surrendering to a mystery one never expects to solve. It also implies that everything one really needs to know about the author—the author's essential spirit—is contained in the works anyway, as the essential nature of God resides in his Word. "Although Shakespeare is so elusive, because so protean, ever changing from one character to another, his spirit permeates the plays," wrote the scholar F. E. Halliday, "and we read them not only for the poetry and the people we meet there, but also for the man he was."

Shakespeare is his texts, a man dissolved into language, word made flesh, flesh made word. One does not need to look for the author, for he is right there! In every line of his works. "Shakespeare" thus becomes a placeholder for the unknown, a name for an absence, even as inquiries into the absence are forbidden.

I met the professor on the quad outside the English Department. He looked like a stock character of the literature professor, with a trimmed beard and a furrowed brow—the sort of professor one sees in movies set on leafy campuses studded with Gothic architecture. Having spent most of his career on one leafy campus, he had transferred some years before to the equally leafy campus on which we found ourselves. Call it Yarvardton, if you like, as in Yale, Harvard, Princeton. It does not matter what it's called. He would rather I not disclose it to you anyway.

The professor parked his bike, and we strolled to a nearby restaurant. The campus was practically deserted. We passed a graduate student on a lawn chair, teaching through a laptop set on his knees. The professor talked wryly of trying to write a book while parenting his homebound children.

Over lunch I asked him, "If you had a graduate student who seriously wanted to do something on the authorship, what would you tell him?"

"I'd say, 'Hold off. Write something else first. Then when you get tenure, you can write about the authorship.' "

"But even tenured professors don't write about the authorship," I pressed him.

"The industry takes over," the professor said with a shrug. "From the top to the bottom—the fat sums for best-selling Shakespeare biographies to the actors in local Shakespeare productions. They don't want to overturn the applecart, which is treating them quite well."

"But do you think universities *should* allow research into the authorship?"

"Absolutely, of course. Why not?"

Why not, indeed? Where did our certainty in Shakespeare come from? *Was* there a concealed author? If so, who? Why vanish so completely? Henry James looked on the authorship mystery as a piece of *Tempest*-like enchantment. But even Prospero's magic, that sweet illusion he spins by "some vanity of mine art," eventually comes undone. Was our belief in Shakespeare perhaps already disintegrating, little holes appearing in the fabric and then growing wider and wider? Was this why scholars were so disproportionately angry, so zealously adamant about their rightness? "When we feel ourselves losing ground in a fight, we often grow more rather than less adamant about our claims—not because we are so sure that we are right, but because we fear that we are not," writes Kathryn Schulz in *Being Wrong: Adventures in the Margin of Error*. "Remember the Warner Brothers coyote, the one who runs off the cliff but doesn't fall until he looks down? Certainty is our way of not looking down." I had a sudden vision of Shakespeare professors running together off a cliff, clutching their books, refusing to look down.

We talked about the professor's book, and we talked about mine, which was then only beginning to form in my head. Should I write it? Did I dare? The taboo was alluring. Still, my contrarian instincts ran up against my old need to win my teachers' praise. Sitting with the professor I cannot name outside the gates of the university I cannot reveal, I realized that I was in some way seeking his blessing, still wanting to be the good little student even as I pursued a question that good little students do not pursue.

"Write it," he urged me.

TWO

Biographical Fiction

IN 1564, IN THE EARLY years of the reign of Queen Elizabeth I, a child was born in the market town of Stratford-upon-Avon (population: approximately 1,500) to John, a glove maker, and his wife, Mary. The exact date of his birth is unknown, but a baptismal record for April 26, 1564, reads, "Gulielmus filius Johannes Shakspere" ("William son of John Shakspere"). Subtracting a few days, biographers locate his birth on April 23, the feast of Saint George, patron saint of England.

How did the boy from Stratford become the world's greatest playwright? Though scholars claim not to participate in the authorship debate—not to recognize it—Shakespeare biographies are entirely about the authorship question. They try to make the case *for* Shakespeare, to explain *how he did it*. They begin like a folktale or the legend of a saint, deep in the heart of England, wrapped in wildflowers and rolling green hills. See, for instance *Will in the World: How Shakespeare Became Shakespeare*, the 2004 *New York Times* best seller by the Harvard scholar Stephen Greenblatt. "Let us imagine that Shakespeare found himself from boyhood fascinated by language, obsessed with the magic of words," Greenblatt begins.

Let us imagine.

It is alluring, inviting, and entirely make-believe. Whether William of Stratford was obsessed with words is unknown—but if you assumed he wrote the works, then he must have been. "There is overwhelming evidence for this obsession from his earliest writings, so it is a very safe assumption that it began early," Greenblatt defends his assumption, "perhaps from the first moment his mother whispered a nursery rhyme in his ear: Pillycock, pillycock, sate on a hill / If he's not gone—he sits there still." On the very first page of his biography, Greenblatt conjures a scene—Shakespeare's mother singing to him—for which no evidence exists.

A few facts are known of the family. His father, John, who came from the nearby village of Snitterfield, was fined for keeping a dung heap outside his house. Across different tellings of the tale, the dung heap takes on a kind of symbolic quality. Anti-Stratfordians recount the detail gleefully—as though to say, this story stinks of shit. Stratfordians, in hagiographic fashion, tend to airbrush out the dung heap. John engaged in various trades around town: in addition to glove maker, he was also a "brogger" (an unlicensed wool dealer), a dealer in timber and barley, a landlord, and a local official, rising from ale taster (responsible for ensuring the quality of bread, ale, and beer) to bailiff (chief magistrate of the town council). He signed documents only with a mark, suggesting that he could not write his name. "Most plain-dealing men in early modern England used marks because the majority of the population was illiterate," explains the historian David Cressy. "More than two-thirds of men and four-fifths of women in the seventeenth century could not write their names." Numeracy, not literacy, was needed to conduct business in Elizabethan England, and reading and counting were taught before writing, so some could read but not write. Of the nineteen elected officials in Stratford while John Shakespeare held office, only seven could sign their names. His wife could not write her name, either.

Next, the biographies usually tell us about the genius's school days. The slight awkwardness is that we don't know if he ever went to school. He may have attended the local grammar school—his father's position on the town council would have allowed him to attend for free—but the school's records have disappeared. In order to write the plays, however, he must have received an education, so scholars assume he attended. They have tried to squeeze the most out of the grammar school, imagining it as the site of a rigorous classical education, but Renaissance writers deplored the quality of the provincial grammar schools—generally one-room schoolhouses in which all levels were taught by a single schoolmaster, and writing materials were so "scarce and expensive" that Latin grammar was instilled by recitation and the rod. If he did attend, it probably wasn't for long. In the 1570s, his father was prosecuted for usury and illegal dealing in wool. By 1576, when William was thirteen, John Shakespeare withdrew from public life. It is suspected that he either fell into debt or lowered his profile to continue pursuing his illegal wool-dealing. Scholars believe William likely left school to help support the family. He had five younger siblings.

At eighteen, he married. Friends of the bride's family signed a financial guarantee for the wedding of "William Shagspere and Anne Hathwey," who was three months pregnant. The surname appears in various forms: Shakspere, Shagspere, Shaxpere. Elizabethan spelling was not standardized. In the Stratford records it appears most often as "Shakspere," with a short "a," though on the title pages of the plays and poems it would generally appear as "Shakespeare" or "Shake-speare."

The couple had a daughter, Susanna, and three years later twins Hamnet and Judith—apparently named after their Stratford neighbors Hamnet Sadler, a baker, and his wife, Judith. Another gap stretches from 1585 to 1592. Scholars refer to these as the "lost years," like the lost years of Jesus from his childhood to the beginning of his ministry. Greenblatt imagines that he spent them as a tutor to a Catholic family in the north of England, where he met a Jesuit priest named Edmund Campion. ("Let us imagine the two of them sitting together . . . Shakespeare would have found Campion fascinating.") But there is no evidence that Shakespeare was a tutor or that this thrilling meeting of minds ever took place.

The biographies are riddled with speculation: Shakespeare "could have," "might have," "must have," "probably," "surely," "undoubtedly," they muse, conjuring baseless scenes and elaborating tenuous theories in an attempt to connect the man to the works. They are the very worst kinds of biography: fiction masquerading as history. Scholars are not unaware of the problem. *Will in the World*, Greenblatt's best seller, was censured by a colleague in the *London Review of Books* as "biographical fiction." But it was beautifully written and vividly imagined, and so, in spite of its liberties, it became a finalist for the National Book Award and the Pulitzer Prize.

Other scholars, encouraged by Greenblatt's success, pumped out more biographies. Despite, or perhaps because of, their fictional qualities, Shakespeare biographies have been popular with readers since the Victorian age, telling a rags-to-riches story of a hero whose early hardships elicit sympathy and whose rise to fame and wealth offers the satisfaction of virtue justly rewarded. The cognitive scientist George Lakoff calls the rags-to-riches structure one of our "deep narratives," recurring again and again in our cultural and political life—in religious stories, fairy tales, and the campaigns of charismatic politicians. Our attachment to it is difficult to shake. The story of Shakespeare's rise from humble origins, from an apparently illiterate family in a provincial town, to literary immortality is cozy, comforting, compelling, a tale with all the warmth, cheer, and assurance of English firesides. But it is an imaginative construction. ("What matters is not the true story, but a good story," wrote the scholar Gary Taylor, reviewing Greenblatt's book.) Over the years, scholars have imagined a Protestant Shakespeare, a secret Catholic Shakespeare, a republican Shakespeare, a monarchist Shakespeare, a heterosexual Shakespeare, a bisexual Shakespeare, a Shakespeare who hated his wife (and thus left her the second-best bed), a Shakespeare who loved his wife (and thus left her the second-best bed), a Shakespeare who, before taking up the pen, must have been a roving actor or a schoolmaster or a lawyer or a soldier or a sailor. Being nothing, Shakespeare can be anything—anything his biographers desire.

In 2016 scholars convened a conference called Shakespeare and the Problem of Biography. "Shakespeare's life exists as a kind of black hole of antimatter in relation to the vast nebula of his fame," Professor Brian Cummings of the University of York observed in his opening remarks. "Could it be that his fame has grown through this very lack of identity to pin a more ordinary life to, so that he is the perfect container for our desire and creative empathy?" Cummings lamented the difficulty of reconstructing

Shakespeare's life, admitting that "the largest lacuna of all is the mystery of how Shakespeare ever got to be a writer in the first place."

At some point, Shakespeare made the journey to London, although precisely when and why are unknown. It has been tempting to imagine that he ran off to the big city to pursue the life of a writer, but recent research into the family finances suggests he first went to London to further his father's business interests. "To survive, the Shakespeare family business had to have a London representative," writes the scholar David Fallow. Who better than the eldest son, who "surfaces in London exactly where and when contacts in the wool trade would have been vital to the survival of the family business?" He first appears in the capital in 1592, loaning £7 to a John Clayton. (He would sue Clayton eight years later in 1600 for recovery of the debt.) "Given John Shakespeare's relative market position in the English wool brokering scene," writes Fallow, "the probability is that William first went to London as a businessman rather than as an impoverished poet."

By 1592, Shakespearean plays had begun appearing on London stages. In his diary, an impresario named Philip Henslowe, who operated various theaters and bear pits, recorded a performance of *Harey the Vj* at his theater, the Rose, on March 3 of that year. This is thought to be the first part of Shakespeare's *Henry VI* trilogy about the Wars of the Roses—the series of bloody civil conflicts between the houses of York and Lancaster for control of the English throne. It had fifteen performances, Henslowe notes, and earned 3 pounds, 16 shillings, and 8 pence, making it one of the most successful plays of the year. But Henslowe did not record the author's name. He listed the titles of other Shakespearean plays in his diary, too (*Henry V*, *The Taming of the Shrew*, *Titus Andronicus)*, also authorless. Nearly a century later, in 1686, an actor named Edward Ravenscroft would record a rumor he'd heard about Shakespeare's *Titus Andronicus*: "I have been told by some anciently conversant with the Stage, that it was not Originally his, but brought by a private Author to be Acted."

How did William of Stratford, a provincial businessman with minimal education, suddenly start turning out plays? When had he written these works? When, for that matter, had he acquired the *knowledge* to write, for instance, an epic saga about English political history?

Scholars of the eighteenth and nineteenth centuries scoured theatrical records looking for some sign of Shakespeare emerging on the scene in the 1580s or early 1590s, but he is nowhere to be found—not mentioned as a member of any company, not recorded on any cast list. Desperate to establish his presence in the theater world, an eighteenth-century scholar named Thomas Tyrwhitt seized on a 1592 pamphlet attacking a presumptuous player—an "upstart crow"—and proclaimed it a reference to Shakespeare. The pamphlet, published as *Greenes Groats-worth of Wit*, purports to be the dying testimony of the impoverished playwright Robert Greene. (Its authorship is uncertain; while Greene was a real writer, scholars think it may actually have been written by another writer, Henry Chettle, which is to say that it is a text plagued by its own authorship question.)

Like most playwrights of the age, Greene was a university-educated scholar who sold his work to whatever playing company would take it. He was hugely resentful of the players, who accumulated wealth as shareholders in their companies, while writers—who supplied the very words they spoke—were tossed a pittance. Addressing his fellow writers, Christopher Marlowe, Thomas Nashe, and George Peele, Greene warns them not to trust players—"those puppets . . . that spake from our mouths." Greene singles out one player in particular who, fancying himself a jack-of-all-trades, a *Johannes factotum*, thinks he can fill out a blank verse as well as the writers: "Yes trust them not: for there is an upstart Crow, beautified with our feathers, that with his *Tygers hart wrapt in a Players hyde*, supposes he is as well able to bombast out a blank verse as the best of you: and being an absolute *Johannes factotum*, is in his own conceit the only Shake-scene in a country." Greene's attack on the upstart with a "Tygers hart wrapt in a Players hyde" echoes the third part of *Henry VI*: "Oh Tygers hart wrapt in a womans hide!" Richard, Duke of York, cries when Margaret waves a cloth dipped in the blood of his murdered son in his face. To Thomas Tyrwitt in 1778, the meaning was clear: the player with the "Tygers hart" who thinks himself "the only Shake-scene in a country" could only be the author of *Henry VI*. "There can be no doubt, I think, that Shake-scene alludes to Shakespeare," Tyrwitt concluded. Since its discovery more than 240 years ago, the passage has formed a foundational chapter in Shakespeare biographies, a primal scene proving that by 1592 Shakespeare had arrived in the world of the theater.

But in 1592, *Henry VI* hadn't been published, and even when it was published in 1594, it was anonymous. How would anyone reading Greene's pamphlet connect "Shake-scene" to "Shakespeare"? And what exactly does the allusion say about him? That he's ruthless to poor writers? That he's a social climber? That he's presuming to write his own lines? By 1592, the author of the *Henry VI* plays had done much more than "bombast" a few lines. He'd penned several plays, including one of the most popular of that year. And what is a "Shake-scene" anyway? The epithet suggests a powerful actor shaking the stage. Greene implies that there are other "Shake-scenes" in England, though this one is arrogant enough to suppose himself the only one ("in his own conceit the only Shake-scene in a country"). This suggests that the term refers to an archetype—a type of actor—not an individual's name. A similar epithet of the period, "shake-rags," was a common word for a beggar. If Shakespeare had become a leading player by 1592—prominent and powerful enough to draw Greene's venom—why is there no record of his involvement with any playing company? "A vast edifice of biographical inference rests on a single sentence of just fifty-nine words," observes the scholar Bart van Es.

Challenging centuries of tradition, some anti-Stratfordians argue that Greene's attack on the upstart crow is not directed at Shakespeare at all but at a man named Edward Alleyn, a star of the Elizabethan stage famed for shaking the timbers of the Rose with his bombastic acting. Contemporaries described Alleyn's "scenical strutting" and "furious vociferation," his "stalking and roaring," his "thundring threats," as he "vaunts his voice upon the hired stage with high-set steps and princely carriage" to "ravish the gazing Scaffolders." Earlier that year, Alleyn had performed the title role in Greene's play *Orlando Furioso.* Brazenly, Alleyn added his own lines to the script, bombasting out his own verse. A few months later, his company produced *Tambercam*, a blank-verse rip-off of Christopher Marlowe's popular *Tamburlaine*, in which Alleyn had starred. Philip Henslowe recorded

Tambercam in his diary as Alleyn's "booke." In short, in the months before Greene's attack, Alleyn, a recognized "Shake-scene," was presumptuously daring to rival both Greene and Marlowe at playwriting. He would have been a natural target of Greene's anger: having started out as a boy player touring the provinces, Alleyn had risen—without a university education or a privileged social background—to wealth and influence. He was a lead shareholder in his company, the Lord Admiral's Men, and a cunning businessman, buying plays, lending money, and comanaging the Rose (and later more theaters and bear-pits) with his father-in-law, Philip Henslowe, with whom he split the profits: the epitome of a shrewd player building his wealth on the backs of writers. *Tygers hart wrapt in a Players hyde.* If Alleyn delivered the memorable line from *Henry VI* onstage, it may have been more associated with the player who spoke it, not the anonymous, unpublished playwright who wrote it. What's more, Alleyn's family was associated with the crow: he was born and raised at his father's inn, "at the sign of the Pye"—not a meat pie but a magpie, a type of crow. *Upstart Crow, beautified with our feathers . . .*

In his pamphlet, Greene urges the writers to desert "those apes," as he calls the players—to punish them by withholding future plays. "O that I might entreat your rare wits to be employed in more profitable courses: & let those apes imitate your past excellence, and never more acquaint them with your admired inventions," he writes, "for it is a pity men of such rare wits, should be subject to the pleasure of such rude grooms." It is hard to see how withholding plays from Shakespeare would punish him: he was not dependent on other writers' plays; he was writing his own, and if other writers withheld theirs, it would only increase the demand for his—hardly a punishment. If the writers withheld plays from Alleyn, however, it would hurt his company and his fortunes, as Greene dearly hoped. The anti-Stratfordian argument for Alleyn as the upstart crow is so strong that it was published in 2020 in *English Studies*, a thoroughly orthodox journal. Nevertheless, scholars still cling to Shakespeare as the upstart crow because there is nothing else—*nothing*—to place William of Stratford in the theater in the early 1590s. The first record of his theatrical activities does not appear until 1595, when he was paid as a member of a newly formed company, the Lord Chamberlain's Men, for performances at court the previous Christmas.

How did he come to join the new company? Many actors were tradesmen. For instance, another member of the company, John Heminges, was a grocer who loaned some of his apprentices to the stage. If Shakespeare came to London as a businessman, it is possible that his business associations led him to the playing company. He never became a star player, but he appears to have been a shrewd businessman. Records show that he dodged taxes, was fined for hoarding grain during a shortage, pursued petty lawsuits, and was subject to a restraining order—another dung heap often omitted from the biographies. "Be it known," the order reads, "that William Wayte craves sureties of the peace against William Shakspere, Francis Langley, Dorothy Soer wife of John Soer, and Anne Lee, for fear of death, and so forth." (Francis Langley, a goldsmith with a slimey reputation, was the builder and proprietor of the Swan Theatre, suggesting that "Shakspere" had perhaps become involved in some shady business in the theatrical underworld.)

In 1596 his son Hamnet died, aged eleven. (The parish register records the burial of "Hamnet filius William Shakspere.") While other writers composed grief-stricken poems on the loss of their children—Ben Jonson wrote, for instance, "On My First Son"—Shakespeare never did. Instead, the years immediately following Hamnet's death saw the production of some of the most cheerful Shakespearean comedies: *The Merry Wives of Windsor, Much Ado About Nothing, As You Like It*. Then, around 1600, *Hamlet*. Most scholars reject the notion that *Hamlet*, a revenge tragedy about regime change, political legitimacy, and political violence, has anything to do with the boy Hamnet. *Hamlet* is based on "Vita Amlethi" ("Life of Amleth"), a thirteenth-century Danish legend, which was translated into French in 1570 by François de Belleforest. By 1589, at least one adaptation of the tale had already appeared on the London stage. (Scholars call this play the "Ur-Hamlet.") In an attempt to connect the play with Shakespeare's life, however, and to compensate for the awkward timing of those comedies, Greenblatt suggests that Shakespeare's grief at Hamnet's death lies at the heart of *Hamlet*: "the coincidence of the names . . . may well have reopened a deep wound," he wrote. But what parent would memorialize their dead child as a depressed man who contemplates suicide and the murder of his uncle, before being murdered himself?

By 1597, Shakespeare had accumulated enough wealth to buy one of the largest houses in Stratford. His father's application for a coat of arms had finally been accepted, which meant he could style himself a "gentleman." Shoring up his new status with further investments, he became a shareholder in the newly built Globe Theatre and, later, in the Blackfriars Theatre, too. Though the early plays were anonymous, by 1598 they started appearing with the name "William Shakespeare" on their title pages. A clergyman named Francis Meres published a book listing Shakespeare among the best English writers and naming a dozen Shakespeare plays: "Shakespeare among the English is the most excellent in both kinds [comedy and tragedy] for the stage." Such evidence proves attribution, not actual authorship. Had this man really written *Richard III*? *Romeo and Juliet*? *The Merchant of Venice*? That same year, a businessman in Stratford wrote (though never sent) a letter to "my Loveinge and good ffrend & contreymann Mr. Wm Shackespeare" requesting help in securing a loan to pay "all the debettes I owe in London." Nothing in the letter suggests that "Mr. Shackespeare" was a major playwright.

The rest of his documented life records similarly banal business matters. In 1600 he took action to recover a loan. In 1602 he purchased a hundred acres of Stratford real estate. ("For much of his life, he was investing in property," notes Stanley Wells.) When James came to the throne, he was listed as a member of the playing company, now called the King's Men, but during the theater season of 1604, numerous records place him in Stratford: He sells malt to a Philip Rogers, lends Rogers two shillings, then sues Rogers to recover the amount plus damages. He invests in Stratford tithes. These are the years when he's supposed to be writing his greatest plays—*Othello*, *King Lear*, *Macbeth*. The name "Shakespeare" also appeared on the title pages of non-Shakespeare plays, such as *The London Prodigall* in 1605 ("by William Shakespeare") and *A Yorkshire Tragedy* in 1608 ("written by W. Shakespeare" and "acted by his Maiesties Players at the Globe"). But these plays weren't included in the 1623 collection of Shakespeare's plays, and no scholar believes the author of *Hamlet* wrote them. Why was the name being used so freely? And if someone was fraudulently using Shakespeare's name, why didn't he protest?

In 1607 his daughter Susanna wed the physician John Hall. The parish register records the marriage of "M. Hall gentleman & Susanna Shaxspere."

In 1608, he had his Stratford neighbor John Addenbrooke arrested for failing to repay £6 and sued him to recover the debt plus damages.

His litigation against Addenbrooke continued in 1609.

In 1611 he leased a barn to a man named Robert Johnson and filed a complaint to protect his real estate interests against default by other lessees.

In 1612 he testified as a witness in a lawsuit in London, where he was identified not as the famous writer but merely as a "gentleman" of Stratford-upon-Avon.

In 1614 he was listed as a landowner in Stratford, and his name appeared in documents concerning the enclosure of nearby pastures.

In 1616 he died, leaving his embarassing will devoid of literary interests. A silver gilt bowl went to his daughter Judith; his "second-best bed" to his wife, Anne; a sword to Thomas Combe; and twenty-six shillings, eight pence to his Stratford neighbor Hamnet Sadler "to buy him a ringe." In an interlinear addition, he also left money to Richard Burbage, John Heminges, and Henry Condell, three actor-shareholders in his company. His other bequests went to wealthy landowners and business associates. But his primary concern seems to have been preserving his assets for a future male heir. The bulk of his estate, including his main house, his various other lands and properties, and the rest of his "goods, chattels, leases, plate, jewels, and household stuff whatsoever" went to his eldest daughter, Susanna, and her potential sons.

He was a rich man but not, by the appearance of his will, an intellectual one. He did not mention any of the possessions typical of a Renaissance humanist: no books, no musical instruments, no maps. He did not remember any writer, though he is said to have associated and collaborated with other writers in the tightly connected world of literary London for more than two decades. For all his wealth, he did not make any bequest to the Stratford grammar school that had allegedly nurtured him, nor any provision for his eight-year-old granddaughter's education. (Other men of letters often made bequests to their alma maters or provided money for children's education.)

Strangest of all, he made no mention of manuscripts or writing of any kind. Scholars have scrambled for explanations. Maybe his books were listed in a separate inventory that has been lost. Maybe he didn't care about the preservation of his works. But then why do they show evidence of revision for the printed page? The sonnets suggest a poet who clearly thought about his legacy: "Not marble nor the gilded monuments/ Of princes shall outlive this powerful rhyme," he writes in Sonnet 55. "Your monument shall be my gentle verse, / Which eyes not yet created shall o'er-read," he boasts in Sonnet 81. What happened to his manuscripts? Why didn't he leave instructions for his unpublished plays? And what of his poetry? Professor Samuel Schoenbaum could not help noting the discrepancy between Shakespeare's meticulous parceling of his assets and his apparent disregard for his literary legacy: "If Shakespeare was indifferent to the ultimate fate of the plays that immortalized him, he showed no similar nonchalance about assembling and passing down his estate."

At his death, supposedly on April 23, 1616 (Saint George's day, again), there was no recorded notice of the celebrated writer's passing. No elegies. No great London funeral. No burial at Westminster Abbey alongside Geoffrey Chaucer, Edmund Spenser, and Britain's other literary dead. On April 25, he was buried quietly at the local church in Stratford-upon-Avon. The only trace of this event is the church's burial register, which reads simply, "Will Shakspere gent."

⁂

No such void exists for other major writers of the period. Though many left fewer documents, the ones they did leave identified them as writers in payment records, manuscripts, letters, and diaries. The poet Edmund Spenser wrote a letter about his "sundrie royall Cantos" that he intended to publish with "many other [of] of my Tracts & Discourses, some in Latin, some in English, some in verse." When he died in 1599, a correspondent wrote that "Spenser, our principal poet . . . died at Westminster on Saturday last." Playwright George Chapman was described in a lawsuit as a man who "hath made diverse plays and written other books." John Lyly, another playwright, wrote to Elizabeth I vowing to "write prayers instead of plays." Thomas Nashe referred in a letter to his frustrations "writing for the stage and for the press." Samuel Daniel wrote that necessity had reduced him to "making the stage the speaker of my lines." A royal patent increased Ben Jonson's pension for "those services of his wit and pen." When he died, a correspondent wrote, "our great Poet, Ben Jonson, is lately dead and was buried on Wednesday last here at Westminster." Theater owner Philip Henslowe, who put on early Shakespeare plays, recorded payments to twenty-seven playwrights—but never Shakespeare. Cuthbert Burbage, another theatrical entrepreneur and shareholder in the Globe, named him merely as one of several "men players," not as the company's playwright. "Perhaps we should despair of ever bridging the vertiginous expanse between the sublimity of the subject and the mundane inconsequence of the documentary record," sighed Professor Schoenbaum. "What would we not give for a single personal letter, one page of diary!"

Even in Stratford, where he spent the last years of his life having supposedly retired from writing, no one identified him as a writer, as Shakespeare scholars themselves concede. Not the town clerk, one Thomas Greene, who stayed at the home of "my cosen Shakspeare" and detailed their exchanges—over mundane land matters—in his diary. Not his son-in-law the physician John Hall, who kept notebooks of his case notes, referring at one point to the "excellent poet" Michael Drayton but saying nothing of his own father-in-law. In *Britannia*, a survey of Great Britain that ran through six editions between 1586 and 1607, the historian William Camden wrote that the "small market-town" of Stratford-upon-Avon owed "all its consequences to two natives of it. They are John de Stratford, later archbishop of Canterbury, who built the church, and Hugh Clopton, later mayor of London, who built the Clopton Bridge across the Avon." Camden was clearly aware of the poet Shakespeare—he referred to him elsewhere as one of "the most pregnant wits of our time"—but he apparently did not regard Stratford as the poet's origin.

And where *did* he acquire the wide-ranging knowledge displayed in the plays? The playwright Christopher Marlowe was born into similar circumstances—his father was a shoemaker—but Marlowe's early signs of genius did not go unnoticed, and he won a scholarship to the King's School, followed by another scholarship to Cambridge. Other playwrights, such as Thomas Nashe, George Peele, and Robert Greene, earned university scholarships, too. Ben Jonson, who attended the Westminster School, wrote an epigram acknowledging his debt to William Camden ("Camden, most reverend head, to whom I owe / All that I am in arts, all that I know"). Jonson also dedicated one of his plays to Camden, "the instructor," for "the benefits confer'd upon my youth." But Shakespeare never recognized any school or teacher, and no one claimed to have tutored him. If he was self-taught, how did he acquire books? The plays draw on hundreds of texts, including some—in French and Italian—that hadn't yet been translated into English. Where did he learn French and Italian? *The Merchant of Venice* is based on *Il Pecorone*, a fourteenth-century Italian tale by Giovanni Fiorentino that did not exist in English. Neither did the sources for *Much Ado About Nothing* (Matteo Bandello's *Novelle*), *Twelfth Night* (the play *GI'ingannati*), *Othello* (Cinthio's *Gli Hecatommithi*), *Hamlet* (François de Belleforest's *Histoires tragiques*), and so on.

Early scholars actually tried to deny the influence of foreign literature on Shakespeare, maintaining that he was unspoiled by European learning. "Shakespeare was nurtured by Nature and his own tongue," one eighteenth-century scholar wrote. "His studies were most demonstratively confined to Nature and his own language." Nineteenth-century scholars agreed: "He was Nature's own child—her favourite son—her beloved offspring," wrote one. "She guided every idea, warmed and perfected every description, and fired every effusion and passion." The weirdly pagan invocation of "Nature"—the inverse of learning or knowledge—was meant to explain the genius of Shakespeare's works, which poured forth from him like holy texts from God's appointed prophets. This romantic mythology fit the conception of the author as a provincial man of humble origins and minimal education, a divinely inspired son of England. By the early twentieth century, however, this fantasy became impossible to maintain, as it became increasingly evident that not only had Shakespeare borrowed stories from foreign texts, but he also imported foreign words and phrases into English. Macbeth hallucinates a dagger with "*gouts* of blood," casually using the French word for drops. "Shakespeare grafts on his own English speech for the first and only time numerous French colloquialisms," noted Sidney Lee. Three scenes of *Henry V* unfold entirely in French. "Frequently we find whole lines translated literally from Italian without the slightest alteration," observed Ernesto Grillo, a professor of Italian at the University of Glasgow. In *All's Well That Ends Well*, the warring Florentines and Sienese are described as being "by the ears," a phrase that makes no sense in English because it is an Italian colloquialism ("*si pigliano per gli orecchi*," meaning "in conflict"). In *The Taming of the Shrew*, Petruchio and Hortensio greet each other in perfect Italian. Shakespeare wrote as one at ease in the multilingual circles of the European Renaissance. In *The Merchant of Venice*, he has Portia make fun of her English suitor Falconbridge because "he hath neither Latin, French, nor Italian."

To make matters worse, some passages in the plays closely parallel passages in ancient Greek tragedies, for which English translations likewise did not exist. "[W]hat can we say when we find some of Aeschylus's thought appearing in Shakespeare's plays?" asked the scholar Gilbert Highet. "The only explanation is that great poets in times and countries distant from each other have similar thoughts and express them similarly," he concluded, skipping the more obvious explanation: that the author read Aeschylus in ancient Greek. Others, too, have admitted "unmistakable" commonalities. The echoes are "strong," Stanley Wells admitted in an address to the 2012 World Shakespeare Congress. (He cited research from an anti-Stratfordian; "we must try not to hold that against him," Wells quipped.) Greek was a language of the universities and of privately educated nobility. When the future Elizabeth I was sixteen, for instance, her tutor Roger Ascham recorded that his pupil spoke French, Italian,

Latin, and "intermediate Greek." Unwilling to give up Shakespeare, Wells suggested that some unknown collaborator helped him.

And what of his knowledge of foreign affairs and foreign lands? French scholars have noted that *Love's Labour's Lost*, which is set at the court of Navarre, in southern France, displays "fidelity to the most minute details of historic truth and local color . . . It would seem likely that its author had spent at least a few months moving in high French society," wrote the critic Émile Montégut. Abel Lefranc, chair of French literature at the Collège de France and a member of the Académie des Inscriptions et Belles-Lettres, agreed, noting that the characters correspond to historical figures at the French court in 1578, when Shakespeare was a fourteen-year-old in Stratford-upon-Avon. Lefranc had no patience for the persistent English belief in the Stratford man. It was plain to anyone acquainted with French history that the play exhibited "virtually impeccable and absolutely amazing acquaintance with aspects of France and Navarre of the period that could have been known only to a very limited number of people," he wrote in 1918, scorning the Shakespeare scholars' "absurd theory." "Neither absence nor paltriness of documents troubles these authors, whose robust faith guides their pens around so many pitfalls they choose to ignore."

Oscar Campbell, a Shakespeare professor at Harvard, conceded Lefranc's findings: the author "adverts to incidents of current social and political life" and "directly satirizes figures well known in that world." Another scholar, Hugh Richmond, later agreed: "It is Shakespeare's genius to have copied, not invented, such psychologies," he wrote. Still another scholar, J. Dover Wilson, confessed his bafflement: "To credit this amazing piece of virtuosity to a butcher boy who left school at thirteen, or even to one whose education was nothing more than what a grammar school and residence in a little provincial borough could provide, is to invite one either to believe in miracles or to disbelieve in the 'man from Stratford.' "

Shakespeare's knowledge of Italy appears more miraculous still, for ten of the plays are set in Italian cities, betraying familiarity with local customs, geography, and landmarks. Early scholars generally concluded that the author must have spent time in the country. It is "the most natural supposition," wrote the nineteenth-century publisher Charles Knight. "Nothing can uproot my belief of his having been there," agreed Charles Armitage Brown. "The milieu of the time and place with regard to Italy is so intimate that it is difficult to avoid the belief that Shakespeare himself actually visited and lived for some time in that country." Shakespeare was "remarkably successful in giving local colouring and atmosphere," wrote E. K. Chambers, citing his "familiarity with some minute points of local topography."

But as no evidence could be found that Shakespeare ever left England, and as other authorship candidates began to be put forward who *had* demonstrably spent time in Italy, scholars began to walk back the idea that the author had any personal knowledge of the country. It fed the flames of doubt. Most modern scholars now insist that he merely imagined Italy, and that the details he imagined are inaccurate, proof that Shakespeare was never actually there. In *The Two Gentlemen of Verona*, for instance, he sends the character Valentine from Verona to Milan—two inland cities—by boat. How silly! In fact, the cities of northern Italy were once linked by a network of canals and rivers used frequently by Renaissance merchants and travelers. When a character says, "I mean thou'lt lose the flood, and losing the flood, lose thy voyage," *flood* refers to the timed rising of water in the locks. In *The Taming of the Shrew*, too, a character refers to "com[ing] ashore" in Padua. "These lines make no sense unless the author envisions inland Padua with a seacoast," scoffs Scott McCrea in his 2004 book *The Case for Shakespeare: The End of the Authorship Question*. But Shakespeare never says anything about a seacoast; *shore* means any land bordering on a sea, lake, or river, and old maps show a river port at Padua. Renaissance travelers recorded going "by water to Padua by river of Brente" and that "one can, if one wishes, go by coach to Padua, but the journey by river is nicer due to the beautiful palaces built along its banks." Had the author—whoever he or she was—traveled the river and canal routes of northern Italy?

In *The Tempest*, too, Prospero describes being hurried "aboard a bark" (a small sailing ship) as he was banished from Milan. "But Milan is not near any river that can carry a bark," counters McCrea. On the contrary, a traveler named Michel de Montaigne confirmed: "We crossed the river Naviglio, which was narrow, but still deep enough to carry great barks to Milan." The errors here are not Shakespeare's but the modern-day professors'.

The examples are endless. For instance, *All's Well That Ends Well* reveals precise topographical knowledge of Florence:

Widow: God save you, pilgrim! Whither are you bound?
Helena: To Saint Jacques le Grand.
Where do the palmers lodge, I do beseech you?
Widow: At the Saint Francis here beside the port.

Stratfordians suggest that these three references—a pilgrimage site called Saint Jacques le Grand, a lodging house called Saint Francis that caters to "palmers" (pilgrims), and a nearby port—are all invented. In fact, a Florentine port flourished on the Arno River; beside it, on the Piazza Ognissanti, was the Saint Francis pilgrims hostel (still standing today); and across the river was the church of San Jacopo Sopr'Arno, dedicated to San Giacomo Maggiore (in French, "Saint Jacques le Grand"). Helena uses French instead of Italian because she's a Frenchwoman. *Othello* refers to the "Sagittary," a street in Venice where arrow makers lived. In *The Merchant of Venice*, the moneylender Shylock tells his wealthy friend Tubal to "meet me at our synagogue." Surely there was no synagogue in sixteenth-century Venice? In fact, there were several. *The Two Gentlemen of Verona* mentions St. Gregory's Well in Milan. Professor Murray Levith of Skidmore College confessed himself "surprised," suggesting that Shakespeare might have learned of the well from a famous 1582 map of Milan. But the well is not on the map. *The Taming of the Shrew*, set in Padua, "displays such an intimate acquaintance not only with the manners and customs of Italy but also with the minutest details of domestic life that it cannot have been gleaned from books or acquired in the course of conversations with travelers returned from Padua," concluded Professor Grillo, who continued to insist—despite the protestations of his English colleagues—that Shakespeare must have visited Italy.

In 2008 Roger Prior, a scholar at Queen's University Belfast, published his discovery of Shakespeare's "detailed knowledge" of an obscure fresco in the town of Bassano del Grappa, ancestral home of the Bassanos. "So specific and accurate are his references to it that it is reasonable to assume he had seen it himself," wrote Prior. The references appear in *Othello.* The name "Otello" also appears to have been exclusive to the town, Prior noted. "We know of ten men of this name, covering three generations from 1430 to 1597, all of whom lived in Bassano at some point." Scholars have puzzled over Shakespeare's source for this name, which does not appear in the original Italian tale; the character is simply called "the Moor." Seeking to keep Shakespeare out of Italy, they have taken to arguing that he acquired his Italian knowledge from books on the country (though they cannot say which) or from Italians living in London (though they cannot say who).

"A curious Shakespeare could have learned everything he needed to know about the settings of his plays from a few choice conversations," James Shapiro wrote in *Contested Will.* But consider what Shakespeare writes about venturing abroad: "Home-keeping youth have ever homely wits," he has Valentine observe, extolling the mind-opening benefits of foreign travel. Would a home-keeping author have written such a line?

The sheer number of problems is fascinating. And the conviction with which so many scholars brush them aside is fascinating, too. In order to maintain the traditional attribution, they are forced to diminish Shakespeare. They rejoice to find him making errors. They deny the depth and accuracy of his knowledge. If necessary, they make things up. And then when all else fails, they appeal to his miraculous "genius." How did he acquire his legal knowledge? Shakespeare shows "the most complete mastery of the technical phrases, the jargon, of the law," wrote the scholar Richard Grant White, noting that "no dramatist of the time . . . used legal phrases with Shakespeare's readiness and exactness." Some argued that his knowledge was not that profound; others that he must have trained as a law clerk. But since there is no evidence he had legal training, they cite "the wonder of his genius" which allowed him "to grasp in lightning speed what could be attained only after dull years of work by ordinary minds."

Could he have written the plays? Could he write at all?

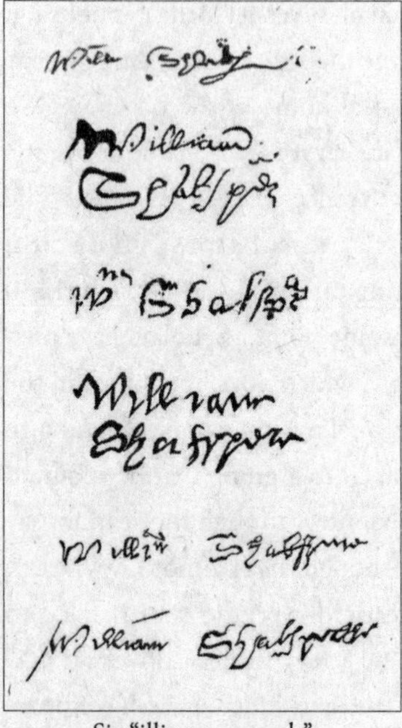

Six "illiterate scrawls"

The only surviving samples of his handwriting are six signatures so poorly formed that some have questioned his comfort with a pen. "Just a mere glance at [his] pathetic efforts to sign his name (illiterate scrawls) should forever eliminate Shakspere from further consideration in this question—he could not write," wrote Mortimer Adler, professor of philosophy at the University of Chicago and chairman of the editorial board of the *Encylopædia Britannica*. Three of the signatures appear on his will; the others on a deposition, a property deed, and a mortgage deed. They are all spelled differently. In 1985 Her Majesty's Stationery Office published an official report on the matter. "It is obvious at a glance that these signatures, with the exception of the last two (on the will), are not the signatures of the same man," wrote Jane Cox, the principal assistant keeper of records at the National Archives. "Almost every letter is formed in a different way in each. Literate men in the sixteenth and seventeenth centuries developed personalized signatures, much as people do today, and it is unthinkable that Shakespeare did not."

Cox raised the possibility that some of the signatures were written not by the Stratford man but by clerks who drew up the documents on which they appeared; thus the discrepancies. In an era of widespread illiteracy, proxy signatures by scribes were legal. Was the man illiterate? Was he simply too ill to sign? (Scholars have reached for this explanation despite the fact that the opening of his will states that he is in "perfect health.") His parents couldn't write, his daughters couldn't write—given the level of illiteracy in the family, was it likely that he could? In a letter to the

Times of London, Cox aggravated the scholars further: "The marked discrepancies between the signatures lend credence to the views of most extreme anti-Stratfordians," she wrote. "Could this man write his own name, let alone anything else?"

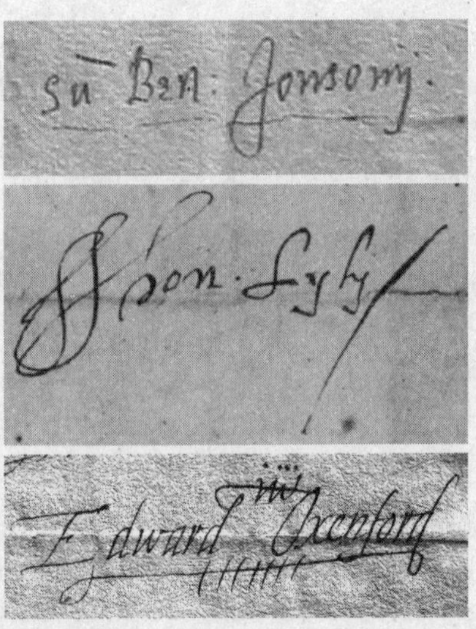

The signatures of Ben Jonson, John Lyly, and the Earl of Oxford

⁂

As I read through the literature on the authorship question—vast, complex, and absorbingly illicit—I kept stumbling across the remarks of writers and thinkers who had contemplated the mystery over the centuries. Writers have a natural interest in the authorship question. Like children seeking knowledge of their paternity, they want to know their forefather—the writer who so shaped them that, in the words of Harold Bloom, they "cannot get outside of him." What's more, they understand from personal experience the relationship between a writer's life and his work; how a writer often transmutes aspects of his life experience—his travels, education, relationships, frustrations, losses—into fiction, leaving his personal mark even on works of fantasy and imagination. But the Stratford man left no mark in the plays; nothing in them reflects his life. For many writers, this disconnect has suggested that they are not his. "I am firm against Shaksper—I mean the Avon man, the actor," Walt Whitman wrote in 1888. Whitman, the poet of democracy, was no snob, but he was convinced that there was another mind behind the plays, referring suggestively to "dim and elusive" facts "of deepest importance—tantalizing and half suspected—suggesting explanations that one dare not put in plain statement." What did Whitman dare not put in plain statement?

Writing to a friend, Henry James confessed, "I am 'sort of' haunted by the conviction that the divine William is the biggest and most successful fraud ever practiced on a patient world." He could not reconcile the author who emerges from the plays—the sophisticated, multilingual artist steeped in Renaissance learning—with the vulgar Stratford businessman, narrowly focused on the bourgeois pursuit of money and real estate. To accept that the author and the businessman were one required believing in "that strangest of all fallacies, the idea of the separateness of a great man's parts," James wrote in a 1907 introduction to *The Tempest*. "His genius places itself, under this fallacy, on one side of the line and the rest of his identity on the other." A keen analyst of character, James could not support this view. "In greatness as much as in mediocrity, the man is, under examination, *one*, and the elements of character melt into each other. The genius is a part of the mind, and the mind a part of the behaviour . . . where does one of these provinces end and the other begin? We may take the genius first or the behaviour first, but we inevitably proceed from the one to the other." With Shakespeare, James argued, we cannot proceed. We are "forever met by a locked door flanked with a sentinel who merely invites us to take it for edifying."

The sentinel guarding the locked door is the figure of the Shakespeare scholar. In 1909, a year before he died, Mark Twain unleashed the full force of his satire on the scholars. "So far as anybody actually knows and can prove, Shakespeare of Stratford-on-Avon never wrote a play in his life," Twain wrote. Shakespeare's biography "is built up, course upon course, of guess, inferences, theories, conjectures—an Eiffel Tower of artificialities rising sky-high." Twain saw right through the scholars' maybes and might-have-beens. "Fact and presumption are, for business purposes, all the same to them," he scoffed. "They know the difference, but they also know how to blink it. They know, too, that while in history-building a fact is better than a presumption, it doesn't take a presumption long to bloom into a fact when *they* have the handling of it. They know by old experience that when they get hold of a presumption-tadpole, he is not going to *stay* tadpole in their history-tank; no, they know how to develop him into the giant four-legged bullfrog of *fact*, and make him sit up on his hams, and puff out his chin, and look important and insolent and come-to-stay; and assert his genuine simon-pure authenticity with a thundering bellow that will convince everybody because it is so loud."

Twain, who delighted in stories of frauds, swindles, and deceptions, did not buy the rags-to-riches fairy tale of the boy from Stratford. He was under no illusion, however, that he would succeed in swaying the believers. "Ah, now, what do you take me for? Would I be so soft as that, after having known the human race familiarly for nearly seventy-four years?" Such is the nature of belief, he wrote, that "when even the brightest mind in our world has been trained up from childhood in a superstition of any kind, it will never be possible for that mind, in its maturity, to examine sincerely, dispassionately, and conscientiously any evidence or any circumstance which shall seem to cast a doubt upon the validity of that superstition." It would be many years, Twain predicted, before the world ceased to believe in the Shakespeare superstition. It took thousands of years, after all, to convince people that there was no such thing as witches, and churches still preached damnation, consigning unbaptized infants to everlasting fires. We treat our superstitions with reverence, he noted. And so, though Stratfordian belief amounted, in his view, to no more than "miraculous 'histories' built by those Stratfordolaters out of a hatful of rags and a barrel of sawdust," no one was eager to examine the artifice too closely. "Disbelief in him cannot come swiftly," Twain concluded. Shakespeare, he suggested, was unlikely to vacate his pedestal for another three centuries at least.

THREE

Crafty Cuttle

But if "Shakespeare" was a fraud—a pseudonym for a concealed author—wouldn't someone have said so?

The Renaissance was a great age of assumed names. The practice of secretly arranging to publish one's work under a pseudonym (a false name) or under an allonym (someone else's name) was not only possible but pervasive. Renaissance plays, poems, and pamphlets often appeared with no name attached. Some were signed "Ignoto" (Latin for "Unknown") or carried mysterious subtitles such as *Dido's Death*, which explained that it was "Translated out of the best of Latin poets into the best of vulgar languages. By one that hath no name."

Some authors' names appeared only as initials, an ambiguity that mixed naming and anonymity. Some reversed their initials—"M.A." for playwright Anthony Munday and "B.N." for poet Nicholas Breton—at once preserving and obscuring information about their identities. Some scrambled their names into anagrams for readers to work out. For instance, Nicholas Breton also appeared as "Salohcin Treboun." Others hid their names cryptically within their works, planting clues to their authorship: "Let no man ask my name, nor what else I should be," the courtier Fulke Greville wrote in an anonymous poem, "For Greiv-ill, pain, forlorn estate doe best decipher me." Another courtier, Edward Dyer, concealed his name in a poem, too: "Die er thowe let his name be known his folly shews to muche." Still others printed their works under obvious pseudonyms such as "Andreas Philalethes" and "Democritus," the latter of whom explained that the pen name allowed him "to assume a little more liberty and freedome of speech." A religious critic like "Martin Marprelate" (sometimes "Mar-prelate"), who in the late 1580s attacked the ecclesiastical hierarchy of the Church of England, had a natural need to conceal his identity. ("Mar-prelate" may refer to his marring of the prelates; his true identity is still a matter of debate.) Satirists and pamphleteers crafted humorous, hyphenated names such as "Simon Smell-knave" and "Thomas Tell-troth." Tracts that defended women against misogynist attacks appeared under female pseudonyms like "Jane Anger" and "Constantia Munda" (the latter Latin for "pure constancy"). One writer, responding to a pamphlet on the evil nature of womankind by a man named Joseph Swetnam, took on the name "Ester Sowernam," playfully reversing Swetnam's name in her surname (*sour/sower* for "sweet") and referencing the biblical heroine in her first name. On the title page of her 1617 pamphlet, she gave only this cryptic clue to her identity: "neither Maide, Wife nor Widdowe, yet really all, and therefore experienced to defend all."

If Renaissance modes of anonymity varied enormously, so did the reasons for employing it. In an age when books were sometimes banned and writers sometimes imprisoned (or worse), writers might choose anonymity for their personal safety. But anonymity could also be useful to the state. Lord Burghley, the Queen's chief advisor and the most powerful man in England, used anonymity to print surreptitious propaganda. In other instances, it was a fashionable stance or a matter of social decorum. In 1589 the critic George Puttenham (who himself wrote anonymously) emphasized the prevalence of anonymity among persons of rank. Members of the nobility were often "loath to be a known of their skill," he explained. "I know very many notable Gentlemen in the Court that have written commendably, and suppressed it again, or else suffered it to be published without their own names to it: as if it were a discredit for a Gentleman to seeme learned and to show him selfe amorous of any good Art." While pious works, learned translations, or historical treatises were respectable, poems and plays were considered frivolous "trifles." Aristocrats circulated them in manuscript for the entertainment of themselves and their friends.

But to publish them—to be seen writing for money—was an act of commercial vulgarity unbecoming of nobility. As the Renaissance jurist John Selden wrote, "It is ridiculous for a Lord to print Verses: 'tis well enough to make them to please himself, but to make them public is foolish." Aristocrats avoided the "stigma of print" by refusing to publish their verse, publishing it anonymously, or disclaiming responsibility for its appearance in print. (When a commoner named Thomas Sackville was elevated to the peerage as Baron Buckhurst, his play *Gorboduc* suddenly became a great embarrassment to the dignity of his new position. Unable to destroy the copies already in circulation, he tried to claim that it had been published without his permission—that the publisher printed it criminally by "fraud and force.") Sometimes others published their work—in miscellanies or posthumously, after the author's death. But the stigma meant that anonymity carried what the scholar Marcy North calls "a paradoxical link to courtly identity."

Between 1475 and 1640, more than eight hundred authors are known to have published anonymously. "The flexibility of anonymity and the multiplicity of meanings that it evokes make it difficult to interpret today, but this flexibility also made it especially popular in early modern England," writes North, a scholar of Renaissance anonymity practices.

Among these modes of authorial concealment, some writers used false attribution, ascribing their work to some other, living person. As North explains, false attribution was "popular and marketable," allowing authors to cultivate a recognizable brand while remaining anonymous. In 1591 the playwright Robert Greene complained of this practice, which he called "underhand brokery," describing poets who "get some other Batillus to set his name to their verses." Batillus was a mediocre Roman poet who tried to claim some verses of Virgil as his own. But where Batillus did so without Virgil's consent, Greene suggested that Renaissance writers intentionally sought out an allonym—a "Batillus"—using that person's name in place of their own to avoid being associated with a publication.

For example, in 1596 the Earl of Essex sought to advance his interests by publishing a self-aggrandizing account of his military exploits at Cádiz, Spain, under someone else's name. (Presumably he thought this would be more effective than publishing it under his own.) First, he sought permission from Fulke Greville, to have his initials ascribed to it. When that failed, Essex's secretary suggested others: "The subscription may [be] DT or some other designed name as you shall thinke good," he wrote. "If he [DT] be unwillinge, you may put RB, which some noe doubt will interpret to be Mr Beale, but it skills not." In 1600 John Bodenham, an anthologist of Elizabethan poetry, identified six courtier poets whose works were to be found "extant among other honorable personages writings"—existing under others' names. They were, he wrote, the Earl of Oxford; the Earl of Derby; Walter Raleigh; Edward Dyer; Fulke Greville; and John Harrington. But in the subsequent edition of 1610, Bodenham's admission was withdrawn. It had perhaps revealed too much.

Even the Queen knew about the use of allonyms. In 1599 Elizabeth I had the historian John Hayward hauled before the Court of Star Chamber to answer questions about a treatise he had published that she did not like. According to an account of the interrogation, the Queen "argued that Hayward was pretending to be the author in order to shield 'some more mischievous' person, and that he should be racked so that he might disclose the truth." As the crown changed hands, authorial concealment continued to be a matter of state interest. Recall Francis Bacon's mysterious letter in 1603: "So desiring you to be good to concealed poets."

Begin at the beginning. The beginning of "Shakespeare" as a literary identity occurred not with a play but a poem. In April 1593 the comic-erotic poem *Venus and Adonis* was entered in the Stationers' Register, a book that functioned as an early form of copyright law. It was entered as an anonymous work, without an author's name. Adapting tales from Ovid's *Metamorphoses*, the poem tells a story of seduction. Venus, goddess of love, is in hot pursuit of "rose-cheek'd" Adonis, a beautiful boy—"the field's chief flower, sweet above compare." Adonis wishes that Venus would just leave him alone so he can go hunt a wild boar with his friends, but Venus is not so easily put off. Though Adonis protests, mumbling womanly objections such as "No" and "Let me go," Venus silences him with kisses and locks her arms around him. "I'll be a park, and thou shalt be my deer," she instructs. "Graze on my lips," she continues cheekily, "and if those hills be dry, / Stray lower, where the pleasant fountains lie."

In the poetic conceit of love as a hunt, it is the woman who is traditionally the hunted deer. Inverting traditional gender roles of pursuer and pursued, the poem parodies tales of women forced into submission by male gods. It gives us instead an effeminate man forced into submission—raped by a goddess. Venus is "sick-thoughted," obsessed with Adonis's lips and why they are not on her lips. The whole poem reads like a pornographic play-by-play of whose lips are where: " 'Touch but my lips with those fair lips of thine,' " Venus commands. " 'Look in mine eye-balls, there thy beauty lies; / Then why not lips on lips, since eyes in eyes?' " Adonis is her prey, and "glutton-like she feeds, yet never filleth; / Her lips are conquerors, his lips obey." Eventually, Adonis escapes her clutches and heads off on his hunt for the wild boar. Sadly, the boar gores him in the groin. As he dies, the blood from his wound spills to the ground and a flower grows. Venus picks the flower—"sweet issue of a more sweet-smelling sire"—and holds it to her breast, rocking it like a newborn baby.

The poem is strange, beautiful, funny, disturbing, and filthy all at once. When it appeared on Elizabethan bookstalls in the spring of 1593, it sold so rapidly that it went into a second printing within a year and fourteen more by 1640. "The younger sort takes much delight in Shakespeares Venus & Adonis," a gossipy critic named Gabriel Harvey noted a few years later, "but his Lucrece & his tragedie of Hamlet, Prince of Denmarke, have it in them to please the wiser sort." In modern-day academia, the poem has given rise to such scholarly articles as " 'Stray[ing] Lower Where the Pleasant Fountains Lie': Cunnilingus in *Venus and Adonis*," "Sexual Perversity in *Venus and Adonis*," and "What It Feels Like for a Boy: Shakespeare's *Venus and Adonis*."

The poem's salaciousness clearly fueled sales. But its popularity might also have had something to do with its dedication. The author dedicated the poem to Henry Wriothesley, the 3rd Earl of Southampton, a dashing young nobleman. Like Adonis, the nineteen-year-old Southampton was a "chief flower" of the court with a "tender spring" upon his unripe lip: "No youth there present was more beautiful or more learned in the arts," recorded an observer, "than this young prince of Hampshire, though his face was yet scarcely adorned by a tender down." Like Adonis, Southampton also had a thing for refusing women. He is known to have refused one in particular: Lady Elizabeth Vere, eldest daughter of Edward de Vere, Earl of Oxford, and granddaughter of Lord Burghley. Scholars generally understand "rose-cheek'd" Adonis—possibly a play on "Wriothesley"—as a figure for the young earl.

"I know not how I shall offend in dedicating my unpolished lines to your Lordship," the author begins, though there is nothing "unpolished" about his lines. If Southampton "seem but pleased" with the work, he vows to "take advantage of all idle hours till I have honoured you with some graver labour." Incredibly, the author describes the poem as his first work—"the first heir of my invention"—the first child or product of his creative faculty. If Southampton is not pleased—"if the first heir of my invention prove deformed"—the author declares, "I shall be sorry it had so noble a god-father: and never after eare so barren a land, for fear it yield me still so bad a harvest." Beneath the dedication is printed the name "William Shakespeare."

How could this highly sophisticated, 1,194-line narrative poem, adapting Ovid's *Metamorphoses* and written in polished stanzas of iambic pentameter, possibly be his first creative endeavor? Besides, the author had already written several anonymous plays. Skeptics see the workings of a carefully constructed pretense: a concealed author debuting as "Shakespeare," making out that this is his first work. How the Stratford man came to meet the fashionable aristocrat, or why he dedicated the poem to him, is another mystery. Biographers tend toward the view that Southampton was Shakespeare's patron, financing his early poetic endeavors. But no mention of Shakespeare has been found in Southampton's papers, and there is no record of payment. Indeed, there wouldn't be: Southampton was still a minor in 1593, not yet in control of his finances and thus unable to patronize anyone. When he did come into his majority the next year, he had already racked up enough bills to be heavily in debt—not a man with money to spare on literary amusements. In any case, it is hard to understand why Southampton would pay a poet who calls him a "poor fool," feminizes him as a deer, and has him speared in the balls—or, for that matter, why a commoner would dare to depict a nobleman this way.

Who was this Shakespeare, bursting onto London's literary scene with a bawdy, instant best seller? What did he mean by *Venus and Adonis*? And why did he dedicate it to the young earl? The moment one begins grasping for Shakespeare, he slips away—already, at the very inception of the literary identity, a ghost.

⁂

Scholars maintain that no one doubted Shakespeare until the mid-nineteenth century—that the authorship question was one of the silly products of the Victorian age, like phrenology or spiritualism. Reading through the literature, I found this statement repeated again and again:

No one in Shakespeare's lifetime, nor the first two hundred years after his death, expressed the slightest doubt about his authorship.

—Jonathan Bate, *The Genius of Shakespeare* (1998)

For more than two hundred years after William Shakespeare's death, no one doubted that he had written his plays.

—James Shapiro, *Contested Will: Who Wrote Shakespeare?* (2010)

No one expressed doubt that William Shakespeare of Stratford-upon-Avon wrote the works attributed to him, give or take some suggestions that some of the plays might have been written in collaboration with other professional

writers, as was exceptionally common at that time . . .
until the middle of the nineteenth century.

—Stanley Wells, *Shakespeare Beyond Doubt: Evidence, Argument, Controversy* (2013)

The scholars are very insistent on this point. Anti-Stratfordians, however, point to a cloud of literary gossip from the Renaissance suggesting that Shakespeare's authorship was suspect in his own lifetime.

Whispers seem to have begun swiftly. Shortly after the registration of *Venus and Adonis*, the critic Gabriel Harvey boasted that he knew the identity of a masked author: "I could here dismaske such a rich mummer," he wrote, "as would undoubtedly make this Pamphlet the vendiblest booke in London." Harvey didn't "dismask" the author, being "none of those, that utter all their learning at once," but he dropped a few hints, writing of "that faire body of the sweetest Venus in print, as it is redoubtedly armed with the complete harnesse of the bravest Minerva." Minerva is the Roman name for Pallas Athena, Greek goddess of war and wisdom, the spear-shaker of classical mythology. She is described in *The Homeric Hymns* "springing from the immortal head of Zeus, shaking a sharp spear." In *The Iliad*, her will shakes the spear of Achilles, enabling him to slay Hector. The *Thesaurus Linguae Graecae* of 1572 recorded that Pallas-Minerva "is said to be a brandisher goddess and indeed a brandisher of the spear." Renaissance poets frequently invoked her as their muse, calling on "Pallas" or "Minerva" to guide their pens as she guided Achilles's spear. (The pen and the spear were poetically interchangeable.) "For Pallas first, whose filed flowing skill, / Should guide my pen some pleasant words to write," one poet wrote. Another: "Go where Minerva's men, / And finest wits do swarm, whom she hath taught to pass with pen."

When Harvey referred to the new "Venus in print" armed by the "bravest Minerva," did he mean the new poem by Shakespeare? Noticeably, Harvey never says it is by William Shakespeare of Stratford-upon-Avon. He does not mention the author's name at all. Instead, he says that the poem is "armed with the complete harness of the bravest Minerva."

Protected, shielded, equipped with a weapon. His language emphasizes Minerva's protective qualities—the complete military "harness"—and implies, perhaps, that the name "Shakespeare" itself is the armor, the shield. In an article published in the journal *Critical Survey* in 2009, the scholar Ros Barber argued that this could be interpreted as evidence of doubt about Shakespeare in 1593—but because the evidence "conflicts radically with a belief that has achieved the status of truth," it had been "quite naturally overlooked."

Anti-Stratfordians suspect that a writer took the Stratford man's baptized name, which was usually spelled "Shakspere," and turned it into "Shakespeare," an allusion to the spear-shaking goddess. Was there an arrangement? Did the poet pay off his "Batillus," according to the custom of "underhand brokery" that Robert Greene described?

In 1594 a writer going by the initials "T.H." (Thomas Heywood) seems to have endorsed the view that the name was a cover for a concealed poet. T.H. published a poem called *Oenone and Paris*, a "shameless" imitation of *Venus and Adonis*, "bristling with travesties and parodies of Shakespeare's poem." Like Shakespeare, he prefaced his poem with a dedication—one that lampoons the language of Shakespeare's dedication to Southampton. T.H. claims the poem is his first—the "Maiden head of my Pen," echoing Shakespeare's "first heir of my invention." He worries that readers might find it "rude and unpolished," mimicking Shakespeare's self-deprecating dismissal of his "unpolished lines." Then he explains that he is offering it under concealed authorship, "hiding himself" like the ancient Greek painter Apelles to see how readers like it before offering a more elaborate work, just as Shakespeare promised to honor Southampton with "some graver labour." The dedication begins:

> Heare you have the first fruits of my indeavours and Maiden head of my Pen; which, how rude and unpolished it maye seeme in your (Eagle-sighted) eyes, I cannot conceive: and therefore, fearinge the woorst, I have sought in some sort to prevent it. *Apelles* having framed any Worke of woorth, wold set it openlie to the view of all,

> hiding himselfe closely in a corner of his Worke-house, to the end, that if some curious and carping fellow came to finde any faulte, he might amend it against the next Market. In the publishing of this little Poem, I have imitated the Painter, giving you this poore Pamphlet to peruse, lurking in the mean-while obscurely till that, hearing how you pleasure to censure [judge] of my simple woork, I may in some other *Opere magis elaborato*, apply my Veine to your humours.

In pretending that *Oenone and Paris* is his first poem, T.H. seems to be making fun of Shakespeare's pretense in claiming *Venus and Adonis* as the "first heir of my invention." Most striking, though, is his playful claim to be hiding himself—"lurking in the mean-while obscurely." If T.H. is imitating Shakespeare, does this suggests that he took "Shakespeare" to be a mask for someone who was also lurking obscurely?

Shakespeare made good on his promise to produce "some graver labour," publishing a second poem, *The Rape of Lucrece*, which drew on Ovid's *Fasti* (in the original Latin) and Livy's *History of Rome* to recount the story of chaste Lucrece's rape by "lust-breathed Tarquin." The author again dedicated the poem to the Earl of Southampton. "The love I dedicate to your Lordship is without end," he professed in weirdly intimate language. "What I have done is yours, what I have to doe is yours, being part in all I have, devoted yours."

Venus and Adonis and *The Rape of Lucrece* made Shakespeare's name, becoming two of the most popular works of the period. That same year, 1594, the author was referenced explicitly for the first time by a third party, in a strange, pseudonymous pamphlet called *Willobie His Avisa*: "Yet Tarquyne pluckt his glistering grape / And Shake-speare paints poor Lucrece rape." The pamphlet's central poem further alludes to Shakespeare's *Rape of Lucrece*, recounting the story of a virtuous maid, a "Brytaine [British] Lucretia," who is given the "fained name" Avisa. She is besieged by a series of suitors, including a "W.S." and an "H.W." Scholars have taken a special interest in the poem, noting that the initials match those of William Shakespeare and Henry Wriothesley. W.S. advises H.W. on how to seduce the British Lucretia, disclosing that she is not as pure as she seems: "She is no saint, she is no Nonne, I think in time she may be wonne." The poem apparently contained sensitive information, for it was banned under the Bishops' Ban of 1599, a sweeping act of censorship that ordered various literary works to be brought to the archbishop of Canterbury and the bishop of London to be burned. Some read it as a commentary, perhaps a libelous attack, on the love triangle of prominent Elizabethans. If "W.S." was the poet Shakespeare and "H.W." was Henry Wriothesley, the Earl of Southampton, who, then, was the British Lucretia, the woman under the feigned name Avisa? Why was the first explicit reference to "Shake-speare" published by a writer hiding behind a pseudonym? And why did that anonymous writer hyphenate "Shake-speare"? It was the first time the name appeared this way. To anti-Stratfordians, the hyphen recalls other hyphenated pseudonyms such as "Tom Tell-troth" and "Simon Smell-knave," suggesting that contemporaries may have viewed the name as a pseudonym. While the hyphenated name "Shake-speare" would appear frequently on title pages over the coming decades, it never appeared hyphenated in the Stratford man's records.

Whoever wrote *Willobie His Avisa* and whatever he or she was saying about "Shake-speare" remains mysterious. Scholars have called the poem "probably the most famous of Elizabethan poetic riddles . . . a tightly shut box of words." What surfaces again and again with Shakespeare is this sense of concealment and mystery—of things said cryptically and then suppressed; of rumors refracted through the obscure, densely allusive language of Elizabethan poetry.

In 1595 a poet named Thomas Edwards described Shakespeare as "deafly masking thro / Stately troupes rich conceited."

In 1597 Joseph Hall, a puritan moralist, published rumors about a hidden poet, someone who was concealing himself like a cuttlefish in a cloud of ink and shifting his identity "on to anothers name":

Long as the craftie Cuttle lieth sure
In the black Cloud of his thick vomiture;

Who list complain of wronged faith or fame
When he may shift it on to anothers name.

Who was the crafty cuttle shifting his fame onto another's name? Hall gave a few hints. The cuttle had an annoying tendency to create hyphenated epithets ("In Epithets to join two words as one / Forsooth for Adjectives cannot stand alone"). *Venus and Adonis* and *The Rape of Lucrece* are overrun with such epithets: for instance, "rose-cheek'd Adonis," a "bold-fac'd suitor," "sick-thoughted Venus," the "love-sick queen," "lust-breathed Tarquin," and "holy-thoughted Lucrece." Hall also mocked the cuttle's fondness for beginning his lines with "Big But Ohs" ("Big But Ohs each stanza can begin"). Many lines in the poems begin with *But* or *Oh*—or both, as in "But, O, what banquet wert thou to the taste." A further characteristic: the cuttle appealed to the god Phoebus-Apollo to help him write. ("Phoebus filled him with intelligence," Hall wrote. "He can implore the heathen deities / To guide his bold and busy enterprise.") Shakespeare's *Venus and Adonis* features a prominent quote on its title page invoking Phoebus-Apollo to guide him: "Let base-conceited wits admire vile things. / Fair Phoebus lead me to the Muses' springs." His poetry, Hall continued, owes a debt to the fourteenth-century Italian poet Petrarch. ("Or filch whole pages at a clap for need, / From honest Petrarch, clad in English weed.") Certain scenes in *The Rape of Lucrece* closely resemble one of Petrarch's poems, *canzone delle metamorfosi*, even mirroring Petrarch's language. Finally, the cuttle's poetry is immoral, Hall prudishly bemoaned—"uncleanly." *Venus and Adonis* and *The Rape of Lucrece* are notoriously filled with sexual imagery. Nicknaming this immoral poet "Labeo," Hall urged him to clean it up: "For shame! Or better write; or, Labeo, write none." Why "Labeo"? The name possibly referenced the Roman poet Labeo Attius, who was disparaged for his "obscene and filthy verse." But "Labeo," Latin for "one who has large lips," is also a genus of fish, making it a fitting name for the crafty cuttle.

Another poet, John Marston, took up Joseph Hall's gibe at "Labeo" in his own satirical poems, identifying "Labeo" even more explicitly with

Shakespeare. "So *Labeo* did complaine his love was stone, / Obdurate, flinty, so relentlesse none," Marston wrote, quoting the language of *Venus and Adonis.* "Art thou obdurate, flinty, hard as steel? / Nay, more than flint, for stone at rain relenteth," Venus complains when Adonis resists her advances. For his own part, Gibson conceded, "We may agree that Hall is patting himself on the back because he has guessed the identity of an author writing under a pseudonym . . . and that he is aiming his satire at this author [Shakespeare]." Since then, however, scholars have tried to back away from the identification, insisting that Labeo must be some other poet, though no one else fits the bill.

When I suggested in the *Atlantic* that doubts about Shakespeare were almost as old as the works themselves, Shapiro accused me of publishing a "falsehood." The *Atlantic*, duly registering Shapiro's complaints, corrected my "falsehood," removing the phrase about doubts being almost as old as the works themselves and inserting new language to clarify that doubts arose only in the mid-nineteenth century. The professor said so, so it must be true.

The problem, of course, is that it is all a matter of interpretation. These are literary texts, capable of multiple possible meanings. The authorship question turns on reading practices. It is a dispute over the exact meaning of Renaissance Scripture—the ordained reading, in which there is no funny business, no doubts or whispers or questions—and the heretical one, in which lay readers have bypassed the priestly interpreters to uncover meaning themselves. Their sin is the old, original sin: the forbidden pursuit of knowledge. But is there hope of "proving" anything with scraps of poetry? This is literature, not data. One can only argue a reading, sweetly coax, and persuade.

In 1599 a Cambridge poet named John Weever published a book of epigrams, proclaiming that to "whip and scourge, my chiefest meaning [intention] is / With seven sour rods laid full seven weeks in piss." In epigram 11, titled "In Spurium quendam scriptorem" ("On Spurious, a certain writer"), Weever mocked an unnamed and spurious ("not being what it purports to be; false or fake") poet who had written "bald rimes of Venus." Scholars say he is referring to a French poet named Clément

Marot, but Marot died in 1544, and Weever specifies in his introduction that his epigrams are topical: "Epigramms are much like unto Almanacks serving especially for the year which they are made." In 1599, when Weever's epigrams were published, *Venus and Adonis* had gone into a fifth edition and was by far the most famous English poem about Venus.

In the early years of the sixteen hundreds, a series of comedies known as the Parnassus plays were staged by the students of Cambridge University. "O sweet Shakspeare! I'll have his picture in my study at the courte," a goofy character called Gullio exclaims. "I'll worship sweet Mr. Shakspeare, and to honour him will lay his *Venus and Adonis* under my pillow." Is the play mocking the idolatry of "Mr. Shakspeare"? Gullio is gullible—literally, a gull.

In another one of the plays, two characters named Will Kempe and Richard Burbage appear. Kempe and Burbage were the real-life names of players in the Lord Chamberlain's Men, the company to which the Stratford man also belonged. The players are depicted as illiterate morons looking for Cambridge students to compose lines for their plays. "Few of the university pen plaies well," Kempe complains, "they smell too much of that writer Ovid, and that writer Metamorphoses, and they talk too much of Proserpina & Juppiter. Whey heres our fellow Shakespeare puts them all downe." Kempe stupidly thinks "Metamorphoses" is a writer. He also suggests that Ovidian influence and classical allusion are the hallmarks of university men—unlike "our fellow Shakespeare." Does he not realize that Shakespeare's *Venus and Adonis* is adapted from Ovid's *Metamorphoses* and that his plays are full of classical allusions to, for example, Proserpina and Jupiter? The Cambridge students deride the players' ignorance, describing them as "leaden spouts that nought do vent but what they do receive." Ignoring the comedic context, Stratfordians treat the text as straightforward evidence that Shakespeare was the Stratford actor. But does it prove his authorship? Or does it lampoon players and implicitly identify Shakespeare as someone who writes like a university-educated scholar?

⁂

In the Renaissance writers were often purposefully ambiguous, building complexity into their poetry as a defense mechanism. The censors were watching. Those writers who gave offense to the Crown could incur punishments such as "fine, imprisonment, loss of ears, or nailing to the pillory, slitting the nose, branding the forehead, whipping in public places, or any punishment but death," according to the records of the Court of Star Chamber. In 1579 the writer John Stubbs published a pamphlet arguing against the Queen's proposed marriage to the French Duke of Anjou. At forty-six, Elizabeth I was too old to bear children, making the marriage pointless, he argued, as well as immoral (for the duke was a Catholic). Stubbs, found guilty of "seditious writing," was sentenced to have his right hand chopped off with a cleaver in the marketplace of Westminster. It took three blows to sever his hand. Ben Jonson was imprisoned twice for plays that gave offense. The precise nature of the first offense is unknown, as all copies of the offensive play, *The Isle of Dogs* (1597), were destroyed. The second offense was an anti-Scottish reference in the play *Eastward Ho* (1605), which displeased the new king, James I, a Scot. Thomas Nashe, who cowrote the first play with Jonson, fled to escape imprisonment. John Marston, who cowrote the second, fled too. Even being slung into prison—where plague was rampant and starvation common unless someone on the outside paid to bring you food—could be a death sentence. The playwright Thomas Kyd never recovered from his time in Bridewell Prison. In 1593 he was tortured to reveal the author of "divers lewd and mutinous libels" that had been posted around London. Having pointed his finger at his former roommate Christopher Marlowe, he was released—but died the next year, aged thirty-five.

The effect of censorship on the writerly psyche was the creation of what the Yale scholar Annabel Patterson calls a "functional ambiguity." If writers wanted to critique powerful figures or expose some sensitive information but also avoid, say, having their nose slit, they had to be creative. Jonson listed a whole range of cryptic devices used by writers of his day to encode meaning and evade the censors, including riddles, anagrams, acrostics, logogriphs, palindromes, eteostiches, telestichs. "What we can find everywhere apparent and widely understood, at least from the middle of the sixteenth century in England onward," explains Patterson, "is a system of communication ('literature') in which ambiguity becomes a necessary creative instrument, while at the same time the art (and the theory) of interpretation was reinvented, expanded, and honed." By constructing lines of double meaning, writers could maintain a certain plausible deniability. An epigram from 1618 praised a judge who understood that an author wishing to write truthfully must sometimes construct lines with two possible interpretations:

A Certain man was to a Judge complaining,
How one had written with a Double meaning.
Foole, said the Judge, no man deserveth trouble,
For Double meaning, so he deale not Double.

Take another scrap of poetry about Shakespeare—a seemingly inconsequential epigram published in 1611 by the poet John Davies. It is titled, "To Our English Terence Mr. Will: Shake-speare." Scholars read it as a nice bit of praise for Shakespeare, comparing him to the Roman playwright Terence, who was known for his comedies. In the Renaissance, however, Terence carried an additional association. He was believed to have been a cover—an allonym for works written by other Roman authors. "It is well-known by good record of learning, and that by Cicero's own witness, that some Comedies bearing Terence['s] name were written by worthy Scipio and wise Laelius," the scholar Roger Ascham wrote. Michel de Montaigne's essays, translated into English in 1603, also noted Scipio and Laelius's decision to "resign the credit of their comedies" to Terence. Which meaning is it? Is Davies merely complimenting Shakespeare? Or is he calling Shakespeare a cover? His epigram appeared in a book called *The Scourge of Folly*, which was subtitled "Consisting of satyricall epigramms, and others in honor of many noble and worthy persons of our land," suggesting there might be something biting or derisive about the line. The epigram becomes, in this light, another piece of literary gossip; a cheeky and defamatory satire winking to those in the know. But it is underhanded, maintaining a plausible deniability. Confronted, Davies could insist that his intended meaning was innocent. "I was merely saying how wonderful Shakespeare is!"

Which raises the question: Were writers forbidden from writing openly about Shakespeare? And if so, why?

Books and poems of the period are strewn with many more allusions, but amongst these allusions to the poet in his lifetime, "there is none," to quote Professor Wells, "that explicitly and incontrovertibly identifies him with Stratford-upon-Avon."

In 1628 a theologian compiling a list of the best English poets (Geoffrey Chaucer, Edmund Spenser, Michael Drayton, and so on) added, in Latin, "that well-known poet who takes a name from shaking and spear." The phrase immediately jumps out from the list of other names. Why not simply give him as "William Shakespeare," like the others? The conspicuous difference suggests something conspicuously different about Shakespeare.

⁂

Among all the references to which anti-Stratfordians point to argue that Shakespeare was an assumed name, their favorites by far are those made by the poet himself. *Shake-speare's Sonnets*, published in 1609, record the speaker's expectation that his identity will be "forgotten." This is not a matter of modesty. The author expects his "powerful rhyme" to outlive the gilded monuments of princes and seeks to immortalize his beloved in verse. But while the poetry will last forever, the poet himself will vanish:

From hence your memory death cannot take,
Although in me each part will be forgotten
Your name from hence immortal life shall have,
Though I, once gone, to all the world must die.
—Sonnet 81

But how could the author be "forgotten"? How could he die "to all the world"? The name Shakespeare was famous by that time. And yet the sonnets suggest that the poet's identity is concealed—and that when he dies, it will be lost for good.

My name be buried where my body is,
And live no more to shame nor me nor you.
—**Sonnet 72**

Why this obsession with being "forgotten" and "buried"? The usual thing in poetry was to write about the possibility of living eternally through verse. Ovid, Shakespeare's greatest influence among the ancient poets, knew that his name would live forever:

Yet in my better part I shall be borne
immortal, far above the stars on high,
and mine shall be a name indelible.
Wherever Roman power extends her sway
over the conquered lands, I shall be read
by lips of men. If Poets' prophecies
have any truth, through all the coming years
of future ages, I shall live in fame.

Shakespeare did not doubt the immortality of his verse. "When all the breathers of this world are dead; / You still shall live, such virtue hath my pen," he writes. But where Ovid knew his verse would make his name "indelible," Shakespeare suggests that, for him, the opposite will be true. His name will be buried; will die with him. His friend should refrain from even repeating his name, lest he be associated with the poet's shame:

Do not so much as my poor name rehearse;
But let your love even with my life decay
Lest the wise world should look into your moan,
And mock you with me after I am gone.
—**Sonnet 71**

At the same time, he suspects his writing reveals him—that in his verse, "every word doth almost tell my name, / Showing their birth, and where they did proceed" (76)—suggesting his name is otherwise concealed. Why is he so intent on concealing his identity? The speaker refers again and again to his shame. He is "in disgrace with fortune and men's eyes," he writes,

I all alone beweep my outcast state,
And trouble deaf heaven with my bootless cries,
And look upon myself and curse my fate.
—Sonnet 29

How to reconcile this with the Stratford man, who, far from being outcast, enjoyed rising wealth and status: a coat of arms, a large house. The poet is "despised," "shamed," and "vile esteemed," he continues. There is a "vulgar scandal stamped upon my brow" (112), he writes of the stigma that shadows him. But what happened? We hear only that "my name receives a brand" (111). It is enough to raise the question: If his name has received a brand, might that compel him to write under another name? After all, the poet's identity *could* disappear if "William Shakespeare" was not his name; if he intended his identity to disappear beneath a nom de plume. "My name is Will," he writes in Sonnet 136, but does he mean his real name or his pen name?

The sonnets are so problematic for the traditional theory of authorship that some scholars have tried to dismiss them, arguing that they are merely poetic fictions—literary exercises through which Shakespeare could display his technical virtuosity—and not about him at all. "It is better to read the sonnets for universal values than to lose their poetry by turning them into riddles about Shakespeare's biography," warned the scholar C. L. Barber. But sonnets—whether John Donne's *Holy Sonnets* struggling with his faith or John Milton's meditation on his blindness—tend to be highly personal poems. Reading Shakespeare's sonnets, William Wordsworth was compelled by their aura of personal confession: "With this key, Shakespeare unlocked his heart," he wrote. C. S. Lewis agreed that the sonnets tell "so odd a story that we find a difficulty in regarding it as fiction." Even the most orthodox scholars have conceded that "it is not unreasonable to look in them for reflections of his personal experience."

Who, for instance, are the other figures in the sonnets? Do they have something to do with the scandal? One is a handsome young man, the "fair youth," thought by many scholars to be Henry Wriothesley, the Earl of Southampton, again. The poet urges him to produce an heir: "Make thee another self for love of me," he writes in Sonnet 10—a bizarre request. He lavishes praise on the man's beauty—but why did Shakespeare address sonnets to a man? The sense of scandal that apparently shadowed the poet in his own lifetime has lingered. One could not read the poems, lamented an eighteenth-century critic, "without an equal mixture of disgust and indignation." Such sentiment "casts a slur on the dignity of the poet's name which scarcely bears discussion," agreed another. The editor of a 1793 edition of Shakespeare's works simply omitted the sonnets because "the strongest act of Parliament that could be framed would fail to compel readers into their service." Scholars continued wringing their hands well into the twentieth century. "The story Shakespeare recounts of his moral—or rather his immoral—predicament . . . must certainly, in the interests of the British Empire, be smothered up," the critic L. P. Smith concluded in 1933.

Other sonnets involve a mistress, the "dark lady." At some point, the youth and the mistress seem to have an affair. A fourth figure hovers over this thorny threesome—a "rival poet." What on earth is it all about? "No capable poet, much less a Shakespeare, intending to produce a merely 'dramatic' series of poems, would dream of inventing a story like that of these sonnets or, even if he did, of treating it as they treat it," wrote the scholar A. C. Bradley. The very weirdness of the sonnets, their obscurity and unintelligibility, suggests they tell "a real story," written "for people who knew the details and incidents of which we are ignorant."

Scholars have tried desperately to unravel the sonnets and identify the figures, publishing studies with titles like *Shakespeare's Sonnets Solved* and *The Secret Drama of Shakespeare's Sonnets Unfolded, With the Characters Identified*. But the sonnets remain opaque. Nothing in them fits the Stratford man's life. "Shakespeare's sonnets are an island of poetry surrounded by a barrier of icebergs and dense fog," wrote the

Harvard scholar Douglas Bush. But the fog itself is suggestive. It is the same fog that surrounds everything to do with Shakespeare. Might the fog lift with the right author?

⁂

The fundamental charge that anti-Stratfordians bring against scholars is that they ignore evidence inconvenient to their belief—that they have been, in fact, *unscholarly*. For to miss the potential meanings of "Our English Terence" or "that poet who takes a name from shaking and spear" they must read shallowly. They must stay unwaveringly on the surface of the text, refusing it the possibility of alternate or double meaning. They must ignore the historical and cultural contexts in which the author wrote. They must cover their eyes and block their ears to allusion. They must, in short, commit literary malpractice.

Have the scholars failed to interpret properly the sacred texts in their care? Have they, blinded by their faith, hopelessly bungled the foremost duty of their office: to *read*?

The single most important text in the authorship debate is the First Folio, the authoritative collection of Shakespeare's plays published in 1623, seven years after the Stratford man's death. Until then, only half of the plays had been published, in individual, pamphlet-like editions called quartos. The Folio collected all thirty-six plays, half of which might have otherwise been lost, and set up Shakespeare as a figure of cultural prestige, hailing him in a series of prefatory pages as the triumph of Britain—a poet "not of an age but for all time!" Scholars argue that this praise of Shakespeare in the First Folio, seven years after his death, confirms the Stratford man's authorship.

(Summing up the scholarly testimony in the 1965 trial, Justice Richard Wilberforce noted that the "slight" evidence of the Stratford man's authorship "rests positively, in the main, on the explicit statements of the First Folio of 1623, and on continuous tradition.")

It is peculiar, however, that the praise was seven years delayed. Other writers were eulogized within weeks or months of their passing. Why not Shakespeare? Anti-Stratfordians argue that the First Folio in fact contains statements hinting at a hidden author. According to this view, the central text of the Stratfordian faith is also its greatest weakness.

Out of 750 copies printed originally, 235 remain today. One was found in a French library in 2014, where it had lain undisturbed for two hundred years. Another surfaced in 2016 in a Scottish country house. In 2020 a First Folio sold at Christie's fetched nearly $10 million, making it the most expensive work of literature ever auctioned.

The largest collection of First Folios is held by the Folger Shakespeare Library in Washington, DC. As I was contemplating a trip to the Folger to see a folio in the flesh, the Supreme Court justice John Paul Stevens died. Stevens was one of several justices who doubted the traditional attribution. "I think the evidence that he was not the author is beyond a reasonable doubt," he told the *Wall Street Journal* in 2009. In an article in the *New Yorker*, James Shapiro announced that he was donating his "treasured correspondence" with the late justice to the Folger Shakespeare Library. The professor and the justice had apparently exchanged letters on the authorship question. In the *New Yorker*, Shapiro explained his decision to make his correspondence with the justice available to the public: "I hope it may be of value to others interested in how one of the finest legal minds of the past century interpreted evidence, read the past through the present, and comfortably embraced a conspiracy theory," he wrote.

Stevens was barely cold in his grave, his family still mourning his passing, and Shapiro was making out that he had been a dupe. What did a discussion of the authorship between an arch Shakespeare defender and "one of the finest legal minds of the past century" really look like?

I decided I would read the correspondence myself.

FOUR

Seeliest Ignorance

THE FOLGER SHAKESPEARE LIBRARY SITS one block east of the Capitol, across the street from the Library of Congress and catty-cornered to the Supreme Court. It looks like a bank or a temple—a large block of white marble in the neoclassical style, like Washington's other buildings. Henry and Emily Folger were Gilded Age philanthropists who spent their fortune obsessively collecting First Folios. Henry had become enamored of Shakespeare as a student at Amherst College. After graduating from Columbia Law School, he joined John D. Rockefeller's Standard Oil Company and married Emily, a kindred Shakespeare spirit. For some forty years, while Henry climbed the ranks of Standard Oil, becoming president and later chairman of the board, the Folgers built their Shakespeare library, sending confidential agents to auction sales in London and New York to acquire the most precious books of the English Renaissance. Their haul eventually came to include eighty-two copies of the First Folio, as well as its later editions: fifty-eight copies of the Second Folio (1632); twenty-four copies of the Third Folio (1663); and thirty-six copies of the Fourth Folio (1685). They also amassed rare Shakespeare quartos, the works of Shakespeare's contemporaries, and works that have been identified by scholars as Shakespeare's sources, so that their collection encompassed all the great documents of the Shakespearean age. It is, as the library boasts, "the world's largest collection of Shakespeare materials."

For years, the couple kept their treasures in bank vaults and Brooklyn warehouses, locked away from the grubby hands of researchers. Childless, the Folgers looked on their collection as their legacy. Henry Folger referred to his books as "the boys." Eventually they decided to share the boys with the public and chose Washington, DC, for their library, wanting to create a monument to Shakespeare in the US capital. "The poet is one of our best sources, one of the wells from which we Americans draw our national thought, our faith, and our hope," Emily Folger explained, drawing on a strain of American literary criticism that saw Shakespeare, paradoxically, as America's poet. He had influenced the founding fathers, who saw in his villains and tyrants the dangers of monarchy and the need for institutional checks on power. Shakespeare's history plays heralded the "inauguration of modern democracy," Walt Whitman wrote, for they put "on record the first full exposé—and by far the most vivid one . . . of the political theory and results" of a feudal system "which America has come on earth to abnegate and replace."

Having bought up and demolished a block of row houses on Capitol Hill, the Folgers built their library. The white marble exterior is ornamented with various Shakespearean inscriptions. Across the top of the building: "For Wisdomes sake, a word that all men love." On the fountain, beneath a statue of the sprite Puck, from *A Midsummer Night's Dream*: "Lord, what fools these mortals be!" The interior, however, is oak-paneled with stained glass windows and Renaissance tapestries evoking Tudor England, or at least one of Henry VIII's hunting lodges. Henry Folger died two years before the building's completion, but Emily saw the project through, installing the collection, hiring staff, and ensuring the library's endowment through donations from her inheritance. She had a master's degree in Shakespeare and a particular interest in Shakespeare's female characters. "His comedies are a revel of feminine supremacy," she noted in a speech at Vassar College.

The opening of the Folger Shakespeare Library on April 23, 1932—Shakespeare's birthday, of course—was attended by President Herbert Hoover and the first lady, the chief justice of the Supreme Court, and the ambassadors from Britain, France, and Germany. King George V sent a message from Buckingham Palace expressing his pleasure. "The Folger Shakespeare Library fittingly takes the place among those other symbols which venerate America's immortals, the Washington Monument and the Lincoln Memorial," the *Evening Star* reported, claiming Shakespeare as an honorary American "immortal" alongside George Washington and Abraham Lincoln. Joseph Quincy Adams Jr., the Folger's inaugural director of research, delivered a commemorative lecture on "Shakespeare and American Culture," emphasizing that Shakespeare had become "the cornerstone of cultural discipline," rising above the rest of the Western canonical heroes. "Not Homer, nor Dante, not Goethe, nor Chaucer, nor Spenser, nor even Milton," Adams insisted, "but Shakespeare was made the chief object of study and veneration."

Entering the building, I passed the doors to the Elizabethan Theatre, which puts on Shakespeare's plays—next up, *The Merry Wives of Windsor*—and entered the Great Hall, a long, stately room used for exhibitions. A copy of the nine-hundred-page, double-columned First Folio sat on display in its glass case. Except when they are brought out for exhibitions, the library's other folios, manuscripts, and rare materials are kept in an underground storage facility that stretches a full block beneath the building—dust-proof, humidity-controlled rooms reportedly protected by a nine-inch-thick steel bank vault door. In 2016, to mark the four hundredth anniversary of Shakespeare's death, the Folger busted out the Folios, touring first editions to all fifty states like a medieval show of saints' bones. When I visited in late 2019, the library was getting ready to close for extensive renovations in preparation for 2023—the four-hundred-year anniversary of the book itself.

A bust of Henry Folger looking dapper in a bow tie was ensconced on the wall. The Folger is ostensibly a bastion of orthodoxy, a temple to Shakespeare, but its modern presentation obscures its founders' sympathies. Henry Folger was a founding member of the Bacon Society of America, which inquired into the theory that Francis Bacon wrote the works of Shakespeare. He collected books on the authorship question as part of his vast Shakespeare library, though his mind does not seem to have been fixed. In 1925, five years after the Earl of Oxford was first proposed as a candidate for authorship, Henry Folger acquired an annotated 1570 Geneva Bible believed to have belonged to Oxford. The acquisition suggests that, in his final years, Henry Folger had become intrigued by the new candidate. In 1928, two years before his death, he wrote a letter admitting that he was "coming towards the end of my interest in Bacon." The letter has been used to claim that Henry Folger ultimately reconciled himself to the Stratfordian faith. He continued to pursue Oxford-related works for his collection, however, suggesting that he had moved not from Bacon to Shakespeare but from Bacon to Oxford.

The Folger does not advertise this aspect of its history, papering over it like an embarrassing stain on the otherwise celebrated narrative of its founding. The library's directors have been, for the most part, staunchly orthodox. Louis Wright, who took the helm in 1948, went so far as to deny the knowledge exhibited in the plays in order to maintain the Stratford man's authorship claim. "The plays show no evidence of profound book learning," he declared, clinging rather absurdly to the myth that Shakespeare was inspired by "Nature." Gail Kern Paster, who reigned from 2002 to 2011, deemed anti-Stratfordian ideas "pernicious," and when John Paul Stevens died, she scolded the late justice for his nonbelief: "While we at the Folger will remember Justice Stevens fondly, we strongly disavow his wrongheaded opinions about Shakespeare." The current director, Michael Witmore, is less dogmatic about the authorship. After he took over, a new statement appeared on the website:

> The Folger has been a major location for research into the authorship question and welcomes scholars looking for new evidence that sheds light on the plays' origins. How this particular man—or anyone, for that matter—could have produced such an astounding body of works is one of the great mysteries. If the current consensus on the authorship of the plays and poems is ever overturned, it will be because new and extraordinary evidence is discovered. The Folger Shakespeare Library is the most likely place for such an unlikely discovery.

The idea was tantalizing: What might lie, secure but lost, in the bowels of the Folger?

"You can't have a collection like ours and say you know everything. It's just wrong," Witmore said when I asked him about the authorship question. But he wasn't up at night worrying about it, he assured me. "I'm much more thinking about the humanities and what role we need to play in the world we live in today." Witmore was friendly and easygoing, accustomed to playing host to all manner of visitors who come to the library seeking Shakespeare. Before taking over the Folger, he had held professorships at Carnegie Mellon University and the University of Wisconsin–Madison. Now he was Shakespeare's ambassador in Washington, advocating passionately for the place of poetry in the civic life of the capital. "I tend to follow the scholarly consensus," he continued. "When it comes time to, I'm sure I'll know my cue." When it comes time to what? I leaned forward. Was Witmore anticipating a shift? Waiting for the pendulum to swing? I pushed him, but he clammed up. "I don't feel compelled to make statements about it, just like I don't feel compelled to weigh in on foreign policy disputes," he said. "I just . . . I don't . . . Are you going to quote me?"

I wandered into the reading room, which continued the Tudor theme: carved oak paneling, a high-trussed roof, Flemish tapestries, a large stone fireplace, researchers hunched like monks over long tables. On one end hang portraits of Henry and Emily Folger in their academic robes, gazing proudly over their children. Their ashes are immured in the wall, behind a memorial plaque. On another wall hangs a large painting of baby Shakespeare surrounded by various allegorical figures in a manger-like nativity scene. It is called *The Infant Shakespeare Attended by Nature and the Passions*, by the eighteenth-century artist George Romney. Nature, glowing like the Holy Spirit, hovers over the infant, blessing and beatifying him, infusing him with genius-poet dust. Baby Shakespeare gazes blankly at the viewer, unmoved. I thought baby Shakespeare looked a bit vapid, but it is a remarkable painting for its barefaced equation of the Renaissance poet with the son of God. Leaving baby Shakespeare to his infant babbles, no doubt very precocious, I wandered over to the circulation desk where I requested to view the correspondence of James Shapiro and John Paul

"Baby Shakespeare" by George Romney, ca. 1791–92

Stevens. It was promptly produced: a thin stack of papers secured in a manilla folder. I sat at one of the long tables and read through them. The letters began with great politesse, a dignified discussion on a matter of literary evidence between a justice and a scholar, both at pains to be on their very best behavior.

Then it unraveled—not on Stevens's side but on Shapiro's. In his last letter, Shapiro cut off the correspondence. Why he had made the letters public, I couldn't understand. Perhaps it made him feel important to be in correspondence with a Supreme Court justice and have his letters in the archives of the Folger. But he didn't come off well. I made copies. Eventually, I wanted to interview Shapiro, and I suspected I would need them.

Returning the letters to the circulation desk, I wandered back into the Great Hall to inspect the First Folio.

* * *

The title page announces, "Mr. William Shakespeares Comedies, Histories, & Tragedies." The first recorded reader—or, more precisely, buyer—of a First Folio was a fashionable gentleman named Sir Edward Dering, who had left his country seat to spend the season in London. Naturally, he did a bit of shopping. In his account book for December 5, 1623, Sir

Edward recorded his purchases: marmalade, boot hose, a boat ride across the Thames, meals for himself and his servant, and two copies of Shakespeare's First Folio. Below the title sits the famous portrait of Shakespeare known as the Droeshout portrait, after its engraver, Martin Droeshout. It is a famously awful portrait. Critics over the years have complained that the head is huge—"much too big for the body." The skull is of "horrible hydrocephalus development." The mouth is too small. The ear is malformed. The hair is lopsided, like a bad wig. The countenance is "pudding faced." One eye is lower than the other. A guild of British ophthalmologists determined that it actually has two right eyes. Light hits it from several directions at once. "I never saw a stupider face," declared the eighteenth-century artist Thomas Gainsborough. The figure has no neck, so its head appears to be floating on top of the ruff. Something funny is going on with his outfit. The shoulder wings are "grotesquely large and vilely drawn." In 1911 an anonymous tailor writing in the *Gentleman's Tailor* pointed out that the figure has two left arms: the doublet "is so strangely illustrated that the right-hand side of the forepart is obviously the left-hand side of the backpart; and so gives a harlequin appearance." This, the tailor noted, "is not unnatural to assume was intentional, and done with express object and purpose." The literary scholar Northrop Frye put it bluntly: the portrait makes Shakespeare "look like an idiot."

A sartorially challenged "idiot"

The suspicion has arisen that the portrait's deformities

were, as the anonymous tailor suggested, intentional—that it is a joke portrait depicting a fool as the author. Two left arms signal left-handed writing, which in ancient tradition is associated with deception. "Writing with the left hand is to make some secret circumvention, to cunny-catch, deceive, or defame," wrote Artemidorus in the second century AD. (His work was translated into English in 1606, and widely read and quoted.) Are the two left arms meant to suggest that the figure is a deceiver—a fake? There is a strange double line running on one side of the figure's jaw, which some skeptics see as an indication that the face is a mask. Scholars have protested that the engraver was merely incompetent. "Droeshout's deficiencies are, alas, only too gross," sighed Professor Samuel Schoenbaum. But it is hard to believe that a professionally commissioned artist would be so inept as to accidentally make two left arms, two right eyes, a huge head, and all of the other alleged deformities. The First Folio was an expensive undertaking, several years in the making. The anti-theatrical puritan William Prynne complained that "Shakespeare's plays are printed in the best crown paper, far better than most bibles." It might have been financed by brothers William and Philip Herbert, the Earls of Pembroke and Montgomery, to whom it is dedicated. (A prefatory epistle explains that the earls showed "much favour" toward the author and his works, though the Stratford man had no documented relationship with them.) If the patrons or the printer did not approve of the portrait, they could have refused it and sought out a better one. They did not. The portrait of the idiot is apparently what they wanted.

The strangeness of the Droeshout portrait becomes especially apparent when placed next to other portraits of the period. The other authors look nicely proportional in their title page portraits. Dignified. Their portraits also tend to be elaborate productions, featuring allegorical figures, personalized mottos, emblems, and inscriptions communicating information about the author's identity and preselecting the author's intended audience. For instance, Ben Jonson's folio of 1616 features a laurel wreath, a motto, and a Latin inscription from Horace explaining that he wrote not for the crowd but for the discriminating few: *Neque, me vt miretur turbo laboro: Contentus paucis lectoribus* ("I do not labor for the crowd to admire me, I am content with a few readers"). Shakespeare's portrait is oddly bare. No motto, no personalizing emblem, no laurels signifying a poet, no coat of arms, though his father had gone to some trouble and expense in acquiring one. His coat of arms on the portrait would have identified him unequivocally as the author. Why omit it? The figure is as stripped of pomp as King Lear crying, "Doth any here know me? . . . Who is it that can tell me who I am?" ("Lear's shadow," replies the Fool.) Nothing in the portrait would even lead one to think he is a poet.

On the page directly facing Shakespeare's portrait—in fact, preceding the portrait—there is a short poem, "To the Reader," by Ben Jonson, advising the reader to look *away* from the portrait:

This Figure that thou here seest put,
It was for gentle Shakespeare cut,
Wherein the Graver had a strife
with Nature, to out-doo the life:
O, could he but have drawne his wit
As well in brasse, as he hath hit
His face, the Print would then surpasse
All, that was ever writ in brasse.
But, since he cannot, Reader, looke
Not on his Picture, but his booke.

The poem describes the portrait not as an image *of* Shakespeare but as a "Figure" cut "for" him and "put" on the title page. (In the Renaissance, *figure* could mean "an imaginary form, a phantasm," according to the *Oxford English Dictionary*.) "The poem undermines the visual power of the portrait by insisting on it as something constructed and 'put' there," writes the scholar Leah Marcus. It is "in the precise sense of the term, iconoclastic." It attacks the portrait's authenticity and credibility. It "abolishes Shakespeare as an entity apart from his writings." Astonishingly, Marcus, who is outwardly a Stratfordian, concedes that "Jonson's poem sets readers off on a treasure hunt for the author: Where is the 'real' Shakespeare to be found?" In his "Booke," the poem tells us—in his plays, his language. "The

First Folio opens with an implicit promise to communicate an authorial identity, which it instead repeatedly displaces: Shakespeare is somehow there, but nowhere definitively there."

I stared down at the image of the hydrocephalic idiot, wondering what Jonson had been up to. Why would he begin this expensive book commemorating Shakespeare with a poem that sends readers off on a "treasure hunt" for the real author? Having been imprisoned twice for his writings, Jonson developed a notoriously ambiguous writing style. He sought to be understood not by the "crowd" but by the "discriminating few," as indicated by the inscription he selected for his own folio. Scholars have described him as "the supreme tactician" and "this most complex of authors," one whose literary techniques and interpretive puzzles "are related in one way or another to the topic of secrecy." He was influenced by the first-century Roman rhetorician Quintilian, who recommended to writers "the very common device . . . in which we drop a hint to show that what we want to be understood is not what we are saying—not necessarily the opposite (as in irony) but something hidden and left to the hearer to discover." When it comes to Shakespeare's First Folio, however, scholars ignore Jonson's reputation for ambiguity. In telling readers to look away from the picture, what does Jonson want to be understood? He deplored the common failure to read carefully, grumbling how "the multitude commend Writers, as they do Fencers, or Wrestlers. . . . But in these things the unskillful are naturally deceived." Lest anyone misunderstand who he considered a poor reader, he continued: "nor think this only to be true in the sordid multitude, but the neater sort of our Gallants: for all are the multitude; only they differ in clothes, not in judgment or understanding."

The Folio proceeds with two letters from John Heminges and Henry Condell, fellow players in Shakespeare's company. In the first, addressed in effusive language to William and Philip Herbert, "the most noble and incomparable pair of brethren . . . Knights of the most Noble Order of the Garter, and our singular good Lords," the players explain that they have collected the plays and are publishing them "without ambition either of selfe-profit, or fame: onely to keepe the memory of so worthy a Friend, & Fellow alive, as was our SHAKESPEARE." In the second, an address "To the great Variety of Readers. From the most able, to him that can but spell," the players acknowledge that readers have the right to censure—that is, judge—the plays: "Do so, but buy it first," they urge. The crass sales pitch rather contradicts their earlier disavowal of profit: "whatever you do, buy," they insist again.

The letters of Heminges and Condell praising their "fellow" Shakespeare are considered incontrovertible evidence of the Stratford man's authorship. To Professor Schoenbaum, their testimony constituted "the most crucial single document in the annals of authorship attribution." But there is a glitch in the testimony. In the eighteenth century, the scholar George Steevens noted that the letters contain numerous parallels to Ben Jonson's writings. He recorded twelve pages' worth of parallels. The letters draw on Roman writers such as Horace and Pliny the Elder, which fits with Jonson, a classics scholar, but not with the actors. Noting that the players were "wholly unused to composition" (indeed, we don't even know if they could write), Steevens concluded that "every word of the first half of this address to the reader, which is signed with the names of John Heminges and Henry Condell, was written by Ben Jonson." Subsequent scholars have agreed. (The letter "so strongly echoes the induction of Jonson's comedy *Bartholomew Fair* that many are convinced Jonson wrote the preface himself," affirms Leah Marcus.) What, then, is the value of this testimony? Read closely, for it is full of ridiculous statements. For instance, the players—or Jonson writing as the players—claim that the plays spilled out of Shakespeare without any need for revision: "His mind and hand went together: And what he thought, he uttered with that easinesse, that wee have scarse received from him a blot in his papers." No scholars take this claim seriously. And a "great Variety of Readers" could not have afforded the folio, certainly not those who "can but spell." (A bound copy cost a pound, about $200 today.) In their dedication to the earls, the players prostrate themselves absurdly, approaching "with a kind of religious addresse" and offering the plays to their lordships as "country hands reach foorth milke, cream, fruits, or what they have" to their gods. Observing that even the "meanest" cakes are more precious when "dedicated to Temples," they "humbly consecrate" the plays to the earls.

Is there something satirical here? Is Jonson's impersonation of the players a kind of parody? Scholars recognize that the Heminges and Condell letters cannot be entirely trusted. As one scholar writes, "The First Folio's omissions, errors, and outright lies have long been common knowledge." When it comes to Shakespeare's authorship, however, scholars want to grant the Heminges-Condell letters the status of affidavits. But they aren't sworn testimony; they aren't even really letters in the sense of private correspondence. They are literary texts, apparently written by Jonson, the "supreme tactician," created to frame our reception of plays that are themselves full of characters who engage in deception and forgery. In *King Lear*, the bastard Edmund forges a letter in the hand of his brother Edgar, with the aim of discrediting him. "It is his hand, my Lord," Edmund tells their father, the Earl of Gloucester, "but I hope his heart is not in the contents." His deception depends not only on the forgery but also on rhetorical manipulation—on his seeming reluctance to incriminate his brother. In *Hamlet*, when the prince discovers that his childhood friends Rosencrantz and Guildenstern are carrying a sealed letter from his uncle Claudius, king of Denmark, ordering his execution, he replaces it with a forged copy ordering their execution instead. And in *Twelfth Night*, when the pompous puritan Malvolio tries to spoil the fun, Maria gets revenge by composing a letter in the handwriting of Olivia, whom Malvolio seeks to marry. The letter convinces him that Olivia loves him and wishes to see him smile constantly and wear yellow stockings cross-gartered (a fashion she actually abhors). Credulously, Malvolio buys the letter. "By my life, this is my Ladies hand: these be her very C's, her U's, and her T's, and thus makes she her great P's." Following its instructions, he makes a fool of himself. The trick depends, crucially, on Malvolio's desire to believe that the letter is from Olivia.

Likewise, scholars desire to believe that the Heminges-Condell letters are genuinely from the two player-shareholders, even though they've discovered evidence that suggests otherwise. They've bought it ("whatever you do, buy"). They have to buy it—because if the portrait is fake,

Jonson's poem iconoclastic, and the Heminges-Condell letters unreliable, then the whole Folio presentation starts to look like a fraud. It is easier to believe that the letters are true. Humans are biased toward truth, inclined to believe that the communication of others is honest. Psychologists call this the "truth-default theory." We default to truth. It is uncomfortable to think we've been deceived, and perhaps especially uncomfortable for scholars to accept that their own subject—their Shakespeare—has deceived them.

But the fraud need not be malicious. Many deceptions in the plays are benevolent, intended to reconcile lovers, teach someone a lesson, or save a character's life. They partake of the tradition of the pious fraud, "a deception practiced for the furtherance of what is considered a good object; esp. for the advancement of religion." Religions employ pious frauds, counterfeiting miracles or falsely attributing sacred texts to holy figures, in order to increase the faith. The First Folio is a kind of sacred text. It marks the birth of a religion. If the author wished to remain unknown or if others had their own reasons for not telling, is it possible that the false attribution of the First Folio might have been a pious fraud, a benevolent lie, practiced for the furtherance of a good object: the preservation and celebration of the plays?

If it is a falsehood, Ben Jonson appears to be very uneasy about the lie. In the Folio's central tribute, a long poem titled "To the Memory of My Beloved the Author, Mr. William Shakespeare," he begins strangely, preoccupied with—of all things—Shakespeare's name. Putting Shakespeare's name in parentheses, he announces that he will not "draw envy" on it; that is, he will not praise Shakespeare's name:

To draw no envy (Shakespeare) on thy name
Am I thus ample to thy Booke, and Fame;
While I confesse thy writings to be such,
As neither Man, nor Muse, can praise too much;
'Tis true, and all men's suffrage. But these ways
Were not the paths I meant unto thy praise.

Why, if Shakespeare's writings cannot be praised "too much," does Jonson refuse to praise Shakespeare's name? He seems to fear that praising Shakespeare's name will be misunderstood and goes on to give three reasons for why he will not use "these ways" to honor the author. The first is that those of "seeliest Ignorance" will read what they want into his words, believing what is wrong as long as it sounds good. (*Seeliest*, from *seely*, means most "foolish, simple, silly.")

For seeliest Ignorance on these may light,
Which, when it sounds at best, but echoes right

The second reason is that those of "blinde Affection" will, in their idolatry, fail to discover the truth, groping hopelessly in the dark for explanations:

Or blinde Affection, which doth ne'er advance
The truth, but gropes, and urgeth all by chance

The third reason is that those of "crafty Malice" will pretend the words praise Shakespeare, though they know better:

Or crafty Malice, might pretend this praise,
And thinke to ruine, where it seem'd to raise.

It is a striking introduction, for which scholars do not seem to have any explanation. Why does Jonson feel the need to begin his tribute to Shakespeare by warning against "seeliest Ignorance," "blinde Affection," and "crafty Malice," all three of which would apparently misconstrue praise of Shakespeare's name? Jonson compares them to a whore praising a dignified, married woman—praise that could only be offensive:

These are, as some infamous Bawd, or Whore,
Should praise a Matron. What could hurt her more?

Between the lines, Jonson seems to be insinuating something he cannot say outright. Is he reluctant to praise the name "Shakespeare" because it is the *wrong* name? Because he perceives that the ignorant, the blindly affectionate, and the malicious will misinterpret the praise to the detriment of the real author? "*What could hurt her more?*" But if true, this raises a fresh set of questions. Why couldn't Jonson say the name outright? Why, if he knew the truth, did he not simply expose the correct author?

After his long preamble warning about praise of Shakespeare's name, Jonson finally begins his tribute properly:

I, therefore will begin. Soule of the Age!
The applause! delight! The wonder of our stage!
My Shakespeare, rise . . .

It sounds almost as though he is now praising a different person: my Shakespeare, not the person more commonly associated with that name. My Shakespeare, rise. (Will the real Shakespeare please stand up?) Addressing the author, Jonson goes on to extol him in the loftiest terms, as a poet who outstripped not only all English poets but all ancient poets, too— "all that insolent Greece or haughty Rome / Sent forth." Britain can now boast a poet to whom Europe should bow: "Tri'umph, my Britain, thou hast one to show / To whom all scenes of Europe homage owe. / He was not of an age but for all time!"

Jonson's eulogy offers little in the way of biographical information. If he wanted to identify the author unequivocally, he might have included details about his family, his hometown, his life. What he offers instead are a few careful clues—for instance, about his knowledge of Latin and Greek: "And though thou hadst [even if you had] small Latin, and lesse Greeke, / From thence to honour thee, I would not seeke / For names; but call forth thund'ring Aeschylus, / Euripides and Sophocles to us." These lines have been read as an insult suggesting that Shakespeare knew little Latin and Greek. But as the nineteenth-century scholar Clement

Mansfield Ingleby argued "though thou hadst" is in the subjunctive voice, the equivalent of "even if you had" or "even supposing that": even if you had small Latin and less Greek, I would still call forth the ancients to honor you. In his typically oblique fashion, Jonson may be acknowledging that the author *did* have Latin and Greek. Shakespeare forged his poetry through careful revision, sweating like a blacksmith forging metal, Jonson continues: for he "who casts to write a living line, must sweat / . . . and strike the second heat / Upon the Muses' anvil." If he did not "strike the second heat"—rewrite and revise—he would win scorn instead of laurels. Jonson's point, contradicting Heminges and Condell, is that Shakespeare's poetry was the product of labor, not divinely inspired nature. "For a good poet's made, as well as born," he writes. "And such wert thou."

Instead of providing more information that might shed light on the life of the poet, Jonson suggests that Shakespeare reveals himself—his "mind and manners"—in his works, as a father's face shines in that of his children. Here Jonson invokes the image of Pallas shaking her spear:

Look how the father's face
Lives in his issue, even so the race
Of Shakespeare's mind and manners brightly shines
In his well-turned, and true-filed lines;
In each of which he seems to shake a lance,
As brandish'd at the eyes of ignorance.

Then, toward the end of the poem, Jonson finally offers something like an identification. Calling Shakespeare a "swan"—a classical image for a poet—he associates the poet with "Avon":

Sweet Swan of Avon! What a sight it were
To see thee in our waters yet appear,
And make those flights upon the banks of Thames,
That so did take Eliza and our James!

Aha! Here at last seems to be the definitive identification of Shakespeare with Stratford-upon-Avon. "Avon," after all, is the name of the river that runs through Stratford. "Flights upon the banks of Thames" seems to reference the performances of his plays in the public theaters, which sat along the Thames. "Eliza and our James" are the two monarchs, Elizabeth and subsequently James, who were apparently very fond of the plays. But, frustratingly, this clarity dissipates on closer consideration. There are nine Avon rivers in Britain. Another problem: monarchs did not attend plays in the public theaters. The "flights upon the Thames / That so did take Eliza and our James" cannot refer to performances at the Globe, Rose, or other theaters on the Thames. Elizabeth and James enjoyed their entertainment at court, where Shakespeare's plays were often staged. ("These dramas, the most treasured jewels of our literary heritage, were *not* composed for the gawkish groundlings of the Globe," writes the scholar Richard Levin, "but for theatres and audiences far more worthy of them.")

The grandest court theater was the Great Hall at Hampton Court, a palace on the banks of the Thames, sixteen miles west of London. Henry VIII mounted elaborate entertainments there for courtiers and visiting dignitaries. During Elizabeth I's reign, huge festivals of plays were put on, and she went often "for her private recreation." James I continued the tradition. Some thirty plays were presented at Hampton Court over the first Christmas season of his reign. They were extravagant productions, involving, for instance, the "painting of seven cities, one village, and one country house." In 2014 an anti-Stratfordian named Alexander Waugh (grandson of the novelist Evelyn Waugh) pointed out that Hampton Court was originally known as "Avon." In 1543 the historian John Leland wrote, for example:

A Stately place for rare and glorious shew
There is, which Tamis with wandring stream doth dowse;
Times past, by name of Avon men it knew:
Here Henrie, the Eighth of that name, built a house
So sumptuous, as that on such an one
(Seeke through the world) the bright Sunne never shone.

Leland's words were quoted in the exhaustive history of Britain published by William Camden, Ben Jonson's tutor. So the description would certainly have been known to Jonson. In another work, Leland explained that "Avon" was a shortening of the Celtic-Roman name "Avondunum," meaning a fortified place (*dunum*) by a river (avon), which "the common people by corruption called Hampton." Raphael Holinshed similarly wrote in his sprawling 1577 book of British history, *Chronicles*, that "we now pronounce Hampton for Avondune." William Lambarde in his *Topographical and Historical Dictionary of England* affirmed that Hampton Court is "corruptly called Hampton for Avondun or Avon, an usual Name for many Waters within Ingland." In "Swan Song," a well-known poem of the period, a poet in the guise of a swan swims down the Thames describing the topography as he goes. When he gets to Hampton Court, he refers to it as the "lofty and conspicuous palace of Avona."

Alexander Waugh suggests that "Sweet Swan of Avon" was purposefully ambiguous: "Jonson was allowing, and probably expecting, some of his readers—those of 'seeliest Ignorance'—to think of Stratford-upon-Avon, home to the late Mr. Will. Shakspere." Others—the discriminating few—would know better. "That the cult of Stratfordianism was spawned from these games is regrettable," laments Waugh, "but for Jonson, at the time, it was a reasonable solution to a difficult and inconvenient problem."

Through the whole of Jonson's eighty-line poem, he never actually mentions Stratford. But several shorter poems follow Jonson's tribute, including one that refers to "thy Stratford Moniment." "Shake-speare, at length thy pious fellowes give the world thy Workes," writes the poet Leonard Digges, as he looks forward to a future

when that stone is rent,
And Time dissolves thy Stratford Moniment,
Here we alive shall view thee still. This Booke,
When Brasse and Marble fade, shall make thee looke
Fresh to all Ages.

A monument to Shakespeare sits on the wall of the local church in Stratford-upon-Avon. It is not known with any certainty who erected it or when, but some version of it must have existed by 1623. It features a bust of a mustachioed man, with an inscription below exhorting passersby to slow down and "read if thou canst"; that is, to figure out its meaning. The inscription proceeds in two parts—a Latin couplet, followed by English verse—but it is notoriously opaque:

IUDICIO PYLIUM, GENIO SOCRATEM, ARTE MARONEM, TERRA
TEGIT, POPVLUS MÆRET, OLYMPVS HABET

STAY PASSENGER, WHY GOEST THOV BY SO FAST,
READ IF THOV CANST, WHOM ENVIOUS DEATH HATH PLAST,
WITH IN THIS MONVMENT SHAKSPEARE: WITH WHOME,
QVICK NATURE DIDE WHOSE NAME, DOTH DECK TH[I]S TOMBE,
FAR MORE THEN COST: SIEH ALL TH[A]T HE HATH WRITT,
LEAVES LIVING ART, BVT PAGE, TO SERVE HIS WITT.

The Latin couplet refers to the judgment of the "Pylian" (Nestor, Greek king of Pylos), the genius of Socrates, and the art of "Maro" (Publius Virgilius Maro, more commonly known as Virgil). Scholars have struggled to explain why an epitaph to Shakespeare references Nestor (who wrote nothing), Socrates (who also wrote nothing—his observations were recorded by others), and Virgil (who, though a poet, was not one with whom the Ovid-loving Shakespeare was associated). The verse below isn't much clearer. Its opening lines, "Stay passenger, why goest thou by so fast, read if thou canst," mirror an epitaph Jonson wrote for a soldier: "If, Passenger, thou canst but read: Stay." Did Jonson write this inscription, too? What is meant by "Read . . . whom envious death hath plast [placed], with in this monument Shakspeare"? "[E]nvious death" cannot have "plast" Shakespeare within the monument, which is far too small to hold a body.

Time will "dissolve" the "moniment," Digges writes in the Folio. In the Renaissance, *dissolve* was used to mean "decipher," "resolve," or "figure out," as in the modern *solve*. ("At last we shall dissolve this Riddle," wrote the playwrights Beaumont and Fletcher.) To anti-Stratfordians, Digges's reference to a future when "Time dissolves thy Stratford moniment" refers to a day when the inscription is (dis)solved, and the poet looks "fresh to all ages." "Fresh" in what sense? New? Renewed?

What did early readers make of the First Folio? In 1640 an anthology of Shakespeare's poems was published, irreverently questioning the Folio's presentation of Shakespeare. It, too, featured a copy of the Droeshout portrait but added a bright light behind his subject's head, suggesting the figure in front is but a shadow. To drive home the point, an accompanying poem called the figure a "shadow" and mimicked the language of Jonson's famous tribute, sprinkling it with sarcastic question marks that contest the legitimacy of the image:

> *This Shadow is renowned Shakespear's? Soule of th'age*
> *The applause? Delight? The wonder of the stage.*

Some of the First Folio's early readers apparently suspected that this was a false image of the author.

⁂

The Droeshout portrait and its accompanying texts stirred a feeling I have often had about the whole mess: that there is something uncannily Shakespearean *about* the Shakespeare authorship question. It is like one of the riddles or charades in the plays themselves—as if the plays have spilled off the stage, and we have all become players in a comedy that the author himself set in motion. Mistaken identities abound in Shakespeare. Reputations are false. Appearances are deceptive. Things are not what they seem. "I am not what I am," says Viola, disguised in *Twelfth Night* as the boy servant Cesario. She winks at her trickery, which allows her to transgress the narrow strictures of femininity, to do and say things that, as a woman, she could not otherwise. The disguise is a deception that frees her, paradoxically, to become more of herself.

But "I am not what I am" is also the villainous Iago's tagline. In his mouth, it becomes an inversion of God's "I am that I am," marking him as the play's devil. He does not really serve Othello but only pretends to—"seeming so for my particular end." The play ends in tragedy because Othello is taken in by the deception: he believes Iago is true when he is false, and he believes Desdemona is false when she is true. In both plays, the audience is wise to the deception, sharing with Viola and Iago an inside knowledge to which the other characters are not privy. We observe the consequences of being taken in: both the comic consequences in *Twelfth Night* and the tragic ones in *Othello.*

Again and again, the plays dramatize the riddle of identity. Perdita, the shepherd girl in *The Winter's Tale*, is actually the lost daughter of the king. Christopher Sly, the drunken peddler in *The Taming of the Shrew*, is fooled by an elaborate prank into thinking he is a lord. High is low, and low is high. The apparent Viola is not the real Viola. The apparent Iago is not the real Iago. "Is the apparent author the real author?" the Harvard scholar Marjorie Garber asks. "Is the official version to be trusted?"

Is it possible that Shakespeare, too, is only "seeming so"?

The problem of "seeming" is pervasive. "I know not 'seems,' " Hamlet declares in the play's opening act, when his mother inquires about his mourning clothes and depressive air. Disgusted by the courtly world's preoccupation with appearances, he rejects seeming, lecturing his mother like a moody, misunderstood teenager:

'Tis not alone my inky cloak, good mother,
Nor customary suits of solemn black
Nor windy suspiration of forced breath . . .
That can denote me truly: these indeed "seem,"
For they are actions that a man might play:
But I have that within which passeth show,
These but the trappings and the suits of woe.

Though seeming cannot denote him "truly," seeming also proves useful. Hamlet later plays at being mad, as Iago plays at being honest, and

Viola and the other cross-dressed heroines play at masculinity. The presentation of the self in everyday life is a kind of theater. "All the world's a stage," observes the melancholic Jaques in *As You Like It*. "And all the men and women merely players; / They have their exits and their entrances; / And one man in his time plays many parts." It is not just that the theater mirrors life, but that our lives themselves are full of seeming.

The Shakespearean preoccupation with deception and illusion is Platonic in origin: the prisoners in Plato's cave mistake shadows dancing on the wall for reality; illusion for the real thing. The theater, a place of flickering visions, resembles Plato's cave. Players themselves are called "shadows," as when Puck addresses the audience at the end of *A Midsummer Night's Dream*:

If we shadows have offended,
Think but this, and all is mended,
That you have but slumber'd here
While these visions did appear.
And this weak and idle theme,
No more yielding but a dream.

But the theater also dramatizes the process by which man leaves the cave of shadows to face reality—or is forced out of the cave or sometimes remains, by his own failings, trapped in the cave, immersed in illusion. Macbeth's realization comes too late:

Life's but a walking shadow, a poor player
That struts and frets his hour upon the stage,
And then is heard no more: it is a tale
Told by an idiot, full of sound and fury,
Signifying nothing.

As in Plato, the fundamental test of character in the Shakespearean world is the ability to see past illusion, to distinguish seeming from reality. When Lear decides in the play's opening scene to divide his realm among his three daughters according to their expressions of love, he engages in a world of seeming. Goneril's and Regan's declarations are the hollow flattery of courtiers, calculated for their own selfish ends. Cordelia, perceiving the deceptive nature of this rhetorical game, refuses to engage. Her decision to "love, and be silent" is a rejection of the illusions that hold her father and the rest of the court captive. Lear fails to understand this until his world is crumbling around him. Dispossessed and mad, he can finally see: "When we are born, we cry that we are come / To this great stage of fools."

In *The Merchant of Venice*, this Platonic test of character manifests as an actual test: the casket test. Portia's suitors are presented with a gold casket, a silver casket, and a lead casket. One of them contains her portrait. To win her hand, a suitor must choose the correct casket. "If you do love me, you will find me out," says Portia.

The first suitor chooses gold, reasoning that the portrait of the beautiful woman must surely lie in the most valuable casket. But he finds only a skull, with this message in its empty eye socket:

All that glisters is not gold;
Often have you heard that told:
Many a man his life hath sold
But my outside to behold:
Gilded tombs do worms enfold.

Portia is relieved. "A gentle riddance," she sighs, sending him on his way. The second suitor arrives and chooses silver. "What's here? The portrait of a blinking idiot!" he cries, opening the casket to discover the portrait of a fool. "How much unlike art thou to Portia! How much unlike my hopes and my deservings." Bewildered, he demands, "Did I deserve no more than a fool's head? Is that my prize? Are my deserts no better?" The message left inside this casket reads,

Some there be that shadows kiss.
Such have but a shadow's bliss.

There be fools alive, iwis [certainly],
Silvered o'er—and so was this.
Take what wife you will to bed,
I will ever be your head.

Defeated, he retreats carrying the portrait of the idiot, which will "ever" be his head. "With one fool's head I came to woo," he groans, "but I go away with two." Amused, Portia compares her suitors to moths drawn to a candle's flame: "Thus hath the candle singed the moth. / O these deliberate fools! When they do choose, / They have the wisdom by their wit to lose."

The third suitor arrives, contemplating the decision he has before him in a long speech. "So may the outward shows be least themselves: / The world is still deceived with ornament," he begins, enumerating a series of ways in which "outward shows" deceive: In court, a false plea "seasoned with a gracious voice" can obscure a guilty subject. In religion, sins are justified with citations of Scripture, "hiding the grossness with fair ornament." In war, men with false hearts and "livers white as milk" hide their cowardice beneath the beards of Hercules and Mars. Among women, beauty is "purchased by the weight" in makeup. "In a word," he concludes, these ornaments and deceptions are "the seeming truth which cunning times put on / To entrap the wisest." He will not be entrapped. Rejecting "outward shows" and "seeming truth," he chooses the dull lead casket and finds Portia's portrait. The accompanying message congratulates him:

You that choose not by the view,
Chance as fair and choose as true!

He solves the riddle and wins the lady's hand by exercising Platonic wisdom—by discerning the difference between illusion and truth, shadows and reality.

Have scholars chosen the right casket? Or are they kissing shadows? *Some there be that shadows kiss. / Such have but a shadow's bliss.* Is the image on the title page of the First Folio indeed a fool's head, like the image selected by Portia's second suitor—a "portrait of a blinking idiot"? Have we been taken in by seeming truth and outward show? Everyone who seeks Shakespeare is a suitor of sorts for his hand. Can Shakespeare be won—found, solved, identified? There have been many kinds of suitors: the early scholars who pored through the archives, searching for records that would illuminate his life; the founding fathers and men of letters who made pilgrimages to Stratford-upon-Avon, slicing "relics" from his chair and falling on their knees to kiss the sacred ground; in later centuries, Stratfordians who wrote biographies, trying to solve the mystery of how he did it, and anti-Stratfordians who saw still different authors by different names.

I had become a suitor, too. I saw the line of Shakespeare lovers stretching back hundreds of years. The suitors approaching cautiously at first, drawn like Portia's moths to the flame, each beginning with a declaration of love for the author; then throwing themselves on the riddle, believing they might, at last, be the ones to solve it; and finally retreating, in one way or another, singed by their suit. In the background, Shakespeare waits, like Portia, watching and smiling. *If you do love me, you will find me out.*

"I looked into it once," a Shakespeare professor of mine, now retired, told me, referring to the authorship. "Because it matters," he added. "Culturally, it matters." He shook his head. His investigations, wherever they had led, never yielded the clarity he sought. "Look," he said, trying to brush it off, "I say it's Occam's razor. Shakespeare wrote Shakespeare." The philosophical principle, attributed to the fourteenth-century friar William of Ockham, asserts that a simple explanation—the explanation requiring the fewest assumptions—is generally preferable. Scholars often cite it to defend the traditional attribution: Shakespeare's name is on the title pages; it is therefore simpler to conclude that Shakespeare wrote the works than that they were written by someone else. I wanted to point out that the simpler explanation—the outward one, the seeming truth—is not always the correct one. But he rushed away from the subject. I could see that he had been a suitor. He had been singed. That "Shakespeare wrote Shakespeare" was not the triumphant conclusion of his search so much as an expression of resignation. He had tried and failed. He was not going to try again.

FIVE

Bardolatry

THE FIRST FOLIO PRESERVED THE sacred writings, but the full adoration—the pious paintings, the pilgrimages to Stratford—flowered over the following centuries. This flowering, however preordained it might seem in retrospect, was not inevitable. For a period, Shakespeare was almost lost. In 1642 civil war broke out in England between Royalists, who supported King Charles I, and Parliamentarians, who sought an end to absolute monarchy. The Puritan-controlled Parliament ordered all theaters closed, condemning plays as "Spectacles of pleasure, too commonly expressing lascivious Mirth and Levity." The Globe Theatre was razed to the ground to build tenements. English drama was cast out along with the English monarchy. In the weeks before his execution on January 30, 1649, Charles I was said to be reading the plays of Shakespeare and Jonson. His beheading would not have been necessary, argued one contemporary, "had he but studied Scripture half so much as Ben Jonson or Shakespeare." Drama was banned in England for nearly twenty years. It returned only with the return of the monarchy. In 1660 the dead king's son, Charles II, who had been living in exile in France (where drama was plentiful), came home to England. Shortly after his own restoration to the throne, he ordered the restoration of English drama, granting warrants for the creation of new playing companies and the construction of new theaters. But what were the new companies to perform? There had been no playwrights in England for two decades. There was no material. Instead of waiting for new plays, they turned to the established masters—to the drama of the old days. With the blessing of the king, the shadowy, half-forgotten Shakespeare rose again—and the work of retrieving Shakespeare began.

As the scholar Gary Taylor writes, the "whole subsequent history of Shakespearian criticism, scholarship, interpretation, and performance is a history of the retrieval, analysis, and synthesis of what seemed lost by 1659."

Shakespeare returned as an ally of conservative powers—of monarchy. As the plays had so pleased "Eliza and our James," so they also pleased Charles II. But after 1660, the plays didn't go to the monarch at court; instead, the monarch went to the plays. Charles II visited the theaters almost daily when he was in London, bringing along his entourage of courtiers. The new theaters—converted at first from old tennis courts—were small, with limited seating and high ticket prices, and so theatergoing became an increasingly aristocratic pastime. The king proposed ideas to the playwrights. He slept with the actresses. Having seen women perform onstage in France, he sanctioned their appearance on England's public stages. Women could finally play the heroines, including the cross-dressing ones who appear in breeches, a novelty that titillated London's theatergoers. In October 1661 the diarist Samuel Pepys recorded seeing a play featuring a woman with "the very best legs that ever I saw; and I was very pleased with it."

The political content of Shakespeare's plays, with their tales of banished rulers (for example, *The Tempest*) or princes unjustly driven into exile (*Pericles*), had an immediate relevance to a nation restoring a banished monarch. *Hamlet* was so popular that in 1695 two rival companies staged simultaneous productions. The Earl of Shaftesbury called it that "piece of Shakespeare's, which appears to have most affected English hearts, and has, perhaps, been oftenest acted of any that have come upon our stage." Did the tale of a prince called to avenge his father's murder have a subliminal resonance for a nation recovering from regicide? By the particular confluence of Shakespeare's political content and the royal favor bestowed on Shakespeare in the Restoration period, Shakespeare became almost synonymous with the Crown. "Shakespear's pow'r is sacred as a King's," wrote the poet and critic John Dryden.

New editions of the collected plays were published—the Third Folio in 1663 and the Fourth Folio in 1685—ensuring Shakespeare's survival in print as well as onstage. The plays of Shakespeare's contemporaries were revived, too, and sometimes saw more performances. It was Shakespeare, however, who was increasingly deified: "We all well know that the immortal Shakespears Playes . . . have better pleased the World than Jonsons Works," wrote Aphra Behn, the first Englishwoman to earn a living by her pen. By the time Voltaire visited in 1728, he noted that Shakespeare "is rarely called anything but 'divine' in England." The Irish writer Arthur Murphy explained: "With us islanders, Shakespeare is a kind of established religion in poetry."

It is hard to say exactly why Shakespeare became "divine," and Jonson or Beaumont or Fletcher didn't. Greatness is nebulous. It depends not only on the intrinsic qualities of a work but also on the extrinsic forces that sweep in to lift it up. Did Shakespeare's divinity lie in the hypnotic power of his language? In his deep understanding of human psychology? Was it something to do with nationalism—his evocation of "this blessed plot, this earth, this realm, this England"? It surely helped that Shakespeare was favored by establishment forces, not just in the seventeenth century but in later centuries, too. Did it also help that women and not just men loved him? Shakespeare's first critic was a woman. In 1664 Margaret Cavendish, the eccentric Duchess of Newcastle sometimes known as "Mad Madge," wrote the first critical prose essay on Shakespeare, marveling at his ability to dissolve entirely into his characters—to embody them, even the women. "One would think he has been Metamorphosed from a Man to a Woman," she wrote, "for who could describe Cleopatra better than he hath done, and many other Females of his own Creating." Women's enthusiasm for Shakespeare helped drive his rising status. In the 1730s a group of upper-class women calling themselves the Shakespeare Ladies Club started petitioning the theaters to stage more Shakespeare plays. Prologues at performances of the plays praised them as mothers responsible for Shakespeare's rebirth, and the London *Daily Advertiser* ran a letter from Shakespeare's ghost "to the Fair Supporters of Wit and Sense, the Ladies of Great Britain," thanking the ladies for reviving "the Memory of the forsaken Shakespear."

Shakespeare's divinity lay in all of these things and more. But who was Shakespeare? If some early readers of the First Folio were skeptical of the author presented in its pages ("This Shadow is renowned Shakespear's?"), others accepted its praise of the "Sweet Swan of Avon" as praise of the man from Stratford-upon-Avon. In 1662 a vicar newly appointed to the village parish mused in his diary on the poet's uneducated genius. "I have heard that Mr. Shakspeare was a natural wit, without any art at all," he wrote. "Remember to peruse Shakespeare's plays," he reminded himself, "and bee much versed in them, that I may not bee ignorant in that matter."

Some years later, a gossip named John Aubrey, compiling his *Brief Lives* of eminent figures, wandered up to Stratford to gather stories about Shakespeare. "His father was a Butcher, and I have been told heretofore by some of the neighbours, that when he was a boy he exercised his father's Trade," Aubrey wrote—swiftly undermining his credibility, for John Shakespeare was a glover, not a butcher. When Shakespeare was "I guesse about 18," he went to London, Aubrey continued vaguely. "He was a handsome, well-shap't man: very good company." In 1709 a playwright named Nicholas Rowe sought more reliable information on Shakespeare to introduce a new edition of the plays. As Rowe explained, "knowledge of an Author may sometimes conduce to the better understanding his Book." Rowe's publisher placed advertisements in the *London Gazette* and the *Daily Courant*, requesting anyone with "serviceable" materials to come forward. No one seems to have done so, for Rowe's introduction, "Some Account of the life &c. Of Mr. William Shakespeare," is largely a critical appreciation of the plays dotted with a few biographical statements. Many of these statements proved to be either inaccurate or unverifiable, but they were repeated for the next 150 years, entrenching a Shakespearean mythos.

Shakespeare's father sent him to the grammar school, Rowe wrote, "where 'tis probable he acquir'd that little *Latin* he was Master of: But the narrowness of his Circumstances and the want of his assistance at

Home, forc'd his Father to withdraw him from thence." This limited education fit with Rowe's perception of the plays as the works of an uneducated genius. "It is without Controversie, that he had no knowledge of the Writings of the Antient Poets," Rowe insisted erroneously. After his marriage, Shakespeare fell—"by a Misfortune common enough to young Fellows"—into the company of deer-stealing hooligans. He was caught poaching in a deer park that belonged to Sir Thomas Lucy of Charlecote, Rowe claimed (though such a deer park did not exist in the sixteenth century). Shakespeare was prosecuted "somewhat too severely," and to avenge himself on Sir Lucy, he wrote a bitter ballad—"probably the first Essay of his Poetry"—but the ballad (which also does not exist) "redoubled the Prosecution against him," such that he was forced to leave Stratford and shelter in London.

The crucial event happens in a puff of smoke. In one paragraph Shakespeare is in Stratford stealing deer; in the next, he's in London penning immortal plays. He became acquainted with the playhouses and rose up through his "admirable Wit." The Queen "without doubt gave him many gracious Marks of her Favour," and his generous patron, the Earl of Southampton, gave him a "bounty" of £1,000, Rowe asserted (though, again, there is no evidence of such a bounty). "His exceeding Candor and good Nature must certainly have inclin'd all the gentler Part of the World to love him," claimed Rowe. In time, Shakespeare ceased writing and returned to Stratford to enjoy "Ease, Retirement and the Conversation of his Friends."

Later scholars would note that much of Rowe's account was merely the stuff of legend. For one thing, his only source was his actor-friend Thomas Betterton, who claimed to have visited Stratford to collect anecdotes about Shakespeare—but another actor contested that Betterton had ever made the trip. If the actor did indeed travel to Stratford, a scholar noted, "perhaps he was too easily satisfied for such [anecdotes] as fell in his way, without making any rigid search into their authenticity." Rowe's account—the first so-called biography of Shakespeare—was a jumble of myths fitted to the archetypal narrative of the hero's journey: from his "fortunate fall," setting him on his adventure and encounter with destiny, to his return home. But it appealed to the sensibilities of eighteenth-century readers, offering an excuse for Shakespeare's unchristian conduct in abandoning his family, a warning about the dangers of "ill Company," and a happy ending whereby his sin turned out to be his salvation. (The deer poaching, "tho it seem'd at first to be a Blemish upon his good Manners, and a Misfortune to him, yet it afterwards happily prov'd the occasion of exerting one of the greatest *Genius's* that ever was known in Dramatick Poetry.")

Though unsubstantiated, Rowe's claims were reprinted and repeated into the twentieth century. The deer-poaching episode is "a satisfying story—an exciting sequence of theft, discovery, punishment, and escape," wrote the scholar Samuel Schoenbaum. "What a dramatic scene!" Never mind that the "exciting sequence" sounds suspiciously like a rewriting of Adonis's hunt for the boar—except that where Adonis is gored by the animal, Shakespeare emerges victorious. Schoenbaum dubbed Shakespeare the "Deerslayer," as though he were a Greek hero. Remarking on the "problem of biography" in 2016, Professor Cummings would note that Rowe's account of Shakespeare's life is "little different in outline from one penned now, 300 years later."

Over the following decades, a few documents turned up—a loan, a real estate investment, the request for a grant of a coat of arms—but none shed any light on what critics were most eager to understand: Shakespeare's literary career and development. One document that should have, Shakespeare's will, was particularly disappointing. The Stratford vicar who discovered it noted that it "appears to me so dull and irregular, so absolutely devoid of the least particle of that spirit which animated our great Poet; that is must lessen his Character as a Writer." Certainly writers can care about money as well as ideas, but how was it possible that the man who wrote *King Lear* also wrote this will? How could Shakespeare have gone from the existential vision of Lear stripped of his lands and power, confronted with his bare humanity, undressing himself on the heath—"Off, off, you lendings!"—to this small-minded, bourgeois preoccupation with real estate? Where were the traces of a life spent devoted to learning and writing?

At the time, the literary world still held on to the hope, in the words of the writer James Boaden, that "a rich assemblage of Shakespeare papers would start forth from some ancient repository, to solve all our doubts." For doubts about Shakespeare were in the air. It was the age of Enlightenment, of empiricism and philosophical skepticism.

"Who wrote Shakespeare?" a character asked in a play staged in London in 1759.

"Ben Jonson," another replied.

"Oh no. Shakespeare was written by Mr. Finis," someone else interceded comically, "for I saw his name at the end of the book." The joke, which appeared in the play *High Life Below Stairs*, by James Townley, is silly. "The passage cannot, however, be taken as accidental; there is no reason to think that Townley could have written 'Who wrote Milton?' instead," notes the historian R. C. Churchill. "There must have been, in the mid-eighteenth century, a certain amount of discussion as to the authenticity of the traditional authorship of Shakespeare." A story published in 1769 featured "a person belonging to the playhouse" who steals literary materials from allegorical characters called Wit, Genius, and Wisdom. "With these (stolen) materials . . . he commenced Play-Writer," the story explained, and "how he succeeded I need not tell you; for his name was Shakespeare." The notion that Shakespeare was a thief, that the plays were not rightly his, recurred again in 1786 in "The Story of the Learned Pig, By an officer of the Royal Navy." The "learned pig" recounting his previous human incarnations claims that, in the Renaissance, he wrote the plays for which Shakespeare took credit. "He has been fathered with many spurious dramatic pieces," the pig complains. "*Hamlet*, *Othello*, *As You Like It*, *The Tempest*, and *A Midsummer Night's Dream*," of "which I confess myself to be the author."

As legends and jokes circulated, devotees began making pilgrimages to Stratford-upon-Avon to pay homage to the divine poet. Hoping to find "relics," they flocked to Shakespeare's large house on Chapel Street. They were particularly drawn to the mulberry tree in the garden, said to have been planted by the poet himself. In 1756 the home's current owner, annoyed by the constant visitors snooping around his property, had the tree cut down. A local tradesman bought the logs and grew rich selling carvings from the tree, like pieces of the true cross. On nearby Henley

Street, a sign outside the windows of a small tenement proclaimed, "The Immortal Shakespeare was born in this house." Some skeptics suspected that the sign was part of a scheme devised by the town to bring visitors to Stratford. Others suggested that it was hung by an enterprising occupant of the house, eager to do a little business showing pilgrims the site of Shakespeare's nativity. Whatever the provenance of the sign, it established the beginning of a tradition whereby the house on Henley Street came to be known as "The Birthplace": a holy site, a shrine of pilgrimage and worship sanctified by the spirit of the poet.

In 1769 David Garrick, the leading Shakespearean actor of his day, organized the Shakespeare Jubilee, a much-advertised, multiday festival in Stratford-upon-Avon to commemorate the bicentennial of the poet's birth. It opened with the firing of thirty cannons and the ringing of church bells. Garrick, who had erected a "Temple of Shakespeare" at his country estate, set himself up as Shakespeare's first great priest, framing the festival's liturgy and leading the people in worship. He performed songs in celebration of the mulberry tree: "And thou like him immortal be!" He blessed Stratford as the holy place of the poet and recited his "Ode to Shakespeare," inviting the congregation to join him in the refrain, "Untouched and sacred be thy shrine, / Avonian Willy, bard Divine." Striding into a small room on the upper floor of the Birthplace, he declared it the precise room where Shakespeare was born—the "Birthroom" of the poet, the holy of holies.

Reported in newspapers throughout Europe, the jubilee cemented the connection between Shakespeare and Stratford and marked the formal beginning of the town's tourist industry. No Shakespeare play was actually performed over the course of the three-day festival. In fact, not a single line of Shakespeare's writings was spoken. The works were drowned out in the frenzy of national celebration. It was what "Shakespeare" signified—the veneration of Shakespeare as, in Garrick's words, "blest genius of the isle"—that dominated the jubilee, for if the eighteenth century was an age of skepticism, it was also an age of rising nationalism. Britain had just handed France a resounding defeat in the Seven Years' War, gaining the bulk of French lands in North America, the colony of Senegal, and superiority over French trading posts in Asia. As a new edition of the plays explained, Shakespeare was "a part of the kingdom's riches" that were "talk'd of wherever the name *Britain* is talk'd of, that is (thanks to some late counsels) wherever there are men." Shakespeare rose with Britain, but Shakespeare was also held up as proof of Britain's cultural superiority—of its right to rule. "England may justly boast the honour of producing the greatest dramatic poet in the world," Garrick declared at the jubilee. Over the course of the following century, the mutually reinforcing mythologies of the nation and its poet, the empire and its hero-god, became intertwined so that the idea of Shakespeare would become inseparable from the idea of Britain itself.

Not everyone was a fan of the Shakespeare Jubilee. Some contemporaries remarked on the "scandalous Behaviour of the very low People of the Town of Stratford, in regard to their Avarice, and shameful Extortions." Certain members of the literati were also conspicuously absent from the festivities, including Samuel Johnson, England's most distinguished man of letters, and his circle, who signaled their disapproval by staying away. Even David Garrick soured on the event. Coaches got stuck in the town's muddy, unpaved streets. The fancy-dress parade was canceled due to rain. Hotels were overbooked. If Stratford wanted to make the event an annual celebration, Garrick recommended some improvements: "[L]et your streets be well pav'd & kept clean," he wrote to the Corporation of Stratford, "do something with the delightful meadow, allure Every body to visit the holy Land, let it be well lighted & clean under foot, and let it not be said, for your honour & perhaps for your interest that the Town, which gave Birth to the first Genius since the Creation, is the most dirty, unseemly, ill-pav'd, wretched-looking Town in all Britain." Garrick scurried back to London, disseminating his "Ode to Shakespeare" and repackaging the festival events as a play, *The Jubilee*, which ran for a record ninety-two nights.

Scholars regard the Shakespeare Jubilee of 1769 as "the point at which Shakespeare stopped being regarded as an increasingly popular and admirable dramatist and became a god." Two hundred years after its break from Rome, England had its own Jesus, Bethlehem, and manger. A visitor to the

Birthplace warned that the worship of Shakespeare threatened to eclipse the worship of God:

Yet steals a sigh, as reason weighs
The fame to Shakespeare given,
That thousands, worshippers of him,
Forget to worship Heaven!

Shakespeare was the "Glory of the British Nation" and the "Prince of Dramatic Poets," but his life was still wrapped in myth. One anecdote, published by the actor Theophilus Cibber, attempted to explain how Shakespeare became involved in the theater: "Driven to the last necessity, [he] went to the playhouse door, and pick'd up a little money by taking care of the gentlemens horses who came to the play." Cibber related the story's chain of transmission: "Sir William Davenant told Mr. Betterton, who communicated it to Mr. Rowe; Rowe told it to Mr. Pope, and Mr. Pope told it to Dr. Newton, the late editor of Milton, and from a gentleman, who heard it from him, 'tis here related." Literary history was being constructed like a game of telephone.

⁂

Reading Rowe's "account" of Shakespeare's life, an Irish lawyer named Edmond Malone was astonished that no one had attempted a more thorough biography of the national poet. He judged Rowe's a "meagre and imperfect narrative," and he saw Aubrey, the gossip, as "a dupe to every wag who chose to practice on his credulity." The absence of anything resembling a literary life motivated researchers like Malone to go in search of documents that testified to the literary Shakespeare, not the social-climbing, money-oriented one. Having given up his law practice, which bored him, Malone devoted himself to literary pursuits, entering into the intellectual circles of late-eighteenth-century London. He befriended the great Samuel Johnson, author of *A Dictionary of the English Language*. He sat to have his portrait painted by the eminent portraitist Sir Joshua Reynolds—sometimes on the same day as King George III, who found time to pose while waging war in the American colonies. Eventually Malone was admitted to "the Club," Johnson's exclusive literary society whose members included the philosopher Edmund Burke, the historian Edward Gibbon, and the economist Adam Smith.

Malone spent forty years trying to extinguish all the doubts. He published a study of the plays' chronology, "An Attempt to Ascertain the Order in Which the Plays Attributed to Shakespeare Were Written"—a title whose circumlocution ("Attributed to Shakespeare") seemed to disclose some vague uncertainties. But his primary ambition was to find enough documents to write a "Life of Shakespeare"—"to weave the whole into one uniform and connected narrative." His early discoveries were promising. He found the diaries of actor Edward Alleyn and impresario Philip Henslowe, both valuable resources for understanding the history of the Renaissance theater. But, of course, they did not shed any light on Shakespeare himself. In 1790 Malone published his edition of Shakespeare's plays and poems. "Despite the most diligent inquiries, very few particulars have been recovered, respecting Shakespeare's private life or literary history," Malone lamented. He issued an advertisement hoping, as Rowe had, that someone with a cache of treasures locked away in the attic would come forward.

The year 1790 also saw the publication of Edmund Burke's famous pamphlet *Reflections on the Revolution in France*, attacking the intellectual underpinnings of the French Revolution and praising British traditionalism—constitutional monarchy, aristocracy, private property, and the wisdom of the ages. His account of the mob's violent treatment of Louis XVI and Marie Antoinette horrified British readers, and the subsequent Reign of Terror—which confirmed many of Burke's predictions—further fed the veneration of British culture in reaction to French radicalism. As the critic Leigh Hunt noted, "the French Revolution only tended at first to endear the nation to its own habits," prominent among which was play-going. While France was awash in bloody massacre, England's elite attended performances of *Hamlet* and *Twelfth Night*, *The Merchant of Venice* and *Richard III*. The defense of British culture provoked by the French Revolution—and the nationalism that surged in the following years of the Napoleonic Wars—served only to glorify

Shakespeare more. He had become one of the illustrious authorities to be protected and preserved, along with the monarchy, the House of Lords, and the Church of England.

The desperation to find literary papers for Shakespeare had grown so acute by the end of the eighteenth century that one man, seeing an opportunity, started forging them. In 1794 William Henry Ireland, a twenty-year-old Londoner, claimed to have discovered documents in the old trunk of a mysterious gentleman collector. The documents provided everything the literary world had longed for: a love letter from a young Shakespeare to Anne Hathaway, in which he had enclosed a lock of his hair; Shakespeare's letters to and from Henry Wriothesley, the 3rd Earl of Southampton; Shakespeare's haggling with a printer over the terms of publication of one of his plays ("I do esteem much my play, having taken much care writing of it. . . . Therefore I cannot in the least lower my price"); a note from the Queen thanking Shakespeare for his "pretty verses" and inviting him to perform for her at Hampton Court; and, mercifully, Shakespeare's Protestant "Profession of Faith," putting an end to the dreadful possibility that the glory of the British nation might have been a secret Catholic. Ireland also "found" Shakespeare's books inscribed with his name and marginal notes. And then, to top it all off, the greatest treasure of all: the original manuscript of *King Lear* in Shakespeare's own hand, including a prefatory note from Shakespeare to his "gentle readers."

The literary world fell for the forgeries, hook, line, and sinker. Men of letters flocked to Ireland's home to view them. (Ireland's father restricted access and charged an entry fee of two guineas.) Scholars congratulated the young Ireland on having afforded "so much gratification to the literary world." The biographer James Boswell kissed the manuscripts. *Some there be that shadows kiss / Such have but a shadow's bliss.* "How happy am I to have lived to the present day of discovery of this glorious treasure," he proclaimed. "I shall now die in peace." Britain's press gushed over the findings, declaring that the papers shed new light on Shakespeare's character: he had "an acute and penetrating judgement with a disposition amiable and gentle as his genius was transcendent." In December 1795, transcriptions and facsimiles of William Henry Ireland's discoveries were published as *The Miscellaneous Papers.* Literary authorities affirmed their conviction that "these papers can be no other than the production of Shakespeare himself." They wanted to believe, so they believed. But Edmond Malone, ever the lawyer, was suspicious.

He got hold of *The Miscellaneous Papers* and began studying it. In the meantime, Ireland, growing cocky with his success, announced to a committee of literary "authorities" that there were additional discoveries: original manuscripts of *Julius Caesar* and *Richard II*; verses addressed to Queen Elizabeth I and notable courtiers; more books annotated in Shakespeare's hand; manuscripts of two "lost" Shakespeare plays called *Henry the Second* and *Vortigern and Rowena*; and, astonishingly, Shakespeare's "brief account of his life in his own hand." The owner of London's Drury Lane Theatre purchased the rights to *Vortigern and Rowena*, and rehearsals began to stage the "lost" play. John Philip Kemble, the actor who played Vortigern, began to doubt the play's authenticity; so, too, did Sarah Siddons, who was cast as Vortigern's wife. Both were regular actors in Shakespeare plays and knew a fake when they saw one. "All sensible persons are convinced that 'Vortigern' is a most audacious impostor," Siddons wrote.

Their suspicions were confirmed in 1796, when Malone published his retort, *An Inquiry into the Authenticity of Certain Miscellaneous Papers and Legal Instruments.* Ireland's papers, he showed, were not even good forgeries. The spelling was at odds with Elizabethan usage. The vocabulary was off, using words that didn't come into currency until the eighteenth century. The dates were wrong. (The Queen's letter was addressed to Shakespeare at the Globe—a decade before the theater was built.) Southampton's signature did not match his signature in other documents that survived in his hand. Siddons dropped out of *Vortigern and Rowena* a week before the play's debut, but tickets had already sold out. On opening night, John Philip Kemble laid heavy emphasis on a certain line in the play—"When this solemn mockery is o'er"—repeating it until the audience erupted in laughter. *Vortigern and Rowena*'s first night was also its last.

Ireland confessed to the forgeries, and Malone's book was a best seller. But Malone died in 1812 without having finished the book he really wanted to write: the life of Shakespeare. He never found enough material. The "one uniform and connected narrative" was not possible. Malone's assistant gathered together the fragments to publish posthumously, apologizing to readers that "in some of the most important parts of his [Malone's] investigations, a chasm must be left." Malone's friend Samuel Johnson, who spent much of his life promoting the genre of literary biography and editing Shakespeare's plays, never finished a life of Shakespeare, either. Though his publisher commissioned him to write one, "he could never be prevailed on to begin it." Johnson's *Lives of the Most Eminent English Poets* includes short biographies and appraisals of fifty-two poets—but Shakespeare, the divine bard, prince of poets and glory of Britain, is glaringly absent.

Johnson's silence seemed to me more interesting than everyone else's noise. Did he decide there simply was not sufficient material to write even a brief biography of Shakespeare? Some of his biographies are as short as ten pages. Or did his study of the plays lead him to understand something else about their author?

⁂

In the early years of the nineteenth century, others picked up Edmond Malone's unfinished investigations. They sifted public records, finding evidence of Shakespeare's business transactions and lawsuits, but the need to find the right documents led, perhaps inevitably, to more forgeries. In 1811 a Welsh writer named Richard Fenton claimed to have discovered a "curious journal of Shakespeare, an account of many of his plays, and memoirs of his life by himself" at an auction in southwest Wales. One of the journal entries helpfully explained something that was troubling scholars: how Shakespeare came to know foreign languages and literature.

"Having an earnest desire to lerne foraine tongues, it was mie goode happ to have in my father's howse an Italian, one Girolamo Albergi," fake-Shakespeare wrote in fake Elizabethan lingo. "He had the breeding of a gentilman, and was a righte sounde scholar. It was he who taught me the little Italian I know, and rubbed up my Latin; we read Bandello's Novells together, from the which I gathered some delicious flowers to stick in mie dramatick poseys." Despite the absurdity of the language, excerpts were republished as evidence as late as 1853.

The most infamous Shakespeare forger emerged in the 1830s. John Payne Collier's literary career was initially illustrious. A successful London journalist, he devoted his leisure time to the study of Shakespeare, producing a three-volume history of dramatic poetry. "On looking back to the life of Shakespeare, the first observation that must be made," he reflected, "is that so few *facts* are extant regarding him: nearly everything interesting is derived from tradition, or depends upon conjecture." The work landed Collier the plum post of librarian to the 6th Duke of Devonshire. Some of his findings were genuine: a record showing that Shakespeare hoarded ten bushels of corn, a suit regarding his failure to pay tithes. These were not the records scholars wanted, so Collier added other "discoveries," apparently uncovered in the duke's library at Bridgewater House. Published in 1835 as *New Facts Regarding the Life of Shakespeare*, the purported treasures included twenty-one new documents. The cream of the crop was a letter from the Earl of Southampton to an Elizabethan official, asking the man to "be good to the poor players of the Blackfriars," including Shakespeare, "my especial friend, till of late an actor of good account in the company, now a sharer in the same, and writer of some of our best English plays."

Collier followed *New Facts* with two more publications of alleged discoveries: *New Particulars Regarding the Works of Shakespeare* and *Further Particulars Regarding Shakespeare and His Works.* "This information is now hardly as scanty as it was formerly represented," he declared. Collier was rapidly becoming Britain's leading Shakespeare scholar, his "discoveries" celebrated and reproduced in popular biographies of the period. In 1852 he would announce his unearthing of a new Folio that featured the author's annotations and revisions. Oddly, he refused to let anyone else look at the Folio, which he guarded at the library of his patron. After the duke's death in 1858, however, the Folio was bequeathed to the British Museum, and Collier's fraudulent claims began to unravel. Experts at the museum concluded that the annotations were modern forgeries imitating Renaissance script. (Microscope analysis revealed pencil annotations underneath the archaic-looking ink.) But it would take years to sort Collier's other fraudulent discoveries from his genuine ones.

As Collier forged, the deification of Shakespeare continued apace. In an 1840 lecture "On Heroes, Hero-Worship, and the Heroic in History," the influential critic Thomas Carlyle declared that it was "impiety" to meddle with Shakespeare. If Dante was the "melodious Priest of Middle-Age Catholicism," Shakespeare was the "still more melodious Priest of a *true* Catholicism, the 'Universal Church' of the Future and of all times." Carlyle perceived that the disparate reaches and peoples of the British Empire needed something to unite them: "And now, what is it that can keep all these together into virtually one Nation, so that they do not fall out and fight, but live at peace, in brotherlike intercourse, helping one another?" he asked, alluding to the loss of the American colonies. The answer, Carlyle argued, was the Universal Church of Shakespeare. "Here, I say, is an English King, whom no time or chance, Parliament or combination of Parliaments, can dethrone! That King Shakespeare, does not he shine, in crowned sovereignty, over us all, as the noblest, gentlest, yet strongest of rallying signs; indestructible; really more valuable in that point of view than any other means or appliance whatsoever?" In language that eerily anticipated Adolf Hitler's "Thousand-Year Reich," Carlyle projected the future of a thousand-year British Empire, imagining Shakespeare "radiant aloft over all the Nations of Englishmen, a thousand years hence." As the Nazis would draw on Germanic myths and folktales to construct an ethno-nationalism of one *Volk* united by "blood and soil," so Carlyle envisioned a global people united under the "rallying sign" of England's hero-god. Men and women from Bombay to Sydney to New York would say, "Yes, this Shakspeare is ours; we produced him, we speak and think by him; we are of one blood and kind with him."

Having reached the very heights of British adoration, Shakespeare's reputation expanded outward. He inspired the music of German, Italian, and Hungarian composers; was translated, adapted, and praised by Russian poets, novelists, and playwrights; and was read and staged across

America—from Boston, to Saint Louis, to the mining camps of California. Goethe adored Shakespeare. So did German philosophers, seeing in him what Hegel called "the infinite breadth of his world-stage." Shakespeare's plays weren't English but universal, representing the essential nature of man. "Deutschland ist Hamlet," wrote the German poet Ferdinand Freiligrath. Even the French submitted. Marie-Henri Beyle, who wrote under the pen name Stendhal, published *Racine et Shakespeare*, praising *Macbeth* as "one of the masterpieces of the human spirit"; Hector Berlioz composed a choral symphony *Roméo et Juliette*; Edgar Degas painted Hamlet, and Alexandre Dumas conceded that Shakespeare was "the artist who has created most, after God."

It is true, of course, that Shakespeare transcends borders and cultures, but as the scholar Michael Dobson has noted, "that Shakespeare was declared to rule world literature at the same time that Britannia was declared to rule the waves may, indeed, be more than a coincidence."

Visitors from around the world now descended on Stratford, eager to pay their respects at the "immortal house," as Victorian guidebooks called it. The visitor arrives "as a pilgrim would to the shrine of some loved saint; will deem it holy ground, and dwell with sweet though pensive rapture, on the natal habitation of the poet," one tourist wrote. Divinity mingled with domesticity. The Birthplace became a site not only for venerating Shakespeare as a god but also for imagining him as a child: a flesh-and-blood boy whose family life and formative experiences took place within those walls. Like the infant Jesus, he was at once god and man, immortal and relatably human, his otherworldly genius "tabernacled in the flesh," as another visitor wrote. The veneration of Shakespeare had become, in a term coined later by Irish playwright George Bernard Shaw, "bardolatry." The Victorians were obsessed with rediscovering Shakespeare's childhood. An 1836 poem, *The Pilgrim of Avon*, captured the raptures of a worshipper longing for a "mighty spell" that could raise visions of the poet's "bygone days":

And was it here! Oh! was it here,
His cry first charm'd a mother's ear?

Here, where his first young wizard thought
To charm the wond'ring world was given. . . .
Oh! That some mighty spell could raise
A vision of the bygone days,
A mirror, like his Banquo's, fling
In its reflecting radiance true,
His childhood's scenes before my view.

Victorian biographers cast that spell gladly, flinging visions of young Shakespeare before eager readers. In 1843 the publisher Charles Knight provided the nation with the first book-length biography of the national poet, *William Shakspere: A Biography*. (Nineteenth-century biographers tended to use "Shakspere," consistent with the spelling on his baptismal and burial records.) The book was an extended Victorian fantasy—a "descriptive reverie," as one critic at the time put it—freely fictionalizing Shakespeare's life, blissfully untethered from scholarly citation or historical fact. Since Shakespeare could not be known through letters, journals, or other personal records, Knight found him in Stratford-upon-Avon—in the streets and village life, the surrounding fields and forests, and in the Birthplace itself. Stratford filled in the gaps—indeed, *became* Shakespeare's biography. The Warwickshire countryside elucidated his love of nature; the half-timbered house on Henley Street, his idyllic childhood. Another writer observed: "From the obscurity in which his life is shrouded, the coeval remains of Stratford-upon-Avon have far greater importance than they would have possessed had Shakespeare received from his contemporaries notice such as has so frequently been lavished on inferior men." Knight, who visited Stratford to gather inspiration for his biography, used the Birthplace to build out scenes of the poet's formative years—those "happy days of boyhood" for which no accounts actually exist. Never mind. Knight imagined them, conjuring the Shakespeare family's cozy domesticity around an evening fireside: "The mother is plying her distaff, or hearing Richard his lesson out of the ABC book. The father and the elder son are each intent upon a book of chronicles, manly reading . . .

and then all the group crowd round their elder brother, who has laid aside his chronicle, to entreat him for a story."

Knight went on to describe the stories that young Shakespeare would recount to his brothers and sisters. It turns out that they bear an uncanny resemblance to the plots of Shakespeare plays (wars, star-crossed lovers from feuding families). He affirmed that the boy would regale his father with "something of his school progress." An accompanying illustration depicted young Shakespeare by the fireside with his parents, leaning against his father's knee. Readers advancing through Knight's reverie would encounter many more happy visions in Stratford: a romantic scene of Shakespeare's betrothal to Anne Hathaway; a pious scene of his Christian devotion before his death. The biography was closer to hagiography, to the lives of the saints, than to any documented historical truth. Critics faulted Knight for building "hypothesis upon hypothesis" and expressed their wish that he would "confine his fancy within the bounds."

It did not matter. The book sold, igniting a rage for Shakespeare biographies. John Payne Collier (whose forgeries had not yet been exposed) published one the next year. The fireside scene became a particular fixation in the Victorian imagination. Another biographer, asserting that the Shakespeare family liked to tell stories by the fire on winter nights, had the decency to admit, "Like most things written about Shakespeare, this is pure speculation." Most dropped the admission, however, proclaiming simply that Shakespeare loved to sit in the chimney nook as a boy. In Stratford, the custodians of the Birthplace milked this fixation, inviting tourists to sit in the chimney nook where Shakespeare once sat. They had it specially dusted every morning for this purpose.

Knight's biography went through multiple editions: a Stratford edition, a pictorial edition, a cabinet edition, a national edition, and an imperial edition. Shakespeare had become a fixture of the Victorian home. No parlor in Britain, or indeed in her colonies, was complete without an edition of the plays and a biography of the national poet. In domesticating Shakespeare, the Victorian biographers made it possible for readers to feel an emotional connection to the poet. He was no longer only a saint or a god to be revered; he was also someone they *knew*—a father, a brother, a son, a friend. Shakespeare is "to us Englishmen, the national, the domestic Poet, whom we love as we love our own homes," proclaimed the bishop Charles Wordsworth (nephew of William Wordsworth) in a sermon on the 1864 tercentenary of Shakespeare's birth. Victorians had developed an emotional relationship to him that superseded any historical data. "Of no person is there a clearer picture in the popular fancy," wrote the Victorian journalist Walter Bagehot. "You seem to have known Shakespeare—to have seen Shakespeare—to have been friends with Shakespeare."

The biographical fictions and fanciful conjectures about Shakespeare were not, in the end, so different from the forgeries. Both were gossamer illusions, shadowy, insubstantial pageants. Writers were eager to pen them, turning the evidentiary void into an opportunity to display their own imaginative power and narrative skill. Publishers were eager to sell them, without regard for their authenticity. Readers were eager to consume them. Coming from "authorities," why would they suspect them? In some ways, the biographies were actually more dangerous than the forgeries, for while the forgeries were eventually discarded, the fictions lasted. Knight's method—filling the literary chasms in Shakespeare's life with speculation—set the model for modern Shakespeare biographies. When the *Oxford Dictionary of National Biography* was compiled at the end of the nineteenth century, Shakespeare received the longest entry, later exceeded only by that of Queen Victoria herself. The dictionary's editor, Sir Sidney Lee, repeated the old myths—even the deer-poaching legend ("a credible tradition"). Expanding his entry on the "hero's life" into a monograph, *A Life of William Shakespeare*, Lee re-entrenched the narrative for another generation of readers. A few critics commented that the material had been "twisted by a master artificer into the cunning semblance of a biography" and that "it is all a record of external events . . . not the exhibition of a human soul." But mostly Lee's book was celebrated, becoming the new Shakespeare biography for the twentieth century.

What is remarkable is not simply that people believed in the shadows but that they created, of their own accord, more shadows to feed their belief.

⁜

I decided it was time to make my own pilgrimage to Stratford—and to visit the esteemed scholar who presides over the Birthplace, Sir Stanley Wells. Wells is Britain's leading Shakespeare authority, the one who declared it "immoral" to question history and "take credit away" from Shakespeare. For many years, he was professor of Shakespeare studies and director of the Shakespeare Institute in Stratford-upon-Avon, as well as chairman of the Shakespeare Birthplace Trust, the organization that oversees the Birthplace. During his chairmanship, he appended a notice to the Trust's website stating that those who doubt Shakespeare's authorship suffer from a "psychological aberration," exploiting prejudices against the mentally ill to discredit anyone who questioned his view. Challenged to validate his claims with empirical evidence, Wells removed the statement.

As doubts about the authorship grew louder, he had begun frantically publishing books with titles like *Shakespeare Beyond Doubt*, *Why Shakespeare WAS Shakespeare*, and *Shakespeare Bites Back*. My favorite section in the latter accused "anti-Shakespearians" of "sucking Shakespeare's blood" and feeding "leech-like" off the truth. Wells denigrates skeptics as "anti-Shakespearian," a clever rhetorical move, making anyone who doubts the authorship "against" Shakespeare, though all the doubters I know love Shakespeare. It is their love that made them look too closely.

In 2014 Wells's crusade spilled into the British tabloids. "Bard Blood at the Palace," the *Daily Mail* announced, reporting that Professor Wells had "crossed swords" with Prince Philip, Duke of Edinburgh. Wells had apparently asked the queen's consort if he was a heretic. Philip, never one to tread lightly, responded, "All the more so after reading your book." Meanwhile, Prince Charles had written to Professor Jonathan Bate, then at Oxford, asking for a list of arguments backing Shakespeare. Was the Prince of Wales plagued by a faltering faith? If he had doubts, it would not be wise to let on—not as president of the Royal Shakespeare Company and not, certainly, as he approached his throne.

I wasn't sure how to approach Professor Wells. Despite having written several books on the authorship question, he apparently did not like to discuss the topic. If I mentioned it upfront, he might refuse to speak with me. I decided to explain that I was a journalist writing a book about Shakespeare and that I wanted to include him in the book. Would he be open to speaking? I didn't specify exactly *what* about Shakespeare, and he didn't ask.

When I arrived in London in June 2021 the papers were cackling over Boris Johnson's much anticipated biography *Shakespeare: The Riddle of Genius*, which had been announced with some fanfare in 2015 and slated for publication in 2016 to mark the four-hundred-year anniversary of Shakespeare's death but which, five years later, had yet to materialize. The *Independent* reported that the prime minister had missed Covid meetings at the beginning of the pandemic in 2020 to write the Shakespeare book. Downing Street denied this. Meanwhile, the *Daily Mirror* quoted anonymous sources explaining that he had to work on the draft or else pay back his $500,000 advance from his publisher, which he could not afford. A period in February 2020—twelve mysterious, unaccounted for days—were cited as time Johnson spent squirreled away at an estate in the country, attempting to punch out *The Riddle of Genius* instead of attending "crucial Covid meetings." The riddle was apparently proving inscrutable. Amazon listed the book as an upcoming title: "From the inimitable, mop-headed, best-selling British journalist and politician, a celebration of the best-known Brit of all time." But it still had not appeared, and the longer it failed to appear the funnier the subject became. The tabloids had begun referring to the whereabouts of the book itself as the "riddle."

Stratford lies two hours northwest of London in the British midlands. Fittingly, this is more or less the heart of England. For the truly devout, there is a waymarked footpath between London and Stratford, "Shakespeare's Way," intended to approximate the route he might have taken to and from his hometown. Passing up the opportunity to squelch my feet in Shakespeare's hallowed footsteps, I caught the train from London's Marylebone Station. It felt slightly surreal to be traveling to Stratford-upon-Avon, like taking the train to Narnia or Neverland. En route, I read the *Stratford Herald*, which reported that Johnson, struggling to crack the riddle of

Shakespeare's genius, had asked a Shakespeare scholar in Stratford to help him write the book—in fact, to "semi-dictate" the content to him. The newspaper noted that Johnson had employed the same ghostwriting method in his 2014 book on Winston Churchill: recruiting an expert to do the work and then slapping his own name on the cover. But the *Herald* missed the great irony of the saga—that Johnson was seeking to pass off as his own a book written by a hidden author, the very thing Shakespeare is suspected of having done.

Alas, the scholar turned down the prime minister. Who was the scholar rebuffing Britain's prime minister? "I've not been approached at all," Jonathan Bate was quoted as saying. "If I find there is any plagiarism, he will be hearing from my lawyers." He added, "LOL." Stephen Greenblatt similarly confirmed that he was not the mystery scholar. "I haven't been approached and do not know who might have been. Have you tried Jim Shapiro at Columbia? If I were the PM, I might ask him." That the prime minister was struggling to unlock the riddle of Shakespeare's genius was, of course, a very good joke. Everyone since Nicholas Rowe had failed to do so. No scholar could help him there.

I pulled out my dog-eared copy of *Shakespeare Beyond Doubt*, which Stanley Wells had coedited with Reverend Dr. Paul Edmondson, a priest of the Church of England and the Birthplace's "head of knowledge." The cover featured an image of the actor Joseph Fiennes from the 1998 movie *Shakespeare in Love*. He looked pensive and brooding, in a loose linen shirt with a quill balanced between ink-stained fingers. A fictional Shakespeare seemed an odd choice for a scholarly book that claimed to present "evidence," though, if you saw the matter from an anti-Stratfordian perspective, as a book presenting a fictional author, it was perfect.

In one chapter, Wells catalogued the Renaissance allusions to Shakespeare (such as Jonson's praise of the "Sweet Swan of Avon"), maintaining these as "clear evidence" of his authorship and calling dramatically on skeptics to disprove it—a challenge they had happily taken up. But some allusions were conspicuously omitted, while others were glossed over hurriedly as "cryptic." Nothing on Labeo, the crafty cuttle hiding in a cloud of ink; nothing on "that poet who takes a name from shaking and spear." I made a note to ask Wells about the allusions he had omitted and flipped to Reverend Edmondson's chapter, which began ominously: "Shakespeare has enemies. Wherever one starts from, the questions and discussions about authorship are basically antagonistic." Edmondson went on at length against "anti-Shakespearians," deeming them "parasitic." He deplored the assumption that it is "always acceptable to challenge or contradict a knowledgeable and expert authority. It is not," he wrote. Questioning the authorship is "ultimately a dangerous phenomenon."

Stratford was quiet and gray when I arrived. I checked into my hotel and went to the hotel restaurant for dinner. It was trendy and modern, with a menu offering, incongruously, the most traditional English fare: potted ham hock and ox tongue, crispy lamb sweetbreads, slow-roast Berkshire pork belly, and roast dry-aged Hereford beef rump. I ordered a large glass of wine and pulled out my notebook to draft my questions for my interview with Wells the next morning. Why were so many of the allusions "cryptic"? What did he think the poet meant in the sonnets when he wrote that he must "die to all the world"? Did he still think it was "immoral" to question history? I didn't expect the professor to admit any doubts, but I was curious to see how he would handle the questions. I had become less interested in *who* Shakespeare was than in how people responded to the ambiguity. Reasonable as the questions seemed to me, I imagined they might sound hostile to him. Should I load the big ones up front in case he gave me only ten minutes before throwing me out of his house? I had been warned that he could become angry when questioned about the authorship.

As I was drafting, my phone buzzed. It was an email from Wells.

Dear Elizabeth

I have just discovered that you are an anti-Shakespearian. As you are well aware, I have consistently and frequently expressed my contempt for this stance. I should prefer not to meet you.

Yours
Stanley Wells

I let the email sit for a while, contemplating my response. He had guessed—presumably having discovered my *Atlantic* article—that I was planning to ask him questions he didn't want to answer. He would be better off avoiding me altogether. The decision was as sensible as it was cowardly. I wrote back expressing my disappointment. I had read his books, I added. I had questions, naturally, but I didn't see why we shouldn't be able to have a pleasant and interesting conversation.

The next morning, I wandered through Stratford, waiting to hear back. The main downtown area was small and pedestrian, centered on the local tourist industry. Most of the buildings were in the half-timbered Tudor style, lending an air of Renaissance authenticity to the town. Quaint street signs helpfully funneled bumbling tourists toward the attractions: "Shakespeare's Birthplace" or "Holy Trinity Church and Shakespeare's Grave." On High Street, I passed the Hathaway Tea Rooms and a pub called the Garrick Inn. Farther along, a greasy-looking cafe called the Food of Love, a cutesy name taken from *Twelfth Night* ("If music be the food of love, play on"). The town was Elizabethan kitsch—plus souvenir shops, a Subway, a Starbucks, a cluster of high-end boutiques catering to moneyed out-of-towners, more souvenir shops. Shakespeare's face was everywhere, staring down from signs and storefronts like a benevolent big brother. The entrance to the "Old Bank estab. 1810" was gilded ornately with an image of Shakespeare holding a quill, as though he functioned as a guarantee of the bank's credibility. Confusingly, there were several Harry Potter–themed shops (House of Spells, the Creaky Cauldron, Magic Alley). You could almost feel the poor locals scheming how best to squeeze a few more dollars out of the tourists. Stratford and Hogwarts, quills and wands, poems and spells. Then again, maybe the confusion was apt: Wasn't Shakespeare the quintessential boy wizard, magically endowed with inexplicable powers?

I had been prepared to find a charming, dreamy village on the banks of the fabled Avon River. Instead, Stratford felt tacky and dingy—like a theme park, but a very drab one. I was reminded of David Garrick's advice after the 1769 Jubilee: that Stratford make improvements so as not to be called "the most dirty, unseemly, ill pav'd, wretched-looking Town in all Britain." The town had been paved and scrubbed since Garrick's time, but it was not difficult to mentally subtract the cafes and shops to picture how wretched it must have been a few centuries back.

On Henley Street, I stopped in front of the Birthplace, the town's central attraction. It was another half-timbered building, yellowed with age. I imagined the pious Victorians who had once lined up outside the house. In the nineteenth century, the tenant of the Birthplace, Mrs. Mary Hornby, did a little business showing and selling "relics" to gullible visitors and spinning tales of the poet. "There is nothing like resolute good-humoured credulity in these matters," the American writer Washington Irving wrote of his encounter with Mrs. Hornby, "and on this occasion I went even so far as willingly to believe the claims of mine hostess to a lineal descent from the poet." Noticing the growing line of pilgrims at the Birthplace, Mrs. Hornby's landlady, Mrs. Court, doubled the rent, then doubled it again, pushing out Mrs. Hornby, who took her little collection of relics to a house on the other side of Henley Street. Mrs. Court, who also owned the neighboring pub, ran a lucrative side hustle showing tourists around the immortal house. She even had business cards printed inviting "the nobility and gentry visiting Stratford-upon-Avon to gratify their own laudable curiosity, and honour her by inspecting the house in which the immortal Poet of Nature was born." But she did not have the relics. Desperate to secure their return, she resorted to threats and bribes. Mrs. Hornby would not budge. The women, bitter rivals in the Shakespeare tourist trade, were regularly seen fighting on their doorsteps, heaping such abuse on each other that a jaded pilgrim was moved to capture the scene in verse:

What, Birthplace here? and relics there?
Abuse from each! Ye brawling blouses!
Each picks my pocket, 'tis not fair,
A stranger's curse on both your houses!

The relics were eventually exposed in an article in *Bentley's Miscellany*, a literary magazine, which observed that four different chairs, each purporting to be "Shakespeare's chair," had been sold over the years, each made by a well-known local craftsman. "As long as this was confined to chairs, tables, jugs, and walking-sticks, and the pious fraud benefited poor people at the expense of rich credulity, there was no great harm done." The real fraud, the article suggested, was the Birthplace itself.

In 1847 Mrs. Court died, and the Birthplace was put up for sale. What was to happen to the shrine of England's immortal poet? Who would purchase it? A national discussion began. There was a great deal of anxiety about the possibility of the property falling into the wrong hands. If foreigners bought it, they might chop it up and sell it off. The *Morning Herald* worried that the Birthplace would be turned into snuffboxes by the French, pipes by the Dutch, or card cases by the Chinese. The real threat, of course, was the Americans. The *Times* reported that "one or two enthusiastic Jonathans have already arrived from America, determined to see what dollars can do in taking it away. The timber, it is said, are all sound, and it would be no very difficult matter to set it on wheels and make an exhibition of it." The American showman P. T. Barnum (of Barnum & Bailey Circus) was circling the property, reportedly intent on shipping it back to the States and making it part of a traveling show. The sacred house would become a vulgar American tourist attraction. The *Athenæum* saw this looming horror as reason for the British public to "save" the house and "rescue a property so sanctified by its associations from the vulgarity of showmanship."

A committee of Shakespeare scholars was formed to purchase the property "for the nation." The committee put up posters and placed advertisements in the papers, asking the British public to donate money to the cause. Donations were construed as an expression of proper veneration: the "last and precious opportunity of showing that we truly revere and love our own glorious Shakspere," the papers emphasized. The campaign to buy the house was complicated, however, by a pesky little question: Was the Birthplace *really* the site of Shakespeare's birth? "[T]he extraordinary sensation caused by the purchase of this shabby sausage-shop deserves a prominent place amongst popular delusions," declared *Bentley's Miscellany.* John Shakespeare had rented and owned several houses in Stratford, any one of which might have been the site of his eldest son's birth—and he bought the house known as the Birthplace only in 1575, when Shakespeare was eleven years old. In a letter to the editor of the *Examiner*, a former inhabitant of Stratford disclosed that the Birthplace was a "deception." A historian affirmed that the "paltry hut" venerated as the Birthplace was a "most flagrant and gross imposition, invented purposely with a design to extort pecuniary gratuities from the credulous and unwary." Another writer mocked the gullibility of a nation pouring forth funds to buy "a rubbishing mass of lath and plaster in which the Poet was no more born than was the Man in the Moon himself."

The belief that the immortal poet was born in the "rubbishing mass" on Henley Street rested on tradition—that is, on the repetition of the belief from generation to generation. "Here we may safely trust to tradition," the antiquarian Charles Roach Smith assured the nation. As one nonbeliever scoffed, "It is the easiest thing in the world to deceive people who themselves wish to be deceived." The auction of the Birthplace went forward on September 16, 1847, the auction room packed with people who wished to be deceived: celebrated artists and men of letters, prospective buyers, curious onlookers, and members of the committee. The committee prevailed, securing the Birthplace for the nation.

After the auction, Charles Knight expanded his biography of Shakespeare, adding that the Birthplace was a sweeter shrine for the very absence of evidence—for the faith it required of its pious visitors. "The want of absolute certainty that Shakspere was there born produces a state of mind that is something higher and pleasanter than the conviction that depends on positive evidence," he wrote. "We are content to follow the popular faith undoubtingly." In 1848 another scholar, James Halliwell-Phillipps, produced his own Shakespeare biography, reaffirming the faith and placing the Birthplace above questioning: "Let not our poetical sympathies be measured by the argument of reality," he urged. "It suffices to know and feel that the spot was trod by Shakespeare, that there he 'prattled poesey in his nurse's arms,' and, more than this, that the associations remain and have not been destroyed. The worldly wise will tell us sympathies such as these are visionary, that our interest has arisen solely from our own imaginations. . . . Breathe not a whisper to dissipate the solemn thoughts of such a power—tell us not how changeable are the records of men."

They knew it was an illusion, but they loved the illusion. It was a beautiful illusion. Plus, the illusion made good economic sense. The purchase of the Birthplace solidified Stratford-upon-Avon as a tourist mecca. The committee became the Shakespeare Birthplace Trust, a formal body of trustees charged with managing and maintaining the property. Extensive restoration works began to make the site more appealing to tourists. A visitor walking down Henley Street in the 1840s recalled being hit with a smell so objectionable that he was compelled to quicken his pace, but not before looking up to discover its source: the gutters of the Birthplace, which were being cleaned. "The people of Stratford are as dirty as ever," he determined.

An inquiry by the Board of Health confirmed the unsanitary and impoverished conditions of the town. This would not do for the most sanctified spot in the whole of the British Empire. Sewers were laid. The focus then turned to the Birthplace itself. Shakespeare's worshippers needed a proper temple and the "shabby sausage-shop" left something to be desired. It was decided that the adjoining premises should be demolished, ostensibly to reduce the risk of fire but also to make the building a more "attractive site." Walls were moved, floorboards replaced, new doorways and staircases created. The Birthplace was transformed into the large, comfortable, detached home of a prosperous Elizabethan family—the building now before me. If I didn't know better, I would have assumed it was authentic. Sir Sidney Lee conceded later that "a murky cloud of misunderstanding" hung over the Birthplace, which was not a Tudor construct so much as a Victorian one, created in the context of the nineteenth-century fascination with "merrie olde England." The Victorians invented the Birthplace, as the scholar Julia Thomas writes, inventing in the process a Shakespearean tradition that still holds power today.

A visitor who had seen the house before the restoration observed, on returning years later, that it "seems to have grown mysteriously." Shakespeare had moved up in the world. Pointing to the handsome house on Henley Street, commentators could now assure Victorian readers, "There can be little doubt that during his childhood, and up to his eleventh or twelfth year, little William Shakespeare lived in careless plenty, and

Shakespeare's Birthplace, squashed between other tenements, before the restoration (1847)

After the restoration, the Birthplace "seems to have grown mysteriously" (ca. 1890–1900)

saw nothing in his father's house but that style of liberal housekeeping, which has always distinguished the upper yeomanry and rural gentry of England." The Victorians had a peculiar fixation with Shakespeare's social status. When Charles Knight was preparing his biography of Shakespeare, he visited Stratford looking for evidence that the poet had been brought up in comfort. A more prosperous childhood made for a more believable author: one who *must* have been educated, who *must* have had access to books. The "restored" Birthplace came to stand as a kind of evidence for Shakespeare—in place of the evidence biographers would have preferred.

At the same time, Shakespeare was held up as a source of inspiration for Britain's working classes; a token of what was possible if you just worked hard enough. In the aftermath of the auction, the *Evening Sun* declared the story of Shakespeare "a brilliant token of the advancement of civilization in these realms, and a lesson calculated to inspire the uneducated mechanic with aspiration beyond those which have, in bygone centuries, been prevalent through the humbler classes of society." Shakespeare's social status thus became synonymous with his moral status. He represented *advancement*, *aspiration*, *education*. To improve yourself, you read Shakespeare. While 65 editions of Shakespeare's works appeared between 1709 and 1810, at least 162 editions were published between 1851 and 1860 alone—that is, in the decade following the auction of the Birthplace. The plays were praised as the "Bible of Humanity," and books such as J. B. Selkirk's *Bible Truths with Shakespearean Parallels* placed Shakespeare quotations alongside Scripture, further reinforcing Shakespeare's standing as a paragon of Christian morality.

Some disdained the Birthplace's new appearance. "I was not prepared to see it look so smug and new," wrote the Reverend John Mounteney Jephson. He hoped that the weather would eventually "tone down the 'neat' look of the house in Henley Street." The British weather certainly did not fail on that front, I thought, looking up at its worn facade. The building gradually lost its "neat look," and the history of the restoration faded from memory. It was not a history that anyone cared to remember.

⁜

I bought a ticket and entered through the Shakespeare Centre, a small museum that acted as a sort of antechamber to the Birthplace, preparing visitors for their entrance to the shrine. It was a strange museum. One of Shakespeare's wobbly signatures was blown up and highlighted in red above a placard explaining helpfully that "William Shakespeare has helped to shape us and make us who we are." There were various modern paintings of Shakespeare by twentieth-century artists, offering their creative renditions of the bard. In large lettering, a famous statement by journalist Bernard Levin of the London *Times*:

> If you cannot understand my argument, and declare "It's Greek to me," you are quoting Shakespeare; if you claim to be more sinned against than sinning, you are quoting Shakespeare; if you recall your salad days, you are quoting Shakespeare; if you act more in sorrow than in anger; if your wish is father to the thought; if your lost property has vanished into thin air, you are quoting Shakespeare; if you have ever refused to budge an inch or suffered from green-eyed jealousy, if you have played fast and loose, if you have been tongue-tied . . .

It went on. Incidentally, Bernard Levin also made another memorable statement about Shakespeare, but it was conspicuously absent from the museum walls: "Stratford permits—indeed encourages—one of the biggest frauds in England to rage unchecked," he wrote in 1965. "I mean those two monumental frauds, 'Shakespeare's' Birthplace and Anne Hathaway's Cottage." In 1892 the Shakespeare Birthplace Trust had acquired in the neighboring village of Shottery a thatched farmhouse said to be the childhood home of Anne Hathaway. For years, tourists had been descending on the house to sit in the "Shakespeare Courting Chair," where Shakespeare allegedly sat while wooing his bride.

I continued to a glass case displaying eight busts of Shakespeare, which dated from 1844 to 2000. Another case featured a Shakespeare beer jug (1933), a Shakespeare action figure (made in China, 2003), playing cards with Shakespeare's face (1974), and a paperweight (2000), which, according to the display label, was "made from stone reclaimed from a wall of the Birthplace during restoration works." A Shakespeare bowl, a mug, another ceramic Shakespeare figure. What on earth was this junk? It looked like the kind of clutter you might find in your grandparents' basement or the back of a secondhand shop—the kind that sat around forever collecting dust. What was it meant to prove? That Shakespeare was important? I was reminded of the Shakespeare "relics" that Mrs. Hornby bandied about the Birthplace before Mrs. Court pushed her out. After the auction and the restoration, new relics were found to help legitimize the house, including a desk said to have been Shakespeare's as a boy. A lady from New York fell on her knees and kissed it.

In 1891 the Birthplace's curator, a man named Joseph Skipsey, resigned his post, explaining that he and his wife "had not held our office more than a few months before we discovered that not a single one of the many so-called relics on exhibition could be proved to be Shakspere's—nay, that the Birthplace itself is a matter of grave doubt." The legends were an "abomination," Skipsey added, which "must stink in the nostrils of every true lover of our divine poet."

There was no Shakespeare drinking cup or Shakespeare goblet or Shakespeare desk at the Birthplace now. The fraudulent relics gone, the museum was making do with this new heap of tchotchkes and trinkets, most of them made in the twentieth century and of no discernible historical value—relics that testified not to Shakespeare's existence but to his importance, which was almost as good.

I moved on from the rubbish relic heap and stopped short at a large bust of a slightly balding man in a starched lace collar. I recognized him immediately. He was Sir Thomas Overbury, a courtier who became embroiled in various court intrigues culminating in his murder in 1613. A portrait of him surfaced in 2006. Stanley Wells claimed it as a portrait of Shakespeare. The Cobbe family, who had owned the portrait for some three centuries, was eager to encourage the identification, which immediately increased the portrait's value. But art historians with expertise in sixteenth- and seventeenth-century portraiture called Wells's claim "codswallop." The portrait does not have any inscription or coat of arms identifying the figure as Shakespeare. Besides, it closely resembles another portrait of Thomas Overbury. Even other Shakespeare scholars agreed that the portrait is of Overbury, not Shakespeare. Nevertheless, the Birthplace Trust adopted the artwork as its official Shakespeare image. It was effectively a rebranding: an image upgrade from the horrible Droeshout portrait to a courtly, sophisticated, educated-looking Shakespeare; a Shakespeare who might believably have written the dramas presented before England's monarchs. In the face of growing authorship questions, it made Shakespeare seem somehow more credible. The Birthplace had emblazoned it on signs and souvenirs and even, I realized, across the cover of the guidebook I had been handed at the entrance. I peered down at the bust's label, which read, "Sculpture based on Cobbe portrait of William Shakespeare, 2014."

It was all a sham, but no one seemed to mind. Around me, the other visitors were moving quietly through the darkened room, examining the displays, murmuring to one another in reverent museum whispers. I wondered if any of them would notice that there was nothing actually *there*—that they were staring at Shakespeare action figures made in China and a bust sculpted in 2014 from a portrait that was almost certainly not Shakespeare. The thinness of the museum gave it away. When the philosopher William James (brother to Henry) visited in 1902, he was struck by the "absolute extermination and obliteration of every record of Shakespeare save a few sordid material details." Far from strengthening his belief, his pilgrimage to Stratford eroded it. "In fact," he wrote, "a visit to Stratford now seems to me the strongest appeal a Baconian can make."

The museum dumped visitors onto a path that wound through an English country garden and up to the house. On either side, waist-high grasses teemed with lavender, rosemary, dog roses, and marjoram. The grounds of the Birthplace had been planted with plants from Shakespeare's plays. They were the loveliest thing I had seen in Stratford, but I resented them, feeling that they were also part of the deception.

In the Birthplace, I shuffled from room to room with the other visitors. Guides posted around the house talked about Shakespeare's childhood. They were trained by their head of knowledge, Reverend Paul Edmondson. I wondered if they believed the stories they told. Were there any disenchanted Joseph Skipseys here? When Henry James heard about the nineteenth-century curator and his wife who'd resigned from the Birthplace in disgust, he recorded the details in his notebook, seeing potential for a short story: "Say they end by denying Shakespeare—say they do it on the spot itself—one day—in the presence of a big, gaping, admiring batch," James wrote. "Then they must go."

The short story he ended up writing, published in 1903 as "The

Birthplace," is far subtler and more interesting. The curator confides his doubts to his wife, who worries about losing their livelihood if he says too much. When he begins tempering and qualifying the tales he tells to tourists, a representative from "the Body" arrives to reprove him. So instead of denying Shakespeare, the curator takes things to the opposite extreme, telling wild tales about Shakespeare's childhood. ("There would be more than one fashion of giving away the Show," he reflects, "and wasn't *this* perhaps a question of giving it away by excess? He could dish them by too much romance as well as by too little.") His wife worries that his sarcastic mythologizing will expose them. But it's exactly what everyone wants! Tourists flock to the house, and the Body, delighted by his performance, doubles his salary.

The story is instructive for curators as well as scholars: dishing the world by too much romance pays. But can a great show of romance also conceal gnawing doubts?

In the "Birthroom," a sign read, "This is the room where we believe William Shakespeare was born in April 1564." Next to the master bed stood a little cradle laid out with blankets and a tiny pillow, encouraging visitors to imagine the baby genius mewling by his parents' side. For the Victorians, the Birthroom offered the mystical possibility of contact with the dead poet. "We are by these means sensuously informed of his actuality, and seem able to expand in affection towards him," one explained. Visitors recorded melodramatic accounts of what they felt on entering the Birthroom. Frequently, they burst into tears. They fell down. They kissed the floor. Some visitors, desiring a more extended communion with the poet, spent the night in the Birthroom.

But others were unimpressed by their visits. Nathaniel Hawthorne reported that he "felt no emotion whatever in Shakespeare's house—not the slightest—nor the quickening of the imagination." Henry James delivered perhaps the most masterful put-down. "If I were to allude to Stratford, it would not be in connection with the fact that Shakespeare came into the world there," he wrote. "It would be rather to speak of a delightful old house near the Avon which struck me as the ideal home for a Shakespearean scholar." The Victorian mock-Tudor on Henley Street was, properly speaking, the dwelling place not of Shakespeare but of Shakespeare scholars—their construction, their fantasy.

To exit the Birthplace, visitors were made to pass through the gift shop, where any lingering sense of piety was met by a tidal wave of consumerism. The shop was selling Shakespeare mugs and Shakespeare breakfast teas and Shakespeare tea towels. Shakespeare rubber ducks and Shakespeare windup toys. Shakespeare Christmas ornaments, Shakespeare baby onesies, Shakespeare tote bags, and Shakespeare luxury chocolates. Standing by a collection of purple Ophelia socks and Ophelia silk scarves, I checked my phone. It was now midmorning, and Wells had not responded. I sent a short follow-up, confessing my surprise that he did not want to talk about a subject to which he has been a leading contributor. "How about tea later this afternoon?" I suggested, banking on the English love of tea to resolve all conflicts. "If you hate my questions, you can chuck the tea at me," I added. "I won't complain."

He responded tersely:

Ok. 4.30.
S

I had several hours now to take in the rest of Stratford's holy sites. I wandered back past the half-timbered buildings of Henley Street and the High Street. After the auction of the Birthplace in 1847, there was a push to make the town look more antique—to transform the brick-fronted dwellings into timber-framed ones and to build new houses in a Tudor style. "Modern progress is decidedly not the 'cue' for Stratford," wrote Marie Corelli, a popular Victorian novelist who had settled in the town. "Its good measures of gold, its full purses, its swelling bank-books, will be best and most swiftly attained by setting its back to the wall of the sixteenth century and refusing to budge." As Corelli astutely perceived, Stratford's commercial potential depended on "regaining" its Elizabethan features—thus the disproportionate number of half-timbered buildings.

I turned onto Chapel Street and approached New Place, which Shakespeare bought in 1597. The house itself does not actually exist anymore. After his death in 1616, it passed to his daughter and then his granddaughter, who died childless, and then out of the family. In 1756 the owner, Reverend Francis Gastrell, destroyed the mulberry tree in the garden, and the townsfolk retaliated by smashing the windows of New Place. The feud escalated when Gastrell's application for permission to extend the house's gardens was rejected. Then his tax was increased. Embittered, Gastrell demolished the entire house in 1759, a show of iconoclasm that enraged the locals, who promptly drove him out of town.

A little museum now stands on the site of New Place. It recounted the excavations of the house, which turned up a few beads and fragments of a pipe but, alas, no manuscripts. There being little to show, most of the space was given over to more gardens, which were artfully scattered with evocative quotes from the plays, hinting at Shakespeare's continued ghostly presence: "I will hide me in the arbour" and "Rest, rest, perturbed spirit." A new mulberry tree had been planted, rumored to be of the "same lineage" as the original. In a little courtyard, I came across sculptures of a small desk and chair.

"What's this?" I asked the guide.

"Well, this is what would have been the Great Hall, and we believe Shakespeare wrote many of his plays here," she explained. "You're welcome to sit if you'd like." She gestured to the chair.

This invitation delighted me enormously, calling to mind the accounts of Victorian curators who invited visitors to sit by the fireplace where Shakespeare had sat. So the tradition continued!

I exited the gardens and started toward Holy Trinity Church, the site of the mysterious Shakespeare monument. As I walked, I thought of the Victorian guidebooks that emphasized how "these walks will ever derive their principal attraction for the thoughtful visitor from the conviction that they may each have been trodden by the feet of Shakespeare; that his eye must have rested on every hill and valley; that every turn of the classic river; every common flower that here takes root, was familiar to him." All was sanctified by the halo of his presence—even the flowers. On the way I passed Hall's Croft, another mock-Tudor structure purporting to be the home of John Hall, Shakespeare's son-in-law, and Susanna, his daughter. Two tourists were staring down earnestly at a plaque in the pavement, reading about the lives of John and Susanna. But there are no records showing that they ever lived there.

⁂

Holy Trinity Church sits right on the banks of the river. A wide, tree-lined path cuts from the street through the graveyard, full of ancient, moss-covered tombstones, up to the church. It is a beautiful old church, parts of which date back to the early thirteenth century. I walked up the aisle toward the altar. The gravestones for Shakespeare and his family lie near the chancel steps. But the slab that marks his burial spot is famously strange. There is no name, no identification of him as a poet, only some junky verse carved into the stone—a curse on anyone who moves his remains:

Good Friend For Jesus Sake Forbeare,
To Digg the Dust Enclosed Heare:
Blest Be The Man That Spares These Stones,
And Curst Be He That Moves My Bones.

Why were Shakespeare's last words to the world a curse? Had the author of *A Midsummer Night's Dream* and *Romeo and Juliet*—of the most enchanting, musical poetry in the English language—really written this mediocre verse? Some have wondered if the curse was meant to deter the curious from investigating the grave. But why? What was in it? When Washington Irving visited in 1815, he spoke to the old sexton, who told him he had peered into the grave while laborers were digging to create an adjoining vault, but he "could see neither coffin nor bones; nothing but dust." The church has refused to excavate the grave in deference to Shakespeare's wishes—that is, in deference to the curse. But in 2016 a team of archaeologists conducted a nonintrusive investigation using ground-penetrating radar. They were hoping to detect objects buried with the body. The grave was empty.

High up on a wall to the left of the altar is the Shakespeare monument. I had thought it would be prominent, but the walls were cluttered with similar monuments and memorials, tombs and plaques, put up by anyone rich enough to afford one: town benefactors, local landowners, a mayor. Scholars have lamented the figure's "heavy unintellectual expression," regretting that it makes the poet look like a "self-satisfied pork butcher." In 1634 a heraldist named Sir William Dugdale visited Stratford and sketched the monument, publishing his drawing—the earliest known depiction of the monument—in his illustrated book *The Antiquities of Warwickshire*.

A "self-satisfied pork butcher"

In the introduction, he stated his intention to "preserve those Monuments from that fate, which *Time*, if not contingent mischief, might expose them to." The monument preserved in Dugdale's sketch appears very different from the one now on the church wall. In the sketch, the figure's arms are strangely elongated, and he holds what appears to be a woolpack—a bag for transporting fleeces. In the current incarnation of the monument, however, the proportions are more regular, and the woolpack has been transformed into a cushion on which rests a piece of paper. A quill—a real feather quill—has been placed in the figure's right hand, creating the impression of a poet in the midst of composition. I asked a docent standing near the altar if the quill was original to the monument.

"No, it's not. It's original to David Garrick," she said, explaining that

Dugdale's sketch, 1634

at the time of the Shakespeare Jubilee, Garrick started the tradition of placing a feather in the figure's hand. "It's actually replaced every year on his birthday," she added. "They have a big parade here and service right around April twenty-third, and the quill is brought in."

Stratford hosts an annual two-day festival known as the Shakespeare Birthday Celebrations. There is street entertainment and pageantry; a ceremony of the unfurling of the flags of nations; the Shakespeare Birthday Lecture, delivered by a notable Shakespeare scholar; the Shakespeare Birthday Lunch, featuring performances from the Royal Shakespeare Company; and the Shakespeare Birthday Service, held at Holy Trinity Church. (No separation between Church and Shakespeare.) The central event, however, is a parade of great fanfare in which the head boy from the grammar school picks up "Shakespeare's quill" at the Birthplace and solemnly carries it through the streets of Stratford to the church, where it is deposited in the hand of the Shakespeare bust.

If the quill is not original to the monument, did the bust originally depict a poet or a local landowner holding a woolpack? Had there been a bit of "contingent mischief"? Anti-Stratfordians suggest that the bust may have been altered or replaced over the years. Parish records show alterations to the church on at least ten occasions from 1649 to 1861. A clue may lie in the bust's mustache. It is an upturned cavalier mustache, a fashion that became popular only in the 1640s and 1650s, suggesting that the bust Dugdale saw in 1634 may have been replaced later with the current one. Scholars maintain that Dugdale's sketch must be inaccurate—that he failed to notice the quill and the sheet of paper. But Sir William Dugdale was a renowned heraldist whose exacting attention to detail was praised by his contemporaries. ("The skilfullest Anatomist that yet Upon an humane body e're did sit, Did never so precisely show his Art as you have yours," one wrote.) Dugdale spent years meticulously researching and preparing his survey of Warwickshire, which was funded partly by subscriptions of the county gentry. Would he have made such flagrant errors? No one seems to have complained he had misrepresented the Shakespeare monument; his book went through several editions without alteration or apology.

I studied the inscription below the bust, with its Latin couplet and English riddle challenging passersby to "Read If Thou Canst, Whom Envious Death Hath Plast With In This Monument Shakspeare." According to Stanley Wells, the inscription "somewhat cryptically calls on the passerby to pay tribute to his greatness as a writer." But Shakespeare cannot be "plast with in" a wall plaque too small to accommodate a corpse. Anti-Stratfordians have suggested their own interpretations over the years. Alexander Waugh, the latest to venture an explanation, points to the space between "with" and "in," arguing that this allows the reader to separate "with" from the phrase "in this monument." The inscription then becomes: "Read if thou canst, whom envious Death hath plast with [in this monument] Shakspeare." Or, in even plainer English: "With whom is Shakespeare buried? Work it out by reading this monument!" The Latin couplet above, he argues, offers the solution. Translated from Latin, it reads:

A Pylian in judgement, a Socrates in genius, a Maro in art
Earth covers, people mourn, Olympus holds.

Waugh suggests that the three names—Nestor (the Pylian), Socrates, and Maro (Virgil)—are sobriquets for three English writers: Francis Beaumont, whose literary judgment was held in such esteem that contemporaries referred to him as "Judicious Beaumont" and a "Judicious Partner . . . a Master of a good Wit and a better Judgement" (like the judicious Pylian); Geoffrey Chaucer, whose philosophical mind was compared to "the heavenly mind of prudent Socrates" and who was described as having "the genius of Socrates"; and Edmund Spenser, who was hailed as the "Virgil of England," an "imitatour" of Virgil who sang "in full Virgilian voice," and "our modern Maro." Francis Beaumont, Geoffrey Chaucer, and Edmund Spenser are buried—precisely in that order—in Westminster Abbey, England's Olympus, the seat of its gods. In the words of the couplet, "Earth covers, people mourn, Olympus holds."

To Waugh, this is the meaning that would be "dissolved" in time: that the poet—the real Shakespeare—is not buried in Stratford's church but in Westminster Abbey, with England's other great poets. Westminster Abbey is, of course, where a great poet *should* be buried. In the seventeenth century, a few writers suggested that Shakespeare lay at the Abbey, not in the Stratford church. A publisher named Samuel Speed wrote of Westminster "where Shakespear, Spenser, Camden, and the rest / Once rising Suns, are now set in the West." Sir John Denham, a poet and courtier, wrote of his friend Abraham Cowley's burial "amongst the Ancient Poets" in Westminster, listing Chaucer, Spenser, Shakespeare, and Jonson, leading a twentieth-century scholar to inquire incredulously, "Did Sir John really think that Shakespeare was buried in Westminster Abbey, as the above line would seem to imply?" Everyone knows Shakespeare is buried in the church in Stratford-upon-Avon. How could they get it so wrong? Or did they know something other people didn't?

It was Portia's casket test all over again: Which casket—which church, which grave—holds the poet? As I wandered back down the aisle of Holy Trinity Church, I made a note to ask Professor Wells why he thought Shakespeare's monument invokes Nestor, Socrates, and Virgil.

SIX

Aberration and the Academy

Sir Stanley Wells lives a few minutes' walk from the church on a street of modest brick row houses. I arrived a little early, anxious about the interview. We were starting out on very tense footing. When a journalist becomes an enemy, it is usually *after the fact*—after the interview, when the subject, who assumes your empathy, discovers that you haven't written what he wanted you to write. He feels that you've betrayed him; that you've been a wolf in sheep's clothing. But the journalist *needs* to appear as a sheep in order to put the subject at ease. I wished for some sheep's clothing. I was knocking on Stanley Wells's door simply as a naked, undisguised wolf.

"Come in," he said, showing me into a small sitting room at the front of the house.

It was slightly shabby in the professorial way, the coffee table scattered with magazines, the walls crammed with books and old records. Wells himself looked very formal, in a blue suit with his white hair and beard neatly trimmed.

"Do sit down," he said, unsmiling. "Would you like a cup of tea?"

He seemed to be struggling between his instinctive contempt for "anti-Shakespearians" and his Englishman's need to perform the requisite social courtesies. I told him I would have tea if he was having tea, but he was not having tea, so we did away with the tea. I immediately regretted it. Without the tea, things suddenly felt very cold. We had nothing to ease our way in, nothing to soften the hard edges of the interview. Instead, we faced each other like two wrestlers in a ring. He settled into an armchair. I perched on the edge of a sofa. Putting on a cheerful voice, I thanked him for seeing me. I was determined not to be the wolf he thought I was.

"Have you been round the sites?" he asked.

I said I'd been to the Birthplace, New Place, and Holy Trinity Church but had not yet made it to Anne Hathaway's cottage, which lay a few miles outside of Stratford. Was it worth visiting?

"Well, it's very charming."

"Is it genuine?"

"Oh yes, yes," he said. "Yes, all the houses we show are genuine." I thought briefly of citing the evidence to the contrary, but I let it go. I was not interested in arguing with him about the houses. "We've had a very difficult time," he went on, lamenting the Trust's loss of income during Covid. "Our normal income in a good year would have been about nine and a half million pounds. We've lost suddenly eight and a half million pounds." A government loan had kept the organization afloat, but "half of our staff were sacked."

Glancing around the room, I took in a picture of Wells smiling with Reverend Paul Edmondson at a parade that looked like the Shakespeare Birthday Celebrations, as well as a painting of Wells wearing his knighthood medal. In 2016 he was knighted at Buckingham Palace for services to scholarship.

The feeble show of small talk didn't last long. "So, what can I do for you?" he asked.

⁂

Sir Stanley Wells, professor emeritus of Shakespeare studies, honorary president of the Shakespeare Birthplace Trust, and Commander of the Order of the British Empire, is an exemplary product of the academic institution of English literature. And so, to understand him, one must understand the rise of the English Department. For strange though it may seem, English as a professional discipline did not exist until fairly late in

English history. At the beginning of the nineteenth century, there were no English departments and no such thing as a degree in English literature. The public enjoyed Shakespeare at the theaters and read Shakespeare recreationally. Percy Shelley, Samuel Taylor Coleridge, and other poets wrote influential pieces of literary criticism. Anglican clergymen at Oxford delivered occasional orations on poetry. And lawyers such as Edmond Malone wrote books on Shakespeare, but they were amateur scholars—self-appointed Shakespeareans. Around the mid-nineteenth century, however, the field began to professionalize. A discipline called English literature arose, founded on and formed around Shakespeare. It arose, first and foremost, as a substitute for religion.

For centuries, Christianity had exerted a pacifying influence on the population, encouraging values of meekness and self-sacrifice, and unifying all classes, from the richest congregant to the pious peasant, under a single ideology. But by the Victorian period, religion was threatened by scientific discovery and social change. Church attendance among the working classes was falling. Social unrest seemed to be building. The church was losing its hold on the masses, and the Victorian ruling class worried that, without religion to encourage morality and restraint, something like the French Revolution could happen in Britain. A new religion was needed; a discourse that could provide the unifying, pacifying function formerly provided by Christianity.

As the scholar Terry Eagleton writes, "If one were to provide a single explanation for the growth of English studies in the later nineteenth century, one could do worse than reply: 'the failure of religion.'"

In 1829 the University of London appointed the first Professor of English—Reverend Thomas Dale, a priest of the Church of England. In 1840 another Anglican priest, F. D. Maurice, became Professor of English literature at King's College London, outlining in his inaugural lecture his belief that the study of English literature would serve "to emancipate us . . . from the notions and habits which are peculiar to our own age," connecting Britons instead with "what is fixed and enduring." Instead of worrying about their small, everyday concerns, they could contemplate the eternal truths and beauties of English literature. In doing so, they could enter imaginatively into the life of the nation, taking pride in the cultural riches of Britain and the achievements of their countrymen. They could feel that they had a stake in the nation, which might—with some luck—keep them from revolution.

In 1854 Maurice founded the Working Men's College to provide laborers with a "liberal" education. Colleges were also founded to train the new body of English teachers. "It seems as if few stocks could be trusted to grow up properly without having a priesthood and an aristocracy to act as their schoolmasters at some time or other of their national existence," wrote the critic Matthew Arnold. As the old priesthoods and aristocracies were losing their power, a new body of priests—teachers drawn from the middle classes and trained "into intellectual sympathy with the educated of the upper classes"—were needed to lead the masses. "If these [middle] classes cannot win their sympathy or give them their direction, society is in danger of falling into anarchy," Arnold warned.

Advocating for state-regulated education, Arnold looked to the study of English literature—the "best culture" of the nation—as the necessary agent of social harmony. It could unify the classes, instilling in them a sense of pride in their national literature, but it could also—like religion—offer moral and spiritual guidance. "The future of poetry is immense," he wrote. (By "poetry," he meant literature broadly.) While creeds and dogmas crumbled, in poetry humanity would find "an ever surer and surer stay. . . . More and more, mankind will discover that we have to turn to poetry to interpret life for us, to console us, to sustain us . . . and most of what now passes with us for religion and philosophy will be replaced by poetry."

Presented with a cosmic perspective, Britons would cease to worry about wages or better working conditions. Literature would introduce the working man to the "intellectual leaders of our race," explained a lecturer at York Training College. It would carry him "above the smoke and stir, the din and turmoil of man's lower life of care and business and debate," helping him to see "that truth is many sided, that it is not identical or merely coextensive with individual opinion, and that the world is a good deal wider than his own sect, or party, or class." Literature, in short, would help to break down class differences, subtly drawing people away from their allegiance to a class or political movement. English helps to "promote sympathy and fellow feeling among all classes," a Victorian teachers' handbook emphasized. Though workingmen could not produce literary masterpieces themselves, they could share in the sense of national accomplishment, knowing that people *like them*—other English people, even other lowborn English people (say, Shakespeare)—had succeeded in doing so.

"The main purpose is not to educate the masses," Lord Playfair emphasized to the London Society for the Extension of University Teaching in 1894, "but to permeate them with the desire for intellectual improvement, and to show them methods by which they can attain this desire. Every man who acquires a taste for learning and is imbued with the desire to acquire more of it, becomes more valuable as a citizen, because he is more intelligent and perceptive." The solitary, contemplative study of literature (like the solitary, contemplative study of the Bible) would keep them from more disruptive, collective activities such as erecting barricades or mounting protests in Hyde Park. It certainly worked on the political dissident Thomas Cooper, who recorded in his memoirs the mollifying effects of literary study: "The wondrous knowledge of the heart unfolded by Shakespeare made me shrink into insignificance; while the sweetness, the marvelous power of expression and grandeur in his poetry seemed to transport me, at times, out of the vulgar world of circumstances in which I lived bodily."

The Victorians congratulated themselves on the success of their project. While Europe was full of students "liable to dangerous explosions of political feeling," another lecturer noted, the men and women of Britain "spend the little leisure they have from their work in life in quiet, peaceful study," immersed in the "civilising, softening charms of the noblest literature in the world."

It was important that women, too, were drawn into the study of English literature—not because the ruling class was eager to support women's advancement, still less their emancipation, but because women were agitating for education. They needed to be placated, and yet they could not possibly be admitted to virile disciplines such as the sciences or the classics. (The study of dead languages was purely scholarly and therefore a masculine pursuit.) English seemed a "convenient sort of nonsubject to palm off on the ladies," as Eagleton puts it. Literary study would confirm women in their proper roles, preparing them for their wifely duties of empathy and understanding. It might be viewed as an attractive addition to the traditional staple of "accomplishments" wealthy women were expected to display on the marriage market. As one report on the education of young women observed in 1868: "Of all the 'solid' subjects . . . those comprised under the name of modern languages and literature are most prized by parents." French, painting, music, needlework, and English literature then—though only with censored, sanitized texts. Bowdlerized editions of Shakespeare, purged of all the indecent innuendo and dirty jokes, rolled off the presses.

The rise of English thus accompanied the founding of women's colleges and the reluctant admission of women to institutions of higher learning, but it was a remedy—an attempt to forestall their desires for more sweeping change. "In America, some are maintaining that they should take degrees and practise as physicians," observed Maurice, who founded Queen's College for Women in 1848. "I not only do not see my way to such a result; I not only should not wish that any college I was concerned in should be leading to it; but I should think that there could be no better reason for founding a college than to remove the slightest craving for such a state of things, by giving a more healthful direction to the minds which might entertain it." Women's colleges followed later at Oxford and Cambridge to provide that "more healthful direction" to female minds, but women were still not full members of the universities, and they were not granted degrees.

The study of English literature thus began as a form of social control: to civilize the restless masses and subdue the tiresome ladies. There was a third group, too, that the Victorians sought to control: the natives that they conquered. In 1853 Parliament passed the India Act, decreeing that the most lucrative and prestigious posts in the civil service should be awarded based on competitive examination. Candidates would be tested in a range of subjects, but "foremost among these, we place our own language and literature," a committee affirmed. Representatives of Britain needed to demonstrate knowledge of Britain's literary treasures. Armed with Shakespeare, secure in a sense of their national identity and cultural superiority, they could venture forth to impose their higher civilization on the natives. (Knowledge of the culture, literature, and languages of the natives themselves was not deemed necessary.) Literary taste—a "taste for pleasures not sensual"—might also, the committee hoped, help the administrators resist the abuses and "scandalous immorality" to which they might be tempted in their foreign posts.

The civil service examinations pressured schools and universities to supply the necessary instruction. In 1878 Cambridge introduced English as a subdepartment of the Board of Medieval and Modern Languages. In 1882 Oxford created a professorship of English Language and Literature. By 1908, the newly formed English Association would publish a pamphlet on *The Teaching of Shakespeare in Schools*, championing Shakespeare as "the supreme figure of our literature" and encouraging teachers to read the plays aloud in the classroom.

Conceived as a replacement for religion, English was institutionalized at the height of the Victorian deification of Shakespeare, swapping the old Judeo-Christian God for one that Britain had ready at hand. "An institution," Ralph Waldo Emerson observed, "is the lengthened shadow of one man." And the academic institution of English literature, as the scholar Nancy Glazener writes, can be understood as a shadow cast by Shakespeare, though this shadow is "an effect of Shakespeare's having been positioned and lit retrospectively."

⁂

To some, however, Shakespeare remained *just* a shadow. Who was the man that cast the shadow called English literature? The same period that saw the rise of English also saw the rise of alternative authorship theories. No account of the first is complete without also understanding the second. For religions define themselves by a set of beliefs, but they also define themselves against a set of heresies. The new church of English literature defined itself, in part, against the Shakespeare heresies.

It is not a coincidence that the first explicitly heretical writings on

Shakespeare followed on the heels of the first Victorian biographies. Discerning readers saw through their fictions. They saw, too, that a void still persisted in the documentary records of Shakespeare's life.

In 1845, just two years after the publication of Charles Knight's biography, an American woman named Delia Bacon began researching the authorship of Shakespeare's plays. Delia was that still-rare nineteenth-century creature: a lady of letters, unmarried (of course), and existing on the margins of a male literary culture that alternately celebrated and reviled her. Born in a log cabin, the daughter of a New England congregational minister, she had a limited formal education. While her brother was sent to Yale, she left school at fourteen to support her family. She tried her hand at fiction, once beating Edgar Allan Poe for a short-story prize, but she made her living teaching Shakespeare to schoolgirls in New Haven. She "seemed to saturate herself with the plays," one student remembered, "to call into imaginative consciousness the loves, hopes, fears, ambition, disappointment, and despair of the characters . . ." Eventually—and unusually for a woman—Bacon became a distinguished professional lecturer. According to one spectator, "she looked and spoke the very muse of history."

In the scholarly currents of her day, Bacon saw exciting discoveries. Biblical scholars were questioning the authorship of the Bible, demonstrating that the Gospel narratives—with their miracles of virgin birth, incarnation, and resurrection—were not eyewitness accounts but myths recorded long after Jesus's death. Classical scholars were questioning the authorship of *The Iliad* and *The Odyssey*, arguing that Homer was merely a preserver and transmitter of oral traditions. "And who is Shakespeare?" a character asked in the 1837 novel *Venetia* by Benjamin Disraeli, a future prime minister of England. "We know of him as much as we do of Homer. Did he write half the plays attributed to him? Did he ever write a single whole play? I doubt it." (The character, Lord Carducis, was based on the poet Lord Byron, suggesting Byron may have "doubted it.")

Delia Bacon doubted it, too. In an age of historical inquiry, how much longer would the world accept the Stratford myth? Seeking to overturn Shakespearean tradition as scholars were overturning biblical and Homeric traditions, she withdrew from lecturing to pursue her theory. When it was published more than a decade later, it would spark an international movement. In the meantime, other skeptics published their own doubts about the authorship.

In 1848 a minor American novelist named Joseph Hart suggested that Shakespeare was a "mere *factotum* of the theatre" and a "vulgar and unlettered man." The plays were collaborative works produced by educated writers whose identities had simply been lost, Hart argued in a digression in one of his novels. In Scotland in 1852 an anonymous article titled "Who Wrote Shakespeare?" appeared in *Chambers's Edinburgh Journal*. "Is it more difficult to suppose that Shakespeare was not the author of the poetry ascribed to him, than to account for the fact that there is nothing in the recorded or traditionary life of Shakespeare which in any way connects the poet with the man?" the author asked. Biographical facts reveal a man "intent only on moneymaking," he continued, floating a theory that the plays were written by "some pale, wasted student . . . with eyes of genius gleaming through despair" who sold the plays to Shakespeare. "What was to hinder William Shakespeare from reading, appreciating, and purchasing these dramas, and thereafter keeping his poet?" the anonymous author wondered. "Well, reader, how like you our hypothesis? We confess we do not like it ourselves; but we humbly think it at least as plausible as most of what is contained in the many bulky volumes written to connect the man, William Shakespeare, with the poet of *Hamlet*." If Shakespeare did not keep a poet, he concluded, then he must have retreated to a cave like a prophet to receive the sacred plays by "divine afflatus."

Delia Bacon was developing a different hypothesis. Drawing on her years of reading and teaching Shakespeare, she saw the plays as radical critiques of tyranny written by a "little clique of disappointed and defeated politicians," who sought to covertly disseminate their anti-monarchical ideas through the medium of the theater. Lear is the "impersonation of absolutism," she wrote, "the very embodiment of pure will and tyranny in their most frantic form." But the plays' political philosophy was obscured by the Stratfordian attribution: "Condemned to refer the origin of these works to the vulgar, illiterate man . . . how could we, how could any one, dare to see what was really in them?"

Delia Bacon suggested that the true authors were a group of courtiers, led by Francis Bacon (though not, as some have claimed, because she thought they were related). In the nineteenth century, Francis Bacon was revered as a philosophical genius, one of the great minds of the Renaissance. "No one reads the works of Bacon without imbibing an affectionate veneration for their author," Emerson observed. A worldly courtier, steeped in Renaissance learning and politics, he seemed exactly the sort of man that Shakespeare *should* have been. His father was a high-ranking official in the Queen's government; his mother, a linguist who translated religious texts from Latin and Italian and debated theology with leading clergymen. Along with his older brother, Anthony, he was educated at Trinity College, Cambridge, under the personal tutelage of John Whitgift, the future archbishop of Canterbury. He displayed a precocious intellect. A painting of Bacon at eighteen features the Latin inscription *Si tabula daretur digna animum mallem* ("If one could but paint his mind"). To further his education, he accompanied the English ambassador to Paris, traveling through France for three years, studying language, statecraft, and diplomacy.

"If one could but paint his mind"

On his return, he entered the Inns of Court to study law, which fit with the legal knowledge scholars were discovering in the plays. For instance, Edmond Malone observed that Shakespeare's "knowledge of legal terms is not merely such as might be acquired by the casual observation of even his all-comprehending mind; it has the appearance of technical skill." John Payne Collier, the scholar-turned-forger, agreed that "proofs of something like a legal education are to be found in many of his plays, and it may safely be asserted that they do not occur anything like so frequently in the dramatic productions of any of his contemporaries."

Launching a career in the 1580s as a writer and public servant, Bacon wrote to his uncle Lord Burghley, "I have taken all knowledge to be my province." By 1594, the Queen had appointed him as one of her "learned counsels." His position at court and his relationship with his brother Anthony, who was a spy for the Crown, put him at the center of a web of intelligence on political, religious, and cultural matters across Europe. In James I's reign, he ascended to attorney general and lord chancellor before falling into disgrace in 1621 under trumped-up charges of corruption. After a short stint in the Tower of London, he decided "to retire from the stage of civil action and betake myself to letters."

Bacon's literary output was prodigious: political treatises, parliamentary speeches, juridical texts, theological meditations, his *Essays*, and philosophical works, including *The Advancement of Learning*, *The New Atlantis*, *Instauratio Magna*, and *Novum Organum*. But there is something of a mystery around the full extent of his literary activities. When Bacon died in 1626, thirty-two eulogies were collected and published, including a remarkable claim about his contribution to drama: "So did philosophy, entangled in the subtleties of Schoolmen seek Bacon as a deliverer . . . he renewed her, walking humbly in the socks of Comedy. After that, he rises more elaborately on the loftier buskin of Tragedy." In what sense did Bacon "walk" in the socks of comedy and tragedy? Along with his brother Anthony, Bacon had employed a team of writers and secretaries—"some good pens which forsake me not," he called them. He also helped organize performances for Gray's Inn law school. During the Christmas revels of 1594, *The Comedy of Errors* was performed by torchlight—the first recorded performance of the play. In his *Advancement of Learning*, Bacon noted that "though in modern states play-acting is esteemed but as a toy, except when it is too satirical and biting; yet among the ancients it was used as a means of educating young men's virtue." The final part of Bacon's *Instauratio Magna*—his project to restore virtue and learning—never appeared, leading Delia to suspect that the missing work survived as the plays of Shakespeare.

From her friend Samuel Morse, an expert on encryption who developed Morse code and the telegraph, Delia learned of Francis Bacon's interest in ciphers. As a statesman, Bacon moved in a world of court intrigue and state secrets in which coded messages were a routine part of diplomatic communication. "Let us proceed then to ciphers," Bacon wrote in *De Augmentis Scientiarum*. "Of these there are many kinds: simple ciphers; ciphers mixed with nonsignificant characters; ciphers containing two different letters in one character; wheel ciphers; key ciphers; word ciphers; and the like." He detailed how to create a good cipher, noting that "the virtues required in them are three: that they be easy and not laborious to write; that they be safe . . . and lastly that they be if possible such as not to raise suspicion." Bacon developed his own biliteral cipher, a substitution cipher in which each letter is replaced by a sequence of five characters. Delia believed that the cipher would hold the key to proving the true authorship of the plays.

In Boston, she befriended Emerson, who was himself baffled by the authorship. Shakespeare "was a jovial actor and manager," he noted in an essay in 1850. "I cannot marry this fact to the verse. Other admirable men have led lives in some sort of keeping with their thought; but this man, in wide contrast." Though Emerson wasn't ready to reattribute the plays to Francis Bacon, he was intrigued by Delia's theory. "Her discovery, if it really be one, is of the first import not only in English, but in all literature." He was also impressed by her insights into the plays: "I have seen nothing in America in the way of literary criticism, which I thought so good." Conclusive evidence about the authorship, Delia argued, would lie in the land of the author's birth. Armed with letters of introduction from Emerson, she sailed for England in May 1853.

England, however, did not welcome her heresy. Thomas Carlyle, the critic who declared it "impiety" to meddle with Shakespeare, was appalled. "Mr. Carlyle came down on me with such a volley," she wrote to her sister. "I did not mind in the least. I told him that he did not know what was in the plays if he said that, and no one *could* who believed that that booby wrote them. It was then that he began to shriek. You could have heard him a mile." Carlyle encouraged her to consult archives for evidence of her theory. Instead, she hung around Francis Bacon's home, St. Albans, hoping to find the manuscripts hidden in his tomb. (Her failure to do proper research is a legitimate criticism, though it's worth remembering that she didn't have the privilege of a university education and probably didn't know how to navigate archives.) London's publishers similarly received her theory with "terror." But Emerson supported her. "All that makes it formidable there should make it popular here," he wrote to the publisher George Putnam. Delia Bacon was staking a claim for the value of American literary criticism—rescuing the plays from "misled" British critics and returning them to American readers as radical texts, precursors of democracy. *Putnam's* magazine agreed to serialize her work. In 1856 the first installment appeared under the modest title "William Shakespeare and His Plays; An Enquiry Concerning Them."

Delia skewered bardolatry. "How can we undertake to account for the literary miracles of antiquity, while this great myth of the modern ages still lies at our own door, unquestioned?" she asked. "This vast, magical, unexplained phenomenon which our own times have produced under our own eyes, appears to be, indeed, the only thing which our modern rationalism is not to be permitted to meddle with." She blamed the critics who "still veil their faces, filling the air with mystic utterances which seem to say, that, to this shrine at least, for the footstep of the common reason and the common sense, there is yet no admittance." Ridiculing the belief in a superhuman genius governed by "its own laws and intuitions . . . not subject to our natural conditions," she deconstructed the workings of the myth: how the emphasis on Shakespeare's humble origins threw into relief his wondrous genius; how the murkiness of the biography suited scholars' purposes, allowing Shakespeare to become "any shape or attitude which the criticism in hand may call for." And although Delia didn't name the real author(s) in her first installment, she suggested it must be someone who knew the world of the court. She identified the author with the courtly Hamlet and the Stratford actor with the actors Hamlet directs—"that dirty, doggish group of players who come into the scene summoned like a pack of hounds to his service, the very tone of his courtesy to them, with its princely condescension, with its arduous familiarity, only serving to make the great, impassable social gulf between them more evident."

Putnam's published the essay anonymously, referring to its author only as a "learned and eloquent scholar." Veiled, Delia was also unleashed, adopting an authoritative voice that departed from that of her ladylike lectures. "What new race of Calibans are we that we should be called upon to worship this monstrous incongruity?" she exclaimed. "Oh, stupidity past finding out!" In her crusade to explode the great myth, Delia was unduly abusive to the poor Stratford man, whom she denigrated as the "Stratford poacher," a "poor peasant," and a "stupid, ignorant, illiterate, third-rate play-actor," taking out her frustration with the "stupidity" of Shakespeare scholars on the object of their veneration, smashing their idol. In doing so, she gave them the perfect ammunition to lob at anti-Stratfordians—the charge of classism—which they still lob today. But as the scholar Gary Taylor notes, the anti-Stratfordian movement wasn't an elitist phenomenon so much as "the revolt of the layman" against academic authority.

Delia's article was only part one of a series, but part two never appeared. *Putnam's* editors asked an American Shakespeare scholar named Richard Grant White to write an introduction to it, and White immediately disapproved. Shakespeare wrote the plays, he insisted, "solely that he might obtain the means of going back to Stratford to live the life of an independent gentleman." They had no higher artistic or political purpose; they were merely moneymakers. (This argument neglected the fact that writing was hardly a good way to make money in Renaissance England.) White succeeded in suppressing Delia's second article and convincing *Putnam's* not to publish anything else by her. "[A]s the writer was plainly neither a fool nor an ignoramus, she must be insane," White wrote later in the *Atlantic*, "not a maniac, but what the boys call 'loony.'" The authorship question was "an infatuation," he insisted, "a literary bee in the bonnets of certain ladies of both sexes, which should make them objects of tender care and sympathy." The implication seems to have been that this "mental epidemic," as he termed it, afflicted women and gay men. That Shakespeare wrote the plays was "certain," White maintained. "We know this as well as we know any fact in history."

White was not a professor. He was a lawyer turned editor and critic. By the mid-nineteenth century, however, the cadre of editors and critics was professionalizing—beginning to sort out who belonged in the emerging priesthood and who did not. As the scholar Nancy Glazener writes, "The professionalization of Shakespearian editing and criticism depended on defining acts of exclusion, and White's exclusion of Delia (which he recounts in explicitly misogynist terms) was one such act." White was a nonacademic, technically as amateur as Delia Bacon, but he shored up his role as an arbiter of legitimate Shakespeare studies by disqualifying her. The move was apparently successful: White went on to edit the first *Riverside Shakespeare* edition of the complete works.

Derided and impoverished, Delia secluded herself in Stratford, suspecting that the manuscripts had perhaps been buried in Shakespeare's grave, protected by the curse. Meanwhile, others were developing their own theories about Francis Bacon. In 1856, shortly after Delia published her article, an Englishman named William Henry Smith published a pamphlet titled, *Was Lord Bacon the Author of Shakespeare's Plays?* Pointing to philosophical similarities between the works of Bacon and Shakespeare, Smith reasoned that as a man of political ambition, Bacon would have had to conceal his authorship of plays. A "degree of disgrace" was attached to the theater, he noted. "Even to have sported with the Muse, as a private relaxation, was supposed to be a venial fault indeed, yet something beneath the gravity of a wise man." But while Smith insisted that "the history of Bacon is just such as we should have drawn of Shakespeare, if we had been required to depict him from the internal evidence of his works," he also emphasized that his theory was intended "merely to initiate inquiry."

The next year, Smith published a book, *Bacon and Shakespeare: An Inquiry Touching Players, Playhouses, and Play-writers in the Days of*

Elizabeth, elaborating his theory. So did Delia Bacon. Emerson, Nathaniel Hawthorne, and other intellectuals still believed that her work deserved to be part of the public discussion. In 1857 Hawthorne himself financed the publication of her 675-page tome, *The Philosophy of the Plays of Shakspere Unfolded*, this time with her name attached. The publication brought "the whole literary pack down on her," Walt Whitman wrote, "the orthodox, cruel, stately, dainty, over-fed literary pack—worshipping tradition, unconscious of this day's honest sunlight!"

Nevertheless, the Baconian theory went global. From Italy to India and Serbia to South Africa, writers debated the authorship question. It even reached a young riverboat pilot on the Mississippi: Samuel Clemens, who would soon adopt the pseudonym Mark Twain. While navigating the river's channels and reefs, Twain argued with his captain, "an idolater of Shakespeare." The captain read Shakespeare aloud as Twain steered, interjecting his readings of the plays with piloting commands. ("What in hell are you up to *now*! Pull her down! More! *More!*") The captain detested Delia Bacon's book. "And he said it; said it all the time, for months—in the morning watch, the middle watch, the dog watch; and probably kept it going in his sleep," Twain wrote. "He bought the literature of the dispute as fast as it appeared, and we discussed it all through thirteen hundred miles of river." The captain did his arguing "with heat, with energy, with violence, and I did mine with the reserve and moderation of a subordinate who does not like to be flung out of a pilot house that is perched forty feet above water." When Twain made a point that the captain couldn't rebut, the captain would grow silent. "I knew what was happening: he was losing his temper," Twain recalled. "And I knew he would presently close the session with the same old argument that was always his stay and his support in time of need . . . the argument that I was an ass, and better shut up. He delivered it, and I obeyed."

In Stratford, Delia was still intent on proving her detractors wrong. A local doctor reported that he found her in a "very excited and unsatisfactory state." According to an account by her nephew, she was taken briefly to a nearby asylum, then transported home to America, where she died two years later in another asylum. Scholars have gleefully seized on this to brand her a madwoman, suggesting that her madness was already implicit in her repudiation of Shakespeare—and that anyone else who denies Shakespeare must be similarly mad. This "eccentric American spinster," wrote Samuel Schoenbaum, "*was* mad." Jonathan Bate called her the "mother" of all anti-Stratfordians and smugly quoted the account of her institutionalization. James Shapiro insisted that she was "responsible for triggering what would come to be known as the Shakespeare authorship controversy." Doubts about the authorship were circulating before she published her article, but it is convenient to hang doubts about Shakespeare on a woman who ended up in an asylum. By situating the emergence of doubts in the nineteenth century, far removed from Shakespeare's lifetime, and pinning them on a "madwoman," scholars can comfortably dismiss them as groundless.

The story of Delia Bacon has become a kind of cautionary tale: go digging into the authorship of Shakespeare and you will go mad—or, at least, the world will make you feel you've gone mad. Was Delia Bacon really mad? Scholars are quick to accept this narrative. But in the nineteenth century, the list of reasons women could be institutionalized included "novel-reading," "masturbation," "politics," and "egotism," as well as "domestic trouble" and "vicious vices." Suffragists were diagnosed with "insurgent hysteria" and locked up to keep them from agitating for voting rights. Any troublesome woman who violated social, sexual, or intellectual norms risked being declared "mad." In any case, many writers and thinkers have done important work despite mental illness. As Shapiro himself concedes, "Delia Bacon's claim that the plays were politically radical was a century and a half ahead of its time. So too was her insistence that some of the plays should be read as collaborative." She anticipated twenty-first-century literary criticism—a remarkable feat for a self-educated nineteenth-century woman. "But she couldn't stop at that point," Shapiro writes, suggesting that she went after the authorship because she "clearly craved . . . fame." In his telling, Delia was erroneously caught up in the intellectual currents of her time—the doubts about biblical and Homeric authorship. The questioning of Shakespeare was a kind of historical accident. Shakespeare "suffered collateral damage from a controversy that had little to do with him."

But did the biblical and Homeric doubts poison people's minds against Shakespeare? Or did they *open* minds to the problems of tradition and anecdote, to the construction and perpetuation of cultural narratives that had not been critically examined? Astute readers saw that the Shakespeare biographies had roughly as much fact in them as the Gospel narratives. Were they so wrong to doubt? After all, the biblical and Homeric doubts turned out to be legitimate.

"We all know how much *mythus* there is in the Shakspere question as it stands to-day," Walt Whitman reflected. Whitman was not at all sure about Francis Bacon, but he returned to the question over the years, convinced that there was another mind behind the myth. " 'Gentle' is the epithet often applied to him," he jotted in his notebook, remembering Ben Jonson's reference in the First Folio to "gentle Shakespeare." ("This Figure that thou here seest put, / It was for gentle Shakespeare cut.") "At that time was not its signification 'like a gentleman,' of high-blood bearing?" Indeed, the primary meaning of *gentle* in the Renaissance was "well-born, belonging to a family of position; originally used synonymously with noble." Whitman suspected an aristocrat, someone like the "wolfish earls" of Shakespeare's history plays, who could portray that ruthless world. "Conceiv'd out of the fullest heat and pulse of European feudalism, personifying in unparallel'd ways the medieval aristocracy, its towering spirit of ruthless and gigantic caste, its own peculiar air and arrogance . . . only one of the 'wolfish earls' so plenteous in the plays themselves, or some born descendant and knower, might seem to be the true author of those amazing works."

⁂

The authorship question had become the literary controversy of the day, generating some 260 books, pamphlets, and articles by the end of the nineteenth century. Francis Bacon was the only challenger to Shakespeare, and Baconians, as they came to be called, presented various proofs of Bacon's authorship. In 1867 a mysterious, fire-damaged manuscript from the

1590s was discovered in Northumberland House, one of London's old mansions, that seemed to tie Bacon and Shakespeare together. The top right-hand corner reads, "Mr ffrauncis Bacon"; below, a mass of chaotic scribblings, including titles of Bacon's essays and speeches, titles of two Shakespeare plays (*Richard II* and *Richard III*), and multiple scrawls of the name "William Shakespeare," along with other random words and names. No one really knows what the Northumberland manuscript means, but Baconians claimed it as evidence for Bacon.

Shakespeare and Bacon, though both exceptional geniuses of the age, never acknowledged or mentioned the other. The reason for this, Baconians suggested, was that they were the same man. Numerous phrases and expressions in Shakespeare's plays also appear in Bacon's writings. (In *Henry VI*, " 'Tis wisdom to conceal our meaning"; in Bacon's notes, "The prudent man conceals his knowledge." In *Timon of Athens*, "Make use of thy salt hours"; in Bacon's notes, "Make use of thy salt hours." In *Macbeth*, "What's done cannot be undone"; in Bacon's notes, "Things done cannot be undone.") Stratfordians argued that these verbal parallels were commonplace phrases. Why, Baconians retorted, would Bacon have bothered to write down commonplace phrases? Stratford-upon-Avon is never mentioned in the entire works of Shakespeare, they emphasized, whereas Bacon's hometown of Saint Albans is named on fifteen occasions. One Baconian pointed out, to the consternation of other Baconians, that Bacon was probably gay, which fit the author of Shakespeare's sonnets. His mother complained about his disreputable companions who were exposing him to scandal (including a Spanish adventurer, Antonio Perez; "that bloody Perez," Lady Bacon wrote, "yea a couch companion, and bed companion, a proud, profane, costly fellow"), and a fellow member of Parliament wrote about Bacon's love for his Welsh servingmen, in particular a "very effeminate-faced youth" referred to as his "bedfellow."

The Baconian theory produced vastly different kinds of arguments. On one end of the spectrum were the writings of lawyers, law professors, and judges such as Lord Penzance, a high-ranking judge who noted Shakespeare's "perfect familiarity with not only the principles, axioms, and maxims, but the technicalities of English law, a knowledge so perfect and intimate that he was never incorrect and never at fault." In his book *The Bacon-Shakespeare Controversy* (1890), Penzance rejected Shakespeare's authorship, believing that the playwright must have had legal training and expertise. "At every turn and point at which the author required a metaphor, simile, or illustration, his mind ever turned first to the law," Penzance observed. "He seems almost to have thought in legal phrases." Scholars cast around for an explanation, suggesting that Shakespeare had perhaps gained legal training as a clerk. Penzance dismissed this silliness, noting that not a single record at the local courts at Stratford or the superior courts at Westminster bore Shakespeare's name. "No young man could have been at work in an attorney's office without being called upon continually to act as a witness [to wills, for example] and in many other ways leaving traces of his work and name," he wrote. Even Richard Grant White conceded that the idea of Shakespeare being a clerk had been "blown to pieces." Besides, the plays showed *advanced* legal knowledge—"not only of the conveyancer's office, but of the pleader's chambers and the courts at Westminster," Penzance emphasized. A legal expert like Bacon, he argued, was the more likely author. Even the Shakespeare scholar Horace Howard Furness conceded the fit: "Had the plays come down to us anonymously—had the labour of discovering the author been imposed upon future generations—we could have found no one of that day but Francis Bacon to whom to assign the crown," he wrote. "In this case, it would have been resting now upon his head by almost common consent."

On the other end of the Baconian spectrum were the cipher hunters, obsessed with using Bacon's biliteral cipher to find hidden messages in Shakespeare's plays. In *The Great Cryptogram: Francis Bacon's Cipher in the So-called Shakespeare Plays* (1888), a US congressman from Minnesota named Ignatius Donnelly applied convoluted code-breaking equations to produce messages revealing Bacon's authorship. (For instance: "Shak'st spur never writ a word of them.") Donnelly's methods were lampooned, and Baconians sought to distance themselves from him, but other code breakers, convinced that Donnelly had merely misapplied the cipher, continued undeterred.

Orville Ward Owen, a wealthy Detroit physician, built a "cipher wheel" that revealed Bacon's secret history: namely that he was the son of the not-so-virginal Elizabeth I. His assistant, a high school teacher named Elizabeth Wells Gallup, developed her own method, studying alternating fonts in the First Folio to decipher the same message: Francis Bacon was the true heir to the throne. The desire to see Bacon claim his rightful place as author of the Shakespeare plays had become a desire to place him, retrospectively, on the throne itself. Having uncovered a message explaining that the manuscripts were hidden behind panels in Canonbury Tower in Islington, North London, Mrs. Gallup sailed for England. Dr. Owen, for his part, was certain that they were buried in waterproof lead boxes at the bottom of the river Wye. He hired men to excavate part of the riverbed. Newspapers covered the search. In 1909 the journal *Baconiana* declared, "The Goal in Sight."

But the cipher hunters never found the Shakespeare manuscripts. On his deathbed, Owen warned another enthusiast to avoid the authorship question: "You will only reap disappointment. When I discovered the Word Cipher, I had the largest practice of any physician in Detroit. I could have been the greatest surgeon there . . . but I thought the world would be eager to hear what I have found. Instead, what did they give me? I have had my name dragged in the mud . . . lost my fortune, ruined my health, and today am a bedridden, almost penniless invalid." Two professional cryptologists working for the US government, William and Elizebeth Friedman, would later examine the Baconian ciphers, exposing the flaws in the cipher hunters' methods. Ignatius Donnelly's number juggling could produce almost any message the decoder wanted. The alternating fonts, which formed the basis of Elizabeth Wells Gallup's method, were, in fact, random; she was likely influenced by autosuggestion. It was still possible that there *were* ciphers in the Shakespeare works, the Friedmans concluded, but not these ciphers.

The cipher-hunting craze was related to other cultural fads of the late nineteenth century: the rise of detective fiction, with its emphasis on hidden clues, and the interest in Spiritualism, which sought to channel the voices of the dead as Baconians sought to "channel" Bacon in the works of Shakespeare. But the cipher hunters badly damaged Baconians as a whole. Sir Sidney Lee assailed the Baconian theory in the *Times* in 1901 as an "epidemic disease," declaring that Baconians were "unworthy of serious attention except from any but professed students of intellectual aberration."

This attack prompted Sir George Greenwood, a British lawyer and member of Parliament, to tease Sir Sidney Lee in his book, *The Shakespeare Problem Restated.* "Why so warm, Sir Fretful?" he asked. "Upon a purely literary question such a nice 'derangement of epitaphs' seems quite uncalled for," especially, he noted, bearing in mind some of the Harvard law professors, distinguished fellows of Trinity College, and barons of the Exchequer included in Lee's "indiscriminate vilification." Greenwood was known in British politics mostly as an ardent supporter of animal welfare reform and the independence of India, but, in the early twentieth century, he also became one of the most prominent advocates of the authorship question. As Greenwood pointed out, "There are the wild Baconians who find Bacon everywhere, but especially in ciphers, cryptograms, anagrams, acrostics, and in all sorts of occult figures and emblems." Then there are the "sane Baconians, who are content to argue the matter—and some have argued it with great knowledge and ability—in the calm light of reason and common sense." The wild Baconians had not only injured the Baconian cause but also "greatly prejudiced the discussion of the Shakespeare Problem as a whole," he wrote. "For in such cases, we are all liable to be 'tarred by the same brush,' and the sanest of 'Anti-Stratfordian' reasoners has, unfortunately, not escaped the backwash of the ridicule which these eccentrics have brought upon themselves."

Greenwood did not think the Baconians had managed to prove Bacon's authorship. He did not think the Stratfordians had proved Shakespeare's authorship, either. Their strident tone exposed a lack of faith in their own position, he argued. The scholars' attitude was "that petulant spirit which cannot examine an argument with calmness, or discuss it with moderation of language." Greenwood begged readers of "candid and open mind" to set aside their prejudices and examine the evidence. In a series of public debates carried on in books, newspapers, and literary journals, he cleverly catalogued the problems with Shakespeare and the follies of the scholars.

"And we, who see the absurdity of all this, are called 'Fanatics!'" he wrote. "But what is 'Fanaticism'? It is the madness which possesses the worshippers at the shrine. These men have bowed themselves down at the traditional Stratfordian Shrine; they have accepted without thinking the dogmas of the Stratfordian faith; they are impervious to reasoning and to common sense; they have surrendered their judgment. . . . Verily, *these* are the real 'fanatics.'"

Greenwood never threw his support behind any alternate candidate, confining himself to a rebuttal of the Stratfordian case. But his agnostic treatment of the subject was widely admired and praised. Henry James recommended *The Shakespeare Problem Restated* to a friend as "an extremely erudite, fair, and discriminating piece of work" and the best expression of his own view on the problem. Mark Twain was taken by it, too, and so was Helen Keller. "Mr. Greenwood's masterly exposition has led to the conclusion that Shakespeare of Stratford is not to be even thought of as a possible author of the most wonderful plays in the world," she wrote in a review. "How long must we wait for the solution of the greatest problem in literature?"

⁂

It is tempting to imagine what might have happened if the emerging Shakespeare professoriate had been willing to distinguish between the wild Baconians and the sane Baconians, or even between the Baconians and the agnostics—if it had brought the saner elements within the new academy, permitting a rational discussion of the authorship question. Banished, the question raged outside the walls. There was no room for doubt in the new church of English literature. English demanded unwavering faith in its clergy and absolute adherence to the Stratfordian creed. You were in, or you were out.

But though English had claimed its place in secondary schools, mechanics' institutes, women's colleges, and civil service examinations, it still had not taken root in the ancient universities. Oxford and Cambridge resisted establishing full departments of English. As a 1887 article in *Oxford* magazine argued, English was a subject fit for women, workers, and Indians. Gentlemen read literature in their leisure time. Why make an academic discipline of it? In 1912, when Sir Arthur Quiller-Couch took up the newly established chair in English literature at Cambridge, he began his lectures with "Gentlemen . . ."—though his audience was made up almost entirely of women.

English literature eventually came to claim its place at the highest seats of learning, its victory ensured by world war. Classics suddenly looked too foreign—unpatriotic. Philology, the study of dead languages, was even more distasteful, as it had emerged from German universities. And what was worse, the Germans had become slightly obsessed with Shakespeare, treating him as one of their own. "They have studied him for a hundred years, and they do not understand the plainest words of all his teaching," argued Sir Walter Raleigh, who held the first chair of English at Oxford. At Cambridge, Sir Arthur Quiller-Couch delivered a series of lectures entitled "Patriotism in English Literature," which was mostly devoted not to praising English literature but to denigrating German attempts to study it. "If only by the structure of his vocal organs, a German is congenitally unable to read our poetry," intoned Quiller-Couch. Shakespeare's "capture by the enemy," as another professor put it, had to be resisted. English literature, understood properly, was part of the national arsenal.

Philology was smeared accordingly as a kind of treason, English literature was brandished with pride, and Shakespeare was reclaimed for the nation. By the end of the war, English literature's survival was ensured. A school of English (not just a chair) was established at Cambridge; at Oxford, there could be no more jeering about English being for women or workers. From being an amateurish, unserious pursuit, it became *the* singular subject Britain needed to heal from the trauma of war. "Do we lay it aside as a pleasant pastime suitable for less hustling days but remote from our present practical needs and purposes," asked the scholar Ernest de Sélincourt in his lectures on English poetry, "or do we turn to it with a keener spiritual hunger, feeling that it can give us not merely a pastime but in the true sense *recreation*?"

Within a year of the armistice, the British government established committees to investigate the state of teaching in four fields: science, classics, modern languages, and English. The English committee, composed of English professors, published its report in 1921 as *The Teaching of English in England.* It proposed rebuilding the entire "arch" of national education around the "keystone" of English. While knowledge of classics tended to serve as a distinction between the classes, an education in English "would form a new element of national unity, linking together the mental life of all classes," the report stated. Since the Russian Revolution of 1917, the threat of widespread working-class uprisings had begun to look far more serious. In 1920, while the English committee was conducting its investigations, the Communist Party of Britain formed. It appeared that the working classes, especially those belonging to the organized labor movement, were "antagonistic to, and contemptuous of, literature," observed J. Dover Wilson, a Shakespeare professor and member of the committee. "They regarded it 'merely as an ornament, a polite accomplishment, a subject to be despised by really virile men,'" classing it with "antimacassars, fish knives, and other unintelligible and futile trivialities of 'middle-class culture'" and suspecting it of being "an attempt to 'sidetrack the working-class movement.'" Wilson expressed his and the committee's alarm at this "morbid condition of the body politic, which, if not taken in hand, may be followed by lamentable consequences." The shadow of Matthew Arnold's domestic anarchy had been replaced, he wrote elsewhere, by a huger shadow: "that of a world anarchy, which threatens to bring the whole structure of civilisation toppling to the ground."

The working classes needed to be made to feel that they, too, were the inheritors of England's literary heritage, Wilson observed, since "what is wrong with our industry is not so much low wages or long hours as its lack of social meaning in the eyes of those performing its operations." Give the working classes a common share in Shakespeare, and they might refrain from following the Bolshevik example. "A humane education is a possession in which rich and poor can be equal without any disturbance to their material possessions," wrote another committee member. "In a sense, it means the abolition of poverty, for can a man be poor who possesses so much?"

The committee recommended English professors, naturally, as the leaders of this campaign, using the threat posed by Communism to make hyperbolic claims for the value of their profession. "The Professor of Literature in a University should be—and sometimes is, as we gladly recognize—a missionary in a more real and active sense than any of his colleagues," the professors wrote. "He has obligations not merely to the students who come to him to read for a degree, but still more towards the teeming population outside the University walls." The fulfillment of the professor's obligations would require "propaganda work"—not just organization and a staff of "assistant missionaries," but also a conviction that literature is "one of the chief temples of the human spirit in which all should worship." The Victorian vision of literature as a new religion was rearticulated for the twentieth century, mingling the language of faith with the zeal of imperialism. In a book titled *English for the English*, committee member George Sampson expanded on this vision, raising the evangelical language to a near-apocalyptic tone:

> *What the teacher has to consider is not the minds he can measure but the souls he can save. . . .*
>
> *At this stage of our national education, what matters is the faith, not the works. . . .*
>
> *[The reading of English literature] is not a routine but a religion. . . . It is almost sacramental. . . .*
>
> *The teacher's hardest struggle is not against pure ignorance but against evil knowledge.*

In his 1922 inaugural lecture at Oxford, Professor George Gordon summed up the spirit of English literature's new mission: "England is sick, and . . . English literature must save it. The churches (as I understand) having failed, and social remedies being slow, English literature has now a triple function: still, I suppose to delight and instruct us, but also, and above all, to save our souls and heal the state." English, Gordon went on, had become "everywhere a sacrament, a holy remedy, and apparently almost the only sacrament left now." It was needed not only to mend the shattered nation and prevent the rise of Communism, but also to avert a second global conflict. An increased focus on the humanities—on Shakespeare—could foster empathy, understanding, and peace.

This is how the institution of English began: as moral guidance for the restless masses; as imperialist propaganda; as nationalist liturgy. In America, too, Shakespeare was held up as evidence that Anglo-Saxon culture was uniquely blessed. When Joseph Quincy Adams delivered his inaugural lecture at the opening of the Folger Shakespeare Library in 1932, he argued that Shakespeare was key to forging a homogenous American nation when "the forces of immigration became a menace to the preservation of our long-established English civilization." Shakespeare became inseparable from mythologies of nation, empire, and culture. And the story of Shakespeare, enshrined in the early days of the discipline, has been repeated and repeated into our own time, passed down as a sacred, unalterable creed.

Belief consists in repetition, observed the twentieth-century French theorist Michel de Certeau. Not merely in saying that something is true but in "narrated reality"—in iteration and reiteration, the constant repeating of the belief. It consists particularly in the narration of experts who "enable us to accept as credible that which *we are told* is true." Certeau called ours a "recited society," for what we believe is founded in citing the authority of others. We believe things because other people do. But citation serves another function, too: to cite is "also to designate the 'anarchists' or 'deviants' (to cite them before the tribunal of public opinion); it is to condemn to the aggressivity of the public those who assert through their acts that they do not believe."

⁂

The Shakespeare expert Stanley Wells was born in 1930, when Britain was recovering from world war, staving off Socialism, and still proclaiming the glories of its empire. He grew up in Kingston-upon-Hull, in northeast

England, the son of a bus traffic manager. Wells's education at the local grammar school would have been shaped by the 1921 report that sought "national unity" through education in English. By the time he enrolled at University College London to take a degree in English literature, England and its allies had vanquished Germany a second time. After university, he worked for several years as a schoolteacher. Then he came to Stratford-upon-Avon to earn his PhD at the Shakespeare Institute.

Wells's career, his life's work, was given over to Shakespeare. For fifteen years, he was a fellow of the institute, teaching courses, supervising PhD students, and publishing academic books and articles. He climbed the ranks of Shakespeare scholars, becoming associate editor of the *New Penguin Shakespeare*, then general editor. In 1977 he left Stratford for Oxford, taking up a position as director of the Shakespeare Department of Oxford University Press, where he was responsible for supervising a new Oxford edition of *The Complete Works*. When he returned to Stratford ten years later, he was appointed professor of Shakespeare studies and director of the Shakespeare Institute. He became chairman of the Shakespeare Birthplace Trust, too, presiding over Stratford's tourist industry for twenty years. He has written and edited countless Shakespeare volumes, and reviewed books for newspapers and magazines, shaping not just the academic discussion of Shakespeare but also the popular one.

In his sitting room, not drinking tea, I told him I wanted to talk about the Renaissance allusions to Shakespeare. If some of these allusions, which Wells described as "cryptic," contained doubts about the authorship, then it would be much harder for scholars to dismiss the question as a nineteenth-century conspiracy theory. "What do you think it was about Shakespeare that people needed to be cryptic about?" I asked.

"Well, they're only cryptic because they were writing for people of the time who would be able to fill in the context of them, I suppose."

"So people of the time would have understood something from them that we don't?"

"Some people would, perhaps, but not necessarily all of them," he replied.

I mentioned the pseudonymous 1594 pamphlet *Willobie His Avisa*, the first use of "Shake-speare" by a third party and the first appearance of the name with a hyphen: "And Shake-speare paints poor Lucrece rape." Wells had called it "deliberately cryptic."

"I've never studied *Willobie His Avisa*," he said. "I just haven't bothered, frankly. A student of mine was once saying he was astonished I hadn't gone into it. I've looked at it, but I haven't anything to say about that."

I was dumbfounded. The first explicit reference to Shakespeare, and he—Sir Stanley Wells, Britain's knighted Shakespeare authority—had not *bothered*, did not have anything to *say.* I tried another allusion: Thomas Vicars's 1628 reference to "that poet who takes his name from shaking and spear." Wells had omitted it from his chapter on allusions to Shakespeare, I pointed out, though his chapter covered allusions up to 1642.

"I don't remember that," he said.

"You don't remember that?"

"No. Where is this?"

"Thomas Vicars, 1628," I repeated, perplexed. Did he really not know it? "Do you take that to be referring to Shakespeare?"

"Well, it sounds like it, doesn't it?"

"What would that mean to you?" I asked.

"Well, it's just a sort of joke, isn't it?"

I tried to explain the context to him: that Vicars lists the other great English poets by name—Geoffrey Chaucer, Edmund Spenser—but refers to Shakespeare in this strange, winking way.

"I don't remember," he said again. "Well, I don't know. I don't know." He was growing slightly cross. "No comment," he added, adopting PR-speak as though he were a politician being questioned about an unpleasant news report.

I had been prepared to hear all sorts of arguments from Wells about the evidence for Shakespeare, but I had not anticipated this: a Shakespeare professor who'd written several books on the authorship question professing total ignorance about basic pieces of Shakespearean history. Did I need to preface each question with a short tutorial on the allusion—when it appeared, who wrote it, what it said? I dropped the Vicars and tried another allusion, *Oenone and Paris*, the imitation of *Venus and Adonis* published by "T.H." in 1594—the one with the funny dedication about the poet "lurking obscurely" and concealing his authorship. Since it's a recognized imitation of *Venus and Adonis*, does that possibly suggest that T.H. thinks "Shakespeare" was also lurking obscurely and concealing his authorship, I asked? What did he make of it?

"I don't remember it, actually."

I tried Joseph Hall's reference to a poet hiding like a cuttlefish in a cloud of ink, shifting his fame onto another's name.

"Do you know about that one?"

"No, I've forgotten it."

I felt as though I was cross-examining a witness who kept claiming amnesia. Could he really not know? It occurred to me that it was possible he didn't know these allusions because he didn't take criticism of his position seriously enough to have thoroughly studied the evidence. As if sensing his weakness, Wells started throwing out bits of counter-evidence.

"What about Barnfield's praise of Shakespeare?" he asked, referring to a 1598 poem in which the poet Richard Barnfield commended Shakespeare's "hony-flowing Vaine." But it was praise of the works, not evidence of the author's identity. "What about Ben Jonson?" he added. " 'Sweet Swan of Avon!' I mean, isn't that enough?"

I pointed out the phrase was rather ambiguous, that there are numerous Avon rivers in Britain.

"Oh, if you say that, you're just playing with meaning," he scoffed.

"But that's what poets do, don't they?" I said.

"Are you a poet?"

"No, but Ben Jonson was."

"Well, that's just . . ." He trailed off, shaking his head.

"There are a number of interesting references to Hampton Court as 'Avon,' " I added, listing them.

He cut me off—"I know, I know"—as though he didn't want to hear them. Then he added, "I think that's one of the things Alexander Waugh suggested."

So he *did* follow anti-Stratfordian research.

"And, of course, Shakespeare's plays *were* performed at Hampton Court," I pressed him.

"Yes," the professor conceded. "But I think it's perfectly clear what Ben Jonson meant: that he came from the Avon that ran through Stratford."

"So you don't think it might refer to Hampton Court?"

"No, I don't," he said. "Well . . ." He paused, considering it. "I don't see why it should. Anyhow, what if it does?" he added, seeming suddenly to accept that it might. But the concession was short-lived. When I probed further into the meaning of Jonson's words in the First Folio, Wells quickly reverted to not knowing. Why did Jonson open with the long preamble warning about praising Shakespeare's name—about those of "seeliest ignorance," "blind affection," and "crafty malice"?

"Well, why not have a preamble?"

"Sure, but why do you think he's warning against those things?"

"I don't know. I don't have any particular theory about that."

I switched to the monument in the church, with its strange inscription listing Socrates, Nestor, and Virgil. Wells had called it cryptic. "I think it's a method of saying this man was as great as the figures of antiquity," he said. Was there a reason it listed those figures in particular? I pushed him.

"Not that I know of, no."

Wells had spent a lifetime contemplating these texts, and yet he couldn't come up with an explanation for Jonson's words or the monument inscription—two of the most important texts in the authorship debate. It seemed like an abdication of his authority as a scholar. If Wells and his colleagues couldn't supply answers, why shouldn't anti-Stratfordians like Alexander Waugh step in? And yet Wells considered Waugh "a wicked man."

"I could become vituperative," he told me when I asked him what he thought of Waugh. "He conducted a campaign against the Birthplace Trust, even to the extent of taking out a full-page advertisement in the *TLS* attacking the Trust. . . . I refuse to have dinner in the same room as him."

Wells was referring to an ad Waugh and other doubters had run in the *Times Literary Supplement* in 2014 offering to donate £40,000 to the Shakespeare Birthplace Trust if it could establish Shakespeare's authorship beyond a reasonable doubt in open, public debate. The Trust declined. "Can you believe it?" Waugh cackled to *Newsweek.* "A registered charity turned down the opportunity of £40,000 to defend the very basis on which they are founded!" The advertisement, splashed prominently in London's leading literary newspaper, was not an attack so much as a challenge, but Wells clearly experienced it as a personal affront.

"Don't ask me why," he continued, meaning why Waugh attacked the Trust. (I hadn't asked.) "I don't know why. Because he's an evil man, I suppose."

"You think it's done out of—"

"Malice," he said.

"Malice against who?"

"Well, against the Trust."

"Why would he hate the Trust?"

"I don't know."

I suggested that Waugh and other doubters were simply interested in the authorship—that they weren't trying to hurt anyone.

"I wouldn't be too sure of that." He narrowed his eyes.

"You think they have some reason to hurt you? It's personal?"

"I think it's impossible to determine psychologically complex motives which may have their basis in class issues, sociological issues, even in jealousy," Wells said. "Alexander Waugh seems to resent the fact that the Trust makes money. . . . What I write about Shakespeare and about his life is based on a belief that I'm correctly interpreting historical evidence, or that if I can't interpret, I'm admitting ignorance, as I quite often do, and that I'm not doing it out of mercenary motives, trying to make money or to make a reputation in an intellectually dishonest way, and that's what Alexander Waugh is accusing us of."

"He thinks it's misrepresenting history," I said.

"Well, I think any idea that the Earl of Oxford wrote the plays is just—I could be obscene." He paused. "It's a load of shit."

His opinion of other prominent Shakespeare skeptics, including the actors Derek Jacobi and Mark Rylance, was similarly low. "They're both bonkers," he said. Between the two of them, Jacobi and Rylance have played nearly every male character in the Shakespeare canon and some of the female ones, too. Jacobi's Lear was "the finest and most searching Lear I have ever seen," one critic wrote, and Rylance's Hamlet "among the near-complete Hamlets," another insisted. "Mark Rylance speaks Shakespeare as if it was written for him the night before," Al Pacino remarked. That famous, award-winning actors who spent their careers immersed in Shakespeare's plays doubted the authorship seemed a sore point for Wells. "I wouldn't go to either of them for scholarly opinions," he said. "It is unfortunate that the authorship question has attracted a lot of eccentric people, from Delia Bacon onwards." He shot me a heavy look. "So beware!"

"So beware of what?"

"Of being eccentric!"

I recalled his statement that anyone who questioned the authorship suffered from a "psychological aberration." "Is that still your view?" I asked.

There was a long pause. "Well, sort of, yes." He paused again, turning over his words. "I see no reason to doubt the authorship, so I suppose I feel that anyone who does so is going against reason." He smiled. "Perhaps I'm too commonsensical."

There were moments in our conversation, however, when Wells seemed to agree with the anti-Stratfordians without realizing it. When we were discussing the sonnets, he pointed to Sonnet 136, where the poet writes, "My name is *Will*." I reminded him of the context, in which the speaker puns playfully on "will": "Will, will fulfill the treasure of thy love, / Ay, fill it full with wills, and my will one. . . . Among a number one is reckoned none: / Then in the number let me pass untold." What did he think it meant?

"I would have thought he's simply saying, 'Let me remain anonymous.' Something as simple as that."

"Well, exactly," I said, startled.

"Shakespeare somehow managed to lead this sort of double life," he remarked later, musing on Shakespeare's life divided between Stratford and London. "That is not true of the other dramatists of the time, all of whom I think it's fair to say are based in London." Did Wells hear how very *anti-Stratfordian* that sounded? Shakespeare's life was, indeed, so "double" that records sometimes showed him back in Stratford during London's busy performance season. I wondered if it was a kind of Freudian slip—an unconscious recognition of Shakespeare's doubleness even while, consciously, he refused to brook any doubts.

I tried to pin him down on the use of pseudonyms and allonyms. Were they common in the period?

"To some degree, yes," he agreed.

Was there a stigma against aristocrats publishing plays?

"I don't know," he said. I quoted the 1589 text about gentlemen who suffered their works to be published "without their own names to it." With the evidence before him, he acknowledged, "Yeah, no, there probably was." But he grew irritated with my questions.

"I think you're making difficulties," he said at one point.

"I'm just asking questions," I said. "Is it bad to ask questions?"

"No, no."

"You said once that it's dangerous and immoral to question history."

"Did I?"

I asked if he still thought it was dangerous to ask questions.

"No, of course not. You're absolutely right to ask questions. But"—he paused—"I think one should always ask *why* one is asking the questions." He launched into a slightly boastful story about a time when, as a young scholar, he had publicly corrected a renowned Shakespeare professor named A. L. Rowse. "I did it in the middle of a broadcast," he recalled, "and he was rather taken aback. He was very patronizing, too." Wells impersonated a high-pitched, pompous voice. "He thought himself the bee's knees, looking down on me." Wells did not seem to realize that he had now become the senior scholar looking down on those asking questions.

I tried to bring him back to the problem of questioning history.

"It's difficult to be confident about the past," Wells said. "But I think it is dangerous, yes."

"Why?"

"Of course it's quite proper to question history in the sense that history is a construct," he said. "History can be theories about the past, and theories about the past, even if they seem historical, if they depend on interpretation, then they're not historical. I mean, interpretation of the past is making a meaning, making a sense out of events of the past, which may vary, I suppose. The interpretation one makes may vary, perhaps, according to one's own subconscious desires and wishes—wishes that the past was as you would wish it to be."

"Do you think that might apply to the traditional view of the authorship, that it's also a subjective interpretation?" I asked. "There is a desire to see Shakespeare as a boy who came from humble beginnings and became this great playwright."

"Well, yes, but then you could say some people have a subconscious desire to see him as an aristocrat," he retorted.

"Then there are subconscious desires in everyone."

"Yes, that is true," he conceded. "It's a matter of balance, I suppose."

"I guess I wonder, if there are so many questions about Shakespeare, instead of saying we're absolutely certain, why not acknowledge we're not sure?" I ventured.

"Well, I think one can acknowledge gaps in a structure without denying the structure itself," he replied. "I feel that the trajectory of Shakespeare's life is not fully visible; is not fully charted. But I feel that the essentials of the trajectory, of the structure we have"—he listed the records of the Stratford man's life, the name on the title pages, the allusions to Shakespeare—"amount to a structure which, although there are gaps in it, are strong enough, firm enough, and adequate enough for me to accept it totally as, as, as"—he reached for the right words—"well, as I say, as a structure which, in spite of the gaps, nevertheless is strong enough to sustain the meaning we provide for it."

⁂

I walked back through Stratford in the evening light mulling "the meaning we provide for it." There was, among certain anti-Stratfordians, a cynical line of thought that Shakespeare professors such as Stanley Wells knew perfectly well that Shakespeare was not the author—that they were maintaining the tradition dishonestly. I did not think this was the case with Wells. He believed in *the meaning we provide for it.* He had, in fact, dedicated his life to the meaning. There was something of the medieval crusader about him—or perhaps the aging knight, now at the end of his life. I thought of the portrait in the sitting room of Sir Stanley Wells with the knighthood medal around his neck. He had fought for the faith. He had done so with a conviction that he was interpreting the evidence correctly and that he was admitting what he did not know.

Naturally, then, those who attacked the authorship, who attacked the Birthplace, seemed to him "malicious" and "evil-minded" enemies, for they were attacking not only the faith but also his integrity. His life's purpose. Shakespeare *was* him—he, too, had come from a humble background; had gone to the local grammar school; had left for London as a young man; and had come to Stratford-upon-Avon to study, raising himself up through Shakespeare, becoming a knight of the British Empire through Shakespeare. Having sunk so many decades into his faith, he could not now give it up. Psychologically, it was not possible, even as he stumbled to explain what all those strange references meant. *I don't know. I don't know.* There was no room for doubt in his belief system. The more one tried to introduce it, planting little seeds here and there, the more he would die fighting for the faith.

I had plans to meet "wicked" Alexander Waugh, so I collected my bags and headed to the train station.

✣

The next day, I received an email from Professor Wells. He had been "pleased" to talk with me, he wrote. "Nevertheless, I find it sad that a person of such clear intellectual ability should give credence to theories that so clearly fly in the face of documentary evidence. . . . I hope you will soon find an enterprise more worthy of your obvious talents."

In my reply, I included the texts of two allusions that Wells had said he didn't remember: T.H.'s dedication about "lurking obscurely" and Thomas Vicars's reference to "that poet who takes his name from shaking and spear." I would be interested to know what he made of the texts once he'd had a chance to read them, I wrote. He never responded.

SEVEN

Wolfish Earls

BY THE TIME OF THE Russian Revolution, eighteen-year-old Vladimir Nabokov had read all of Shakespeare in the original English. He would take pleasure in translating Shakespeare passages into Russian and invoke Shakespeare in his novels throughout his life. "The verbal texture of Shakespeare is the greatest the world has known," he wrote. Forced to flee Russia in 1917, the Nabokovs settled briefly in England, where Vladimir attended Trinity College, Cambridge, then relocated to Germany. Somewhere along the way, Nabokov began to doubt Shakespeare's identity. In 1924, when he was twenty-five, he published the poem "Shakespeare." "You easily, regretlessly relinquished / the laurels [. . .] / concealing for all time your monstrous genius / beneath a mask," he wrote. "Reveal yourself, god of iambic thunder, / you hundred-mouthed, unthinkably great bard!"

No! At the destined hour, when you felt banished
by God from your existence, you recalled
those secret manuscripts, fully aware
that your supremacy would rest unblemished
by public rumor's unashamed brand,
that ever, midst the shifting dust of ages,
faceless you'd stay, like immortality
itself—then vanished in the distance, smiling.

It's not clear what exactly precipitated Nabokov's heretical poem. He may have read some Baconian text, but it's also possible that he had stumbled across a newer heresy. By 1924, the field had expanded. Skeptics who doubted Shakespeare but remained unconvinced by Bacon were casting around for other candidates. They looked to aristocrats—those "wolfish earls"—arguing that Shakespeare wrote from an upper-class perspective. Even his language and imagery drew from privileged pastimes—falconry, hawking, horsemanship, bowling, royal tennis. Did he study up on tennis, a popular game among nobles, to toss off good metaphors or was he drawing on personal experience? "Shakespeare seems to have had the instincts of a born courtier," the scholar Northrop Frye noted. He was "interested in chronicle, the personal actions and interactions of the people at the top of the social order." Others pointed out that Shakespeare tended to lampoon lower-class characters, making their ignorance a source of comic relief and giving them undignified names such as Snout, Bottom, Wart, Mouldy, and Dogberry. Ben Jonson, by contrast, lampooned the nobility with names such as Lady Haughty, Sir Paul Either-side, Sir Amorous La Foole, and Sir Epicure Mammon. Was Shakespeare an upper-class snob?

Some skeptics singled out Roger Manners, the 5th Earl of Rutland. In 1907 an anti-Semitic German writer, Karl Bleibtreu, declared him *Der Wahre Shakespeare* (*The Real Shakespeare*). A Belgian Socialist, Célestin Demblon, followed in 1912 with *Lord Rutland Est Shakespeare.* Rutland seemed to fit the profile. He was a courtier of intelligence and sophistication who had studied at Cambridge and traveled through Italy. He was close to the Earl of Southampton, the dedicatee of Shakespeare's early poems. At the University of Padua, he registered alongside two Danish students, Rosencrantz and Guildenstern, whose names would famously appear in *Hamlet.* And in 1603 he traveled to Elsinore Castle, the setting of *Hamlet*, as part of the English delegation to Denmark. The play contains bits of local color: the castle's environs, Danish terms such as *Danskers* [Danes] and *Switzers* [Swiss guards], and the Danish court's custom of making toasts to the accompaniment of artillery fire. ("No jocund health that Denmark drinks to-day, / But the great cannon to the clouds shall tell.") But Rutland was awfully young to be Shakespeare—only sixteen when *Venus and Adonis* was published—and he had no recorded talent for poetry or involvement in theater.

In 1918 a new heresy emerged. Abel Lefranc, the distinguished chair of French literature at the Collège de France, published *Sous le Masque de William Shakespeare*, pointing to William Stanley, the 6th Earl of Derby, as the man beneath the mask. Was this the book that the young Nabokov (trilingual in French, Russian, and English) encountered? Having studied the plays for some thirty years, Lefranc felt insulted by Shakespeare scholars, whose adamant faith made, he thought, a mockery of literary and historical scholarship. In his research, he came across a series of articles by an obscure nineteenth-century archivist who had discovered letters from 1599 reporting that the 6th Earl of Derby was "busied only in penning comedies for the common players." But where were Derby's plays? The letters had been sent from London by a Jesuit spy who was sniffing out whether Derby, a suspected Catholic, might seek the throne after the Queen's death. To his disappointment, the spy found that the earl was devoted entirely to literary pursuits. The letters had been intercepted by Elizabeth's government and ended up in Britain's state papers. As he began researching Derby, Lefranc noted parallels to Shakespeare. What's more, he learned that the nineteenth-century archivist who had discovered the letters noted the same parallels. Before he died, the archivist had written an article advocating research into the possibility that Derby had penned the plays of Shakespeare. But amid the noise of the Shakespeare-Bacon dispute, no one paid it any attention.

Derby was raised at his family's estates in the north of England where his father's troupe of players, Derby's Men, performed frequently. After studying at Oxford, he toured Europe: visiting the French court in Paris; journeying south, possibly to the court of Navarre, which is so faithfully reflected in *Love's Labour's Lost*; continuing to the Spanish court, where he fought a duel and fled disguised as a friar (the same disguise used by the duke in *Measure for Measure*, Lefranc noted); and venturing through Italy, Greece, and, according to some rumors, as far east as Russia. Tales of his adventures were turned into a popular ballad. Exactly where Derby went is not clear, only that he was gone for several years. He was accompanied by his tutor, Richard Lloyd, the author of a tedious poem about the "Nine Worthies" of history. In *Love's Labour's Lost*, a pedantic schoolmaster named Holofernes proposes to entertain the court with a stilted production of the "Nine Worthies." What could be more natural, Lefranc argued, than for the young Derby to caricature his tiresome tutor?

On his return, Derby studied law. Through the late 1580s and early 1590s, his elder brother, Ferdinando Stanley, sponsored a troupe of players that performed some of Shakespeare's early plays. When Ferdinando died suddenly in 1594 of suspected assassination by poisonous mushrooms, the troupe reorganized, becoming the Lord Chamberlain's Men—Shakespeare's company. In *Love's Labour's Lost*, the king of Navarre (based on Henry of Navarre) is called Ferdinand instead. The name reappears in *The Tempest*, where the romantic hero who marries Prospero's daughter is also Ferdinand. Lefranc suspected that Prospero, the magician who has mastered sorcery through deep philosophical reading, was based on John Dee, the Queen's court astrologer, a teacher of Hermetic philosophy renowned throughout Europe for his esoteric knowledge. Dee influenced many poets and courtiers, but he appears to have been particularly close to Derby. In Dee's diary, Lefranc found numerous entries recording their meetings.

The Derby theory produced a small, international following of Derbyites who elaborated it over the years, pointing out the plays' topographical references to places around the north of England, where Derby grew up. Plus, his name was "Will," like the "Will" of the sonnets. The theory is somewhat confounded, however, by Derby's long life span. He lived until 1642, three decades after *The Tempest*—one of Shakespeare's last plays—was performed at court. Derbyites suggest that he retired, renouncing his art as Prospero renounced his magic. Little is known of Derby's later life. He seems to have been close to the dedicatees of the First Folio, the Earls of Pembroke and Montgomery, naming them as trustees of his estates. After his death on the eve of the English Civil War, his family seat at Lathom House was destroyed, along with whatever papers it held.

Though the Earl of Derby has been absorbed into various group theories, the Derbyite theory was soon eclipsed by another. In 1920, while Nabokov was studying at Cambridge, an English schoolteacher named John Thomas Looney published *"Shakespeare" Identified in Edward de Vere, the 17th Earl of Oxford*. Over the years, the Oxfordian theory has won an impressive following: Sigmund Freud, the Greek scholar Gerald Rendall, the Pulitzer Prize–winning historian David McCullough, the Nobel Prize–winning physicist Roger Penrose, even several justices of the US Supreme Court. Alexander Waugh is one of its most active advocates today. He lives near the town of Taunton in the Somerset countryside. Having a two-hour journey through England's rolling green hills, I thumbed through Looney's *"Shakespeare" Identified*—and a few of the innumerable articles, books, and newsletters it spawned.

⁂

Looney (the name wouldn't make things easy for him) was in his forties when he began searching for the real Shakespeare. It was actually the second crisis of faith he'd experienced in his life. The first came in his twenties. Raised in a religious family, in what he described as a "strongly evangelical environment," he had trained to become a minister. In the course of his religious studies, however, Looney lost his faith and abandoned his vocation. He became a teacher instead, one of the new body of middle-class missionaries teaching English to schoolboys, and he read widely, searching for a philosophy that could fill the void of his lapsed faith.

He found it in the writings of Auguste Comte, the nineteenth-century French founder of positivism, a philosophical movement that emphasized reason and empiricism over faith and mysticism. Comtean positivism was influential in Victorian England, attracting philosophers, scientists, novelists, and social reformers. Its scientific outlook, dispensing with supernatural forces in favor of rational observation, appealed to Looney. He corresponded with other positivists and joined Comte's Religion of Humanity, a sort of secular church that replaced veneration of God with veneration of humanity. (Congregants praised the "teachers of mankind," which included Moses and Saint Paul as well as Homer, Dante,

Shakespeare, and Descartes.) But in the course of teaching Shakespeare's plays, Looney lost his faith in Shakespeare, too. He looked to positivism to solve the mystery. "[I]t taught me to apply the principles, criteria & methods of science to all vital human problems," he wrote later. "It is, at any rate, from this standpoint, that I should wish my Shakespeare researches to be judged."

Looney was not impressed by the existing anti-Stratfordian theories. Though the Baconian theory had helped to popularize doubt about Shakespeare, it also promoted "a misleading method of enquiry: a kind of pick-and-try process" and set up "an inferior form of Shakespearean investigation, the 'cryptogram,'" he wrote. What was needed was a "systematic search for the author." Looney's methodology, which he laid out in his book, resembled that of a crime unit, drawing deductions about the author from the evidence: the plays and poems in which he had left "more or less unconscious indications of himself." The profile he assembled suggested: a matured man of recognized genius; apparently eccentric and mysterious; of intense sensibility; not adequately appreciated; of pronounced and known literary tastes; an enthusiast for the world of drama; a lyric poet of recognized talent; and of superior education—a classical one—and the habitual associate of educated people. These were followed by a more specific set of special characteristics: for instance, that the author was an enthusiast for Italy, a lover of music, a follower of sport, and a member of the higher aristocracy. He probably nursed Catholic sympathies, a suspicion shared by traditional scholars (in *Hamlet*, the ghost is in purgatory), but was "touched with scepticism." His treatment of the dark lady suggested a "conflicting attitude toward women." ("I have sworn thee fair, and thought thee bright, / Who art as black as hell, as dark as night," the poet writes in Sonnet 147.) And he was likely "loose and improvident in money matters." While Shakespeare's heroes have a free-spending attitude toward money, Looney noted that his villains tend to be penny-pinchers. But finding a man who had deliberately concealed his identity would be challenging: it required "circumventing a scheme of self-concealment devised by one of the most capable of intellects."

Looney singled out one feature to guide his search—that the author must have been a lyric poet of talent—reasoning that the man who published *Venus and Adonis* must have written earlier poems with the same formal structure. Poring through an anthology of sixteenth-century lyrics, he zeroed in on a poem by someone he had never heard of: Edward de Vere, the 17th Earl of Oxford. Little was known of Oxford in the early twentieth century. In an entry in the *Oxford Dictionary of National Biography*, Looney read, "Oxford, despite his violent and perverse temper, his eccentric taste in dress, and his reckless waste of substance, evinced a genuine taste in music and wrote verses of much lyric beauty." The entry happened to be written by the preeminent Shakespearean Sir Sidney Lee, who in his description of Oxford inadvertently gave aid to the enemy. "Puttenham and Meres reckon him among the best for comedy in his day; but though he was a patron of players no specimens of his dramatic productions survive," Lee continued. "A sufficient number of his poems is extant to corroborate Webbe's comment, that he was the best of the courtier poets in the early days of Queen Elizabeth, and that 'in the rare devices of poetry, he may challenge himself the title of the most excellent amongst the rest.'" Elsewhere, oblivious to the implications of what he was saying, Lee noted that Oxford and Shakespeare wrote verses "in a kindred key."

Looney's interest was piqued. He proceeded to study the surviving examples of Oxford's early poetry. In one poem, Oxford lamented the "loss of my good name," a theme that recurs in Shakespeare's sonnets. "Personally, I find it utterly impossible to read this poem of Edward de Vere's and the sonnets . . . without an overwhelming sense of there being but one mind behind the two utterances," Looney wrote. He was further impressed by the "coincidence" that Oxford's early poems survived, but his plays had been lost, while Shakespeare's plays survived, but his early work was lost. Where was Shakespeare's juvenilia? Without some youthful stabs at poetry, the torrent of masterpieces that poured out of the Stratford man in the 1590s were, in Looney's view, literally unbelievable. Meanwhile, it appeared that Oxford stopped writing around the time the works of Shakespeare began to appear. But would a man considered "among the best for comedy" and "most excellent" in poetry suddenly drop his pen at the age of forty? The dates of Oxford's poems and Shakespeare's plays "fit in exactly with the theory of one work being but the continuation of the other."

Having worked from the plays to a suspect, Looney reversed the process, working from the suspect to the plays to see if Oxford's life might be reflected in the works of Shakespeare. Did they align? Could that famously enormous gulf between the man and the works be closed by putting Oxford in place of the Stratford man? One can argue with some of Looney's deductions about the author. (Was Shakespeare necessarily aristocratic? Did he really have a "conflicting attitude" toward women?) One can also criticize him for not casting a wider net. He expected to run through many candidates before he hit on the right one. But the biographical parallels he discovered between Oxford's life and Shakespeare's plays were, in his view, "so amazingly strange and wholly unique" that they justified "a very strong belief that the Shakespeare plays are the lost plays of the Earl of Oxford."

Looking around for a publisher, Looney found one who offered to pay him a substantial sum but only on the condition that he adopted a pseudonym. Such a heretical theory could not possibly be put forward under the unfortunate name of Looney. He refused. He was not going to compound a case of pseudonymous authorship with further pseudonymous authorship. Delivering a sealed envelope containing a description of his discovery to the director of the British Museum to establish his priority, Looney continued looking. Two years later, a publisher finally accepted him undisguised, marketing his book as a rational, evidence-based inquiry that contained "no cipher, cryptography, or hidden message connected with his reason or his discovery."

I wasn't particularly interested in the Oxfordian theory when I started out. It had failed for a century to persuade Shakespeare scholars, so I assumed there wasn't much to it. Besides, it was hard to get excited about the idea of Shakespeare being a high-ranking aristocrat. But as I learned about the case for Oxford—set forth first by Looney, then expanded by subsequent researchers—I began to see why the majority of Shakespeare skeptics today are Oxfordians. I also began to see why the case encountered such resistance—and not just resistance but visceral disgust: No one wants the story of Shakespeare as a member of the 1 percent. Born to incredible wealth and privilege, scion of "the longest and most illustrious line of nobles England has seen" (according to the nineteenth-century historian Thomas Macaulay), Oxford was everything the Stratford man wasn't. His ancestors came from France before the Norman Conquest. He stood for rank, lineage, feudal nobility. And while William of Stratford enjoyed an inspiring ascent from humble beginnings, Oxford's story was one of decline. He was among the most brilliant young noblemen at Elizabeth's court, the subject of much attention and expectation, but he was proud, extravagant, eccentric, and scandal ridden, and he fell into ruin and disgrace. In 1872, when the scholar Alexander Grosart republished some of Oxford's forgotten poetry, he noted that "an unlifted shadow somehow lies across his memory."

Born in 1550, fourteen years before Shakespeare, Edward de Vere was raised at the ancestral seat, Hedingham Castle, where the family's company of players lodged when they weren't on tour. His grandfather, the 15th earl, had patronized the company and commissioned the dramatist John Bale to write plays, one of which—*King Johan*—was a source for Shakespeare's *King John*. (Scholars have wondered how Shakespeare came into possession of Bale's unpublished manuscript.) His father, the 16th earl, continued to sponsor the players (who were once rebuked by the bishop of Winchester as "lewd fellows.") His uncle Henry Howard, the Earl of Surrey, was one of the fathers of the English sonnet, pioneering the form adopted later by Shakespeare. His other uncle, Arthur Golding, translated Ovid's *Metamorphoses*, the source for *Venus and Adonis* as well as the inspiration for many passages in the plays. His early education was supervised by Sir Thomas Smith, a renowned Greek scholar and Regius Professor of Civil Law at Cambridge. Only eight, de Vere entered as an *impubes*: an immature student. (In 1923, the scholar Frederick Boas would note that Shakespeare used slang specific to the students of Cambridge University.) But the boy's life was upended by the sudden death of his father. In 1562, at age twelve, Edward de Vere became the 17th Earl of Oxford and Lord Great Chamberlain of England.

Now a ward of the Crown, he was placed under the guardianship of the Queen's chief advisor, William Cecil, who, as master of the Court of

Wards, held guardianship of aristocratic boys whose fathers had died before they reached maturity. The young earl rode from his father's funeral into London "with seven score horse all in black." Looney saw an immediate parallel to *All's Well That Ends Well*, in which the young Count Bertram, whose father has died, is brought to the court by his mother and left there as a royal ward. (Count is the French equivalent of earl.) Against his wishes, Bertram is married to a lowborn woman named Helena, daughter of the king's physician, just as Oxford would be married to Anne Cecil, his guardian's daughter. Bertram agrees reluctantly to the marriage only after the king promises to elevate Helena to a title. Just before Oxford's marriage, the Queen elevated Anne Cecil and her family to nobility. (Thus William Cecil, by arranging his daughter's marriage to his ward, became Lord Burghley.) In the play, Bertram refuses to consummate the marriage, declaring, "I will not bed her," and runs off to Italy. Oxford and Anne remained conspicuously childless for the first several years of their marriage, before Oxford absconded to Italy.

The story was so like Oxford's that if he wasn't the author, it must have been someone who knew him well, Looney reasoned. Then he came across an item that further seemed to confirm the parallel. In *All's Well That Ends Well*, Bertram is tricked into sleeping with Helena when she switches places at night with another woman—a ploy from folklore known as the "bed trick." Oxford allegedly fell for the same trick. A servant later recorded that Lady Anne "was brought to his bed under the notion of his mistress, and from such a virtuous deceit, she [a daughter] is said to proceed." This was hard to believe, Looney noted, but whether it actually happened didn't really matter. The significant point was that early gossip connected Bertram's story with Oxford's.

Looney saw other traces of Oxford's early life in the Shakespeare canon. Oxford was classically educated under his guardian's regime. Burghley employed Arthur Golding, who tutored his nephew at Cecil House while he was translating Ovid's *Metamorphoses.* (Golding praised his pupil's zeal for learning about ancient history as well as contemporary events.) As a royal ward, Oxford spent time at the Queen's court at Windsor Castle—the setting of *The Merry Wives of Windsor*, a play that exhibits detailed familiarity with the area's lands and traditions. "The play which furnishes the most precise Shakespearean topography gives not the environment of William Shakespere's early poetic life, but of Edward de Vere's," Looney noted. One character wishes for "my Book of Songs and Sonnets," referencing the posthumous book of *Songes and Sonnettes* by Oxford's uncle Henry Howard. Another character is named "Dr. Caius," like the Cambridge professor John Caius (who died in 1573—long before William of Stratford could have met him).

Oxford's mother remarried after her husband's death. In *Hamlet*, the prince of Denmark mourns the loss of his father and scorns his mother's remarriage with "most wicked speed" to another man. "Now reigns here / A very, very—pajock," Hamlet complains to his friend Horatio. The rhyme is supposed to end with "ass." Why does Hamlet substitute "pajock" (a derogatory term for *peacock*) instead? "Our scholarly Shakespeareans have written much in seeking a reasonable explanation of the substitution, but not with much success," Looney noted. "When, however, it is remembered that Oxford's stepfather was Sir Charles Tyrrell, and that the peacock's tail is the distinctive feature in that Tyrrell crest, the obscurity disappears." The Oxfordian theory made sense of things that the Stratfordian one couldn't.

Hamlet's resentment of his stepfather was Oxford's resentment. Hamlet's friend Horatio recalls Oxford's cousin Sir Horace de Vere (sometimes called Horatio). Hamlet himself—"the expectancy and rose of the fair state, The glass of fashion and the mold of form," possessing "the courtier's, soldier's, scholar's eye, tongue, sword"—resembles the young Oxford, a courtier, soldier, and scholar who, by age twenty-five, had "more followers and was the object of greater expectation than any other man in the realm." So reported the French ambassador.

Oxford dazzled the court, taking the prize in a jousting tournament before the Queen. He served in a military campaign in Scotland. (Shakespeare's plays display military knowledge: "It is clear that [Shakespeare] had an extraordinary knowledge of soldiers," wrote the twentieth-century scholar G. B. Harrison, though William of Stratford had no military record.) He took "singular delight," according to one contemporary, in "books of geography, histories, and other good learning." Another warned him against the temptation of being "too much addicted that way." He was granted honorary master of arts degrees by Oxford and Cambridge, where the scholar John Brooke noted that the honor was awarded "by right" of his "excellent virtue and rare learning." Like other young noblemen, Oxford entered the Inns of Court to study law and was involved in legal affairs throughout his life. (In 1586 he would sit on the trial of Mary, Queen of Scots, who conducted her own eloquent defense—a model, Looney suggested, for Portia's speech on the "quality of mercy" in *The Merchant of Venice.*)

His expense accounts record his purchase of volumes in French and Italian, Chaucer, Plutarch, Cicero, Plato, and a Geneva Bible—all recognized sources of influence on Shakespeare. His devotion to learning drew scholars to him, and he became a patron, financing a great range of literary and philosophical works—for example, a translation of a Latin text on overcoming grief called *Cardanus Comforte*, "published by commandment of the right honorable the Earl of Oxenford" in 1573. Looney noted that it had been identified by scholars as "Hamlet's book." Before Hamlet delivers his "To be, or not to be" speech, he is seen "poring upon a book" from which he takes his philosophy. *Cardanus Comforte* "seems to be the book which Shakespeare placed in the hands of Hamlet," wrote one scholar, citing passages that "seem to approach so near to the thoughts of Hamlet that we can hardly doubt that they were in the Poet's mind when he put them into the mouth of his hero." (See, for instance, "death is not accounted other than sleep, and to die is said to sleep," a passage echoed in Hamlet's "To die, to sleep—to sleep, perchance to dream." Or "[T]here is nothing that doth better or more truly prophecy the end of life, than when a man dreams that he doth travel and wander into far countries . . . and that he travels in countries unknown without hope of return," echoed in Hamlet's "dread of something after death, the undiscovered country, from whose bourn no traveller returns.") Oxford prefaced the book with a letter explaining that he had "long desired" to see it published in English "to comforte the afflicted, confirme the doubtful, encourage the cowarde, and lift up the base minded man."

But if the scholarly, philosophical Hamlet resembles Oxford, so does the mad Hamlet who puts on an "antic disposition." Oxford had "an addell heade and a railing tongue," one contemporary remarked. In the same year that Oxford financed the publication of "Hamlet's book," he led his servants in a mock-ambush on Burghley's servants, lying in wait at Gad's Hill and attacking the men who were bringing money for the Exchequer along the road from Rochester to Gravesend. In *Henry IV*, Falstaff and his men ambush messengers bringing money for the Exchequer along the road from, well, Rochester to Gravesend. (In the play, one of Falstaff's men is called Gadshill, underlining the parallel.) Burghley received a letter complaining of his son-in-law's "determined mischief."

And what about Burghley? As far back as 1869, scholars recognized that Polonius, the king's scheming advisor in *Hamlet*, is a caricature of Burghley, the Queen's scheming advisor. Burghley had written "precepts" for his son Robert, which closely echo the words of advice that Polonius delivers to his son Laertes: "Neither a borrower nor a lender be," "This above all: to thine ownself be true," and so on. ("In some of these the identity of language with that of Polonius is so close, that Shakespeare could not have hit upon it unless he had been acquainted with Burghley's parental advice to Robert Cecil," noted the scholar George Russel French.) But how could Shakespeare have gotten hold of Burghley's unpublished precepts? And how could he have dared to satirize the Queen's chief minister without repercussions?

There are other parallels, too. When Laertes leaves for France, Polonius sends servants to spy on him. Burghley, who also had a penchant for spying, worried about his son's activities in France. Hamlet calls Polonius a "fishmonger," apparently mocking Burghley's passionate promotion of a bill to make fish eating compulsory on Wednesdays. In the first quarto of the play (Q1) Polonius is called Corambis, meaning "double-hearted," a play on Burghley's armorial motto, *cor unum, via una* ("one heart, one way"). Seeking to understand why the name Corambis was changed to Polonius, the scholar E. K. Chambers wondered, "Can Polonius have resembled some nickname for Burghley?" Alexander Waugh has offered an answer: when Oxford visited the University of Oxford in 1566, a poet gave an oration praising Lords Burghley and Leicester as "poles" (as in axis poles): "Long may you live in joy and health, O Poles!" Hearing his distinguished guardian called a "pole"—a slang term for *prick*—in front of an audience of dignitaries must have been "singularly amusing" to a sixteen-year-old.

Since Oxford emerged as a candidate, scholars have tried to walk back their identification of Polonius with Burghley. It's too dangerous, for there is nothing to connect Burghley with the man from Stratford. Oxford, by contrast, grew up under Burghley's thumb. He had the motive to mock his father-in-law and the rank to get away with it. In the play, Hamlet accidentally stabs Polonius. In real life, a teenage Oxford stabbed one of Burghley's servants—a drunk under-cook who stumbled into his fencing practice. An Oxfordian reading of the play (which is also a Freudian reading) might suggest he fantasized about murdering his father-in-law instead.

Since his marriage, Oxford had been itching to travel. In 1574 he bolted to the Continent without permission and was dragged home under threat of penalties. The Queen promised him a license to travel if he pledged good behavior. She "delighteth more in his personage and his dancing and his valiantness than any other," observed one courtier. "If it were not for his fickle head, he would pass any of them shortly." Despite his fickle head, the Queen provided Oxford with letters of introduction to foreign rulers the next year, lauding him "not in the usual way but from my heart, on account of his outstanding mind and vertue." To finance his trip, Oxford sold some of his estates. (Oxfordians like to point to Jaques in *As You Like It*, who sells his own lands "to see other men's.") He was presented at the French court in Paris, then passed south, probably through Roussillon, the setting of *All's Well That Ends Well*. (The Dowager Countess of Roussillon had a daughter named Hélène, like the heroine Helena in the play.) He made his way to Milan and Venice, traveling through Italy for a year—through the settings of Shakespeare's Italian plays. Portia's estate in *The Merchant of Venice* has been identified by the Italian scholar Noemi Magri as Villa Foscari, near Venice. (Curiously, a sixteenth-century fresco of Portia graces the walls of the estate, which still stands today.) *Venus and Adonis*, Magri further argued, uses imagery from a painting of the tale by

Titian, which was on display in Titian's studio in Venice when Oxford visited in 1575. He discovered not just Italian cities and customs but also the Italian Renaissance—its art, poetry, and theater, the *commedia dell'arte*, an improvisational theatrical form with colorful stock characters (star-crossed lovers, madcap servants, women dressed as men, nobles dressed as paupers). Scholars consider the Italian *commedia* a major influence in Shakespeare's comedies. For Oxfordians, Oxford's trip to Italy is a landmark event in literary history: a formative experience for the young artist who would bring the Italian Renaissance back to England in the form of Shakespeare's plays. In 1576, his creditors after him, Oxford borrowed money from a wealthy Genoa merchant, Benedict Spinola. Is it just a coincidence that in *The Taming of the Shrew*, the wealthy wheeler-dealer of Padua is called Baptista Minola? Or that London's first permanent public theater, the Theatre, was erected on the Italian model just after Oxford's return? "It is said that a Great lord had it built," a contemporary recorded.

When he traveled back across the English Channel, Oxford was attacked, robbed, and stripped naked by pirates. ("Naked we landed out of Italy, enthralled by pirates, men of no regard," one of his companions recalled, "horror and death assailed nobility.") Hamlet, in a passage that has no known source, similarly claims to have been attacked by pirates in the English Channel and "set naked" upon the shore. While Oxford was abroad, his wife had given birth to a daughter, but a rumor reached him that the child was not his. The scandal had become the "fable of the world," he complained to Burghley. Spurning his wife for her alleged infidelity, Oxford refused to live with Anne for five years. They reconciled later and had several more daughters (as well as a son who died in infancy), but Anne Cecil's life has a tragic cast. Though apparently devoted to her husband, he ostracized and humiliated her, and she died young, just thirty-one years old. Oxfordians see their marriage—and Oxford's grief and guilt—reflected in the plays: in *Othello*, where the jealous Moor kills his wife on hearing a rumor of her infidelity, then regrets his actions on discovering her innocence; in *Cymbeline*, where a young nobleman hears whispers of his wife's infidelity while traveling in Italy, returns wrathfully seeking revenge, and later begs forgiveness; and in *The Winter's Tale*, where the insanely jealous King Leontes of Sicily wrongfully accuses his wife of infidelity and denies paternity of his daughter. When Oxford rejected his daughter, the Countess of Suffolk wrote to Burghley with a scheme to soften Oxford: "Bring in the child as though it were some other child of my friend's, and we shall see how nature will work in him to like it, and tell him it is his own after." In the play, a similar scheme is hatched to present the baby to Leontes in the hope that the father might "soften at the sight o' the child." At the end of the play, a repentant Leontes gazes on the statue of his wife, who has died of a broken heart, and longs to see her live again. "Would you not deem it breathed? And that those veins did verily bear blood?" he cries. "No settled senses of the world can match the pleasure of that madness." In one of the strangest scenes in Shakespeare, the statue comes to life—the innocent, persecuted wife resurrected through art.

Oxford was proud, eccentric, and temperamental. His sister Mary said she "could not rule her brother's tongue, nor help the rest of his faults." He got into a fight with Philip Sidney on the tennis court (in the

"A passing singular odd man."

course of which he reportedly called the poet a "puppy"). When the Queen asked him to dance for visiting French ambassadors, he refused on the grounds that he "would not give pleasure to Frenchmen." In a poem called "Speculum Tuscanismi" ("The Mirror of Tuscanism"), Gabriel Harvey lampooned Oxford's obsession with Italy, ostentatious fashions, and "womanish" works, calling him "a passing singular odd man." Harvey was subsequently summoned by the Court of Star Chamber to answer charges of libel against Oxford. But what did Harvey mean by "womanish" works? The phrase recalls a passage in the writings of a soldier named Barnabe Rich, who recorded seeing an unnamed, ostentatiously dressed man looking "very womanly." The man's eccentric, European fashion has led some to suspect it was Oxford.

He was "riding towards me on a footcloth nag, apparelled in a French Ruff, a French Cloak, a French Hose, and in his hand a great fan of Feathers, bearing them up (very womanly) against the side of his face," Rich wrote. Thinking it "impossible that a man might be found so foolish as to make himself a scorn to the world to wear so womanish a toy," Rich thought at first that "it had been some shameless woman that had disguised herself like a man."

Even as contemporaries remarked on Oxford's eccentricity, they lauded his learning and literary skills. He was "a fellow peerless in England," Harvey conceded, "not the like discourser for Tongue, and head to be found out, not the like resolute man for great and serious affairs, not the like Lynx to spy out secrets and privities of State, eyed like to Argus, eared like to Midas, nos'd like to Naso, wing'd like to Mercury." Naso is Ovid: Publius Ovidius Naso, Shakespeare's favorite poet. He was "of spirit passing great," agreed the playwright George Chapman, one who "writ sweetly or of learned things." The poet John Soowthern noted Oxford's enthusiasm for astronomy, classical literature, languages, and music:

For who marketh better than he,
The seven turning flames of the Skie:
Or hath read more of the antique.
Hath greater knowledge in the tongues:

Or understands sooner the sounds,
Of the learner to love Musique.

"Of French and Italian muses, the manners of many peoples, their arts and laws you have drunk deeply," Harvey saluted him in a Latin address at Cambridge in 1578. "Pallas will instruct your heart and spirit as Apollo cultivated your mind in the arts. Your English poetry has been widely sung. Let your courtly epistle—more polished than even the writings of Castiglione himself—witness how greatly you excel in letters. I have seen many of your Latin verses, and even more of your English verses are extant." Oxford's poems circulated in manuscript, and a few turned up in miscellanies (under the initials "E.O." or "E. Ox."). Urging Oxford to put down the pen and take up the sword against England's enemies, Harvey invoked the image of Pallas-Minerva guiding the spear of Achilles at Troy: "Minerva lies hidden in your right hand. . . . / Thine eyes flash fire, thy will shakes spears. / Who would not swear that Achilles had come to life again?" he asked.

The proper duty of a nobleman was the defense of Crown and country, not writing poetry. But Oxford's focus remained the arts. At thirty, he revived the family tradition of maintaining an acting company and supported various companies throughout the 1580s, making him for a period—the crucial period before the emergence of Shakespeare—one of the most important patrons of theater among the English nobility. In 1583 he acquired the lease on England's first public indoor theater, the Blackfriars, transferring it to his secretary the playwright John Lyly, whose mannered, courtly style influenced Shakespeare's early comedies. ("In comedy Lyly is Shakespeare's only model," notes the scholar R. W. Bond.) By 1586 the critic William Webbe wrote that "in the rare devices of poetry . . . the right honourable Earl of Oxford may challenge to himself the tytle of most excellent among the rest." Later, Oxford's company would perform in the yard of the Boar's Head Tavern, the rowdy pub featured famously in Shakespeare's *Henry IV* plays.

There are records suggesting that Oxford spent lavishly on entertainment for the Queen as well. In his later years, he would remind his brother-in-law Robert Cecil of his "youth, time, and fortune spent in her Court."

The French ambassador recalled a comedy that Oxford presented—"*une belle comedie qui se conclust par un mariage* [a beautiful comedy that concludes with a marriage]"—apparently involving a shipwreck. Oxford's other secretary, the playwright Anthony Munday, described "a brave and comely ship brought in before her Majesty wherein were certain of her noble Lords, and this ship was made with a gallant devise that in her presence it ran upon a rock & was despoiled. This credit was the bravest devise that I ever saw, and worthy of innumerable commendations." Oxford, who had concealed himself in the ship, danced his way toward the audience, where he presented Elizabeth I with a jewel. Another record lists a lost manuscript by Oxford, described as "a pleasant conceit of *Vere*, Earl of Oxford, discontented at the Rising of a mean Gentleman in the English Court, circa 1580."

The performance involving a shipwreck and the manuscript about the rising of a gentlemen both contain elements of *Twelfth Night*, suggesting to some Oxfordians that this might be an early version of Shakespeare's play. Other hints of Shakespearean works also crop up on the theatrical radar in the 1580s: writers referred to plays about Timon of Athens in 1584 and Hamlet in 1589 (the so-called "Ur-Hamlet")—long before Shakespeare is thought to have written them. Scholars argue that Shakespeare must have adapted other writers' works; Oxfordians suggest that these are simply Oxford's early versions of those plays.

That Oxford was writing plays in the 1580s seems clear. In 1589 George Puttenham praised him "for Comedie and Enterlude." Nine years later, the clergyman Francis Meres listed him among the "best" for comedy. Despite this acclaim, his plays are not known, perhaps because he didn't put his name to them. Puttenham suggested as much: "and in her Majesties time that now is sprung up an other crew of Courtly makers, Noblemen and Gentlemen of her Majesties owne servants, who have written excellently well as it would appear if their doings could be found out and made public with the rest, of which number is first that noble Gentleman *Edward* Earle of Oxford."

In the 1580s Oxford was also mired in scandal. He was reported to have embraced Catholicism during his time in Italy. Begging for the Queen's mercy, he repudiated Rome and denounced a group of English Catholics as traitors. They retaliated by producing a hundred pages of invective, accusing him of being an atheist, murderer, homosexual, alcoholic, practitioner of bestiality and necromancy, traitor, and "monstrous adversary . . . who would drink my blood rather than wine." Two of the Catholics claimed that he had abused boys and submitted testimony from his alleged victims—but another refused to corroborate the claim: "I cannot particularly charge my Lord with pedication [pederasty]," insisted Francis Southwell, who also declined to support the other charges against Oxford, except heresy, grandiose talk, and "lewdness [in] speeches." Oxford was apparently an outrageous storyteller, telling tales that threw his companions into fits of laughter. (Among them were references to the "Jews of Italy" and a feud "between two families" in Genoa.) "This lie is very rife with him," Charles Arundell, one of the Catholics, wrote of Oxford's elaborate fictions, and he "glories greatly" in telling it. "Diversely hath he told it, and when he enters into it, he can hardly out, which hath made such sport as often have I been driven to rise from his table laughing. So hath my Lord Charles Howard and the rest." Oxfordians suggest that this description of Oxford aligns with Jonson's description of Shakespeare. In a notebook published after his death, Jonson wrote that Shakespeare "flowed with that facility that sometime it was necessary he should be stopped . . . His wit was in his own power: would the rule of it had been so too. Many times he fell into those things [that] could not escape laughter . . . But he redeemed his vices with his virtues. There was ever more in him to be praised, than to be pardoned."

While the Catholics were imprisoned, nothing came of the charges against Oxford, but his name continued to be associated with scandal. In 1581 the Queen threw him in the Tower of London for impregnating one of her maids of honor, Anne Vavasour, who bore his illegitimate son. Oxford was imprisoned for three months, then placed under house arrest. Various duels ensued between Oxford and his mistress's uncle, Sir Thomas Knyvet, in which both men were wounded and one of Oxford's men died. Looney noted a parallel to the brawls between the Montagues and Capulets in *Romeo and Juliet*, in which Juliet's cousin Tybalt challenges Romeo to a duel, and one of Romeo's men, Mercutio, ends up dead.

In 1585 Anne's brother, Thomas Vavasour, still seeking revenge, tried to provoke Oxford into another duel. "I fear thou are so much wedded to that shadow of thine that nothing can have force to awake thy base and sleepy spirits," he wrote in a letter. "But if there be yet any spark of honor left in thee, or iota of regard for thy decayed reputation . . . meet me thyself alone . . . For the weapons, I leave them to thy choice." No one quite knows what Vavasour meant by "that shadow of thine," but it is clear that Oxford was now looked upon, at least by some, as a dishonorable man.

His reputational decay was compounded by financial ruin, a disgraceful state for a premier nobleman. Oxford was extravagant, spending on clothing and finery, but, as a patron, he was also generous, draining his accounts to support other writers. Robert Greene praised him as "a worthie favorer and fosterer of learning" to whom "scholars flock." His "exceeding bountie" was remembered after his death: "It were infinite to speake of his infinite expense, the infinite number of his attendants, or the infinite house he kept to feede all people," wrote the poet Gervase Markham. "The bountie which Religion and Learning daily took from him" are as "trumpets so loude that all eares know them." Some apparently exploited his generosity. Brought to insolvency by the "over many greedy horse-leeches which had sucked too ravenously on his sweet liberality," as the poet Henry Lok wrote, Oxford was forced to sell more of his estates. Oxfordians see his situation mirrored in Shakespeare's *Timon of Athens*, in which a nobleman lavishes his wealth on parasites and flatterers until they abandon him, and, impoverished, he retreats into solitude. "We have with Timon a perfect fit to Oxford's biography," wrote Looney, noting that Timon's epitaph ("Here lies a wretched corpse, of wretched soul bereft. Seek not my name . . .") mirrors Shakespeare's demand, "My name be buried where my body is . . ."

In 1586 the Queen issued a mysterious privy seal warrant ordering the Exchequer to pay Oxford an annuity of £1,000. The warrant didn't specify any purpose for the annuity and stipulated that there be no account of expenditure—no paper trail—making Oxford's use of the funds effectively a state secret. What was this about? Stratfordians maintain that Elizabeth I was merely relieving Oxford's embarrassing financial situation but, at the time, the Exchequer was depleted by wars, and the parsimonious queen was not known to hand out money for nothing. ("Money was the one thing that Queen Elizabeth could not bring herself to give away," noted the historian Lawrence Stone.) Her usual way of enriching her lords was to give appointments to lucrative offices, grants of lands, or monopolies on the licensing of certain commodities, not funds from her own treasury. In fact, Oxford petitioned repeatedly for such preferments, and she repeatedly denied him. So why would the miserly queen instead execute a privy seal warrant to give an enormous stipend to a disgraced nobleman—indefinitely and requiring no accountability? The Oxfordian who discovered the warrant, Bernard Ward, suggested that she was paying him for theatrical work on behalf of the Crown. A "policy of plays" was one of the "secrets of government," the playwright Thomas Nashe wrote in 1592, explaining that stage adaptations of English chronicles were "very necessary" to encourage virtue and patriotism. Shakespeare's history plays, which are stage adaptations of English chronicles, are generally regarded as patriotic propaganda showing the dangers of civil war and celebrating the Tudor dynasty. (Walt Whitman suspected that they were "the result of an essentially controlling plan. What was that plan? Or, rather, what was veil'd behind it?") Was this where Oxford's £1,000 annuity went? In 1662 the Stratford vicar recorded a rumor that Shakespeare "had an allowance so large, yt hee spent at ye rate of 1000/a year, as I have heard." But, of course, there is no record that William of Stratford had any such allowance.

According to the Oxfordian theory, Oxford spent the 1590s—the last decade of his life—writing and revising his plays, which appeared anonymously at first and then under the name "Shakespeare." Though Oxford was closely tied to all the writers said to have influenced Shakespeare—from Anthony Munday, to John Lyly, to Robert Greene—he was, oddly, never tied to Shakespeare. Why didn't the great patron of theater and the great playwright ever cross paths?

In 1592 Oxford remarried and had a son, Henry de Vere, who would become the 18th Earl of Oxford. In 1593, while Lord Burghley was trying in vain to arrange Southampton's marriage to Oxford's eldest daughter, Elizabeth Vere, *Venus and Adonis* appeared, with its dedication to Southampton from "William Shakespeare" and its bawdy tale of a young man spurning the goddess of love. The poem's printer, a man from Stratford named Richard Field, also printed works for Burghley. When Southampton rejected Elizabeth Vere, she married William Stanley, the 6th Earl of Derby, instead. "Thimperfections of her father shall be no blemishe to her honour," assured a well-wisher. (It was while Derby was staying at Hedingham Castle in 1599 that he was reportedly "penning comedies for the common players.") Burghley proposed that Oxford's second daughter, Bridget, marry William Herbert, one of the Folio dedicatees, but negotiations fell through, and she married someone else. His third daughter, Susan, married Philip Herbert, the other Folio dedicatee. Oxfordians see the First Folio as a "family affair." In short, the three dedicatees of Shakespeare's works were all connected to Oxford's family.

Oxford's reputation seems never to have recovered. "I find comfort in this air," he wrote to Burghley from the countryside, "but no fortune in the court." Despite his rank, he was never elected to the Order of the Garter, the most senior order of knights, and the Queen never granted him the lucrative posts he petitioned for. He disposed of Hedingham Castle, leaving it to Burghley, who held it in trust for Oxford's three daughters. (Oxfordians see a parallel to the aging Lear dividing his lands among his three daughters.) When the Queen died in 1603, Oxford was deeply affected, writing to his brother-in-law Robert Cecil, "I cannot but find a great grief in myself to remember the mistress which we have lost, under whom both you and myself from our greenest years have been in a manner brought up." It is a distinctly poetic letter, cited by Oxfordians as evidence of a Shakespearean-sounding command of language. "In this common shipwreck, mine is above all the rest," he continued, "who least regarded though often comforted of all her followers she hath left to try my fortune among the alterations of time and chance, either without sail whereby to take the advantage of any prosperous gale or with anchor to ride till the storm be overpast."

Oxford's own health was failing, and he died a year later in June 1604, aged fifty-four. On the day of his death, there was a strange panic in the court; Southampton was arrested and his house searched. What were the authorities looking for? Were documents destroyed? Oxford's will was never found. He was buried in St. Augustine's church in Hackney, but in a manuscript history of the de Vere family, Oxford's cousin Percival Golding suggested that he was later reinterred at Westminster Abbey: "Of him I will only speak what all men's voices confirm: He was a man in minde and body absolutely accomplished with honourable endowments. He died at his house at Hackney in the moneth of June Ao 1604 and lieth buryed at Westminster."

Between 1594 and 1604, an astonishing sixteen Shakespeare plays were published, culminating with *Hamlet*. In Hamlet's dying lament for his "wounded name," Looney heard Oxford's voice:

> *O good Horatio, what a wounded name,*
> *Things standing thus unknown, shall live behind me!*
> *If thou didst ever hold me in thy heart*
> *Absent thee from felicity awhile,*
> *And in this harsh world draw thy breath in pain*
> *To tell my story.*

Looney saw in Oxford "the picture of a great soul, misunderstood, almost an outcast from his own social sphere, with defects of nature, to all appearances one of life's colossal failures, toiling on incessantly at his great tasks, yet willing to pass from life's stage leaving no name behind him but a discredited one: at last dying, as it would seem, almost with the pen between his fingers, immense things accomplished, but not all he had set out to do."

After Oxford's death, the stream of publications stopped. No new Shakespeare title appeared for four years. Only four new plays would be published in quarto (*King Lear* in 1608, *Pericles* and *Troilus and Cressida* in 1609, and *Othello* in 1622). While the pre-1604 quartos regularly appeared with notices on their title pages explaining that they were "newly augmented," "newly corrected," "newly amended," and "enlarged" by their author, no post-1604 quarto was advertised this way. Had the author suddently stopped revising his plays? The rest were published in the First Folio of 1623. Oxfordians see these as posthumous publications, in some cases finished by others. Looney suspected that *The Tempest*, for instance, was "one of those composite productions, upon which it was not uncommon to employ a group of court writers and stage experts," he wrote in a letter to George Greenwood, pointing to Oxford's son-in-law, the Earl of Derby, as "just the man to have had a foremost hand in the editing of the Folio, and to have been the author of some of the non-Shakespearean parts of it."

To Looney, Oxford's death in 1604 was "one of the strongest links in our chain of argument." Early scholars, noticing the 1604 break in publications, had suggested that there was some sort of crisis in Shakespeare's life in that year. ("Something had happened" to Shakespeare, wrote Sir Arthur Quiller-Couch.) They also suggested that some of Shakespeare's later plays were altered or completed by others, which Looney pointed out was more consistent with an author who had passed away, not one who was very much still alive. William of Stratford lived until 1616. There was no known "crisis" in his life in 1604, and no reason why he should have let other writers complete his life's work. In 1605 the author of an anonymous pamphlet actually suggested Shakespeare was dead. "I am with the late *English* quick-spirited, cleare-sighted *Ovid*: It is to be feared Dreaming," he wrote. Shakespeare was the English Ovid, who wrote about the fear of dreaming ("To die, to sleep — / To sleep, perchance to dream. Ay there's the rub, / For in that sleep of death what dreams may come"). But William of Stratford obviously couldn't be described as "late" in 1605. Alexander Waugh noted that "quick-spirited" and "clear-sighted" Ovid recalls Harvey's description of Oxford as "winged like to Mercury," "eyed like to Argus," and "nos'd like to Naso [Ovid]." For Oxfordians, Oxford's death in 1604 also explains why the name "Shakespeare" started appearing on non-Shakespeare plays (*The London Prodigal* in 1605, *A Yorkshire Tragedy* in 1608, and so forth): the author was gone, and someone was fraudulently using the name.

When *Shake-speare's Sonnets* was published in 1609, the publisher Thomas Thorpe added a dedication praising the poet as "ever-living," a word used to refer to the divine or the dead, who have passed into eternal life. In Shakespeare's *Henry VI Part 1*, it is used to describe the deceased king: "That ever-living man of memory, Henry V." When the playwright John Fletcher died, he was referred to as "the deceased, but ever-living Author . . . Fletcher." The dedication "has been telling us, for three hundred years in the plainest of terms, that the poet was already dead," Looney wrote.

Indeed, if Shakespeare was alive, why didn't he write his own dedication? Would a publisher have been so impertinent as to write a dedication for a still-living author? Scholars have sometimes explained this by suggesting that the sonnets must have been published without the author's consent, though there is no evidence that Shakespeare protested their publication.

The poet describes himself in the sonnets as "lame"; in his letters, Oxford deplored his lameness. The poet is old, too, describing himself as "beated and chopp'd with tann'd antiquity" (Sonnet 62), having reached the age "when yellow leaves, or none, or few, do hang" (Sonnet 73). This is a stretch for the Stratford man, who was still in his late thirties in the early sixteen hundreds. Oxford was fourteen years his senior. Oxford's "decayed reputation" and recurring scandals also fit, with a poet who suffered from "vulgar scandal."

Looney knew that he didn't have all the answers and that additional research would be needed, but he considered the evidence for Oxford overwhelming, "A few coincidences we may treat as simply interesting; a number of coincidences we regard as remarkable; a vast accumulation of extraordinary coincidences we accept as conclusive proof." Recognition of Oxford's authorship was no longer merely about solving a mystery. It took on, for Looney, the quality of a moral imperative. It was a "long overdue act of justice and reparation to an unappreciated genius who, we believe, ought now to be put in possession of his rightful honours; and to whose memory should be accorded a gratitude proportionate to the benefits he has conferred upon mankind in general, and the lustre he had shed upon England in particular." Three hundred sixteen years after his death, the time had come for Oxford to claim his crown.

⁂

Except, of course, that it hadn't. Shakespeare scholars were no more willing to accept the Oxfordian heresy than they had been to accept the Baconian one. Looney's book was "a sad waste of print and paper," Alfred Pollard wrote in the *Times Literary Supplement* in March 1920, setting the tone for the academic dismissal of the Oxfordian theory. "Almost any man's life could be illustrated from Shakespeare's plays," insisted Pollard, a professor at the University of London. (If that is so, Looney responded in a letter, please explain why "it has been impossible to do anything of the kind for either William Shakespere or Francis Bacon.") Critics made the predictable jibes about Looney's surname (What a looney!), attacked skeptics as snobs, dismissed the biographical parallels to Oxford's life as mere coincidences, and maintained that Shakespeare's works were the product of his miraculous imagination.

Their main argument was that Oxford's death in 1604 ruled out his authorship, based on the assumption that the plays were written between roughly 1590 and 1612. But the dating was originally suggested to fit the life span of the man from Stratford. As the scholar E. K. Chambers wrote, it is "a hypothesis which . . . is consistent with itself and with the known events of Shakespeare's external life." No one knows exactly when the plays were written, only when they were published and sometimes when they were performed. Scholars disagree among themselves about dates of composition. Sidney Lee gave *All's Well That Ends Well* a composition date of 1595; others placed it earlier, around 1590–92, and still others as late as 1602—a twelve-year span. Scholars see jokes about "equivocation" in *Macbeth* as a reference to a series of trials in 1606, which rules out Oxford, but the term *equivocation* was already in use in trials in 1581 and 1595. As Nicholas Brooke, who edited the Oxford University Press edition of *Macbeth*, writes, "There is no evidence to contradict 1606, but there is also very little to support it." *The Tempest*, which features a shipwreck on an island, is dated to 1610–11 based on a 1609 letter describing a real-life shipwreck on the island of Bermuda. But there were many accounts of shipwrecks that could have inspired the play—and the 1609 letter wasn't published until 1625 anyway, making it an unlikely source. (Oxfordians argue that the play was more likely based on *Decades of the New World*, a series of reports published in 1511 about voyages to the Americas.) If scholars don't know exactly when the plays were written, how can they be certain Oxford's death ruled him out?

Coverage of Looney's book was wildly uneven. While English professors trashed it, reviewers outside of academia praised it. "This is a remarkable book," the *Bookman Journal* reported. "It is to be hoped that those who have preconceived opinions will attempt to put them aside and judge the work without prejudice." The *Halifax Evening Courier* wrote that Looney "makes a far stronger case for Oxford than has ever been made out for Bacon." The *Nottingham Journal and Express* deemed it "a case deserving of serious consideration." In Kingston-upon-Hull, the hometown of Stanley Wells, the *Hull Daily Mail* found that Looney "almost proves that Shakespeare's works were written by Edward de Vere."

In 1922 Looney and George Greenwood, the agnostic lawyer, came together to found the Shakespeare Fellowship. Abel Lefranc, the French Derbyite, joined as vice president. If English departments refused to study the authorship question, they needed an organization that would. Though shunned in the academy, Looney's book had caught the attention of other intellectuals. The Nobel Prize–winning novelist John Galsworthy called it "the best detective story I've ever read." James Joyce, who was in Paris finishing *Ulysses*, wrote Looney's theory into his novel. His characters debate the candidates, dispatching Francis Bacon ("Good Bacon: gone musty"), running through others ("When Rutlandbaconsouthamptonshakespeare or another poet of the same name in the comedy of errors wrote *Hamlet*..."), and exclaiming at the mystery ("I believe, O Lord, help my unbelief"). One comments, "Manner of Oxenford," suggesting that Shakespeare wrote in the manner of Oxford, who signed his name "Earle of Oxenford." The Oxfordian theory apparently stayed with Joyce, because in *Finnegans Wake* (1939), his stream-of-consciousness masterpiece, he referenced it again: "Loonacied! Marterdyed!" a character exclaims, presumably referencing the attacks on Looney. A few lines later comes de Vere himself: "my dodear devere revered mainhirr was confined to guardroom." ("Mainhirr" appears to be a multilingual pun on the Dutch and German expressions for "my dear sir": "mijin heer" and "mein herr." "Confined to guardroom" may reference de Vere's confinement in the Tower of London.)

In Vienna, Sigmund Freud read *"Shakespeare" Identified*, then read it again. "I must confess, I am very impressed by Looney's investigations," he wrote to his disciple Ernest Jones. "If this aristocrat, of whose life much is known and even more can become known, really was Shakespeare, then we have much to modify in our analytic constructions, perhaps also much to gain. It would surely repay an analyst's interest to look into the matter."

If, for instance, Hamlet's resentment of his stepfather—what Freud would term his Oedipus complex—was actually Oxford's resentment, what did that reveal about human psychology? What did it reveal about its relation to art? *Lear* could only be understood psychologically as Oxford's creation, Freud wrote in another letter, noting that "the figure of the father who gave all he had to his children must have had for him a special compensatory attraction, since Edward de Vere was the exact opposite, an inadequate father who never did his duty by his children. A squanderer of his inheritance and a miserable manager of his affairs, oppressed by debts, he could not maintain his family, did not live with them, and left the education and care of his three daughters to their grandfather, Lord Burghley." *Othello*, too, could now be explained along psychoanalytic lines, he added, pointing to Oxford's disastrous marriage. "If he was Shakespeare, he had himself experienced Othello's torments."

Jones, conscious of the scholarly ridicule heaped on skeptics, urged Freud not to publicize his Oxfordian allegiance. Freud didn't care. When he was awarded the Goethe Prize in 1930, he referenced the "nobly born and highly cultivated, passionately wayward, to some extent declassé aristocrat Edward de Vere," perceptively highlighting what would become a problem for the Oxfordian theory: that Oxford was not always admirable, that he replaced the charming myth of a merry country lad with the sometimes distasteful details of an aristocrat's troubled life. The effort to know a great author—to bring him nearer to us—"tends in effect towards degradation," Freud noted. "And it is unavoidable that if we learn more about a great man's life we shall also hear of occasions on which he has in fact done no better than we, has in fact come near to us as a human being." The Oxfordian theory elevated Shakespeare to an aristocrat, but it also humanized him. It made him a person who had done bad things—stabbed a servant, abandoned his wife, denied his daughter's paternity, engaged in extramarital affairs, dueled in the streets, allegedly practiced pederasty, squandered his fortune, lost his ancestral estates, and generally represented the worst tendencies of aristocracy—all the things the English did not want and, as the empire declined, could not afford in their national hero. But for Freud, the likability of the author was irrelevant. It was the psychology that mattered. Writers cannot help giving themselves away, and Oxford had given himself away.

Though English departments rejected the Oxfordian theory, it would be wrong to suggest that it didn't exert an influence. Just as the emerging academy of the nineteenth century defined itself against the Baconian "aberration," so, too, did twentieth-century scholarship contort itself against Oxfordianism. In 1923 Alfred Pollard, the scholar who had dismissed Looney's book as "a sad waste of print and paper," sought to counter the Oxfordian challenge by arguing that Shakespeare's handwriting could be identified in the surviving manuscript of a play called *Sir Thomas More*. The play, which is anonymous, is thought to have been written primarily by Anthony Munday (one of Oxford's secretaries), but it shows revisions by multiple hands. Pollard tried to argue that one of the hands, labeled "Hand D," matched Shakespeare's signatures. If the match could be proved, anti-Stratfordian theories would "come crashing to the ground." But as the Folger Shakespeare Library points out, Shakespeare's six signatures are "too small a sample size to make any sort of reliable comparison." (Not to mention that they may not even be his.) Nevertheless, some scholars have continued arguing for "Hand D" as Shakespeare's. The case has become, as the scholar Paul Werstine puts it, "a very successful resistance movement against anti-Stratfordians."

While Pollard was looking for Shakespeare's hand in other plays, some scholars were looking for coauthors in Shakespeare's plays. They suspected, based mostly on their subjective personal judgments, that certain passages weren't Shakespeare's. Often they used the idea of other hands to explain the bad bits: Shakespeare couldn't have written a mediocre verse; must have been someone else. In a 1924 address to the British Academy, E. K. Chambers railed against this "disintegration" of Shakespeare, decrying the inclination to parcel out the plays to various hands and clinging to the romantic image of a solitary genius. Scholars were allowing an "alien invasion" of writers to overrun Shakespeare's plays, Chambers warned. It was insulting to Shakespeare to suggest that he collaborated with others. It diminished his godlike status. Shakespeare was "the rock" beaten by the waves of criticism, and the rock needed to be defended.

Was the rock also England, the blessed isle? Did the language of "disintegration" have to do, in some sort of psycho-colonial way, with the gradual disintegration of the empire? Why were the other writers—all of them English—an "alien invasion"? The main problem, in Chambers's view, seems to have been that the disintegrationists were doing something awfully anti-Stratfordian: they were looking in Shakespeare's plays for clues to other men. "Their heresies," as he termed their findings, "offer results hardly less perturbing than those with which the Baconians and their kin would make our flesh creep."

Chambers's thundering defense of the rock of Shakespeare put a halt to scholarly inquiry into Shakespeare's coauthors. It was too dangerous, too close to the other heresies flourishing outside academic walls. What was to stop a partial questioning of the traditional attribution from accelerating into a total questioning? If the hands of coauthors could be hidden in Shakespeare, who was to say that "Shakespeare" was not himself a hidden hand? Oxfordians were more open to the idea of collaboration. After all, Oxford had surrounded himself with other writers—employed them as his secretaries, financed them, and even housed them. George Greenwood suspected that the plays were the work of "many pens and one Master Mind." Bernard Ward suggested that the secretive annuity pointed to a propaganda group, led by Oxford, to write the history plays. Gilbert Slater, an economist, proposed a theory of "seven Shakespeares," with Oxford at the helm. Freud, too, thought Oxford's plays were finished by friends.

There was tremendous excitement in the early days of the movement. Taking up Looney's call for additional research, a small army of Oxfordians added to and expanded his initial body of arguments. Gerald Rendall, an esteemed professor of Greek, published four books. An American woman named Eva Turner Clark published four more, including her discovery of a book with a mysterious image on its cover: the hand of a concealed writer emerging from behind a curtain. The book was *Minerva Britanna* (*British Minerva*), a book of anagrams published in 1612 by the poet Henry Peacham. The concealed writer has written the words, "*MENTE.VIDEBOR*," or, "By the mind I shall be seen." Who shall be seen? What can the mind perceive that the eye does

From the title page of *Minerva Britanna*, 1612

not? The quill nib at the end of the phrase looks like another *i*, perhaps making the phrase *MENTE.VIDEBORI*, which is nonsensical in Latin, but Eva Turner Clark saw an anagram: *TIBI NOM. DE VERE*, or "Your name is de Vere." "By the mind I shall be seen" turns out to be a pun, Oxfordians argue: the extra *i* will be seen by the alert reader who applies his mind to see who is concealed: Edward de Vere.

Oxfordians circulated their discoveries in newsletters, discussed them at meetings of the Shakespeare Fellowship, and attracted prominent acolytes to the Oxfordian cause. By 1941, the Oxfordian theory had entered popular culture. In *Pimpernel Smith*, a British war movie, a Nazi-fighting archaeologist (played by Leslie Howard) mentions in passing that he has "been doing a little research work . . . on the identity of Shakespeare" that "proves conclusively that Shakespeare wasn't Shakespeare at all. . . . He was the Earl of Oxford." But just as the Baconian movement had produced "wild" Baconians and "sane" Baconians, so the Oxfordian movement, too, begot wild offshoots. A journalist named Percy Allen suggested that Oxford's dark lady was Elizabeth I, with whom he fathered an illegitimate son, the fair youth of sonnets. Allen argued that this secret, which touched on the greatest matters of state—the Queen's virginity, the succession to the throne—explained the suppression of Oxford's authorship. Looney was annoyed by Allen's "extravagant & improbable" hypothesis, worrying that it was "likely to bring the whole cause into ridicule." Freud rejected it, too. But Allen persevered, announcing that he would seek "a solution to the mystery of the authorship by psychic means." In *Talks with Elizabethans*, Allen relayed his spirit communications with Oxford, Bacon, and Shakespeare. Members of the Shakespeare Fellowship were not impressed. Allen, who had been elected president of the fellowship, was quickly forced to stand down.

After the initial burst of enthusiasm, the Oxfordian movement fell off—partially, perhaps, because it had been tarnished by its wilder elements. Another theory postulated that Oxford was actually the Queen's son and rightful heir to the Crown, as Hamlet is heir to the Crown of Denmark. (Some Oxfordians still embrace this theory today, while others reject it.) With London under Nazi bombardment, meetings of the Shakespeare Fellowship were suspended. Looney wrote to Eva Turner Clark, expressing his belief in humanity's enduring need for Shakespeare in its darkest hour:

> *This is where our interest in Shakespeare and all the greatest poets comes in. In the centuries that lie ahead, when the words Nazi and Hitler are remembered only with feelings of disgust and aversion and as synonyms for cruelty and bad faith, Shakespeare, Wordsworth, Tennyson & Shelley will continue to be honoured as expressions of what is most enduring and characteristic of Humanity.*
>
> *Amidst the darkness of the present time, we shall do well therefore to make a special effort to keep alive every spark of interest in their work. More even than in normal times, we need them today, however incompatible they may seem with the tragedy that overshadows us. My own work "Shakespeare" Identified was largely the result of an attempt to do this during the last war: a refusal to be engulfed by an untoward environment even when suffering most poignantly from the loss of many who were dear to me.*
>
> *This then is the part of our share in the present-day struggle: to*

> *insist, even in the slaughter and distress of battle-fields and bombardments by sea and air, on the supremacy of the things of the human soul.*

Looney died in 1944. "I will never again believe in the conventional representation of Shakespeare; there has to be more to it than *that,*" the *New Yorker* critic Hamilton Basso wrote, reviewing the American edition of "*Shakespeare" Identified* a few years later. His article "The Big Who-Done-It" appealed to the magazine's readers to take Looney's proposition seriously: "If anybody in the class is on the verge of cackling, I earnestly urge him not to," Basso wrote. "Mr. Looney is no crank. He is an earnest, levelheaded man who has spent years trying to solve the world's most baffling literary puzzle. I don't say that he has solved it, mind you. There are gaps in his argument and more than one flaw. But if the case were brought to court, it is hard to see how Mr. Looney would lose. The various 'mysteries' that surround Shakespeare—why is there such a lack of information about him, where did he get his education, how did he acquire his plainly first-hand knowledge of courtly practice and behavior, whence came his obviously intimate acquaintance with Italy, why did he never bother to publish his plays, and a hundred other matters—are mysteries no longer if the man we know as Shakespeare was really Edward de Vere."

A Shakespeare Oxford Society was established in America. In 1959 an article in the *American Bar Association Journal*, "Elizabethan Whodunit: Who Was 'William Shake-Speare'?" noted the evidentiary components of the question and suggested it should be of interest to lawyers. A flurry of letters and replies in the journal followed. But having failed to persuade Shakespeare professors, the movement lost its momentum. "We are talking to each other, converting the already converted," Oxfordians lamented in one newsletter. The "sheer volume of heretical publication appalls," Professor Schoenbaum wrote in 1970. It was all "rubbish, some of it lunatic rubbish." Oxford remained in the shadows, his name unmentionable in the halls of English departments. When Charlton Ogburn, a writer and former official of the US State Department, published an article in *Harvard* magazine in 1974 insisting that Shakespeare was Oxford, a Harvard professor responded by inquiring if the magazine would next run a piece demonstrating that Queen Victoria was a Peruvian transvestite. Ogburn had "embarrassed those of us who attempt to teach Shakespeare" and done "a very real disservice to a community dedicated to *veritas*," he wrote. In the following years, however, Ogburn would succeed in pulling Oxford back into the spotlight.

The problem, in Charlton Ogburn's view, wasn't the evidence but getting people to listen to the evidence. "English faculties, abetted by a generally subservient press, show how far entrenched authority can outlaw and silence dissent in a supposedly free society," he wrote in a Shakespeare Oxford Society newsletter. Ogburn knew a thing or two about entrenched authority. He was among the first State Department officials to warn against US military involvement in Vietnam. His memo was ignored. "What I was saying was not the thing to say," he recalled later. "The State Department had the authority. Who was I?" During Richard Nixon's presidency, belief in authority had become even harder to sustain. "We are dealing here with an intellectual Watergate," Ogburn insisted to his fellow Oxfordians, "and it greatly behooves us to expose it." In 1984 he published *The Mysterious William Shakespeare: The Myth & the Reality*, reintroducing the Oxfordian theory to a new generation of readers. "This brilliant, powerful book is a major event for everyone who cares about Shakespeare," the Pulitzer Prize–winning historian David McCullough wrote in a foreword. "The strange, difficult, contradictory man who emerges as the real Shakespeare, Edward de Vere, 17th Earl of Oxford, is not just plausible but fascinating and wholly believable." But the professors did not budge—except to throw eggs from the windows of their lecture halls at anyone who defamed their poet.

Richmond Crinkley, a director of programs at the Folger Shakespeare Library in Washington, DC, quietly observed the conflict from the sidelines. "As one who found himself a contented agnostic Stratfordian at the Folger, I was enormously surprised at what can only be described as the viciousness toward anti-Stratfordian sentiments expressed by so many otherwise rational and courteous scholars," he wrote in the *Shakespeare Quarterly*. "Is there any more fanatic zealot than the priestlike defender of a challenged creed?" Crinkley perceived the fundamentally religious nature of the controversy. "Orthodox scholarship defends its inherited wisdom from the exalted position of a clerisy somehow attuned to special knowledge," he observed. "One wonders, sometimes, who really are the snobs—the anti-Stratfordians who think a nobleman wrote the plays, or the ostensibly democratic Stratfordians who heap such abundant abuse on their opponents?"

Ogburn concluded that the best place to challenge the orthodoxy was in court. In Washington, DC, on September 25, 1987, Shakespeare was put "on trial." Three justices of the US Supreme Court presided. A thousand spectators convened to hear the arguments: busloads of students, Shakespeare professors, assorted Oxfordians, Washington VIPs, and journalists. The *New Yorker* sent a reporter. C-SPAN carried the trial. The *New York Times* reported that the ruling "could go either way." David Lloyd Kreeger, a wealthy lawyer and philanthropist who bankrolled the event, opened by acknowledging his love for Shakespeare, a love nurtured by reading the complete works "in my early years after law school, during the two hours I spent each day on the Pennsylvania Railroad commuting to a law firm in Newark." His reverence for the works led to "a wish to know more about the genius who had created them," and that wish led him into the authorship controversy, which, he noted, turned on circumstantial evidence and therefore "might profitably be subjected" to legal argument.

Justices William Brennan Jr., Harry Blackmun, and John Paul Stevens filed in, decked out in their courtly robes. Security officers carrying walkie-talkies shuffled at their sides. The audience applauded. Brennan announced that the burden of proof would be on the Oxfordian side, since it was seeking to overturn long-established tradition. "You didn't clear that with the rest of us," Blackmun objected. From the beginning, Oxfordians would later lament, the trial was stacked in favor of the orthodoxy.

A professor from the American University School of Law presented the case for Oxford, arguing that "Shakespeare" was a pseudonym used to conceal the fact that he had written poems for publication and plays for public performance—"something the customs of the time effectively prohibited a nobleman from doing." The justices broke in periodically with questions. Charlton Ogburn looked on anxiously. When his time was up, the Oxfordian lawyer took his seat, and the Stratfordian counsel, another law school professor, rose to speak on behalf of "my client, Shakespeare the actor and theatrical entrepreneur from Stratford." At one point, he ticked off Oxford's various misdemeanors: affairs, imprisonment, duels, bankruptcy. "Sounds like the conduct of a playwright," Justice Stevens quipped, eliciting laughter from the audience. Rebuttals followed. Then the court recessed to consider its verdict.

When the justices returned, each delivered his finding in turn. Brennan began by reviewing Shakespeare's so-called errors, like having his characters travel from Verona to Milan by boat. (Oxfordians would note, with irritation, that Brennan had simply repeated discredited Stratfordian arguments.) The case for Oxford "was not proved, as I saw it," he concluded. Blackmun agreed that this was the "legal answer," but "whether it is the correct one causes me greater doubt." Oxfordians had "come closer to proving" their case than any of the other dissenters, he said, and his mind was "tossing on the ocean." Stevens was more uncertain still. Though he delivered a legal verdict for Shakespeare, he confessed to "gnawing doubts that this great author may have been someone else," adding that "if the author was not the man from Stratford, then there is a high probability that it was Edward de Vere." Turning to the Oxfordians, he offered them a bit of advice: "I would like to suggest that the Oxfordian case suffers from not having a single coherent theory of the case." Some argued that Oxford's use of the pseudonym was a secret arrangement. Others that it was known to a small circle, including the Queen and Ben Jonson. Still others that it was common knowledge among London's writers. Oxfordians needed to "put together a concise, coherent theory" of why Oxford concealed his authorship and why it continued to be suppressed after his death. Stevens imagined that such concealment was most likely "the result of a command from the monarch."

Finally, Stevens concluded, "I would remind you that, although we've done our best, and we agree on the ultimate outcome, the doctrine of res judicata does not apply," meaning the decision was not a final judgment. It could be relitigated if new evidence came to light.

Ogburn viewed the verdict as a "clear defeat." But his disappointment was premature, for two of the justices later revised their opinion. "The Oxfordians have presented a very strong, almost fully convincing case for their point of view," Blackmun wrote to Ogburn after the trial. "If I had to rule on the evidence presented, it would be in favor of the Oxfordians." Stevens undertook his own research into the matter. In 1992 he published an article in the *University of Pennsylvania Law Review*, applying legal principles to support the view that the author was most likely Edward de Vere. Justice Lewis Powell, who had not sat on the trial, nevertheless followed the debate. "I have never thought that the man of Stratford-on-Avon wrote the plays of Shakespeare," he wrote to Ogburn. "I know of no admissible evidence that he ever left England or was educated in the normal sense of the term. One must wonder, for example, how he could have written *The Merchant of Venice*." By the end of the twentieth century, the Oxfordian movement had achieved something extraordinary: three of the four US Supreme Court Justices who had expressed a view on the matter declared against Stratfordianism.

In London a descendant of Oxford's named Charles de Vere Beauclerk organized a similar trial at the Inner Temple with three lord justices presiding. Stanley Wells appeared as an expert witness. England, as usual, remained less receptive to heresy. The lords couldn't see why Oxford would take the name of a real person—a man acknowledged as an "actor manager" in the theater. Nor could they understand why no one had proposed him as the author until 1920. Orthodoxy prevailed. Nevertheless, the mere staging of the trials signaled a concession that there were legitimate grounds for doubting the traditional attribution.

The stagnant Oxfordian movement surged back to life. Beauclerk went on the lecture circuit in America, making the case for his ancestor's authorship. In 1989 PBS ran a *Frontline* documentary, "The Shakespeare Mystery." The *Atlantic* followed in 1991 with a cover story, "Looking for Shakespeare," setting the case for Oxford against the case for Shakespeare. *Harper's* magazine published its own issue in 1999. Lewis Lapham, the magazine's legendary editor, explained that he found the Oxfordian theory "congenial" because "I could more easily imagine the plays written by a courtier familiar with the gilded treacheries of Elizabethan politics than by an actor peeping through the drop curtains." And in the post-Watergate era, he added, it wasn't hard to believe in the possibility of a governmental cover-up.

Stories about Oxford and the authorship question ran in *Time*, *Life*, *Newsweek*, the *New Yorker*, the *New York Times*, and the *Washington Post*. Ogburn had succeeded in bypassing the entrenched authority of the English faculties, but he had not succeeded in swaying those faculties themselves. "Academics err in failing to acknowledge the mystery surrounding 'Shake-speare's' identity," wrote Mortimer Adler, the University of Chicago philosophy professor and encyclopedist. "They would do both liberal education and the works of 'Shake-speare' a distinguished service by opening the question to the judgment of their students, and others outside the academic realm."

In 2001 a graduate student at the University of Massachusetts Amherst became the first person to receive a PhD on the basis of an Oxfordian dissertation. (The news was splashed in the *New York Times*: "A Historic Whodunit: If Shakespeare Didn't, Who Did?") Roger Stritmatter pursued his heresy in the university's Comparative Literature Department, astutely circumventing the English Department. The contortions necessary on the part of orthodox scholars to defend the traditional attribution had resulted in a "sometimes fabulously constricted and deformed knowledge of [their] own subject," he wrote.

A crunchy-granola bohemian from the West Coast, Stritmatter is now a professor at Coppin State University, a historically black college in Baltimore. (When I met him at his home earlier that spring, he had thoughtfully laid out actual fruit-and-nut granola bars for me.) Among Oxfordians, he is a kind of hero. His Twitter profile reads, "Like almost everyone, I was born a Stratfordian. Then I studied and realized I'd been wrong." He supported Elizabeth Warren for president, and he speaks about the corruption of the Shakespeare establishment the way that Warren speaks about the corruption of the banking system: entrenched interests, a rigged game, the need to speak truth to power. "I didn't realize how dishonest they were going to be," he said, referring to the early days of his research, "but it doesn't surprise me anymore."

His dissertation examined handwritten annotations in Oxford's 1570 Geneva Bible, showing their correspondence to biblical allusions, quotations, and themes in Shakespeare's works. For example, in Oxford's Bible, an obscure phrase in 2 Samuel 21:19, describing Goliath's spear "like a weaver's beam," is underlined. In *The Merry Wives of Windsor*, Falstaff cites this verse: "I fear not Goliath with a weaver's beam."

"Who reads their Bible looking for odd details like that?" Stritmatter exclaimed to me. "Shakespeare!" Scholars agree that the Geneva Bible is the version Shakespeare used most. The *New York Times* noted that 158 verses and 10 Psalms marked in Oxford's Bible had been cited by scholars as influential on Shakespeare. And the more times Shakespeare alludes to a given verse, the greater the likelihood the same verse is marked in Oxford's Bible. Oxford marked only 13 percent of verses Shakespeare echoed just once, but 88 percent of verses Shakespeare echoed six times.

The significance of the dissertation might be measured by just how much it irritated scholars. As word of Stritmatter's research got out, his department started receiving calls and complaints. Scholars tossed out contradictory arguments in an attempt to rebut his findings. Yes, the handwriting in the Bible was Oxford's, Alan Nelson, a professor at the University of California, Berkeley, agreed, declaring himself "99 and 44/100 percent certain," but he rejected any connection to Shakespeare: "I myself do not believe in it," he wrote. (Was it a matter of belief?) No, the handwriting in the Bible was *not* Oxford's, the president of the Shakespeare Association of America insisted, ignoring the fact the cover was stamped with Oxford's heraldic badge—a blue boar—and that a bill of sale confirmed Oxford's purchase of a Geneva Bible in 1570. Professor Nelson then reversed his position, declaring that the hand *wasn't* Oxford's, despite his having been "99 and 44/100 percent certain" that it was.

"From the beginning, it was the reactions of people that interested me," said Stritmatter. "I thought, 'That's not rational.'" (Stritmatter already had a master's degree in anthropology from the New School for Social Research when he arrived at UMass Amherst, which seems to have lent an anthropological angle to his view of the authorship debate.) It was, of course, possible that some Oxford relative or descendant had made the annotations, which appeared in three different colors of ink. He had the Bible independently examined by a board-certified forensic documents analyst, who concluded that it was, indeed, "highly probable" that the handwriting was Oxford's. The words written most frequently in the margins were "almes," "poor," and "give to the poor," which aligned, Stritmatter noted, with Oxford's reckless generosity. UMass awarded Stritmatter his doctorate, and Justice Stevens wrote to congratulate him: "In time, more and more traditional scholars will be compelled to recognize the force of the evidence you have assembled in support of the Oxfordian position."

That praise, from however high a source, has been meager compensation. "I thought I was going to be homeless when I got out of graduate school," Stritmatter told me. Ostracized by other scholars, relegated to a little-known university, Stritmatter has chosen the hardest possible path in the already doomed humanities—in a field where even mainstream scholars sometimes struggle to make a living. "The authorship question is the key to reviving interest in Shakespeare and the Renaissance," he said. "This is the thing that I think they're missing and that, at some point, the smarter ones are going to start to realize."

There is something monkish in Stritmatter's stubborn commitment to the cause. His house was plain, almost spartan; his files tidily organized and labeled. He was raised by Quakers, I jotted in my notebook.

"I've had to be modest in my academic aspirations and live with marginalization, realizing that my biggest impact on scholarship will probably be posthumous," he admitted. Stritmatter has managed to publish some of his research in traditional scholarly journals (for instance, articles arguing that *The Tempest* could have been written using pre-1604 sources). He simply omits mention of Oxford, a strategy he calls a "mousetrap" approach. Overtly Oxfordian arguments are roundly rejected, consigned to places such as the *Oxfordian*, a journal published by the Shakespeare Oxford Fellowship. "The best Oxfordian scholarship has an immense heuristic value for reading and comprehending the plays," he explained. "When you join it to the best traditional scholarship, you start to see what the plays are actually *doing*."

Stritmatter insists that his heart is in Coppin State and its students. But it is hard to believe that a part of him would not have liked a more prestigious career. When I asked him why he has persevered with the authorship question all these years, he struggled to explain. "Part of the answer is that before you've studied the history, you don't know how serious the suppression has been," he wrote to me later, "so you are kind of like the frog in the pot of water. If you had known how hot it was really going to get, you would have hopped out sooner. But, then, you're not a frog in a pot of water, so you get angry that you're playing a rigged game. You start to see how the history of deception in this topic is just like the histories of deceptions in so many other topics. You see people like Delia Bacon or J. T. Looney, visionary, powerful thinkers who have been ignored or beaten to a bloody pulp by twenty-first-century 'scholars.'" He put 'scholars'" in scare quotes. He wanted justice. He cared about the "larger principle at stake": the truth. The reward for his suffering was his sense of "true intimacy" with Shakespeare; of knowing the man behind the words. "Don't underestimate the psychological value of that feeling of direct connection with the author as a compensation for what might seem like worldly sacrifice required by heresy."

The irony of Stritmatter's quest for justice—of the whole Oxfordian cause—is that if Oxford really did write the works, he did not seek recognition. The most important underlineation in Oxford's Bible, Stritmatter told me, is a verse in the Gospel of Matthew about modesty and self-effacement: "Be careful not to practice your righteousness in front of others to be seen by them. If you do, you will have no reward from your Father in heaven" (Matthew 6:1). To Stritmatter, it "explains scripturally the motive and justification for the pseudonym." So does an underlined passage in the book of Micah about the prophet sitting in darkness because he has sinned, he continued, drawing a parallel to Oxford sitting in darkness—in obscurity and anonymity—because he had sinned. "Really, the whole story is underlined or in other ways present in the Bible, which is something it has taken me years to see as clearly as I now do," he explained. "He's sitting in darkness, and his life's work has been put out under another man's name. That's what Jesus told him to do in Matthew."

But if Oxford did not seek recognition, why seek it for him?

EIGHT

Purple Robes Distained

I DO BLAME DE VERE IN many ways," said Alexander Waugh, sitting in his home in the English countryside. "He decided that he wanted to cover up his name, but he did it in such a way that the truth was always there. It has been right under our noses." Waugh is almost the complete inverse of Stritmatter: an Englishman of conservative leanings, descended from aristocrats on his mother's side and literary royalty on his father's. While Stritmatter battles in the academic trenches, Waugh stands "deliberately and happily outside of the academic thing. I'm really quite happy to step right over all those screaming, petty academics," he told me. "These bossy, boring, wrong people"—by which he meant Shakespeare scholars—"just go on and on and on, without any sense of responsibility to the truth. Personally, genuinely, I think they're such fools. I can't be bothered with them, in a way. I really don't care. To me, it's about getting the facts out. They're so obviously on the wrong side. It's just a question of time before they crumble."

Waugh is a classic in the venerable tradition of the English eccentric, with hair flying up wildly around a bald crown like an electrocuted scientist, and an impish, amused expression, as though a smirk is always twitching at the corners of his mouth. He wore khakis, a button-down shirt, and a blazer—all wrinkled and disheveled in the manner of a man too immersed in Renaissance literature to bother with appearances. If Puck, the mischief-making sprite of *A Midsummer Night's Dream*, had been allowed to grow into middle age and let loose in modern-day England, he would surely have looked like Alexander Waugh.

I first came across him on YouTube, debating the authorship question against the eminent Oxford professor Sir Jonathan Bate. "And who is this scrofulous idiot on the other side?" Waugh asked by way of introducing himself. Describing the Shakespeare professoriate as a "tight world of whipping and censorship and dogma," Waugh commended Bate for his willingness to engage in open debate. But he pulled no punches when it came to the substance of the arguments. When the professor claimed that the plays use Warwickshire dialect, an old Stratfordian argument, Waugh cited an article published in 2016 in the *Journal of Early Modern Studies*, debunking the claim. "You haven't been reading, Jonathan!" he cried, scolding the Oxford professor as if he were a lazy schoolboy. Waugh's moral indignation is matched only by his wicked, irreverent wit. Like his literary forefathers, he is a scourge of pomposity, specifically Shakespearean pomposity.

Evelyn Waugh, Alexander's grandfather, is best known today as the author of *Brideshead Revisited*, but he rose to fame in the 1930s with best-selling comic novels that ruthlessly satirized the social pretensions and follies of his contemporaries. "Nobody ever wrote a more unaffectedly elegant English," the critic Clive James remarked. "Its hundreds of years of steady development culminate in him." Evelyn Waugh was a celebrity in a time when novelists could still be celebrities—a regular subject of interest in the gossip columns, a fashionable guest at country estates, a high-profile foreign correspondent for the newspapers. His later conversion to Catholicism and utter disregard for niceties and social conventions led to a popular conception of him as an elitist snob.

"Why do you expect me to talk to this boring pig?" he would shout at his hostess about a fellow guest. "He is common, he is ignorant, and he is stupid, and he thinks Picasso is an important artist." People feared him. "He was a small man—scarcely five foot six—and only a writer, after all, but I have seen generals and chancellors of the Exchequer, six foot six and exuding self-importance from every pore, quail in front of him," his son Auberon Waugh recalled. When Evelyn Waugh died in 1966, the British novelist Graham Greene likened his death to the loss of a commanding officer, calling Waugh "the greatest novelist of my generation." His requiem mass at Westminster Cathedral, which coincided with the state opening of Parliament, was packed with members of Parliament who chose to pay their final respects to the novelist rather than sit through the Queen's speech. "It is simply that he was the funniest man of his generation," Auberon explained shortly after his father's death.

"What nobody remembers about Evelyn is that everything with him was jokes," agreed the novelist Nancy Mitford. "That's what none of the people who wrote about him seem to have taken into account at all."

Auberon Waugh took up the family profession: relentlessly teasing people who take themselves too seriously in stylish, witty prose. His format was chiefly newspaper columns, where he railed against busybodies, politicians, and anyone who told anyone else what to do. The "great English joke," he held, is that "all seriousness—personal, religious, political—is reduced to absurdity." He hated the police (especially when they tried to prevent drunk driving), insisted that the dangers of smoking were overreported, insisted that the dangers of "passive hamburger eating" were underreported, warned that computer games "produce all the symptoms and most known causes of cancer," criticized attempts to ban foxhunting, and detested Ezra Pound's "disgusting" poetry. "To anyone who gets the essential joke of life, Auberon Waugh was the greatest journalist of the 20th century," an obituarist wrote at his death in 2001.

Though he tended to be identified with conservatism, his politics were essentially "liberal anarchist," his son Alexander clarified. "Once, walking into Westminster Abbey for a memorial service, his eyes alighted on a circular traffic-style notice: a picture of an ice cream with a diagonal red line drawn through it. 'Fascists!' he said as he walked past. If he had had time, I am sure he would have doubled back to buy an ice cream and lick it noisily during the service."

Alexander Waugh is Auberon's eldest son. Though he delayed following in the family footsteps, citing an "element of intergenerational competition," he, too, became a writer: an opera critic for the London papers, a journalist in the Wavian vein, and the author of critically acclaimed books on classical music, time, God, the Wittgensteins, and, of course, the Waughs. ("I suppose, when I think of it, all of us Waughs only became writers to impress our fathers," he writes in his family autobiography.) He is also the general editor of *The Complete Works of Evelyn Waugh*, a forty-three-volume scholarly edition published by Oxford University Press, and a senior visiting fellow at the University of Leicester. His credentials make him an uncomfortable opponent for Shakespeareans. He is part of the literary establishment but undermining its foundation.

"It pisses them off big-time. I mean, fucking hell, I'm an out-and-out anti-Stratfordian," he said. "I literally waited until my contract was signed with Oxford University Press before coming out of my closet, as it were. I said, 'Right, now I'm going to tell you about Shakespeare.' It rather terrified them." Subsequently, two of the scholars working with him on *The Complete Works of Evelyn Waugh* confessed to him that they were anti-Stratfordian, too.

We were sitting in the parlor, in front of an enormous, ancient-looking inglenook fireplace. The Waughs—Alexander and his wife, Eliza (their three children are grown)—live in a seventeenth-century farmhouse, or rather three farmhouses fused into a little maze of old rooms and creaky, uneven floors, fireplaces, paintings, sagging armchairs, frayed carpets, heavy, dusty drapes, and books—books crammed into every nook, books spilling off the shelves. Full sets of Jonson, Dryden, Milton, Spenser, Shakespeare (obviously). Early Evelyn Waugh editions. Books on music, religion, philosophy, Renaissance history. For years, Waugh favored the Oxfordian theory but resisted pinning himself to Oxford, feeling that the case lacked the essential element: contemporary evidence from the time identifying Oxford as Shakespeare. Then, in 2013 he made a discovery. While studying *Polimanteia,* a book published in 1595 by a clergyman named William Covell, he noticed that "Sweet Shak-speare" had been printed as a margin note beside a sentence that included the word "Oxford" and the oddly hyphenated phrase "courte-deare-verse." The phrase, he realized, was a perfect anagram of "our-de-vere a secret." "I thought, 'Bloody hell. A secret!' I tell you, I nearly died." He went to tell Eliza, who was less intrigued. "One of the most wonderful things about her," he continued, "she's never impressed by anything. So, she said, 'Oh yeah, that's quite interesting.' I said, 'No, it's more than that! Four hundred years!' And I said, 'Now, look, can you remember what it is I've shown you?' Because I suddenly got a terrible panic that I'd drop dead, and it'd be another four hundred years until anyone found it. And she said, 'Oh, something in a book called . . .' " Waugh trailed off, laughing.

He emailed the discovery to Stanley Wells, who "wrote back very, very sniffy," according to Waugh. " 'Well, he's certainly being cryptic. I'm not claiming I understand what he's saying'—that was interesting—'but you're just playing Scrabble, really, my boy.' I said, 'Yeah, I am playing Scrabble, but God, wouldn't the Elizabethans have loved Scrabble if they had it? But no, seriously, look, you guys have had four hundred years to work out what that note means." He asked Wells for his interpretation.

" 'If you think I'm wrong, you tell me what "Sweet Shak-speare" is doing alongside "our-de-vere a secret." What purpose is it serving?' And he said, 'Well, I suspect it's a compositor error.' You know, he loves saying 'error.' And I said, 'Okay, fine. It's an error. So it's not supposed to be against that line. Can you tell me which line of all these lines "Sweet Shakspeare" is meant to be written against?' I said to him, 'Look, I've given you a resolution of this problem which makes perfect sense. You might not like it because you don't like the idea that Edward de Vere is Shakespeare. I get that. But until you can find another explanation that makes as much sense as that, I'm afraid my one is going to sit on the top of the pack.' At which point he ended the correspondence."

The technique of hiding a person's name anagrammatically was a not-uncommon Elizabethan device. Plenty of writers did it. Was Covell doing it? His strange phrase "courte-deare-verse" appeared in an essay praising the universities—Oxford, Cambridge, and the Inns of Court—and their alumni. All the authors that Covell refers to attended one of the universities. The appearance of "Shak-speare" in this context is anomalous, since the Stratford man did not attend university. No scholar has managed to explain it.

News of Waugh's discovery appeared in the *Times* and the *Sunday*

Times, rousing the hornet's nest. He was besieged by vituperative Shakespeare defenders. "Shakespeare was a nom de plume—get over it," he wrote in the *Spectator*, explaining that Covell "revealed in words not especially ambiguous by Elizabethan standards" that "Shakespeare" was the alias of the courtier poet Edward de Vere. "Now, a lot of people have been saying this for a very long time—so stale buns to that, you may think—except that no one has yet noticed that the matter was revealed in a book as long ago as 1595, so that makes it an important discovery." Waugh went back through the early Shakespeare allusions, discovering cryptic references to Oxford. "That's when the whole thing just opened up," he said. He has taken to presenting these discoveries in videos that he posts on YouTube, where he has fifteen thousand subscribers. The videos seem to be making converts. A July 2021 issue of the magazine *New English Review* ran an epigram, "On Alexander Waugh" by the American poet Jeffrey Burghauser:

Exhausted by the weight of heresies
I can't but feel reveal the Truth,
(How they have multiplied since youth!)
I now must find the space in which to squeeze
  Another one. It brings me no delight
  That Alexander Waugh is likely right.

Every time Waugh posts a video, he is deluged by responses—people sending in their comments, their decryptions, their theories and speculations. "They're in love with this subject," he said.

"Why is it, you think?"

"I think it's that tantalizing sense that there's a mystery, and it needs to be solved, and we're so near to it, and it's taking us back in history. It's escapism," he said. "The more odious one finds the modern world, the more relaxing and comforting it is just to dwell in the imagination of the 1590s."

Tackling every single Renaissance allusion to Shakespeare is a gargantuan undertaking, so for the last several years Waugh and Stritmatter have joined forces, compiling the allusions into a massive compendium, which they hope will blast apart the Stratfordian myth once and for all. They'd permitted me to read a draft of their manuscript, which they titled "The New Shakespeare Allusion Book." It is nothing less than a total overhaul of Shakespearean history. For each allusion, they provide the orthodox interpretation, followed by their Oxfordian commentary. The embedded critique is that the orthodox attempt has been deficient. "[S]ince it is openly acknowledged by orthodox scholars that many of the contemporary allusions to Shakespeare are 'cryptic,' why is so little done within this incurious community to discover what it was about him that was being secretly or covertly conveyed?" they ask. The cryptic nature of the allusions is "prima facie evidence that something about Shakespeare was prohibited from overt expression by his contemporaries."

Take the Parnassus plays, staged at Cambridge around 1600. When the character Gullio requests to hear a poem in the style of Shakespeare, Ingenioso begins reciting, "Faire Venus, queene of beutie and of love." Gullio approves, exclaiming, "Noe more! I am one that can judge according to the proverb, *bovem ex unguibus.*" Waugh and Strimatter observe that there is no proverb *bovem ex unguibus.* Gullio has altered the Latin proverb *leonem ex unguibus* ("to recognize a lion by its claws"), replacing *leonem* with *bovem*—the lion with an ox. "Scholars in the audience would have understood immediately that Gullio's reaction to the Shakespearean parody . . . implies that Gullio has recognized in these quasi Shakespearean verses the hand of the Earl of Oxford," they write. Contemporaries sometimes referred to him as "Ox," with one complaining, for example, about being confined "while Ox was grazing in the pastures."

Or take the 1595 poem about Shakespeare "deafly masking thro / Stately troupes rich conceited." The author, Thomas Edwards, goes on to describe an unnamed poet who has been "distaind" (dishonored or disgraced), whose "power floweth far," who should have been the age's "only object and the star":

Eke in purple roabes distaind,
Amid'st the Center of this clime,
I have heard say doth remaine,

One whose power floweth far,
That should have bene of our rime,
The only object and the star.

Well could his bewitching pen,
Done the Muses objects to us,
Although he differs much from men,
Tilting under Frieries,
Yet his golden art might woo us,
To have honoured him with baies.

Scholars have not identified who this poet is. Waugh and Stritmatter argue that it's Oxford—a nobleman ("in purple roabes"*) of great influence ("whose power floweth far"), but who is disgraced ("distaind"). He wields far-reaching literary power ("his bewitching pen") and should have been an icon to all poets ("should have been of our rime / the only object and the star"). The disgraced poet is eccentric ("differs much from men"), recalling Harvey's description of Oxford as "a passing singular odd man," and he is known to fight duels at the Blackfriars ("Tilting under Frieries"), where Oxford fought bloody duels.

When a second edition of the sonnets was issued in 1640, they were prefaced with a poem by John Warren praising Shakespeare as "twise liv'd" and "Virbius like." *Virbius* comes from the Latin *vir*, for "man," and *bis*, for "twice"—a twice man or double man. Every line of the fourteen-line poem contains ten syllables, except the third line, which contains only eight. Two syllables are missing:

What, lofty Shakespeare, art again reviv'd?
And Virbius like now show'st thy self twise liv'd,

---

*According to a Sumptuary Law of 1573, the only people outside the royal family who could wear purple were "dukes, marquises, and earls who may wear the same in doublets, jerkins, linings of cloaks, gowns, and hose."

Tis__ __ love that thus to thee is shown,
The labours his, the glory still thine owne.

But who does "his" refer to? Whose labor? Stanley Wells, recognizing the problem of the missing two-syllable name, inserted the surname of the publisher John Benson ("'Tis Benson's love that thus to thee is shown"), implying that Benson had undertaken all the labor of publishing the poems, while Shakespeare still retained the glory. But why would Warren bother praising the publisher's labor? Besides, if Warren intended Benson's name, why didn't he write it?

Waugh and Stritmatter suggest that "Virbius-like" provides a clue to the name that should go in the blank: the Latin *vir* puns on Vere, and the blank happens to fall on the seventeenth word of the poem, suggesting the 17th Earl of Oxford. "To the learned and attentive reader who is able to complete John Warren's opening quatrain by restoring two syllables omitted from line three and by placing 'Oxford's' as the seventeenth word, the sense of Warren's hidden message becomes immediately apparent":

What, lofty Shakespeare, art again reviv'd?
And Virbius like now show'st thy self twise liv'd,
'Tis [Oxford's] love that thus to thee is shown,
The labours his, the glory still thine owne.

Oxford undertook the labor, while William of Stratford reaped the glory, they argue. Waugh reminded me that in his *Oxford* edition of *The Complete Works*, Stanley Wells had inserted "Benson's" in the two-syllable gap, without any editorial acknowledgment that he had altered the original text. "Little ratty cheats," Waugh muttered.

At two volumes and some 1,200 pages, the manuscript is nothing if not comprehensive. It attempts an answer for nearly every objection scholars have raised to the Oxfordian theory. Why, in 1598, did the writer Francis Meres publish a book praising both Shakespeare and Oxford as "best" for comedy? Does this prove they were two different people? Did Meres not know that Oxford had begun using a pseudonym? Was he playing along with the ruse? Waugh and Stritmatter argue that he did know—and indicated as much. Meres, who believed in "heavenly arithmeticke" (or numerical order), doled out his praise in carefully balanced, symmetrical lists, comparing three Greek poets, for instance, to three Latin poets and three English poets. In his list for comedy, though, he set sixteen classical playwrights against seventeen English playwrights. Why is the symmetry off? Balance is restored, Waugh and Stritmatter argue, if you recognize that two names on the list of seventeen English playwrights—Oxford and Shakespeare—represent one person.

In 1599 the publisher William Jaggard published an anthology of poems called *The Passionate Pilgrim*, attributing them on the title page to "W. Shakespeare," though only a few are considered authentically Shakespearean. In 1612 he reissued an expanded edition, adding poems by Thomas Heywood. But Heywood protested the publication of his poems under Shakespeare's name. "I must acknowledge my lines not worthy his patronage," he wrote, adding "the Author I know [was] much offended with M.Iaggard (that altogether unknowne to him) presumed to make so bold with his name." Does this mean Shakespeare, the offended author, was alive in 1612? Waugh and Stritmatter suggest that Heywood is alluding to the author's earlier objection, in 1599, when Jaggard first used the name. In 1612, eight years after Oxford's death, Jaggard "reissued it in the knowledge that a deceased author could no longer raise an objection." If Oxford was "the Author"—they note that Heywood declines to name him—that would also explain why Heywood refers to his "patronage." William of Stratford never acted as a patron.

The manuscript continues in this fashion, turning one allusion after another into corroboration of Oxford's authorship. John Weever's 1599 epigram "Ad Gulielmum Shakespeare" ("To William Shakespeare") begins by "explicitly raising the question of attribution," they note. Weever swears that Apollo begat Shakespeare's works:

Honie-tong'd Shakespeare when I saw thine issue,
I swore Apollo got them and none other

Their rosie-tainted features clothed in tissue,
Some heaven-born goddesse said to be their mother.

That could be read merely as a compliment to Shakespeare—your works are like the fruit of the gods—except that Apollo, god of the arts and leader of the muses, was a common epithet for Oxford. "As a high-ranking leader and chief patron of poets in his age, Oxford was compared by his contemporaries to Phoebus-Apollo more than any other contemporary," they write, listing a half dozen examples: "Apollo has cultivated thy mind in the arts," Gabriel Harvey wrote of Oxford; George Chapman called him "liberal as the Sunne," Apollo also being god of the sun; John Soowthern described Oxford as Apollo; Edmund Spenser referred to Oxford as beloved of "th'Heliconian imps" (that is, the muses); and the playwright Thomas Nashe referred to a leader who "repurified Poetrie from Arts pedantisme, & . . . instructed it to speake courtly. Our Patron, our Phoebus [Apollo], our first Orpheus or quintessence of invention he is." In swearing that Apollo begat Shakespeare's issue, Weever "hints not only at Shakespeare's pseudonymity," they write, "but at Oxford as the author of Shakespeare's works."

Waugh brought out a copy of the First Folio and laid it in front of me. Flipping through the pages, he stopped at the Droeshout portrait. "Look at the bright light on the forehead and the great rays coming out from his collar," he said, pointing at the figure's bulbous forehead, which is oddly highlighted. I hadn't noticed before that the markings on his collar look like sun rays. "It's the great Phoebus-Apollo, the patron god, hiding behind the mask of a player. He's so bright that the light seems to be bursting through!" Waugh exclaimed excitedly. After the preamble warning about praise of the author's name, Ben Jonson begins his tribute on the seventeenth line, befitting the 17th Earl of Oxford. And he proceeds to describe Shakespeare as an Apollo surrounded by his muses:

And all the Muses still were in their prime,
When, like Apollo he came forth to warme
Our eares, or like a Mercury to charme!

As Apollo, Shakespeare outshines the muses: "how far thou didst our Lyly outshine, / Or sporting Kyd, or Marlowe's mighty line." "I think to contemporaries, 'Shakespeare' meant Oxford," Waugh went on, "but it very much meant Oxford as the patron, the head of the group, and he owns, if you like, this name 'Shakespeare,' but I'm not an absolute Oxford purist. I think in those plays there's other input, but he's in command of it."

Piecing together rumors and whispers from the period, Waugh has built a picture of Oxford as a sort of Titian in his studio, leading a team of writers. When Gabriel Harvey accused Nashe of "obscure lurking in basest corners," Nashe—the writer who knew about the secret "policy of plays"—responded in a pamphlet: "I lurke in no corners but converse in a house of credit as well governed as any College, where there bee more rare qualified men, and selected good Schollers than in any Noblemans house that I knowe in England. If I had committed such abominable vilanies, or were a base shifting companion, it stoode not with my Lords honour to keepe me."

Who was "my Lord," who was keeping "rare qualified men" and "selected good Schollers" in his house? It's pretty obvious, Waugh argues. Nashe dedicated his pamphlet to this mystery patron, referring to him by the pseudonym "Gentle M. William," and betraying his identity with the not-so-subtle line "Verilie, verilie all poore Schollers acknowledge you as their patron, providitore and supporter." (*Vere* means "truly" or "verily.") The patron is further described in terms that fit Oxford: as an "infinite Maecenas (patron) to learned men," a prolific poet who has lately run out of money, and who keeps three "maides" (his daughters?) under his roof.

Who else lived in this college? The poet Thomas Churchyard wrote in a letter that Oxford had promised to pay the rent for rooms—but the rent was apparently delinquent. In 1593 the playwright Thomas Kyd confessed to collaborating on plays with Christopher Marlowe for "my Lord . . . whom I have servd almost these six years, in credit until now." The playwright Thomas Dekker wrote later about the writers who were worthy to eat at the table of Apollo: "the children of Phoebus," he called them, "at the Chapell of Apollo," which included "learned Watson, industrious Kyd, ingenious Atchlow [with] Marlowe, Greene and Peele laughing to see Nashe that was but newly come to their college."

Was Oxford simply supporting these writers? Or were they collaborating on plays? Oxfordians suspect that this "college" could explain why scholars are increasingly discovering other hands in Shakespeare's plays. In 1986 Stanley Wells and a younger, rebellious American scholar named Gary Taylor defied E. K. Chambers's warning against the "disintegration" of Shakespeare by crediting coauthors in several plays based on stylistic similarities to their known works. They identified Thomas Middleton, an Oxford-educated playwright, in *Macbeth*, *Measure for Measure*, and *Timon of Athens*; George Wilkins, a pamphleteer with a criminal record, in *Pericles*; unknown writers in *Henry VI, Part 1*; and John Fletcher, a Cambridge-educated playwright, in *Henry VIII* and *Two Noble Kinsmen.* Suddenly, with the imprimatur of Oxford University Press, Shakespeare was no longer a singular author-god. The edition "repeatedly shocks its readers, and knows that it will," Taylor wrote.

Not everyone welcomed this development. A British professor named Brian Vickers was appalled. But by 2002, Vickers had published his own book, *Shakespeare, Co-Author*, acknowledging evidence of collaboration in five plays. Collaboration among playwrights was common in Renaissance England, just as collaboration among Hollywood screenwriters is common today. In 2016 Gary Taylor led a team of scholars in publishing *The New Oxford Shakespeare*, which used something called "computational stylistics"—computer-aided analysis of linguistic patterns—to discover even more writers in Shakespeare's plays: not just Middleton, Wilkins, and Fletcher, but also Marlowe, Nashe, Peele, Heywood, and Jonson. The algorithms, it claimed, could tease out individual hands in the plays. Scholars and readers have "an ethical obligation" to give these writers credit, Taylor argued in his introduction. At times, he comes astonishingly close to anti-Stratfordian claims. "Identity can be simulated, and identifications can be mistaken," he wrote, acknowledging that authors are not always identified correctly and that Shakespeare may have been "alert to the potential for fraudulent imitation of an author."

The new edition bulged with data, diagrams, and algorithms: Delta tests, Zeta tests, Iota tests—a hideous display of mathematics nauseating to the mass of happily innumerate literary scholars. "Shakespeare has now fully entered the era of Big Data," Taylor announced in a press release. The findings of *The New Oxford Shakespeare* were reported in newspapers around the world. There was particular excitement around the discovery of Marlowe's hand in Shakespeare's early *Henry VI* plays, which replaced the romantic vision of the solitary genius with another kind of romance: two geniuses working together. But for some, the edition went too far. Professor Vickers, who had been so appalled by the 1986 edition, found himself newly appalled and called for the creation of a Committee for the Protection of Shakespeare's Text.

"We predict Vickers will get over this new shock as he did the last one," Taylor and company replied. Some scholars dispute the legitimacy of the algorithms. Can they really tell the difference, for example, between Marlowe's hand and Shakespeare experimenting in Marlowe's style—imitating him, parodying him, perhaps, or merely being influenced by him? Others see Nashe's hand or Kyd's instead of Marlowe's. The dispute betrays an extraordinary cognitive dissonance. While scholars insist there is no authorship debate, they engage in their own authorship debate, squabbling about the minor contributions of coauthors while studiously avoiding the issue of the central author. Are they deflecting it or inching toward it? Will disintegrating Shakespeare save Shakespeare? Or will it lead, in the end, to his fall?

In Waugh's view, the discovery of these other hands inadvertently supports the Oxfordian theory. Many of these writers were—in his reconstruction of events—part of Oxford's circle. As Oxford ran out of money, he argues, the circle collapsed, and the writers scattered. "I am quite undone through promisse breach. . . . One drone should not have driven so many bees from their honeycombs," Thomas Nashe wrote, complaining that he was "in most forsaken extremities." George Peele was driven "to extreme shifts" for a living. John Lyly described himself as a "miserable example of misfortune," comparing himself to one that can "only live on dead hopes." Marlowe was arrested for counterfeiting money. Robert Greene died in poverty, issuing in the last year of his life the famous warning to playwrights not to trust an "upstart crow." They were looking for a new patron, Waugh argues, and Greene warned them not to trust Edward Alleyn.

"It makes total sense," Waugh said. He thinks the anonymous quartos that started appearing were the work of Oxford's collapsed studio. "It's as though someone goes out with a handful of sheaves of different plays under their arm, and they start saying, 'Well, look, we've got these *Henry VI* plays.'" Based on the sudden issuing of "corrected" and "amended" versions, Waugh suspects Oxford was not happy. "I think he was trying to sweep up what was a mess. We hear quite a lot about these corrupted versions. (In the First Folio, Heminges and Condell refer to "diverse stolne, and surreptitious copies.") "A bastard version of *Hamlet* went out. Oxford was furious and quite quickly put out another version. Same with *Romeo and Juliet*."

"So you don't think he was behind the publication of some of the early quartos?" I asked.

"I suspect he wasn't. Because they were followed by a better version quite quickly. We don't know. It's a lot of speculation. To try and make sense of the data we have—that's the way I would make sense of it."

I realized Waugh was reconstructing an alternate history to rival the histories of the Shakespearean biographers. In allusions, marginalia, pamphlets, and letters, he had unearthed another structure that could sustain the meaning we provide for it. The structure depended on psychological insight—on storytelling—as much as it did on literary analysis. Was it the right structure? The right meaning? After the circle collapsed, Waugh thinks Oxford spent the last decade of his life revising the plays alone until he died, and others finished the work he'd left undone. Scholars generally see coauthors at the very beginning of Shakespeare's career and then again at the end. Parts of *Macbeth*, for instance, resemble Thomas Middleton's play *The Witch*, suggesting that Middleton revised the play.

"Some Stratfordians say, 'Oooh, that means Shakespeare sat down with Middleton.' Nonsense, no evidence for that," said Waugh. "I would say he kitted the play out in Jacobean times and added some of his script to it after Oxford's death. What they've singularly failed to prove these people, the Stratfordians," he went on, "is that any of those writers—Wilkins, Middleton—ever met or had anything to do with Stratford Shakspere."

"What is your conception of the relationship between Stratford-

Shakspere and Oxford?" I asked. One of the missing bits in the Oxfordian theory—a crucial missing bit—is the nature of their connection.

"That is the six-million-dollar question, isn't it? Of course, the one bit you'd really like to know that you don't know." He ventured that perhaps they bumped into each other through the theater. The Stratford man was "a wheeler-dealer," said Waugh. Given his involvement with theater and investing, "I think it's inconceivable he wouldn't have come across the Earl of Oxford at some point, wouldn't you? I wouldn't be surprised if Oxford borrowed money off him from time to time. Who knows." He sees a trace of their connection in places such as Sonnet 81, about "your name" living forever. "I believe Sonnet 81 is written to William Shakespeare," he said. The only name made famous by the sonnets is, in fact, "Shakespeare":

Your name from hence immortal life shall have,
Though I, once gone, to all the world must die:
The earth can yield me but a common grave,
When you entombed in men's eyes shall lie.

The conversation unfurled that afternoon from one room to another, a feverish, unending elaboration of this counter-history. Waugh leapt around the house, pulling books from shelves to show me an image or an obscure bit of text. He paused to give thoughtful answers to my most skeptical questions. I began to feel that maybe the heretics were the true keepers of the Shakespearean tradition.

"There's nothing I can't answer with confidence," he said. "But then I'll tell you, I'm now going to have to speculate. So, you know the question which always, always comes up: Well, why did he want to keep his name a secret? I can't answer that. But I can give you my theories." Waugh talked about the scandals around Oxford and the stigma associated with an aristocrat selling plays to the general public. "Never would he or anyone else say, '*Hamlet* by the Earl of Oxford.' That would never, never happen." Plus, Waugh continued, the plays contain allusions to "everything from his bankruptcy, to his affairs, to his illegitimate children, which ties in to why his name didn't come out even after his death." Oxford's descendants, who were "pretty powerful people," must have been eager to distance themselves from his scandals, restore honor to the family name, and avoid association with playwriting.

"Why would he be airing that stuff in public?" I asked. What kind of writer would choose to dramatize his appalling bankruptcy or failed marriage on the stage?

"Because his favorite poet was Ovid, and Ovid confesses his life through his works, and that is precisely what Shakespeare does," said Waugh. "His works are not only his gift to mankind but his atonement of his own sins." Once you understand that, he insisted, you realize "what an absolutely beautiful story this is."

According to Stratfordian tradition, Shakespeare wrote plays to make money. But in the Oxfordian reconstruction, the plays were sacramental: writing as confession, atonement, redemption.

⁂

Over lunch, Waugh continued laying out his theory. It would be the easiest way to bring all the anti-Stratfordians together, he suggested, "because, yes, there was a group, and that group could well have included Bacon, it could have had Mary Sidney in it—I don't see why it shouldn't—and Marlowe is certainly in it. So, they're all right, to that extent. But I think what's so difficult," he continued, "is to deny now, with the evidence we have now, that the name Shakespeare was connected to Oxford. It really was. There's just no way out of it now."

Eliza had laid the table with venison, courgettes, omelet, sausages, and salad.

"You must be tired of Shakespeare, Shakespeare, Shakespeare, all the time," I commented to her.

"Well, I like it when everyone is enthusiastic," she said, "particularly Alexander."

"Yes, I am very enthusiastic about it," he said. "It can't be denied."

"He can't be denied!" She laughed.

"And the reason being that one keeps finding new stuff. I remember ages ago, when I started on this trail, I thought, 'What's the point? You're not going to find anything new.' People have squabbled about this for—but amazing new things are being found; I think greatly helped by the computer, of course, and the fact that we can all look at original source material rather than have to be a professor to get access."

One of the things Oxfordians like to find are anagrams. They find "ever"—an anagram of "Vere"—threaded through the Shakespeare mystery. In the sonnets, for instance: "every word doth almost tell my name, / Showing their birth, and where they did proceed." But is de Vere concealing his name in "*every* word"? Or is it a fantastical vision, a religious sign picked out by those who want to see it, like an imprint of the Virgin Mary in a piece of toast? There is some evidence that writers used "ever" to refer to de Vere. A manuscript containing one of his early poems describes the poem as "the best verse that ever th'author made," wittily playing on "ever" as an anagram of "Vere." It crops up again in a strange epistle prefacing Shakespeare's *Troilus and Cressida*: "A never writer, to an ever reader. Newes." What does that mean? Waugh and Roger Stritmatter suggest this may be read as "an E.Ver writer to an "E.Ver reader"—a note from Oxford to readers before his death.

They see other poets anagramming the name, too. In 1638 William Davenant, who succeeded Jonson as poet laureate, published an ode "In Remembrance of Master William Shakespeare," warning poets not to "tread the Banks of Avon." Instead, "reach the Map; and looke if you a River there can spie," Davenant recommends. The reading turns on "River" ("our Vere" or "R-ver"): "Davenant invites the reader to spot 'our Vere' in 'a River' " write Waugh and Stritmatter. "And for a River your mock'd Eie, will find a shallow Brooke," Davenant concludes. A few miles northeast of Stratford, on the banks of the Avon, was the home of Fulke Greville, Lord Brooke, an inferior, shallow poet. Those who go to Warwickshire in remembrance of Shakespeare will be "mock'd," for they will not find our Vere but only a shallow Brooke.

"There is a prejudice against anagrams," observes the scholar

Christopher Ricks, noting that today they're easily derided and dismissed. In the Renaissance, however, anagrams were seen as being "a true assistance to art," he writes. Anagrams were viewed as a kind of verbal alchemy—the dissolution of a word into its elements and the reconstitution of those elements into a new word, which would cast light on a divine truth hidden within the original name or phrase. It was seen as providential, for example, that Pontius Pilate's question to Christ, "*Quid est veritas*?" ("What is truth?"), is also an anagram of Christ's response, "*Est vir qui adest*." ("It is me.") The answer was contained in the query. Courtiers honored Elizabeth I with Latin anagrams of her name: *Elissabet Anglorum Regina* (Elizabeth Queen of the English) became *Multa regnabis ense gloria* (By thy sword shalt thou reign in great renown). Her successor, James Stuart, was frequently rendered as "A just master." The lawyer Thomas Egerton was honored through the anagram *gestat honorem* (he carries honor). But anagrams could be created to insult as well as to honor. When the Countess of Somerset, Frances Carr (née Howard), was found guilty of murdering Sir Thomas Overbury by sneaking arsenic into his jellies and tarts, she was anagrammed as "Car findes a whore" (from her maiden name, Francis Howard, with the *e*'s not counting). It was, as Ricks writes, "the heyday of the anagram."

Across the channel, François Rabelais published his first book in 1532 under the anagrammatic pseudonym "Alcrofribas Nasier." King Louis XIII hired a royal anagrammatist, compensated for his wordplay at a salary of 1,200 livres. The reformer John Calvin, who published under various pseudonyms, sometimes used "Alcuinus," an anagram of "Calvinus" (where $v = u$). Meanwhile, scientists transposed their discoveries into Latin anagrams to lay claim to them before they were published. Galileo turned a phrase announcing his discovery of the rings of Saturn in 1610, *Altissimum planetam tergeminum observavi* (I have observed the most distant planet to have a triple form), into the ridiculous term *smaismrmilmepoetaleumibunenugttauiras*. Robert Hooke was rather more concise. He published Hooke's law, *Ut tensio, sic vis* (as the extension, so the force), as *Ceiiinosssttuv*.

Anagrams became such a fad in the Renaissance that scholars tried to set down rules to regulate anagram formation. William Camden, Jonson's tutor, devoted nine pages to the elucidation of anagrams, including forty-seven examples in four languages, terming the anagram "the only Quintessence that hitherto the Alchymy of wit could draw out of names," a skill that "the French exceedingly admire," and affirming that "names are divine notes, and divine notes to notifie future events; so that events consequently must lurk in names, which can only be pryed into by this mystery." Camden derided those who did not take anagrams seriously as the "sour sort." If we dismiss anagrams, do we risk being the "sour sort"? But then how to recognize intended anagrams from imagined ones, real signs from hallucinations?

"One has to be a little bit careful with the evers, as fun as they are," Waugh admitted. "Have I just found Oxford's name here because I want to find Oxford's name here?" It was true. "The name 'Vere' is a bit easy. I've seen Oxfordians tripping on this. 'Oh look, it says "ever" there, it says "ever" there!' Yeah, yeah, calm down." He laughed.

"Every word doth almost tell my name," I repeated the sonnet line.

"That's more than just the word *ever*. If you say, 'Every *word* doth almost tell my name,' then I think you better start looking at all the words!" he exclaimed. Stratfordians sourly dismiss the notion that "ever" might signify "Vere," but they play the same game, claiming that a line in Sonnet 145 puns on the surname of Anne Hathaway: " 'I hate,' from hate away she threw, / And saved my life, saying 'not you.' "

The difficulty of Waugh and Stritmatter's analysis is that it involves a degree of decryption, bringing back memories of the doomed Baconian ciphers, inviting ridicule that could throw the Oxfordian cause into further disrepute. If other writers thought Oxford wrote the works, why didn't they just say so, I pressed Waugh.

"I think they weren't allowed to say outright, simple as that," he said. Oxford was a high-ranking nobleman. To name him as the author of plays would have been libelous. "Nobility and men of mark" were regarded as "the flowers that stand about the Prince's Crown garnishing and giving grace to it," according to records of the Court of Star Chamber, so "to deface any one of them is an open injury to the Crown itself."

Despite his claim that he "can't be bothered" with Stratfordians, Waugh has tried to engage with them. But their interactions have quickly devolved. During their debate, Jonathan Bate suggested that all Waughs "love an aristocrat," insinuating that Alexander's arguments were rooted in snobbery. Stanley Wells has simply refused Waugh's proposals to debate.

"He was very rude to me on one occasion. He said, 'I have no respect for your low grade of scholarship.' I said, 'Look, Stanley, as you know very well, I have no respect for *your* grade of scholarship, so that's not going to help us advance, saying things like that. Why don't we do a debate together?' And he said, 'I can't cause I'd get too angry.'" Waugh chuckled. In a show of good faith, he tried to arrange a lunch with Paul Edmondson, the Birthplace's head of knowledge. "He's the one who writes things saying that anti-Stratfordians are like boils and pustules," said Waugh. "I felt there's a nasty, rancorous atmosphere, and, frankly, is it necessary?" But according to Waugh, Edmondson refused to meet. Ditto James Shapiro, who has turned down all invitations to participate in literary festivals and radio interviews where Waugh is present, which is not entirely surprising. After Shapiro published *The Year of Lear: Shakespeare in 1606*, which argued that Shakespeare wrote several plays in 1606, after Oxford had died, Waugh and two other Oxfordians published *Contested Year: Errors, Omissions and Unsupported Statements in James Shapiro's "The Year of Lear,"* accusing Shapiro of assorted blunders.

Eliza was an old hand at authorship clashes, familiar with all the main characters, the ins and outs of the arguments, the bits of evidence and counterevidence, and she chimed in, alternately laughing and shaking her head.

"I'll tell you an opinion of Jonathan Bate's that I got from his wife," Waugh went on. He happens to be friends with Bate's wife, Paula Byrne, who wrote a best-selling book on Evelyn Waugh. "He said to his wife, 'When Stanley Wells dies, there will be a huge shift.'"

I raised my eyebrows skeptically.

"Whether that means a shift to believing that Oxford wrote it or something else, but just a shift in attitude to the whole thing. I think it's already moving a bit. Maybe they'll open up and talk about it. When

Stanley Wells pops his clogs . . . I don't know why they've got so much for him, the old fuddy-duddy."

After lunch, Waugh suggested a walk so that I could see the surrounding countryside. We set off, the three of us, down a dirt path, over a fence, and into the fields, Waugh leading the way. It was a hot, clear day, and the open view over the Somerset hills was quaint and charming and very English. Waugh pointed to some spot in the distance where Coleridge had written and Wordsworth had visited, but we quickly reverted to Shakespeare. I mentioned the popular argument that it doesn't matter who wrote the plays.

"Then none of history matters!" Waugh bellowed into the countryside. He was walking in front of me, Eliza behind me. The grasses were waist-high, and I realized how ridiculous we must have looked, this odd threesome wading single file through the fields, shouting about Shakespeare. "And anyway—"

Waugh turned around to face me. His forehead was sweating, and his shirt had come untucked. "If they don't *care* about it, then they should stop *hogging* the subject!" He stomped his foot. "Scholars are supposed to get to the truth! That's what they're paid for. I'm not even paid for it!" He caught his breath and carried on. "They don't want to go where truth might be flickering. That's the bit that worries me. Because I would have thought truth is like a kind of magnet, and, wherever it is, you're pulled toward it. But to just sit and ignore it—it's incomprehensible to me."

As we rambled farther into the countryside, Waugh launched into a story about a party where he found himself in conversation with a woman from Stratford-upon-Avon. After some minutes of jolly chatting, she asked his name. "I said, 'Alexander Waugh.' And she said, 'Not *the* Alexander Waugh.' I said, 'Oh, I don't know what that means, but I'm Alexander Waugh.'

"She said, 'Oh, shit, I live in Stratford-upon-Avon! Your name is absolutely—if anyone knew I'd been talking to you, they'd be furious.' And I said, 'Well, okay . . . I'm so sorry that the most appalling thing you've ever done is speak to me.' She suddenly was almost sort of shaken. I think I've really pissed them off. But it's high time, you know," said Waugh. "C'mon, you've spent a life talking bollocks! You've all got it totally wrong!"

He laughed. "Anyway, so be it. But I'm sure they kind of all know. They all know. And you can tell by the way they debate it, when they do debate it, so high-octane emotion and very low facts. They're scared, these Stratfordians. They're terrified. They don't want to find anything that doesn't allow them to just continue in their wealthy mist of mythology." It wasn't just their faith they feared losing, he suggested, but also their status. "It's a sense that they are personally ashamed and personally threatened because of their livelihoods and the respect that other people show them for their opinions. Nobody really gets cross about anything, really, nobody loses their temper much, unless they sense that they're on weak ground. You know, if they were that confident, there'd be absolutely no need to be rude and abusive and silly. Every one of their reactions is a sign that they know they're on weak ground."

We were parched and sweaty by the time we got back to the house. Waugh went to lie down, and I was left to my own devices. I felt slightly giddy to be roaming freely. When are journalists ever left on their own in a subject's home? I took out my notebook and wandered through the rooms. There was a print of Edward de Vere above one of the staircases (a gift from his son, Waugh told me later), a bust of Evelyn Waugh in a room they called the Long Room, and, along the rafters, a delicate, decorative painting of images from *Venus and Adonis*: the flower, the boar. I recognized another strange beast, too: the mythological calygreyhound, which adorns the First Folio, part of the decorative headpiece just above the catalogue of plays. The calygreyhound also features in the Vere coat of arms and in carvings above a door at Hedingham Castle. In their book, Waugh and Stritmatter quote a heraldist, who noted that the creature was "quite unknown in the heraldic menagerie" outside of its use by the earls of Oxford. It was used on linens of the 14th Earl of Oxford and on the tombstone of the 15th. Edward de Vere used calygreyhounds as supporters on his family arms, prepared at the time of his marriage to Anne Cecil. What were they doing in Shakespeare's First Folio?

I examined Waugh's bookshelves. All the major Stratfordian books were there. E. K. Chambers's four-volume set on *The Elizabethan Stage.* Schoenbaum's books. Shapiro's books. Bate's books. If Stratfordians weren't reading Waugh, he was certainly reading them. I pulled down a copy of *Contested Will,* in which Shapiro had attacked Oxfordians by attacking the originator of the Oxfordian theory. J. T. Looney was, in Shapiro's telling, a deeply conservative reactionary who despised democracy and seized on an aristocratic author who embodied his antidemocratic values. Thus, anyone who embraced Oxford must also harbor antidemocratic values. To be Oxfordian was to be *a bad person.*

The argument was a bit desperate. Looney's political beliefs, whatever they were, are irrelevant to the evidence for Oxford's authorship; the evidence stands or falls on its own merits. And Looney never said he despised democracy. Shapiro seized on and twisted a few of Looney's letters to arrive at this characterization. During World War II, for instance, Looney suggested that the war was less a struggle between democracy and dictatorship than one "between the human soul and elemental brute force." Shapiro saw this as evidence that Looney opposed democracy, but Looney's point seems to have been that even democracy can threaten liberty. ("'Majority rule' might be as tyrannically repressive of spiritual liberty as any other form of government," he wrote, no doubt recalling that Hitler rose to power in 1933 through democratic elections.) Shapiro further suggested that Looney was anti-Semitic, but when Freud arrived in London in 1938, Looney sent him a letter of welcome, writing that he was "shocked at the inhuman treatment being meted out" to Jews, was "in sympathy with the whole of your people," and felt "indignation at the persecution." Shapiro was clearly aware of the letter. He refers to it in his book. But he conveniently omitted these lines, preferring to paint Looney as a crypto-fascist.

It was a smear campaign disguised as scholarship and a distraction from the actual arguments of the Oxfordian case. And it made little sense. Did Shapiro think William of Stratford embodied democratic values? His involvement in land enclosure in Stratford—a process that deprived peasants of their rights to access common land—didn't look particularly democratic. Were Shakespeare scholars democratic? The originators of the discipline were racist, classist, and sexist, bent on suppressing social unrest and upholding Shakespeare as proof of Anglo-Saxon superiority. Silly as all the bickering was between the scholars and the heretics, I understood why the heretics got upset: they felt that the scholars played dirty—and because they had endowed chairs at prestigious universities, they got away with it.

I pulled down Waugh's copy of another famously anti-Oxford book, *Monstrous Adversary: The Life of Edward de Vere, 17th Earl of Oxford* (2003) by Alan Nelson, the professor at Berkeley who had reversed himself on the issue of the handwriting in Oxford's Bible. Nelson had apparently taken the Oxfordian threat very seriously. While most biographers pursue their subjects out of love or admiration, Nelson had written a 548-page biography of Oxford fueled by undisguised enmity. The book painted Oxford in the most despicable light. Treating the libels against him by his Catholic former allies as documentary fact rather than wild, unsubstantiated slanders, Nelson made Oxford out to be a murderer, misogynist, deadbeat dad, pedophile, spendthrift, and syphilitic philanderer. The chapters had titles such as "Necromancer" and "Sodomite." Even the book's title, *Monstrous Adversary*, was taken from one of the attacks ("my monstrous adversary . . . who would drink my blood rather than wine"). The implicit argument was that such a degenerate could not possibly have written Shakespeare.

For good measure, Nelson added that Oxford's youthful verse was "atrocious" and "numblingly repetitive," marked by an "egocentric, crybaby attitude." Though early scholars praised Oxford's poetry, since the rise of the Oxfordian theory, it had become popular to denigrate it.

Nelson's choice of title was revealing. Oxford may have been the Catholics' "monstrous adversary" in the sixteenth century, but he had become Nelson's monstrous adversary by the twenty-first.

Waugh had marked up his copy with heavy underlinings and marginal notes. "Twat!" was scrawled next to one paragraph. "Rubbish—No!" by another. Refreshed from his nap, Waugh wandered into the room and spotted Nelson's book in my hands.

"He's the biggest dickhead who ever lived," he spat.

I asked him to elaborate.

"Everything he does, Nelson puts a vicious motivation on it," said Waugh. "I mean, even trying to say in military terms he was a coward. I mean, that's just really below the belt and nonsense. He wanted a dangerous position in the Armada." Waugh turned to a chapter in which Nelson quoted only a few lines from the Queen's letter commending Oxford to foreign heads of state. "The minute I saw that, I said, 'Where's the rest of the letter?' " Waugh went to the Cambridge University archives and dug out the full text, in which the Queen lavishes praise on Oxford's intellect and virtue. Nelson had cut it. He also left out the references to Oxford's work existing under other people's names. "How can he ignore that, writing a whole biography on the Earl of Oxford?" Waugh demanded. "We know how. It was just absolutely not what he wanted to say.

"The funniest thing is this chapter on Edward de Vere's bad Latin. It's hysterical." Waugh flipped the pages. Nelson had tried to show that Oxford was not well versed in Latin, but Waugh had gone through all the examples and discovered that it was Nelson who was making Latin errors. "Doesn't know what he's talking about." Waugh shook his head.

Nelson seemed almost to hate Oxford, I observed.

"Oh yes, they hate him. He's shattered their dreams because he's not the Shakespeare they thought. But it's a very comical situation because Oxford was self-effacing. He wrote himself out of it. Now he's on the rise, and Nelson's trying to tear him down."

To Waugh, Oxford was a victim, maligned in his own lifetime and maligned again in his death. If Nelson hated Oxford, Waugh loved him, grew defensive of him, felt he had been misunderstood, as his grandfather had been misunderstood. His studies of Evelyn Waugh and Ludwig Wittgenstein had formed his conception of the character of genius. "All three were extraordinarily tricky people; that's the one most obvious characteristic trait. All three had a very wide circle of very loyal friends and, equally, a large circle of quite vicious enemies," he said. "I suspect geniuses—I know this of Waugh and Wittgenstein—they suffer acutely from boredom, from impatience, so that's partly why they can be quite tricky. And all three of them were unquestionably artists striving for truth, so they can be quite rude and abrasive if they find dissembling or bullshitting." He told the story about Evelyn yelling at his host when he was sat next to someone boring at dinner. "If everybody did that, the world would be an intolerable place. But if nobody did that, I think it would be a far less exciting and interesting place."

Waugh went on recalling his grandfather's eccentricities. "He was at an embassy once, and the Danish ambassador was standing very close to him, with his face very, very close and talking very earnestly, and Evelyn said, 'Look, if you're going to kiss me, would you do it quickly and get it over and done with?' "

There was coffee that afternoon to pick us up, then more wine to keep us going. Waugh pulled me into his study to show me his most treasured book: a first edition of *Cardanus Comforte*—Hamlet's book, prefaced with a letter by Oxford and published by his "commandment" in 1573. He had stumbled across it while browsing an auction catalogue for Evelyn Waugh's letters. "I said to myself, 'I've simply got to buy this. I mean, I've simply got to.' Hamlet's book! I think its valuation was something like £2,500, but I was panicking, and I was prepared to pay a lot." In the course of bidding for the book, he accidentally also acquired two paintings of Alexander Pope. "I said, 'Eliza, you're going to kill me. I just bought two pictures of Alexander Pope by mistake. All I can say is, I got them way under estimate.' " The Popes watch over Waugh's desk from which he produces his YouTube videos, disseminating the Oxfordian truth to the far corners of the globe.

"That's a little sketch by Arthur Waugh," he said, seeing me staring at a drawing by his great-grandfather. In the early twentieth century, Arthur Waugh (Evelyn's father) ran the publishing house Chapman & Hall, which published Dickens, Anthony Trollope, William Makepeace Thackeray, and, incidentally, some essays by J. T. Looney. "Those are just some silly people," he said, waving at a group of paintings. "That's a satire by Evelyn Waugh." Throughout the house, Evelyn Waugh paraphernalia vied with Edward de Vere paraphernalia. Were his father or grandfather Oxfordians? They never made any public statement to that effect.

"Of course, they were aware of the authorship question," he reflected.

"I remember once at table it coming up, and my father was about to give an answer, which I probably would have found quite interesting. But my mother interrupted, 'Ah that's absolute rubbish.' " Waugh's mother, the novelist and translator Lady Teresa Waugh, deeply disapproves of his Oxfordian activities. "She said to me, 'I don't care who Shakespeare is so long as he's not an earl!' I said, 'What do you mean? Your *father* was an earl! What's so evil about earls that they can't be good at writing?' "

As soon as some people hear "earl," they start "writhing a bit," he continued. "But I think that earls are very different things nowadays to what they were then, in the sense that an earl had an absolute, rigid, inborn duty. He felt he owed all his privilege to the state and had to work for the commonwealth and the good of Crown and country."

I asked what was happening with his book. Had they found a publisher?

"That's a very funny story, too," Waugh began. He had shown a draft to Oxford University Press, where he sits on the board of the Evelyn Waugh edition. "I said to the commissioning editor there, 'Jacqueline, I'm going to send you a book I've written, and guess what?' She said, 'What?' I said, 'You're not going to publish it. Doesn't matter. You come to stay in my house. You know I'm a scholar you revere and like, and I think it would just be impolite not to send it to you. But you're going to turn it down, so all I'm asking you is two things: Can you turn it down quite quickly and not sit on it for ages? And can you write me a couple of pages on why you're turning it down?'

"She went bright red. She said, 'What are you talking about? What do you mean? Why do you want it?' She was so frightened," he said, snickering. "And I said, 'Well, I want it because it's a part of the history. Because, to me, it's completely fascinating that an enormous scholarly publishing empire like Oxford University Press is too scared to deal with what is essentially the biggest scholarly controversy of our times concerning William Shakespeare. I think it's just absolutely fascinating that you're too scared to deal with it, and I want to hear in your own words. Obviously, you're not going to say, "We're scared." You're going to try to say my book's rubbish. I'd love to see how you do it because obviously I've put a lot of effort into making sure it's correct and isn't rubbish. Anyway, I can't wait.'" Oxford University Press sent it off to a scholar to be reviewed, as is the customary practice, and Waugh and Stritmatter received a letter roundly rejecting their manuscript. "I'd love you to quote my letter."

"You want me to quote your rejection letter?"

"It's hysterical," he said. "One pathetic page saying sort of stupid things like the book is anti-Semitic."

"What? Why?"

"Because it uses the phrase 'orthodox scholars.'"

I read the letter. It began by acknowledging that "a great deal of work has gone into this volume" and admiring the "sheer effort" of its authors—before continuing into the predictable dismissal. "I'm afraid in no circumstances can I recommend publication." The reviewer bemoaned their "wilful distortions of the evidence," and noted that anti-Stratfordian arguments have "long been analysed and dismissed as eccentric . . . by scholars from Schoenbaum to Shapiro to Wells." So that was that. It ended, indeed, by taking issue with the term *orthodox* and warning darkly of the "long association" between anti-Stratfordianism and anti-Semitism—an association that doesn't exist. There was the anti-Semitic German who published a book in 1907 and a right-wing columnist named Joseph Sobran, who was fired from the *National Review* in the 1990s amid charges of anti-Semitism, but they were hardly representative. It was the old trick of seizing on a couple of outliers and pretending they stood for the whole movement—pathologizing the heretics instead of addressing the substance of their arguments. Not to mention that the word *orthodox*, in the sense of "traditional," is widely used by historians to distinguish between traditional and nontraditional interpretations of history. "They're supposed to publish the *Oxford English Dictionary*!" Waugh cried. "If they don't know what *orthodox* means, that's pathetic."

Waugh shared the letter with Jewish members of the Oxfordian movement and took great pleasure in reporting back to Oxford University Press that they were "absolutely furious." He laughed and went on lambasting the peer-review system. "They say things like, 'There's no particular reason why we should believe your theory because it's never been properly published in a peer-reviewed journal.' Yeah, well, that's because they won't let us! So it's a circular argument!"

Next up was Harvard University Press. Waugh lunched with the director, George Andreou, performing the same song and dance. "'The book is really, really interesting,'" he told Andreou, "'but you're not going to publish it.' And he said, 'Well, I hope you'll send it to me.' And I said, 'No, there's no point. You're not going to publish it.' And he said, 'I will!' And I said, 'You won't!'" Andreou begged. Waugh sent it. Then: silence.

Waugh's literary agents, from the prestigious Wylie Agency, bumped into Andreou at the London Book Fair and reported back that the director "spoke with great admiration of what you have achieved in *The New Shakespeare Allusion Book.* However, he regrets that he does not feel able to take things forward at Harvard. There would be opposition from the syndics, and to fight them he would require either a more established tenure at the house [he is still new] or the support of a major Shakespeare authority."

The agents also shared the manuscript with an editor at Bloomsbury Publishing, who remarked that "aristocracy has never produced genius (apart from arguably Rochester), so the Earl of Oxford is wildly unlikely to have produced this work, and the really great scholars are not interested in anything but the greatness of the texts, which is all I am interested in, and feel is all we should all be interested in." Waugh could not resist responding. "Surely you have heard of Ronsard, Byron, Tolstoy, Leopardi, Turgenev, Montaigne, Tasso, Toulouse Lautrec, Pushkin, Francis Bacon, Philip Sidney etc., etc.?" he wrote, listing aristocrats of genius. The Bloomsbury editor conceded his point but maintained that "Shakespeare is too dear to my heart to be kidnapped by someone else."

Waugh laughed gleefully at the entire debacle. He wasn't angry or disheartened that a two-volume, 1,200-page book to which he had devoted several years of his life was being rejected. He was amused. He had taken, I realized, the long view—that this would only make the eventual, inevitable triumph of Oxfordians more brilliant, the cowardly, close-minded obstinacy of the Stratfordians more pathetic, and the whole thing a better story, a better struggle. That's why he brandished the rejection letters like badges of honor. They were part of the history, which would one day be written, of this strange, protracted war for the truth about the god of English literature.

And the truth, Waugh is certain, will triumph. He spoke with admiration of the writers who had planted the clues to that truth—"those people, those amazing people" whom he saw as "planting an oak tree. . . . They'll never see it in their lifetimes, but they've planted the truth," he said. "I have this belief as firmly as they did, that truth is impossible to hide now. I just think you can't hide it. Well, you can, but truth will always come out in the end."

Did he think they planted it *for* some purpose? I asked. Why not come out with it earlier?

"Well, I have thought about this quite a lot," he said, sighing, "and I don't think they buried the truth *for* it to be uncovered. I think that they buried the truth because they couldn't go to their graves knowing that they had told a whopping great lie. So that's why they buried it. But at the same time, they had this almost mythological belief that time would uncover it. And I don't think it mattered a fig to them whether it was uncovered in twenty years or a hundred years or a thousand years. They just believed that time would uncover the truth—this total belief that truth can never be hid forever. Shakespeare himself said it." *Time's glory is to calm contending kings, to unmask falsehood, and bring truth to light.*

Waugh and Stritmatter plan to try a few other publishers. If those fail, they will self-publish. An anonymous investor has contributed $50,000 to their endeavor. "We're going to send copies to all these brutes—and to all the university libraries," he said.

"But Stratfordians aren't going to respond," I replied.

"I don't care. I really don't care. It's a weird thing. I just want to slightly annoy them. Because I know—I'm absolutely certain—that a lot of them are *tortured* about this. But they can't admit that they've totally ballsed it up, really, really badly."

⁂

I had been holding back one question in particular, which I knew Waugh would not like. No one seems to have noticed it—and he certainly wasn't advertising it—but I was pretty sure that Waugh was descended from

Oxford, not through the literary men of the Waugh line but through his grandmother Laura Herbert, who had married Evelyn Waugh. Herbert is a conspicuous name in English history. Mary Sidney Herbert, the Countess of Pembroke, had two sons, William and Philip Herbert, the dedicatees of the First Folio, the latter of whom married Susan Vere, Oxford's youngest daughter. If my reading of family lineages was correct, Waugh was descended from that line—from Oxford through Philip Herbert and Susan Vere. Was it just a coincidence that a descendant of Oxford had become Britain's leading Oxfordian? I decided at dinner that it was time to bring it up.

"Wasn't your grandmother Laura Herbert?" I asked. He looked at me, and I could see he knew what I was getting at. "You don't want this public, do you?"

"No, because I know the Stratfordians will be so pathetic!" he cried. They would use it to claim that he was merely advocating for his ancestor; that his research was distorted by a desire to claim Shakespeare for his own. But Oxford wasn't the only candidate in Waugh's ancestry. "Francis Bacon is a great-uncle of mine," he said. "I'm directly descended from Mary Sidney, obviously. And I'm directly descended from Henry Neville. So I've got a choice, okay?"

I laughed, taken aback. His defense against my insinuation that he might have a familial bias for Oxford was that he was also related to several of the other candidates. How strange—or, how perfectly, incestuously aristocratic. Despite his enthusiasm for nearly everything to do with the authorship question, he seemed only mildly amused by these connections. He wasn't interested in blood. "I could happily be rude about my grandfather or my parents or anybody," he assured me. "It's not a sort of mad loyalty."

As I watched him over dinner—pouring wine, gabbing away about the authorship—I started trying to mentally compose my portrait of him. It would be incredibly easy, I saw, to paint him as an upper-class snob moaning about the odiousness of the modern world, nostalgic for the past, surrounded by his Evelyn Waugh books and busts, infatuated by his literary ancestors, and eager to claim another—the big one—for his lineage. To make matters worse, in 2019, three years after the Brexit referendum, he had run to represent his district as a Brexit Party candidate.

(He hadn't been "really heated" about Brexit, he explained when I asked about this. "We'd been living under EU rule for quite a long time, and it's been fine. What really stirred me was when the vote went for the Brexit, and then the British government just started worming and needling and doing everything to stop it. I thought, 'This is really dangerous now.' We're in very dangerous territory when we just start saying, 'Well, actually fuck democracy, damn what the people want. We know best. We're the leaders.' So it was that, much more than the Brexit itself.") Waugh wasn't elected, but this detail would surely form a part of the portrait, another stroke against him. That would be the portrait a Stratfordian scholar would paint, I was sure. But it would be a cheap portrait, a caricature. It would be used to invalidate Waugh's arguments without actually addressing their substance. And it would leave things out: for instance, that Waugh was deeply devoted to literature—that he really loved Shakespeare and had made some possibly important contributions to understanding Shakespeare. A true portrait would have to hold all of it—hold side by side, for instance, that Waugh both cared about the truth *and* was descended from Oxford.

"If Oxford was Shakespeare," I wondered aloud, "wouldn't that knowledge have been passed down through his family?"

"Well, I always wonder about the Pembrokes," said Waugh, referring to his distant cousins who had inherited the earldom of Pembroke. In 1743 the 9th Earl of Pembroke, Oxford's great-great-grandson, commissioned a Shakespeare statue for their home, Wilton House. It's the twin of a Shakespeare statue erected in 1740 in Westminster Abbey. In the Westminster statue, Shakespeare leans casually against a stack of books and points to a scroll, which features a variant of Prospero's lines from *The Tempest*:

The Cloud capt Tow'rs
The Gorgeous Palaces,
The Solemn Temples,
The Great Globe itself,
Yea all which it Inherit,
Shall Dissolve;

And like the baseless Fabrick of a Vision
Leave not a wreck behind.

The Pembrokes' statue at Wilton House is nearly identical, except that it quotes from *Macbeth*:

LIFE's but a walking SHADOW
a poor PLAYER
That struts & frets his hour
upon the STAGE
And then is heard no more!

Shakespeare's hand points directly at "SHADOW." Of all the grand country houses and important places in Britain where the statue could have been erected, why there? Of all the words in the Shakespearean corpus it could have pointed at, why "shadow"? "It's utterly inconceivable to me," said Waugh, "that the Earl of Pembroke didn't deliberately do that." Was it meant to suggest that Shakespeare was a shadow—a phantasm, an illusion? "It's all too exciting for words," he said. "It really is."

Wilton House, it turned out, was only an hour and half drive away. It is still privately owned, occupied today by the 18th Earl of Pembroke and his young family. Their part of the residence is closed to the public, but the rest of the house and grounds are open to visitors. "Shall we go to Wilton tomorrow?" Waugh suggested. "Or we can hang about here talking about the wicked doings of four hundred years ago."

NINE

Some Heaven-Born Goddess

IT WAS GRAY AND DRIZZLY when we set out for Wilton the next day, and the traffic was terrible. Eliza drove. Wilton is very close to Stonehenge, and the police had blocked off the roads to deter large groups from gathering for the summer solstice.

"Look what they've done!" Waugh piped up from the back seat as we passed more orange police cones. "Can you believe this? They're so boring."

Eliza read a sign along the side of the road. " 'Summer Solstice Canceled.' They think they can *cancel* the summer solstice?!"

"Sheer bossiness," Waugh proclaimed. "We live in such a bossy world."

"Try not to think about it," said Eliza. "Think of Shakespeare."

We reached the little town of Wilton, parked, and made our way up toward the house. Wilton House is majestic, a grand, Palladian-style manor set on a vast expanse of carefully landscaped grounds and gardens. It put me in mind of Pemberley, Mr. Darcy's fictional country estate in Jane Austen's *Pride and Prejudice.* Actually, the Pemberley scenes for the 2005 movie adaptation starring Keira Knightley and Matthew Macfadyen were filmed here. The house is a popular set for period films and TV series. *The Young Victoria*, *The Crown*, *Emma*, *Bridgerton*—anything that needs to look lavishly English and aristocratic seems to be filmed at Wilton House.

One is not allowed to wander through the house unsupervised, so we bought tickets and dawdled in the courtyard garden—roses; little, precisely trimmed hedges; a circular fountain—waiting for the tour to begin. The tour guide, a petite woman with very English teeth, ushered us through the doors of an imposing central tower. Directly inside the front hall, facing the doors as if waiting to greet visitors to the house, stood the Shakespeare statue. The figure leaned on a stack of books, his left index finger hovering over "SHADOW." It was larger than life, towering over the little members of our tour group who shuffled around the statue, looking up at the paintings that lined the walls. They were portraits of the many earls of Pembroke and their countesses. High up on one wall, amid all the portraits of the men in their ruffles and robes and swords, was a portrait of the current earl, looking very out of place in an open-collar suit. On the opposite wall hung the portrait of his wife, the current countess, a young blond woman. After welcoming us and discussing the many earls, the tour guide finally directed our attention at the statue, recounting the (unverified) legend that Shakespeare had come to Wilton and produced *As You Like It* in the courtyard. The statue, she explained, was commissioned in 1743 by Henry Herbert, the 9th Earl of Pembroke, and erected to honor Mary Sidney, who'd been a Renaissance "literary lady."

"Really?" I thought. The statue of Shakespeare was erected *for* Mary Sidney? Believers in Mary Sidney's authorship would be thrilled. But if the statue was commissioned some 120 years after Mary Sidney died, how did anyone know it was erected for her? After the tour guide finished speaking, I went up to ask her, opening my notebook in the hope that she would have some useful details to share.

"Mary Sidney was a literary lady," the tour guide repeated.

"Yes, no, I understand that," I said. "But how do we know the statue was erected for her?"

"It's a historical fact," said the tour guide.

"But where did it come from?" I tried again. I had never come across it.

"It's a historical fact," she repeated. She was growing slightly flustered. "It's a historical fact!"

Realizing I was getting nowhere, I let it go, and the guide moved on gratefully into the house. But the interaction was instructive—symbolic, even, I thought, as we wandered down the grand halls. It encapsulated the whole problem of "knowing" history. We take our knowledge of the past from sources we trust, few of us going back to check how a "historical fact" was arrived at, whether it's correct. This is only practical: we cannot stop to check every piece of information we encounter over the course of a day. But we repeat the fact, and so we pass down as truth what might actually be closer to legend, at once creating and consuming history, rarely stopping to question it. That the Shakespeare statue was erected to honor Mary Sidney was one of Wilton's traditions, a bit of lore that had been repeated and repeated over the years until it landed in the mouth of a tour guide who no longer knew its origin. But why commission a statue of Shakespeare to honor Mary Sidney—unless she had something very important to do with Shakespeare? Or had the statue been commissioned, as Alexander Waugh argued, as a quiet nod to Oxford; a memorial to the Pembrokes' ancestor? Or something else entirely?

As we moved through the rooms of Wilton House, I thought about the figure of the Renaissance "literary lady." Mary Sidney was one of the first Englishwomen to gain significant notice as a poet and patron of poets, but she was preceded by a lineage of other literary ladies in England and Europe. In the 1390s a young Venetian widow named Christine de Pizan became a writer for the French court, supporting herself and her family through her production of ballads, political treatises, epistles, and prose tales. She sparked controversy by critiquing popular, misogynistic stories for their portrayal of women as seducers. In her most famous work, *The Book of the City of Ladies* (1405), she mounted a defense of her sex, creating an allegorical city of women—warriors, scholars, inventors, artists, prophetesses, saints—who form the city's walls and towers, representing women's achievements and contributions to society. Men's stereotypes of women could be sustained, de Pizan argued, only if they kept women from entering the public discourse. She published the book under her own name, but when it was translated into English in 1521 it was attributed to a man.

The *querelle des femmes*, a debate about women—their nature, abilities, virtues, whether they should be permitted to study or write or rule like men—raged across Europe during the Renaissance. Were women inherently inferior? According to Christian teaching, God created man first, and women were daughters of the temptress Eve, responsible for original sin. Women's souls were "naturally seductive," argued Saint Augustine, who feared their potential to corrupt. But as the Catholic Church came into question, so did its teachings about women. Others pointed to classical Aristotelianism, which held that women were defective and incapable of reason. Defenders of women emphasized that both men and women were created in God's image—that both were reflections of the divine. The German polymath Heinrich Agrippa suggested that men didn't oppress women because of some natural law but to maintain their social power.

In this climate, entering the literary sphere was a provocative thing for a woman to do. Some of the women who dared to write were courtesans—intellectual, upper-class prostitutes such as Tullia d'Aragona and Veronica Franco, who wrote poetry and philosophy, moving freely in Italian literary circles and sparring with male intellectuals of their day. Others wrote in an explicitly religious vein. "May the holy nails now be my quills," wrote the Italian noblewoman Vittoria Colonna, dedicating her poetry to the suffering of Christ. "And may his precious blood be my ink." In France, Marguerite de Navarre wrote *The Mirror of the Sinful Soul*, her mystical account of the soul as a woman yearning for Christ as her father-brother-lover. Theologians at the Sorbonne condemned the work as heresy, but her brother—who was, conveniently, the king—had the charges dropped.

The very piety that was used to suppress women's speech also gave them a voice—a virtuous way of entering the male world of letters. Even then, some women concealed their authorship. In 1560 a Protestant woman named Anne Locke became the first person in England to publish a full sonnet sequence, "A Meditation on a Penitent Sinner." But she prefaced the sonnets with a letter claiming they weren't hers; they were "delivered me by my friend with whom I knew I might be so bolde to use and publishe it as pleased me." A classic excuse! For years, scholars assumed the "friend" was a male writer. The sonnets weren't ascribed to Locke until 1989, when scholars compiled evidence of textual parallels between the sonnets and her letter.

Locke's disavowal of her authorship can be seen as an instance of the modesty topos. Anonymity in women was a "relic of the sense of chastity," observed Virginia Woolf. They "did homage to the convention, which if not implanted by the other sex was liberally encouraged by them . . . that publicity in women is detestable." Hence their use of pseudonyms such as "Constantia Munda" or "Jane Anger," who identified herself only as a "gentlewoman at London," concealing her identity even as she lashed out against misogynist depictions of women. "It was ANGER that did write this," she explained in *Her Protection of Women*, pointing out that men misrepresent women because "they think we will not write to reprove their lying lips." Her polemical pamphlet was published in 1589—on the eve of the decade that saw the explosion of Shakespeare's plays, radically rewriting the representation of women.

In 1593 the critic Gabriel Harvey referred cryptically to an "excellent gentlewoman" who was writing "strange inventions and rare devices." Her style is "the tinsel of the daintiest Muses and sweetest graces, but I dare not particularise her Description . . . without her license or permission," he wrote. Still, he couldn't help heaping praise on her. "She is neither the noblest, nor the fairest, nor the finest, nor the richest lady, but the gentlest, and wittiest, and bravest, and invinciblest gentlewoman that I know." Of her writing, he noted that "all her conceits are illuminate with the light of Reason; all her speeches beautified with the grace of Affability. . . . In her mind there appeareth a heavenly Logic; in her tongue & pen a divine Rhetoric. . . . I dare undertake with warrant, whatsoever she writeth must needs remain an immortal work, and will leave, in the activist world, an eternal memory of the silliest vermin that she should vouchsafe to grace with her beautiful and allective style, as ingenious as elegant."

Who was the excellent gentlewoman writing "immortal work" in 1593, the very year Shakespeare's name first appeared in print? Some scholars have suggested that she was just a fiction created by Harvey. Others have wondered if she was Mary Sidney. According to Harvey, the gentlewoman had written sonnets as well as a comedy. Were women writing plays?

Mary Sidney was first proposed as an authorship candidate in Gilbert Slater's *Seven Shakespeares* (1931). Slater thought some of the plays "showed feminine rather than masculine intuition," and suspected that unruly Rosalind, the heroine of *As You Like It* who disguises herself as a man, was "a self-portrait of the authoress." He conceived of Sidney as a collaborator in a group of writers led by Oxford, postulating that she functioned as Oxford's literary executor after his death, "completing his unfinished work and adding to it."

The case for Mary Sidney rests on much of the same arguments as the cases for other candidates: that she knew the court intimately, that she was multilingual and highly educated, and that she had noted literary interests. Her mother, a lady-in-waiting, had nursed Queen Elizabeth I through smallpox. Her uncle Robert Dudley, the 1st Earl of Leicester, was the Queen's longtime favorite and suitor for the royal hand. When Mary's younger sister died, the Queen wrote a letter of condolence to her parents, suggesting that since God had left them yet "one daughter of very good hope," she should come to live at court. At thirteen, Mary Sidney became one of the Queen's maids-of-honor.

That summer, her uncle threw a spectacular three-week bash at Kenilworth Castle in his desperate attempt to woo the Queen. Mary was likely in attendance. It featured fireworks, Italian tumblers, barges of musicians, dancing, hunting expeditions through the surrounding hills and dales, and men dressed as mythological figures spouting poetry and songs to the Queen from the middle of the lake. ("Triton" rode on a giant mechanical mermaid and "Arion" on a mechanical dolphin.) Scholars have noticed that *A Midsummer Night's Dream* contains detailed allusions to these magical sights. "The playwright's imagination drew on the scene at Kenilworth," Stephen Greenblatt writes in his biography of Shakespeare.

After her marriage at fifteen to Henry Herbert, the 2nd Earl of Pembroke, Mary Sidney became the Countess of Pembroke and mistress of Wilton House. In 1580 her older brother, Philip Sidney, came to visit, writing a long pastoral romance, *The Countess of Pembroke's Arcadia*, apparently to entertain her. She was "such a sister," Philip wrote, "as no Englishman, for aught I know, had ever possessed before." In one of Wilton's stately rooms, the guide indicated painted paneling featuring scenes from Sidney's *Arcadia*. Philip and Mary were an intriguing brother-sister duo. Their mission, according to their biographers, was to lay the foundations of a body of English literature that could stand next to the great works in Greek, Latin, French, and Italian. "We remember how much the

Florentine Renaissance owed to the Medici, but we forget that a similar debt was owed by the English Renaissance to the Sidneys," wrote one scholar. "They first produced what in the highest sense may be called the academic spirit in English letters," affirmed another.

Philip, otherwise known for his tennis court quarrel with Oxford, wrote a sonnet sequence, *Astrophil and Stella*, which circulated in manuscript, igniting the Elizabethan vogue for sonnet writing. The subject of his ardour was Penelope Rich, a court beauty with eyes of "beamy black" who had been married, against her will, to the coarse Baron Rich. Sidney was Astrophil—star-lover—and Penelope was Stella, his star. He braided her surname into his sonnets: "Towards Aurora's court, a nymph doth dwell, / Rich in all beauties which man's eye can see. . . . Rich in the treasure of deserved renown, / Rich in the riches of a royal heart, / Rich in those gifts which give th'eternal crown." Despite these little clues, scholars didn't recognize that Stella was Lady Rich until 1935, an indication of just how long Renaissance secrets can stay hidden.

When he wasn't pining for Penelope Rich, Sidney also began translating the Psalms into English. On a military campaign against the Spanish in 1586, however, Sidney's poetic pursuits were cut short. A militant Protestant, he had joined the Battle of Zutphen in the Netherlands, where a musket ball shattered his thigh bone. He died of gangrene twenty-five days later, just thirty-one years old.

Mary took up her brother's literary mantle, completing the work he had left unfinished. She revised and completed his English versification of the Psalms, displaying, in the words of one scholar, a "technical virtuosity in inventing verse forms [that] can scarcely be exaggerated." (At his death, Philip had translated only 43 of 150.) The Psalms constitute "a virtuoso performance," writes another, "almost like a cadenza in a concert." Scholars believe she translated them from the original Hebrew. The courtier John Harrington suggested she must have had help from her bishop, insisting that "it was more than a woman's skill to express the sense so right as she hath done in her verse, and more than the English or Latin translation could give her." Mary may have been showing off, but it was work undertaken in the name of God—and her heroic dead brother. Though her final version circulated only in manuscript, not print, copies reached the libraries of the poet Edmund Spenser and Queen Elizabeth and influenced the religious poetry of John Donne, who hailed her genius.

Mary also reworked her brother's *Arcadia* and published it. She prepared and published his sonnets, fixing errors that had gone out in a pirated edition. She was instrumental in the printing of his *Defence of Poesy*, a work of literary criticism arguing that poetry is better at rousing readers to virtue than history or philosophy. She was able to pass off her literary audacity as a woman by dressing her efforts as a tribute to her brother's memory. At the same time, she turned Wilton House into a literary salon—what one scholar has called "a workshop for poetical experimentation, the seedbed of a literary revolution"—gathering writers around her, supporting them, and assigning them works to write. "She enjoys the wise Minerva's wit and sets to school our poets everywhere," wrote the poet Thomas Churchyard. The poet Samuel Daniel credited her with having taught him, calling Wilton "my best school." His *Tragedie of Cleopatra* was "the worke the which she did impose," he wrote in his dedication, hailing Mary Sidney as "the starre of wonder, which my labours chose / To guide their way in all the course I use." Her literary patronage was celebrated in dozens of dedications. By the early 1590s, she also became a patron—with her husband—of a playing company, Pembroke's Men, which performed some of Shakespeare's early plays. Though she was commended by or connected to most major poets of the day, from Ben Jonson to John Donne, the Stratford man seems never to have known her.

Sidney produced her own work, too, writing poems that circulated in manuscript and translating works from French and Italian. (Translations, seen as inferior to original writing, were therefore appropriate for women.) When she published *The Tragedy of Antonie*, her translation of a French play, she became the first woman to publish a play in English. The play was never performed, of course, but it is thought to have influenced Shakespeare's *Antony and Cleopatra*.

The interest in Mary Sidney as a Shakespeare candidate derives its force from the question: What *else* did she do? "The complete body of her works eludes us," writes the scholar Margaret Hannay, noting that "much of what she wrote and translated has disappeared." One reason may have been "some reluctance to put her original works into print, despite her boldness in printing her translations under her own name." Sidney stayed just within the bounds of propriety for an aristocratic woman even as she challenged them, exerting her influence mostly under the cover of men: God, her brother, the male writers she translated, and the male poets she supported and instructed. Is it conceivable that she exerted some influence on Shakespeare, too? It's hard to see the pious Mary Sidney writing the pornographic *Venus and Adonis*—or if she did, she would certainly have required a pseudonym. But could she have had a hand in the early genesis of the plays? In the shaping of female characters? Or perhaps later in an editorial capacity, revising the plays and preparing them for publication as she had revised and prepared her brother's work? A portrait from 1618, when Sidney was fifty-seven, suggests that she wanted to be remembered as a writer. She holds her translation of

"She enjoys the wise Minerva's wit"

the Psalms, and her collar is embroidered with swans, the classical symbol of a poet—as in the "Sweet Swan of Avon." (Slater asked: "Does the title 'Sweet Swan' better fit the money lending maltster of Stratford or the 'peerless Ladie bright' of Wilton?") She died in September 1621. An epitaph, attributed to Ben Jonson, hailed her memory:

Underneath this sable hearse,
Lies the subject of all verse,
Sidney's sister, Pembroke's mother.
Death, ere thou hast slain another
Fair and learned and good as she,
Time shall throw a dart at thee.

Shortly after her death, the printing of the First Folio began. The dedication to her sons, William and Philip Herbert, constitutes the strongest link between the works of Shakespeare and Mary Sidney.

When the *New York Times* asked the novelist Joyce Carol Oates which writer, dead or alive, she would most like to meet, she replied, "We would probably all want to meet Shakespeare—or so we think," adding parenthetically, "We could ask the man if he'd really written all those plays, or if, somehow, he'd acquired them from—who?—Sir Philip Sidney's sister, perhaps?"

⁂

The idea of a female Shakespeare can easily be dismissed as a kind of modern feminist fantasy—a desire to replace the father of English literature with a mother. But the feeling of something weirdly female about Shakespeare is old. When John Weever wrote of Shakespeare's "issue" in 1599, he said they were born not only of Apollo but also of "some heaven-born goddesse":

Honie-tong'd Shakespeare when I saw thine issue,
I swore Apollo got them and none other,
Their rosie-tainted features clothed in tissue,
Some heaven-born goddesse said to be their mother.

Said to be their mother, as though it were a rumor, a half-heard whisper at court. Why did Weever bother writing about a mother? Why not leave it at Apollo? *Did* the works have a mother as well as a father? I remembered Margaret Cavendish's evocative pronouncement in 1664: "One would think he has been Metamorphosed from a Man to a Woman," she wrote, "for who could describe Cleopatra better than he hath done, and many other Females of his own Creating." Virginia Woolf also thought Shakespeare had an androgynous mind—a "man-womanly mind," she called it. The Victorian critic John Ruskin remarked on the virtue of Shakespeare's female characters, compared with the tragic flaws and foibles of his men, and concluded: "Shakespeare has no heroes—he has only heroines." Orson Welles, who acted in and directed numerous Shakespeare productions, observed that "Shakespeare was clearly tremendously feminine."

"Was it possible that women were involved in Shakespeare?" I had posed the question some months back to Carol Symes, the Shakespeare-doubting historian at the University of Illinois, and as I looked out onto Wilton's courtyard, where, according to legend, *As You Like It* was once performed, I thought back on our conversation.

"Oh, yeah," said Symes. "This is one of those things that's probably always going to be unprovable precisely because of the undocumented nature of women's work." Symes's own scholarship as a historian of the theater has suggested to her that the plays were likely a collaborative effort, not only because early modern playwrights tended to work collaboratively but also because of the "extraordinary variety of expert knowledge and expert epistemologies" exhibited in the plays. Though the group was probably led by "somebody with extraordinary vision," she thought it was impractical to compress all that knowledge into one person. The involvement of a woman—or women—would "make a ton of sense," she added. "The seemingly embodied understanding of women's positionality and plight just shines through those plays amazingly."

If history gets distorted by tradition, it also gets distorted by assumptions that documented history is the whole history; that recorded truth is the complete truth. Since only men's names are included on lists of known commercial playwrights, and only men (and boys) joined playing companies, the Elizabethan theater was long assumed to be an exclusively male realm. But more recent scholarship has shown that women were actively involved in theater. Aristocratic women acted as patrons of playing companies. Women from the middle classes supported the day-to-day business, creating costumes and stage props, collecting entrance fees, and lending money for productions. Some women performed as actors in local festivals, private productions, and courtly masques. At least one woman—Mary Frith, alias Moll Cutpurse, a smoking, cross-dressing pickpocket from the London underworld—delivered a notorious performance at the Fortune Theatre in 1611.

And though women weren't identified as commercial playwrights, that doesn't mean they weren't writing. They wrote liturgical drama and royal entertainments. When a young noblewoman named Jane Lumley translated Euripides's *Iphigenia*—she was the first person ever to translate a Greek play into English—she listed speakers, suggesting that her play, though unpublished, may have been intended for private performance. In France, Marguerite de Navarre was writing comedies that were performed for the court. In Italy, women were writing plays as well as acting in them—and a few Italian troupes traveled across the channel to play for the Queen and popular audiences. What did Englishwomen make of the European example? If French and Italian women were writing plays, it's hard to believe that Englishwomen weren't. By 1613, Elizabeth Cary had become the first Englishwoman to publish an original play, *The Tragedy of Mariam*, though even then she was discreet: the title page identified her only as "that learned, virtuous, and truly noble Ladie, E.C." The play wasn't performed on a public stage, but scholars argue that it could have been staged at a private residence.

The ideological constraints in which women operated are much more likely to have prevented acknowledgment of a woman's authorship than to have actually prevented them from writing plays, argues the scholar Phyllis Rackin. In other words, the constraints "make it more, rather than less, likely that some of the many plays whose authorship is anonymous were actually written by women and also that women collaborated in writing plays whose authorship was attributed only to men." Renaissance households were not simply domiciles but places of production in which every resident had a part, she notes: "The household of a baker produced bread; the household of a glover produced gloves. The household of a playwright is likely to have been organized on similar principles." The theatrical business, like other businesses, was "often a family affair." Plays could have been "the product of his wife's or daughter's work as well as—or instead of—his own."

I was contemplating playwriting as "family affair" when we entered the Double Cube Room, an opulent, gilded stateroom that could pass as the Palace of Versailles, and came face-to-face with a colossal painting of Philip Herbert and his family. Susan Vere had married Philip in December 1604, six months after her father's death. That season of Christmas festivities included performances of seven Shakespeare plays at court; a tribute, Oxfordians suggest, to the bride's late father. If—*if*—Oxford was Shakespeare, what role might his daughters have played in guarding his legacy? Did they hold the manuscripts? So many of the late plays turn on father-daughter relationships: Lear and Cordelia, Leontes and Perdita, Prospero and Miranda. At least one Oxfordian has suggested that Oxford's eldest daughter, Elizabeth Vere, might have had a hand in some of the plays along with her husband, the Earl of Derby: a "tripartite collaboration." Meanwhile, Ben Jonson praised the youngest, Susan Vere, as "the light, and mark unto posterity." In the painting (ca. 1634), by the Flemish artist Anthony van Dyck, Philip Herbert stands in the center, his children around him. To his left is a woman clad in black, staring with a pale, vacant expression. Susan Vere had died of smallpox a few years before, and the pale figure in black represented her as a kind of ghost. Waugh, who knew the painting, was anxious that the tour guide would get it wrong and mistake the figure for Philip Herbert's second wife. When the guide named her correctly, he practically pranced, clapping his hands in delight.

As the tour ended, we were released out onto the grounds. A central path unfurled from the house toward the gardens, the wide lawns with their ancient cedars spread out on either side. Wandering along a little river that ran through the estate, I imagined Mary Sidney roaming the grounds, her red hair flashing against the expanse of green, Philip composing his *Arcadia* and his lovelorn sonnets to the black-eyed Penelope Rich. Some suspected she was also the subject of Shakespeare's sonnets: the dark lady with eyes of "raven black." Philip Sidney was certainly not the only courtier enamored by her. "So many hearts she hath already slain, / As few behind to conquer do remain," wrote another admirer. She was compared to Venus, goddess of love and beauty. Sidney wrote of her "wearing Venus badge in every part of thee." Other poets praised her talent for singing and lute playing: "The basest notes which from thy voice proceed / The treble of the Angels do exceed." Musicians dedicated books of songs to her: "On account of her rare gifts she can do better justice to them than anyone else I know," wrote a French composer, presumably referring to not only her musical gifts but also her linguistic gifts, since his songs were in French and Italian. Penelope Rich's excellence in languages was widely admired. Writers dedicated works to her, praising her "magnificent mind wherein all virtues have their proper seat." King James commended "the fineness of her wit, the invention and well-writing" of her letters. "This heart-stealing goddess charmed their ears," wrote another poet, "to hear her fluent wit, they blush at theirs."

Shakespeare's dark lady is a talented musician, too. In Sonnet 128, the poet watches her perform, calling her his "music," envious of the keys caressed by her hand:

How often when thou, my music, music play'st,
Upon that blessed wood whose motion sounds
With thy sweet fingers when thou gently sway'st
The wiry concord that mine ear confounds,
Do I envy those hacks that nimble leap
To kiss the tender inward of thy hand,
Whilst my poor lips, which should that harvest reap,
At the wood's boldness by thee blushing stand!

Penelope Rich was the first woman ever put forward as the dark lady—first proposed in 1888 by the Stratfordian Gerald Massey in his book *The Secret Drama of Shakespeare's Sonnets*. How Massey thought William of Stratford could be romantically tied to a high-ranking noblewoman, goddaughter to the Queen, is unclear. But Oxford writing about an illicit relationship with Lady Rich could be plausible. Penelope Rich was transgressive. She began an affair with another man and bore his children—another reason for her notorious association with blackness. Perhaps she had other affairs, too. She was deemed a "fair woman with a black soul," the succubus of the court. Even her bedchamber was adorned in black: black velvet trimmed in gold lace and silver damask. (What a strange thing history is that we can know with certainty the color of Penelope Rich's bedding but entertain grave doubts about the authorship of Shakespeare.) In the sonnets, Shakespeare presents the lady's darkness as an inversion of the old hierarchy, which prized fairness. In her, nature has wrought a miracle, setting blackness above all other beauty:

In the old age black was not counted fair,
Or if it were, it bore not beauty's name;
But now is black beauty's successive heir,
And beauty slandered with a bastard shame.

In 1605 Baron Rich sued his unfaithful wife for divorce, and she admitted publicly to adultery. The divorce was granted, but her request to remarry was denied. She married her lover anyway, in defiance of canon law, and was banished from the court by King James. At the end of her life, Penelope Rich was hauled before the Court of Star Chamber, branded "an harlot, adulteress, concubine and whore." Outcast and stripped of her titles, she died in disgrace in 1607, her burial place unknown.

I couldn't help liking her. She flouted the patriarchal morality of her time, and the descriptions of her "magnificent mind" and "fluent wit" hint that there was much more to her than mere beauty. Could the muse have been more than muse? Could she have taken up the pen herself? *Some heaven-born goddesse said to be their mother.*

In 1973 a scholar named A. L. Rowse declared that Emilia Bassano was the dark lady. Bassano was born in London in 1569, but her family came from Bassano del Grappa—the very town in northern Italy where a Shakespeare scholar had discovered the obscure fresco detailed in *Othello*, and the same town that was also overrun with men named "Otello." The Bassanos were musicians and instrument makers, specializing in recorders. They had left Bassano del Grappa for Venice, where they played for the doge. When Henry VIII was looking for musicians for his fourth wedding, his diplomat in Venice reported that the Bassanos—Emilia's father, Baptista, and his brothers—were "all excellent and esteemed above all other[s] in this city." Recommending them to the English court, the diplomat wrote, "It shall be no small honor to His Majesty to have music comparable with any other prince or perchance better and more variable." In 1539 the Bassano musicians left Italy and entered the service of the king, forming a consort of recorder players at court that would, through their sons and grandsons, last ninety years.

Shakespeare's plays abound with musical references. In *Hamlet,* for instance, the prince of Denmark tries to teach Guildenstern how to play the recorder. "'Tis easy as lying," says Hamlet. "Govern these ventages with your fingers and thumb, give it breath with your mouth, and it will discourse most eloquent music. Look you, these are the stops." Guildenstern is no good at it, sending Hamlet off on a tirade about how he dares to "play upon" Hamlet yet cannot play the recorder.

Baptista Bassano purchased buildings and land in Shoreditch, then a suburb outside the City of London with a dissolute reputation—a place of brothels, taverns, and England's first theaters. His daughter was likely born here, to an Englishwoman named Margaret Johnson. When Emilia was seven, however, her father died, and she was sent to live with Susan Bertie, the Dowager Countess of Kent, a childless widow who believed strongly in the education of girls. The practice of sending middle-class children to be brought up in aristocratic households was common, affording them opportunities beyond their families' means. The countess ensured that her young ward received a humanist education. Emilia remembered her later as "the Mistris of my youth, / the noble guide of my ungovern'd days."

Through the countess, or perhaps through her recorder-playing relatives, Emilia was exposed to the world of the court. A document from 1584 about the arrest of two Bassano men records their indignant response: "We have as good friends in the court as thou hast and better too. . . . Send us to ward? Thou wert as good kiss our arse." (The document, interestingly, describes them as "black," probably a reference to their Mediterranean complexions, which looked dark to the pale-skinned English.) By eighteen, Emilia had become the mistress of a powerful nobleman forty-three years her senior: Henry Carey, Lord Hunsdon, the Queen's cousin and Lord Chamberlain in charge of court entertainment. Emilia was "favoured much of her Majesty and of many noblemen and hath had great gifts and been made much of," wrote a lecherous astrologer named Simon Forman who lusted after her. "The old Lord Chamberlain kept her longue," Forman recorded. "She was maintained in great pomp." In 1594 the "old Lord Chamberlain" would become the patron of the Lord Chamberlain's Men, the newly formed company that performed Shakespeare's plays. In 1592, however, the twenty-three-year-old Bassano, pregnant with Lord Chamberlain's child, was married off "for colour" to a court musician named Alphonso Lanier, becoming Emilia Lanier. The Lord Chamberlain gave her "monie & Jewells," Forman noted, but "her husband hath dealt hardly with her and spent and consumed her goods."

The contours of Bassano's life, like the lives of most Renaissance women, are sketchy. In 1611, at the age of forty-two, she became the first woman in England to publish a volume of poetry, *Salve Deus Rex Judaeorum.* Its long title poem is religious, yet startlingly radical, arguing that Eve was wrongly blamed for original sin. Attacking the Christian theology on which the spiritual and social inferiority of women was founded, Bassano makes a plea for women's "libertie" from male oppression:

Then let us have our libertie again
And challenge to yourselves no sovereignty.
You came not in the world without our pain,
Make that a bar against your cruelty;

Your fault being greater, why should you disdain
Our being your equals, free from tyranny?
If one weake woman simply did offend,
This sinne of yours hath no excuse, nor end.

She sounds remarkably like one of Shakespeare's heroines, railing against the patriarchal beliefs of her world—and not just railing against them, but also identifying and deconstructing their biblical origins. Brilliantly, she turns the Bible back on men. Adam, not Eve, was "most to blame" for the Fall, she writes, for the Bible depicts him as stronger than Eve. Shouldn't he have been more capable of resisting temptation? "If Eve did erre, it was for knowledge sake," Bassano argues, positioning her as the bearer of knowledge, which she shared, out of love, with Adam. Men have wrongly taken credit for knowledge ever since, she suggests: "Yet Men will boast of Knowledge, which he tooke / Frome Eves faire hand, as from a learned Booke."

Dedicating the volume to ten noblewomen, including Mary Sidney, Bassano forged a kind of female literary community. She urged women to see themselves not as men see them—as weak, sinful, inconstant—but as worthy and virtuous, equal to any man. And she chided those women who "speake unadvisedly against the rest of their sexe," suggesting that they "refer such points of folly to be practised by evil disposed men, who forgetting they were borne of women, nourished of women, and that if it were not by the means of women, they would be quite extinguished out of the world: and a finall ende of them all, doe like Vipers deface the wombes wherein they were bred." Rescued from obscurity in the late twentieth century, Bassano's poetry is now treated as one of the earliest expressions of feminism in English literature.

But what was she doing between her marriage in 1592 and the publication of her poetry in 1611? Did she write that single volume at the age of forty-two and nothing else? Advocates of Bassano point out that variants of her family name crop up in the plays: there's Bassianus in *Titus Andronicus* and Bassanio in *The Merchant of Venice.* And in *Othello*, a character named Emilia delivers a rousing feminist speech arguing against the tyranny of husbands shortly before her own husband, Iago, kills her. Could she account for the plays' feminism? For their knowledge of Italian and that obscure Italian town? In 2018 the Globe premiered a new play, *Emilia,* which imagined Shakespeare as a plagiarist, stealing Emilia Bassano's words to write the feminist speech in *Othello.* By 2022, Routledge Shakespeare Studies published a book on Bassano "as Shakespeare's co-author."

But all of the mother-candidates, all of the female Shakespeares, are haunted by another female Shakespeare—a purely fictional one. Turning from the river into the gardens, I thought about Virginia Woolf's famous 1929 essay, *A Room of One's Own*, in which she imagines Shakespeare's sister—doomed by virtue of her sex never to write a single word. The equal of her brother in talent, Shakespeare's sister—Woolf calls her Judith—is constrained by the strictures of her life. While young William goes off to school, Judith is kept home to mend the stockings and mind the stew. When she tries to join the theater, she is laughed away at the theater door. She ends up pregnant by the theater manager and kills herself in desperation, her poetry strangled before it has begun. The thrust of the anecdote serves to illustrate Woolf's central thesis: that in order to write, a woman needs £500 a year and a room of her own; that intellectual freedom depends on material things. But even as she reaches this conclusion—that given the social and economic conditions of Elizabethan life, a woman could not have written Shakespeare—Woolf seems to doubt her own claims. Looking at her shelves, she notes that all the history books are about men, war, the church, politics, and agriculture. History "seems a little queer as it is, unreal, lop-sided," she reflects. What about the lives of women? Who wrote all of those old, anonymous texts? "I would venture to guess that Anon, who wrote so many poems without signing them, was often a woman," she writes.

Woolf's ambivalence fascinated and frustrated me—in one breath concluding that a woman's circumstances would have prevented her from writing Shakespeare and in the next acknowledging that there is so much about Renaissance women that she does not know. And the one thing she does know is that they would have written anonymously. Anonymity, she continues, would have been a refuge for women, who "are not even now as concerned about the health of their fame as men are, and, speaking generally, will pass a tombstone or a signpost without feeling an irresistible desire to cut their names on it, as Alf, Bert, or Chas must do in obedience to their instinct." She goes on about Shakespeare's androgynous, man-womanly mind. In her novel *Orlando*, Woolf literalized this man-woman, imagining a poet at the Elizabethan court who magically changes sex from man to woman—a cross-dressed, quintessentially Shakespearean figure. But no, no, no, a woman absolutely could not have written Shakespeare.

Woolf is very hard on women: "You have never made a discovery of any sort of importance," she lectures. "You have never shaken an empire or led an army into battle. The plays of Shakespeare are not by you, and you have never introduced a barbarous race to the blessings of civilization. What's your excuse?" But Woolf knew perfectly well about the empires of Cleopatra, Isabella I of Castile, Elizabeth I, Catherine the Great, Victoria. The discoveries of Ada Lovelace and Marie Curie. The armies led by Boudica, the Welsh warrior queen, and Joan of Arc. Boudica became famous in the Victorian era as a kind of ancient counterpart to Queen Victoria. Tennyson wrote a poem about her. Several ships of the Royal Navy were named after her. In 1902 a sculpture of Boudica in her war chariot leading an uprising against the Roman forces was erected at the north end of Westminster Bridge. Woolf, who loved nothing more than walking through London, could not have missed it.

Was she being tongue-in-cheek? Was her assertion that women could not write the plays of Shakespeare, in the same breath that she said women did not shake empires or lead armies, a rhetorical device—a means of subtly suggesting the converse? "Lies will flow from my lips," she warns. She encourages us to challenge her narrator: "You have been contradicting her and making whatever additions and deductions seem good to you," Woolf writes. "That is all as it should be, for in a question like this, truth is only to be had by laying together many varieties of error." But her errors are pointed: in contradicting her, we summon forth formidable women—and if it is possible to contradict the statements about women not making discoveries, shaking empires, or leading armies, does Woolf intend us to contradict the part about women not writing Shakespeare, too? Is she trying to goad us into considering whether women *were* involved in Shakespeare?

I wandered beneath an arch of golden-green laburnum, contemplating the anecdote about Shakespeare's oppressed sister. Of course she didn't stand a chance of becoming a great poet; she didn't receive an education. The anecdote had a hole: What about the women who did receive an education, who had £500 a year and rooms of their own? Through the arch, I stumbled onto a Japanese garden, complete with pink flowers and lotus leaves and delicate, red oriental bridges set over a pond. (One of the earls had apparently been a Japanese enthusiast.) Suddenly I remembered *The Tale of Genji*, a novel written in the eleventh century by the Japanese noblewoman and lady-in-waiting Murasaki Shikibu. It is sometimes called the world's first novel. When it was first translated into English in 1925, Woolf reviewed it in British *Vogue*. "She knew!" I thought. "She knew perfectly well what women had done. Why did she pretend she didn't?"

At one point in the essay, she remarks that she cannot remember any instance in the course of her reading where two women were depicted as friends until Jane Austen's day, which is to say, until female authors did so. Had she completely forgotten Hermia and Helena, Rosalind and Celia, Beatrice and Hero, Desdemona and Emilia, Hermione and Paulina? I couldn't believe that. Woolf read Shakespeare obsessively throughout her life and alluded to his plays throughout her novels. Were we meant to contradict her again? To wave our arms and say, "Well, what about Shakespeare?" And if she considered the depiction of female friendships characteristic of a woman's authorship, then Shakespeare . . .

I approached the Whispering Seat, a semicircular stone bench set back amid the cedars. The bench was designed so that a whisper issued from one corner can be heard in the other but cannot be heard outside the seat. I sat in one corner and wondered if that was it—if Woolf had been whispering. Perhaps she felt it was too dangerous to say aloud what she suspected about Shakespeare—look what had happened to Delia Bacon, to Thomas Looney. And they had stuck with male authors! In one of her novels, Woolf created a character, Mrs. Hilbery, who toys with the idea of female authorship, evolving "a theory that Anne Hathaway had a way, among other things, of writing Shakespeare's sonnets." She floats the idea "to enliven a party of professors, who forwarded a number of privately printed manuals within the next few days for her instruction." Mrs. Hilbery comes half to believe her joke, "which was, she said, at least as good as other people's facts." But she also senses that the theory is a dangerous one: it implies "a menace to the safety of the heart of civilization itself."

I smiled at Woolf's description of the professors forwarding manuals for Mrs. Hilbery's instruction. She seemed to loathe Shakespeare professors, who fell into the category of people she dubbed "middlebrows": faux intellectuals driven by social ambition, interested in culture not for its own sake but for how their acquisition of culture makes them appear. A condescending reviewer had suggested that Woolf was a "highbrow," which prompted her to write a comical letter to the editor of the *New Statesman* on the "Battle of the Brows." A highbrow is "the man or woman of thoroughbred intelligence who rides his mind at a gallop across country in pursuit of an idea," she explained. She was happy to be accused of being a highbrow—though highbrows, she added, are "wholly incapable of dealing successfully with what is called real life." (Byron slept with one woman, then another, before "dying in the mud," Woolf wrote. Charlotte Brontë was "the worst governess in the British Isles." Sir Walter Scott went bankrupt, leaving "together with a few magnificent novels, one house, Abbotsford, which is perhaps the ugliest in the whole Empire.")

Being incapable, highbrows depend on lowbrows, who gallop across life much more practically—in pursuit of a living, not an idea. She loved lowbrows; her problem was with middlebrows, who amble "in pursuit of no single object, neither art itself nor life itself, but both mixed indistinguishably, and rather nastily, with money, fame, power, or prestige." She described the archetypal middlebrow as a professor of English who makes "money in teaching and in writing books about Shakespeare," who calls "both Shakespeare and Wordsworth equally 'Bill.' " (Walter Raleigh, one of the first professors of English at Oxford, referred to Shakespeare and Wordsworth as "Bill" in his lectures.) The middlebrows' desire to downplay greatness—to see Shakespeare as an everyman, as "Bill"—is coupled with their belief that displaying cultural knowledge will raise their own social status. "[H]ow dare the middlebrows teach you how to read—Shakespeare, for instance?" She pointed with alarm to the spread of their "fungoid growth": "Middlebrow on the cabbages? Middlebrow infecting that poor old sheep?" Concerned that "middlebrow seems to me to be everywhere," she advised highbrows and lowbrows to "band together to exterminate a pest which is the bane of all thinking and living." Going by his plays, Shakespeare didn't like middlebrows, either, she added. (But wasn't the social-climbing Stratford man the quintessential middlebrow?) In conclusion, she requested that reviewers everywhere call her a highbrow. "If any human being, man, woman, dog, cat, or half-crushed worm dares call me 'middlebrow,' I will take my pen and stab him, dead. Yours etc., Virginia Woolf."

I walked back up the long path from the Whispering Seat to the house and over to the parking lot, wondering what Woolf really thought about the authorship. Did she agree with the middlebrow professors for whom she expressed such disdain, with whom she swore she never wanted to be associated? Or was she whispering, between the lines of her too-obvious errors, some other truth?

⁂

The most prominent person championing the idea of female authorship today might be Mark Rylance, the actor and founding artistic director of Shakespeare's Globe. Over the course of his forty years working in theater and film, Rylance has come to the conclusion that Shakespeare's female characters surpass the female characters of any other male playwright—even Ibsen, Chekhov, and Euripides. "So now, for me, however the works of Shakespeare were created, the creator had not only extensive book learning, languages, vocabulary, and life experience, but also the greatest understanding of women any playwright has ever displayed," he wrote in the *Atlantic*, before adding rhetorically, "What would be the next question you might ask?"

I first met Rylance at the Globe at an annual meeting of the Shakespearean Authorship Trust, formerly known as the Shakespeare Fellowship, the society founded in 1922 by J. T. Looney and Sir George Greenwood. Rylance is a trustee. Unlike other authorship societies, which are dedicated to a particular candidate, the Shakespearean Authorship Trust favors no candidate. All are welcome to present their research, including believers in the Stratford man. At the conference, I was surprised to discover a few Stratfordians in the audience. Rylance, I learned, is key to maintaining this spirit. He is a peacemaker. During his tenure as artistic director of the Globe, he held "concerts for peace" at the theater and spoke at protests against the Iraq War. More recently, he resigned from the Royal Shakespeare Company, where he had been an "associate artist" for thirty years, over its sponsorship deal with British Petroleum. "I do not wish to be associated with BP any more than I would with an arms dealer, a tobacco salesman, or anyone who wilfully destroys the lives of others," he told the *Guardian.* "Nor, I believe, would William Shakespeare." Shakespeare is not a job for him or even a passion. It is a philosophy, a way of living that is not separable from modern politics.

Rylance lives in Brixton, a neighborhood of South London known for its open-air Afro-Caribbean market and multiethnic community. Back in the city, I wandered through the noise and chaos of the market and into quiet streets lined with typical English row houses.

Rylance was smiling and shy when he opened the door. Profiles of him almost invariably mention his gentleness, the "twinkle in his eyes," his trademark fedora. Before we could speak, an energetic Jack Russell terrier launched into the front hall, yapping at my incursion. Rylance soothed Apache, the terrier, and motioned me into the house. He was dressed in shorts, his head uncharacteristically fedora-less.

In the kitchen, I greeted his wife, Claire van Kampen, a vibrant blond woman in a sundress. In the eighties, van Kampen became the first female musical director of the Royal Shakespeare Company and the Royal National Theatre, where she met Rylance. When the Globe opened, she was appointed Director of Theatre Music. She shares Rylance's interest in the authorship question.

We went out to the garden and settled into lawn chairs in the sun.

Rylance brought mugs of tea and slices of fruit tart. Apache rested on an ottoman in the house, watching us.

The son of English teachers, Rylance grew up visiting Stratford-upon-Avon with his parents. He spent his formative acting years, from the age of twenty-two, with the Royal Shakespeare Company in Stratford, performing in the gardens of New Place, wandering along the Avon, soaking up the myth. His crisis of faith was gradual, almost accidental.

"I was an ardent Stratfordian," said Rylance. "It was my dream to act in Stratford. I'd done whole seasons there in '82, '83, '84. It wasn't until I came back again in '88 that I had this experience of seeing behind that monument." He was playing Hamlet and Romeo back-to-back—*Hamlet* matinees, followed by evenings of *Romeo and Juliet.* He worried that his characters were bleeding into each other. "People were saying, 'You're coming on too depressed, too dark as Romeo,'" he remembered, "and I was sensitive to—maybe am I bringing too much of Hamlet to my Romeo?" But the play suggested to him that Romeo was in a "classic melancholia" at the beginning. "I have a soul of lead," he says. Walking home at night along the banks of the Avon, Rylance ran into actor friends talking excitedly about Shakespeare's use of alchemical imagery: the transformation of base metals into gold. He had assumed alchemy was just a "charlatan's conceit," but his friends explained that alchemy had a philosophical dimension in the Renaissance. It referred to spiritual ennoblement: the transformation of the soul from lead to gold, from baseness to gilded splendor.

He asked his friends where they had learned this. At the Francis Bacon Research Trust, they said. "I'd seen pamphlets on stage doors over the years and thought, 'Oh this is just cranky, crazy people,'" recalled Rylance. "But it was so winning to me." The Francis Bacon Research Trust, a Baconian society that had survived long past the peak of Bacon's popularity, was looking at the plays through the eyes of an author who was well educated and well traveled, and connected to the philosophical discussions and ancient wisdom flooding into Europe. Rylance was not interested in the authorship when he began attending the lectures. He simply wanted to understand Renaissance philosophy. "It was just very practically helpful—helpful in terms of the choices I had to make every evening," he explained.

In *Romeo and Juliet*, for instance, he realized that Shakespeare was using alchemical imagery to show Romeo's spiritual transformation from a "soul of lead" to silver when he's gazing on Juliet to, finally, gold. At the end of the play, Romeo and Juliet's parents erect gold statues in their memory. "That's not just a cynical action, but in the myth of the story, it's a sign that they've become gold, that their service, their action, is loving—a journey from lead to gold."

At the same time that he was attending the Baconian lectures, Rylance was also reading the Stratfordian biographies, trying to imagine the poet's life in the old market town. "As an actor, my training is to imagine a motivation and an obstacle to that motivation, which necessitates the words and actions of characters I play," he explained. He wondered about Shakespeare's motivation for writing. Biographers claimed Shakespeare's motivation was money, but the plays' philosophical depth did not seem to him to manifest that motivation. Nor could he find the obstacle in the Stratford man's life that provided the necessary pressure for creating such profound works. Slowly, "it dawned on me that the face which came to mind whenever I imagined Shakespeare was changing its appearance."

The breakdown of belief wasn't alarming. It was thrilling. "I thought, 'My God, this is all wrong. All these books I've read, it's all not true. This is a fantastic thing.' " He invited the Baconian lecturer to speak to the Royal Shakespeare Company at the Swan Theatre in Stratford, naively expecting that the cast would be as thrilled as he was to explore an alternate theory. "They weren't at all. They were furious with me."

"It really set the cat amongst the pigeons," said van Kampen. "And again at the Globe, it really was a divisive thing."

The modern reconstruction of the Globe—a project many years in the planning—opened in Southwark, on the south bank of the Thames, in 1997. It was a controversial undertaking. Sam Wanamaker, the actor-director who led its re-creation, committed to using original materials, original hand carpentry where possible, and the latest scholarship about the original theater. Inspired by Wanamaker's faithful reconstruction, Rylance—elected artistic director at age thirty-five—wanted productions, too, to follow what he called "original practices." They turned to scholarship on clothing, props, and period instruments. The company was all-male, as in Shakespeare's day. "Groundlings" stood in the yard for five pounds, the modern equivalent of the penny originally charged. By denying themselves modern sets, lighting, and even—for some of the audience—seats, Rylance and van Kampen hoped to discover the relationship between actor and audience informed by the original architecture. For all their heresy, they were in some ways quite purist, committed to exploring the theater of Elizabethan England.

"I was attracted to the idea of the plays being a force for good in society," Rylance explained. He wanted Shakespeare to be a spiritual experience, like the initiation rites of the ancient mystery schools, awakening the soul, raising consciousness.

Against expectations, the Globe drew huge audiences. The open-air Elizabethan theater was a hit with tourists and locals, who could now "get" their Shakespeare in London instead of having to take a two-hour train to Stratford to see the Royal Shakespeare Company. But then, to complicate matters, the artistic director announced that he held a reasonable doubt about the authorship of the plays. London's theater critics were incensed. The Globe's chief executive and the board called him in to express their concerns. "They tried to get me coaches on how to deal with the press, trying to tell me what I could and couldn't say," Rylance recalled. He attempted to place a few books on the authorship question in the theater's gift shop, but they would summon him to a committee room—a half hour after he finished a performance of *Hamlet*—to listen to some scholar explain why the book was not right for the gift shop. "It would be argued that 'We're the workplace, we're not interested in the biography, we're interested in the work.' I said, 'Okay. I went down to the shop this morning. There were thirteen biographies of the Stratford man.' We were selling plague rats in the shop. We were selling everything just to make money. And you're saying I can't have one authorship book saying maybe there's a question here?"

"There was a prevailing view that because he was an actor, not a scholar, Mark's opinion carried no weight," said van Kampen.

"I remember Stanley pulling my beard," said Rylance. Stanley Wells was a trustee of the Globe. At a reception, he approached the heretical director, tugging at his whiskers. "'Who's a naughty boy?' That kind of thing," said Rylance. "It was a very old-fashioned, Shakespearean thing to do." The stance also made him an easy target in the British papers. Reporters, eager for a cheap laugh, mocked and misquoted him. He was the "David Icke of British theatre," Icke being a sports commentator who spouted New Age conspiracy theories, including that the Earth had been hijacked by a race of shape-shifting reptilians.

But scholars couldn't deny that Rylance had a deep knowledge of the plays. He was performing in nearly every season at the Globe, solidifying his reputation as—in the words of the *New Yorker*—"an actor whose affinity for Shakespeare's works is unparalleled." Were his views about the authorship influencing his acting, setting him apart, giving him something that other Shakespearean actors didn't have?

Rylance understands why people hate the thought that Shakespeare was an aristocrat. They're concerned with "a noble defence of the middle classes," he wrote in the *Times*. "This is an old and proper wrong to be upset about. It goes back to William the Conqueror and the aristocratic families descended from the sellouts and pirates that sided with that cruel William the Bastard, families who still own almost all the land we live on and, in some cases, work to maintain the appallingly unequal society we all endure. For me to suggest that one of these apparently ruthless villains wrote the works of humble Will Shakespeare is an appalling theft." He sympathized with their sense of injustice. "My critics are concerned for the unwitnessed, hardworking, some would say suppressed part of themselves that fears it will never be capable of genius, that it will always be in the middle of the crowd, and, if it raises its head above that crowd, will be duly robbed."

But he also put his finger on the strange ways people project themselves onto Shakespeare: "They see those of us who question whether the man from a small Midlands town could have written these works of genius as directly suppressing their own unrecognised genius."

Wasn't it strange, I asked, that a country that still maintains a royal family in the twenty-first century—that seems anachronistically steeped in reverence for aristocracy—despises the idea of an aristocratic Shakespeare? Sixty-two percent of Britons still support the monarchy.

Van Kampen suggested that the stubborn persistence of the British class system had bred "tremendous antipathy" toward the aristocracy, leading to what she considered a kind of "inverted snobbery": "Aristocrats are stupid, they're inbred, they're not part of the intelligentsia, they wouldn't know how to write a play." Shakespeare was wrapped up in Britain's class resentment. Besides, he was supposed to be an everyman. He "confirms our identity as British people," she emphasized. "He's been created that way because we have an emptiness that we've filled with myth."

"What's the emptiness?" I asked.

She talked about the invasion of Britain over the centuries by different peoples and cultures, about the gradual consolidation of Britishness. "You can see this with the whole Brexit thing and how powerful people's emotions are about having a British identity," she continued. "Shakespeare is up there as embodying an idea of something like the heart of Britishness. If you take that away, what is there?" She told a story about going to dinner with friends when Rylance mentioned the authorship question. Two of the women became very upset. "One started crying, 'I don't want to hear about this. I've learnt at school that it was this. I don't want to hear about it.'

"And don't forget," she went on, "I think it's also to do with the Reformation. The cutoff from the Church caused a tremendous amount of anguish. Recusants carrying on Catholic religion secretly; then in the next regime, it came back; then in the next regime, it was changed again. Tremendous instability about religion and myth in this country." Shakespeare, she suggested, became the unifying myth. "I think there's something there. Otherwise, why would it be so emotional?"

Rylance was listening quietly, nodding along, sipping his tea. As we talked, he gazed up at birds flocking to a bird feeder in the trees. "I get such pleasure when birds come and eat food you put out for them," he said. To Rylance, the authorship question is a "beautiful question," just as the question of God is a beautiful question, a beautiful mystery. There is no urgency for him in alighting on a fixed and certain truth. Francis Bacon was his entry into the authorship question, and he still sees Bacon's philosophy reflected in the plays. (In 2019, Routledge Studies in Shakespeare published *Francis Bacon's Contribution to Shakespeare*, using a new stylometric method to argue that Bacon made small but significant contributions to *The Comedy of Errors*, *Love's Labour's Lost*, and *The Tempest*.) But Rylance has not held exclusively to the first candidate he encountered. He thinks Oxford's trip to Italy is "fundamental" to the works. He's interested in the case for Derby. He sees Mary Sidney as "crucial" to getting the women right.

"For me, Mary Sidney seems very much to have been involved," said van Kampen, referencing the statue at Wilton House. "I feel she was a part of this. Her interest in drama and dramatists was so proactive."

"I really like that there are different windows into these plays," said Rylance. "That's my image of it, really. The Shakespeare works are a house, and you can go and look in one window or another. Each case provides a different perspective and reveals a different quality in the works." He liked exploring the haunted Shakespeare house, visiting the different rooms with their different authors. "The Stratford biography is actually a welcoming front door, but you can get no further than a front hall with a lot of locked doors. Bacon's window looks into a study with musicians playing and mysticism. With Oxford you see Italy and this extraordinary psychological torment and passion. I wander around the question in that way, without feeling that I want it to be one big room," he explained. "I don't want to have a modern architect come in and knock all the walls out. I like that each one is different, and I love being welcomed into each room and hearing what people say. Oh, you want me to come into that room! I love this room! Let's hang around in this room for a while."

It almost sounded as though he didn't ever want to arrive at a conclusion about the authorship, I said.

He didn't care so much who it was, he admitted. He cared about understanding how the plays were made. "That's the important question for me, because I want to make better plays today. How were they created? Unfortunately, the orthodox account is very misleading for theater makers."

"I don't know that you can completely ignore the influence of Elizabeth I, actually," van Kampen interjected. Most playwrights of the period ran afoul of the Crown at some point in their careers. They were fined or jailed or tortured. But Shakespeare escaped such punishment, despite writing arguably seditious material. "And you have to look at why," she said. "Who were the powerful forces at work protecting him?"

Elizabeth, the theater-loving queen, looms over the whole Shakespeare mystery. How did her reign shape Shakespeare's plays? A husbandless female monarch sat on the throne for forty-four years, ruling over the scheming, flattering men of her court, seeing off threats from Catholic Europe, and setting in motion the overseas expansion that would lead to the creation of the British Empire. The court was the ultimate theater, and the Queen was the consummate actress, manipulating her gender in the interests of power. "I know I have the body of a weak and feeble woman, but I have the heart and stomach of a king, and of a king of England too," she declared, rallying her troops as they braced for the invasion of the Spanish Armada. A king's heart in a woman's hide, a woman in a man's role. Scholars have sometimes seen flashes of her in Shakespeare's headstrong queens: for instance, in Titania, the queen of the fairies in *A Midsummer Night's Dream*, and Cleopatra. Ultimately, though, she was his audience. How many of the plays were crafted with her in mind?

Accepting, in his open-armed way, all (or at least many) of the candidates, Rylance favors a collaborative view of the authorship. "There are such interesting phases in the creation of the plays," he said, referring to the different genres: the histories, comedies, tragedies, and late romances. "There are clearly different influences that come in. Obviously, the development of the verse writing, too." The traditional blank verse of the early plays becomes, by the late plays, irregular and varied. "It's so much more human and broken and interesting, the way they're using verse to express emotional states. I always imagine different members of the group joining or rising in influence." He sees the anonymity as a philosophical position. "If you're writing plays that you want to emulate nature, to mirror nature, to be as credible and real as nature—we don't know the author of nature. We may believe there is a god or a goddess, but we don't really know. God is anonymous."

"Yes, I think it's philosophical," said van Kampen. "You see it in music.

People forget to look at the rest of Renaissance culture. They did sincerely believe that the muse sat on your shoulder, and you were inspired. So therefore you can't put your name to it. So many pieces of music in the Renaissance are anonymous for that reason—left unsigned because it was the inspiration of the muse. It's such a Renaissance way of thinking. Later, in the age of Enlightenment, it's all about ownership of the idea. 'This is my book, this is my painting.'"

But it was "important," Rylance insisted, that the Stratford man was the face of it. "They wanted it to be accessible," he said, "to be grounded, not be floating in the air but really grounded in the flesh of a person who was a common man." He paused. "And maybe they also just had a sense of humor about it. I think the wit of the author is the most sublime part. There's a good joke going on."

"You value the disguise," I realized.

"Yeah, it has a value and a beauty." Rylance compared it to a Hopi Indian tradition in which the elders don masks and appear as spirit beings, imparting important truths to the youth. When they come of age, there is an initiation. The spirit beings take off their masks, and the initiated see behind the disguise—see that the "gods" were, in fact, their tribe elders. "I think that is something that, in time, will come of the Shakespeare plays," he said. Some anti-Stratfordians want to see the Birthplace dismantled immediately, which Rylance finds "a bit Protestant-Puritan, like doing a production where Rosalind is herself the whole time. If the plays say anything, they show that disguises are a useful way to get to the truth." He isn't concerned with ripping off the mask or taking down Stratford. "We're not meant to kill it, we're not meant to deny it, we're meant to go through it," he insisted. "And I've written to Stanley about this. Why do we have to be in conflict? Why can we not accept Stratford as the attributed home and face and name of the author and then look at how that happened?" It would be brilliant, he suggested, if the Birthplace had exhibits devoted to the alternate candidates. "Why not have bus trips to Oxford's house and Bacon's?" He went on, imagining an authorship utopia where everyone coexisted harmoniously. "We would see that we're all children of Shakespeare."

After leading the Globe through its first decade, Rylance resigned, exhausted by arguments with the Education Department and the literary community. The more successful the Globe became, the more the papers seemed to attack him. He'd had enough of "what I kind of felt was abuse." Still, Rylance's departure was mourned enormously. "It was the fall of Rome," Dominic Dromgoole, his successor, recalled. "Mark ran the most successfully controversial theater in the world." At his farewell performance of *The Tempest*, people were sobbing in the foyer. Even James Shapiro had to agree. "On the one hand, I think it was a mistake to have someone who wasn't a Stratfordian running the Globe," he told the *New Yorker*. "On the other hand, he did a terrific job."

Another person had wandered into the garden, but we were so absorbed in conversation that I didn't see her until she was standing over us. It was Juliet Rylance, van Kampen's daughter and Rylance's stepdaughter, a slim, blond woman, also a Shakespeare actor. She had played Perdita and Cressida, Juliet and Desdemona, Rosalind and Miranda.

I wandered back into the house with van Kampen and Juliet. They were talking and laughing about the play *I Am Shakespeare*, which Rylance had written after leaving the Globe. It was about a former star Shakespeare scholar, Frank, who has lost his job after becoming obsessed with the authorship question. He hosts a Webcam chat show in which several of the authorship candidates join him as guests. Each tries to argue that he or she wrote the works—that they are the real Shakespeare. When the play opened in 2007, Rylance played Frank, and Juliet played Mary Sidney. It concluded with crescendoing music from *Spartacus*, the 1960 film epic about a slave rebellion against the Roman Republic. In the movie, the Roman senator Crassus demands that the true Spartacus come forward, or he and all the men fighting alongside him will be killed. As Spartacus, played by Kirk Douglas, rises to reveal himself, the other men stand, too, shouting, "I am Spartacus!," confounding the authorities' attempt to find him. Onstage, the authorship candidates shouted, "I am Shakespeare!" To their surprise, van Kampen and Juliet recalled, members of the audience started rising to their feet, too, shouting, "I am Shakespeare!" The play had tapped into the deep, unconscious ways in which we identify with the author.

"I believe whoever wrote Shakespeare's work hid himself—or herself—purposefully to allow each of us to be a creative author ourself rather than subject to a presiding authority," Rylance explained in the *Atlantic*. "Our uncertainty about who wrote these plays is a very positive aspect of them. It allows us to identify deeply with them."

At the end of the play, the audience cast their votes for the author. Astonishingly, Juliet's Mary Sidney got half the votes. "Because she comes out, after Oxford and Bacon and everyone, and says, 'Come on, guys, we know it was all of us!' " Juliet laughed.

We drank wine and talked about Elizabethan women—the educated women who had access to their fathers' libraries, read the classics in Greek and Latin, and wrote unpublished verse and closet dramas. "One often catches a glimpse of them," Virginia Woolf wrote, "whisking away into the background, concealing, I sometimes think, a wink, a laugh, a tear." They were there and not there, increasingly known and yet still unknown. A translation of the Roman historian Tacitus had been revealed, only in the past year, to be the work of Elizabeth I. How do we put women back in the historical picture when they've been systematically written out? Who was Jane Anger? Who was the excellent gentlewoman? Within the sociology of knowledge, there is a field called agnotology, the study of deliberate, culturally induced ignorance, from the Greek *agnosis* ("not knowing" or "unknown"). "How should we regard the 'missing matter,' knowledge not yet known?" asks the sociologist Robert Proctor. Despite the most heroic efforts of feminist scholars, women of the past will always be, to some degree, "missing matter."

TEN

The Reckoning

In 1925 a tenacious Harvard scholar named Leslie Hotson was researching Chaucer in the archives of the English Public Records Office when he stumbled across a key piece of missing matter—the 1593 coroner's report on the death of Christopher Marlowe.

Marlowe first surfaced as an authorship candidate in 1895, during the heyday of the Baconian theory, when an Ohio lawyer named Wilbur Zeigler published *It Was Marlowe: A Story of the Secret of Three Centuries.* The book was a novel, but Zeigler clearly intended his theory to be taken seriously. In the preface, he argued that Bacon and Shakespeare were very different kinds of writers, and that Shakespeare's style was, in fact, much closer to Christopher Marlowe's. That in itself was not a controversial claim. Scholars long agreed that Marlowe, the most popular playwright of his day, exerted a strong influence on Shakespeare. But Zeigler suspected that Shakespeare wrote like Marlowe because Shakespeare *was* Marlowe.

Marlowe was born in Canterbury in 1564—the same year as Shakespeare—to a cobbler. But the cobbler's son was soon receiving a first-class education. A scholarship to the prestigious King's School, where students were required to "never use any language but Latin and Greek," gave him the skills to earn another scholarship to Corpus Christi College, Cambridge. While at Cambridge, scholars suspect he was recruited as a spy—an "intelligencer" to help undermine plots against the Queen's life. College records show that Marlowe was absent from the university for unusually lengthy periods. When he was in attendance, he spent more than he could have afforded on his scholarship income alone. He studied Latin and translated Ovid's *Amores*, receiving his bachelor's degree in 1584. By 1587, a rumor was spreading that he intended to go to the Jesuit seminary at Rheims, in France, a site of Catholic plotting. Upon hearing of his Catholic defection, Cambridge hesitated to award him his master's degree. The Privy Council intervened, explaining that Marlowe was engaged in unspecified "affaires" on "matters touching the benefit of his country." Was Marlowe working for Privy Council member Francis Walsingham, the Queen's spymaster? The council ordered Cambridge to award Marlowe his degree, as the young man "had done her Majesty good service, & deserved to be rewarded for his faithful dealing." Moreover, it was "not Her Majesties pleasure" that persons employed as Marlowe "should be defamed by those who are ignorant in th'affaires he went about."

For six short years, from 1587 to his reported death in 1593, Marlowe embarked on a spectacular literary career. He wrote a popular lyric, "The Passionate Shepherd to His Love" ("Come live with me and be my love"); a longer narrative poem, *Hero and Leander*, which is so similar in style, language, and imagery to Shakespeare's *Venus and Adonis* that scholars assume Shakespeare must have had access to Marlowe's manuscript; and six plays, introducing the use of blank verse onstage and developing the soliloquy, both of which would become key features of Shakespearean drama. His plays, especially *Tamburlaine* and *Dr. Faustus*, were wildly successful. His *Edward II,* about the homoerotic relationship between the king and his favorite, Gaveston, was one of the first English history plays—a genre further developed by Shakespeare. In fact, Shakespeare's *Henry VI* plays are so Marlovian in style that scholars over the years have attributed them in part to Marlowe. Marlowe "haunts Shakespeare's expression, like a figure standing by his shoulder," notes one scholar. What "Marlowe had begun . . . Shakespeare would complete," agrees another. Marlowe was "curiously difficult for the young Shakespeare to exorcise completely," observed Harold Bloom. Shakespeare "only became Shakespeare because of the death of Marlowe," writes Jonathan Bate, suggesting that Marlowe's death gave Shakespeare a chance to emerge from Marlowe's shadow, even as he remained "peculiarly haunted" by that death.

To Zeigler, the curious relationship between Marlowe and Shakespeare—the ghostly haunting—could be explained if the two writers were one. The birth of "Shakespeare," he noted, coincided perfectly with the "death" of Marlowe.

In the spring of 1593, Marlowe's dangerous activities seem to have caught up with him. Various "lewd and mutinous libels" threatening Protestant refugees had been posted around London. One of them, the "Dutch church libel," written in iambic pentameter and alluding to Marlowe's plays, was signed "Tamburlaine." Did Marlowe write it? Was it an attempt by some enemy to set him up? The Privy Council ordered the arrests of those responsible for the libels. Marlowe's former roommate, the playwright Thomas Kyd, was arrested and his papers—"vile heretical conceits"—seized. Under torture, Kyd "affirmeth that he had [them] from Marlowe." On May 18, the Privy Council issued a warrant for Marlowe's arrest. The charge was atheism. Since the monarch was the head of the Church of England, atheism was treason, a high crime for which the ultimate penalty was to be burned at the stake. An informer, priest, and double agent named Richard Baines drew up a note "containing the opinion of one Christopher Marly concerning his damnable judgment of religion, and scorn of God's word." The note, notoriously known as the "Baines Note," recorded outrageous things Marlowe had apparently said: "Christ was a bastard and his mother dishonest"; "the woman of Samaria and her sister were whores, and Christ knew them dishonestly"; "St. John the Evangelist was bedfellow to Christ and leaned always in his bosom"; religion was invented "to keep men in awe"; "the sacrament . . . would have bin much better being administred in a Tobacco pipe"; and "all they that love not Tobacco & Boies [boys] were fools." Someone wanted Marlowe to go down. Atheism and heresy were sufficient to have him executed but, for good measure, he was also gay.

On May 20 Marlowe, who had been staying with his patron Thomas Walsingham (a cousin of Francis the spymaster), presented himself to the Privy Council. But instead of being immediately arrested and imprisoned, he was let go, instructed to "give daily attendance on their Lordships, until he shall be licensed to the contrary." Ten days later, he was dead, at twenty-nine. Within weeks of his death, fellow poets paid tribute. George Peele remembered him as "Marley, the Muses' darling." Michael Drayton wrote that he "had in him those brave translunary things / That the first poets had." Thomas Nashe lamented the death of his friend, "poor deceased Kit Marlowe."

But contradictory rumors circulated about the precise circumstances of his death. He was stabbed in the eye. No, he was stabbed in the head. It happened "in London streets." It happened "at Detford, a little village about three miles distant from London." There were two knives involved. Or was it just one? Marlowe was killed by his own knife. Marlowe was killed by his assailant's knife. Who was the assailant? He was "one whom he met in a streete in London." Elsewhere, "one whom hee ought a grudge unto" and "purposed to stab." Francis Meres claimed it was "a bawdy serving-man, a rival of his in his lewd love," who stabbed Marlowe to death as punishment for his "epicurism and atheism." Centuries later, in the *Oxford Dictionary of National Biography*, Sir Sidney Lee would write that Marlowe was killed in a drunken tavern brawl.

Noting the mystery surrounding Marlowe's death, Zeigler suggested he had faked his death and gone on to write under the name Shakespeare. Shortly after Marlowe's disappearance that spring, the name Shakespeare appeared in print for the first time, attached to *Venus and Adonis*. The theory received support from an unexpected source: a physics professor at what would become Ohio State University. Thomas Mendenhall had developed an early method of quantifying the style of different authors by counting the number of letters in every word of their works. Writers had a predisposition to use words of certain lengths, and graphs of the characteristic curve of each revealed that no two were alike. In 1901 a wealthy Baconian urgently requested that Mendenhall compare Bacon and Shakespeare. Several women were employed to perform the tedious task of counting the letters of more than two million words dredged from the works of Shakespeare, Francis Bacon, Christopher Marlowe, Ben Jonson, and others. As they began to plot the curves, it became clear that

Shakespeare and Bacon didn't match. Bacon's graph showed consistent use of much longer words. The others didn't match, either. But when they plotted Marlowe's curve, something "akin to a sensation" rippled through the group, Mendenhall wrote. "In the characteristic curve of his plays, Christopher Marlowe agrees with Shakespeare as well as Shakespeare agrees with himself."

A few other writers took up Zeigler's theory, but it lay mostly dormant—until Leslie Hotson's discovery. Far from putting the Marlovian theory to rest, the discovery of the coroner's report gave new life to the case for Christopher Marlowe.

The report records that Marlowe spent the day of May 30, 1593, in the tavern of Mrs. Eleanor Bull in Deptford, a neighborhood on the south bank of the Thames. He was in the company of three shady men: Robert Poley, Nicholas Skeres, and Ingram Frizer. Poley was a government agent employed by the Privy Council, an "expert dissembler," and the "very genius of the Elizabethan underworld," according to historians. Skeres was a con man and informer who had also worked for the Queen's spymaster Francis Walsingham. Frizer was a business agent for Thomas Walsingham. These three men were the only witnesses to what happened. Two days later, at an inquest, they testified that they had met with Marlowe in a private room around ten in the morning "& there passed the time together & dined & after dinner were in quiet sort together & walked in the garden belonging to the said house." Around six o'clock, they returned to the room. Frizer and Marlowe got in a fight over the bill—famously described as the "reckoning"—and exchanged "divers malicious words." Marlowe grabbed Frizer's dagger, which he was wearing "at his back," and struck him twice on the head. In the struggle that ensued, Frizer stabbed Marlowe in the right eye, killing him instantly. The stabbing was ruled an act of self-defense, and the body was buried hastily in an unmarked grave. Frizer, pardoned by the Queen, returned immediately to the service of his master, Thomas Walsingham, whose friend and "admired poet" he had apparently just killed.

Hotson published the full text of the coroner's report in his book *The Death of Christopher Marlowe* (1925), in which he raised the possibility that the three witnesses—Frizer, Skeres, and Poley—had "concocted a lying account of Marlowe's behaviour, to which they swore at the inquest, and with which they deceived the jury." Others began to suspect as much as well. The three witnesses were effectively professional liars, all tied to the Walsinghams and the Elizabethan underworld. What was Marlowe, who was supposed to be reporting daily to the Privy Council, doing in their company? Was he really killed in a fight over the bill? Could a knife wound to the eye even cause instant death? Why wasn't Eleanor Bull, the tavern owner, or one of her servants called to testify? Did anyone besides the three witnesses identify the corpse? "There is something queer about the whole episode," wrote another scholar, acknowledging that Hotson's discovery "raises almost as many questions as it answers."

To this day, scholars remain divided on the circumstances of Marlowe's death. Some take the report at its word, believing that Marlowe was killed in a fight over the bill. Others suspect that it was an assassination, and the report a cover-up. The three witnesses were a "profoundly slippery trio," writes the scholar Charles Nicholl, and the only evidence for Marlowe's attack on Frizer is "the testimony of a pair of professional deceivers." Though these scholars acknowledge the "queerness" of the report, they do not give credence to the third theory: that facing trial and almost-certain execution, Marlowe was spirited away with the help of his spy mates.

⁂

"They don't want to take it on because of what it might mean," Ros Barber told me, "because of what would happen next. If he's alive, there's a possibility he wrote the works of Shakespeare."

Barber, a poet, novelist, and scholar in her fifties, with long blonde hair and watchful eyes, is cautious when it comes to the authorship question. She speaks in possibilities, not certainties. She doesn't possess Alexander Waugh's utter conviction, but she does think Marlowe is the best candidate.

Unlike most other authorship theories, the Marlovian theory has the advantage of a nonaristocratic candidate. Proponents cannot be accused of snobbery. On the other hand, it depends on what certainly feels like a conspiracy theory: a faked death. In 1955 an American theater critic and press agent, Calvin Hoffman, popularized the Marlovian theory with *The Man Who Was Shakespeare.* A British schoolteacher, A. D. Wraight, took up the cause in *The Story That the Sonnets Tell.* A stained glass memorial window to Marlowe was unveiled in Poets' Corner in Westminster Abbey, with a question mark over his death date: 1564–?1593, reflecting the serious doubts about the coroner's report. Stanley Wells and Paul Edmondson have called several times upon the dean of Westminster to remove the question mark. Nevertheless, the question mark remains. In 2001 the BBC and PBS aired a documentary, *Much Ado About Something,* which introduced a new generation of skeptics to the Marlovian theory. Barber was a single mother, writing poetry and teaching creative writing classes, when she saw the documentary.

"I thought, 'Oh my God, this is really something.'" She recalled a scene in which Jonathan Bate, "very angrily digging his vegetable garden, said, 'It's a ludicrous idea, but it would make a great novel.' And I went, 'Ding! Light bulb!' Imagine being the greatest writer of all time but nobody knows. You can't say because if you do, you'll put your life and the life of people you love at risk! I thought, 'What a great story! I love this story.' But it was for a novel, just for a novel."

We were walking along the beach of Brighton, Britain's famously (or infamously) bohemian seaside town. People were jogging and dog-walking and sipping their coffees. A pier stretched out in front of us into the sea. Beyond it, the rotting skeleton of a Victorian fun fair. After watching the Marlowe documentary, Barber had dug into the authorship question, writing her novel while earning her PhD in English literature at the University of Sussex. *The Marlowe Papers,* an award-winning "noir thriller in doublet and hose," imagined the version of history in which Marlowe escaped into exile to write the works of Shakespeare. If Shakespearean biography was highly fictional, why couldn't Marlovian fiction be highly biographical? Examining the blurry line between fiction and biography, Barber used her PhD to argue that multiple versions of history can be told using the same data—that history is a story, and the story we find may depend on the story we're looking for.

"I could not believe how unsupported the orthodox story was," she recalled. The evidence was "incredibly flimsy—some slightly dubious interpretation of a text that has at least one other, possibly more valid interpretation." Scholars had interpreted the data to tell a Stratfordian history, but the same data could be used to tell a Marlovian one. It was the first doctorate in Britain and the second in the world (after Roger Stritmatter's) to examine the authorship question. "By the end of it," said Barber, "I was a committed anti-Stratfordian."

Today Barber teaches at Goldsmiths, University of London, and sits as director of research at the Shakespearean Authorship Trust. She signs off its newsletters, "Together in doubt." It is nearly impossible to wade into the authorship question and remain uncommitted. The human propensity to order data into a narrative, to create a story, is too strong, and dwelling in uncertainty—in the space of simply not knowing—is too uncomfortable. Humans are hardwired to avoid uncertainty, which can cause tremendous anxiety and distress. According to psychologists, the brain even prefers physical pain to uncertainty. (In one study, participants who knew they would receive a mild electric shock were calmer than those who were told they had only a 50 percent chance of receiving the shock.) Unusually among both Stratfordians and anti-Stratfordians, Ros Barber has tried to make a virtue of uncertainty. "Evidence is everything," she said. Her parents were physics teachers. Her first degree was in biology. Before she turned to literature, she worked as a computer programmer. Her relentless skepticism makes her a formidable opponent for Stratfordians. She takes apart the traditional beliefs and arguments with the calm, unemotional detachment of a surgeon, cutting here and there until the entire edifice of orthodoxy falls apart, a little pile of unexamined assumptions at her feet.

In 2013 Stanley Wells and Paul Edmondson invited her to join them for their launch of *Shakespeare Beyond Doubt*—a live event in Stratford followed by a webinar called "Proving Shakespeare." Barber had just published *The Marlowe Papers.* But as the book was fiction, they apparently didn't realize she was a genuine anti-Stratfordian. In front of a packed live audience in Stratford, Barber politely and forensically challenged their claims about Shakespeare. "She's bloody sharp," Waugh told me. "She absolutely ran circles around them." Wells grew red with rage. Edmondson tried to disinvite her from the webinar that followed, which was to be broadcast live around the world. Barber cheerfully insisted on going through with it. A recording was uploaded online. Waugh and his family play their favorite parts on repeat.

"It's hysterical. I mean it's absolutely hysterical," Waugh told me. "You can tell he's getting tenser and tenser as he realizes it's going all wrong for him." In the recording, Edmondson suggested—somewhat sexistly—that Barber was a modern-day Delia Bacon. "Is that fair?" he asked. "No, I would think that's not at all fair," she responded. "I mean, for a start, she was self-taught . . . whereas I've done an MA and a PhD." They disinvited her from dinner that evening, silently dropping her back at her hotel.

But Barber turns her skepticism on other anti-Stratfordians, too.

"I came into this trying to understand how beliefs are formed," she told me. "The problem I see—and I see it in different camps—is that people just become convinced. They're convinced it's one person or another person or a group of people. But they become convinced by a single theory, and they immediately become subject to confirmation bias, and the more convinced you are, the harder it is for you to think straight and to think critically and to read the evidence in an unbiased way. I went to an Oxfordian conference, and just the way they talk—'When Oxford wrote *Hamlet* . . .' If you're starting from that point of view, you're never going to see anything clearly! You're going to read every little scrap, every little thing that supports your point of view—that's why every time they see 'every' or 'verily' they decide it's about Oxford. The great thing about doubt," she went on, "is when you doubt—when you fully doubt—you see lots of stuff that other people aren't seeing. Sure, have doubts about Shakespeare, but have doubts about your own candidate, too. Doubt everything. Have doubts about this piece of evidence or that argument. Drill into it. Go 'Where does that come from? Is that true? Is that really what that text means?' It matters, it really matters. Otherwise, we go down the tramlines of our own thinking and end up in the bin."

Barber thinks that arguing for any particular candidate—whether Oxford or Marlowe or someone else—is the wrong strategy. First, the incumbent has to be unseated. "Otherwise, it just turns into infighting, and that really does help the Stratfordian case," she said. Stratfordians often argue that the sheer number of different candidates proves that the whole thing is absurd. "It's a ludicrous argument," she continued. "The reason why there are so many candidates is because there's so clearly so much to doubt. And people like certainty, and they want to rush to put someone in that place." She tries not to be too publicly critical of her fellow anti-Stratfordians' claims, although she does admit that "sometimes I doubt them and doubt their methods."

She doubts, for instance, Alexander Waugh's interpretation of William Covell's phrase "courte-deare-verse," to mean "our de vere—a secret."

"You don't think it contains an anagram?" I asked.

"No. Covell puts Shakespeare in a chapter about university writers," she said, referring to the printing of "Sweet Shak-speare" in the margin of the text. "He clearly thinks Shakespeare is of the university." She agreed with Waugh that Covell's inclusion of Shakespeare cast doubt on the authorship, but not that it pointed to Oxford. "I'm a scientist by background," she said, shaking her head. "I'm not just going to be swayed by your first interpretation of the text. As a writer as well, I know there are multiple layers, especially with poetry."

Barber sees another layer in the Covell text. "Sweet Shak-speare" is printed in the margin next to "courte-deare-verse," but it is embedded in a string of phrases: "All Praiseworthy Lucrecia. Sweet Shak-speare. Eloquent Gaveston. Wanton Adonis. Watsons heyre [heir]." "Lucrecia" and "Wanton Adonis" appear to reference Shakespeare's poems *The Rape of Lucrece* and *Venus and Adonis*, which were the only works bearing Shakespeare's name that had then appeared. But what is meant by "Eloquent Gaveston" and "Watsons heyre"? Some scholars have suggested that "Gaveston" is simply an error, incorrectly listing the poem *Piers Gaveston* by Michael Drayton among Shakespeare's works. Barber sees another explanation: that Covell might have been thinking of Marlowe's Gaveston, who opens and dominates his play *Edward II*. "I think he recognizes Marlowe's style," she said. "He says 'Watson's heir.' Marlowe is undoubtedly Watson's heir." Marlowe was nine years younger than his friend the poet and playwright Thomas

Watson, who was also probably a spy. Watson had traveled through Europe for seven years and died under mysterious circumstances in 1592, just a year before Marlowe. A month after his death, his friend "CM" (probably Marlowe) saw one of his works through the press. When Covell wrote "Watsons heyre," did he mean Marlowe? "Let's say Covell sees Shakespeare's works come out, brand new, the first two poems. He recognizes Marlowe's style in Shakespeare and he links him. You can absolutely read that as Covell *hasn't* made a mistake. Covell thinks that's Marlowe."

Despite their interpretive differences, Waugh and Barber are friends, and she does at times admire his analysis, such as his decrypting of the Stratford monument to uncover the allusions to Chaucer, Beaumont, and Spenser.

"That was really a fantastic piece of scholarship. He really is a very clever man, well educated." But after he published his interpretation of the Covell text, it became "an absolutely public commitment to Oxford," she said. "He put himself in a position where he *has* to be right, do you know what I mean? You can't change your mind when you've made that level of commitment, when you've committed as hard as that. It's the same kind of commitment Stanley Wells has made with the books he's written. There's no coming back from that. There's no 'I was wrong' from that. You're now at the kind of passionate, extremist end of things."

Instead of advocating passionately for Marlowe, Barber's focus is on getting the authorship question accepted as a valid academic subject. She thinks the academy will evolve slowly. "It's like the Max Planck quote that science advances one funeral at a time," she said. "The old guard will die out." And perhaps the democratization of knowledge will help speed the transition. "I think the Internet has allowed the spread of doubt. I think doubt is more prevalent now than ever before, and people are more able to inform themselves of the reasons to doubt. There's more material out there. So, there will be a slow shift."

I kept hearing that, I said, but it's hard to see much softening—except in a few cases, such as William Leahy, the "bog-standard" Shakespeare professor who began questioning the authorship.

"Well, there won't be any softening in individuals who are committed to their beliefs," said Barber. "Bill defected, and he is extraordinary in that regard. That's proper scholarship! Being prepared to change your mind. Most people are not that way, and I forgive them all. We're all deeply flawed."

She talked about the social psychology of belief formation, which begins when we're just a little convinced of an idea. We argue for it, and if someone argues against us, we often become more committed to our side, strengthening our original position. We start gathering evidence to defend it. We seek out information that supports our belief. By the time we have the argument again, we're even more committed, and when we encounter evidence that runs counter to our beliefs, instead of reevaluating what we've believed, we tend to reject the incompatible evidence. Psychologists call this "belief perseverance." Facts that suggest our belief is wrong feel threatening, like an attack, especially if the belief is aligned with our personal identity. And when we feel attacked, it becomes extremely difficult to hear another point of view. We fend off the attack by rejecting the threatening evidence and reaffirming our original belief.

"I mean, I'm subject to confirmation bias. No one is immune," said Barber, "but committed Stratfordians—their whole careers are built on this. They can't possibly change their minds." She pointed to parallels in the sciences. In his landmark 1962 book *The Structure of Scientific Revolutions*, the philosopher of science Thomas Kuhn argued that there are periods of "normal science," in which scientists work in a settled paradigm or framework, but these periods are interrupted by the discovery of "anomalies," which leads to periods of revolutionary science, the questioning of old data, and paradigm shifts. (The Copernican Revolution, moving away from the Ptolemaic, geocentric model of the universe to the heliocentric model, is one such paradigm shift.) Barber sees something similar going on here.

"Most people are doing the 'normal science,' which is Stratfordianism," she explained. "They're working within the paradigm. Those of us outside the paradigm are seen as absolutely ridiculous, just like the guy who discovered tectonic plates moving, just like the guy who discovered what oxygen actually was." It's lonely at first, but "then more and more people get persuaded by your arguments, and, at some point, the balance shifts, and they're the old guard, and now their ideas are irrelevant."

Shifts in the humanities are trickier than those in the sciences. Scientists are at least dealing in quantitative data, in numbers and measurements; literary scholars deal with text, and text—good text—is always open to interpretation. But even scientists fall prey to confirmation bias. A study of lab scientists that found they threw away results that didn't support their hypothesis. "That's scientists!" she exclaimed. "What chance do humanities scholars have!?"

Barber believes that the dismantling of the incumbent has to be done in scholarly ways, without accusing anyone of idiocy. It has to be done piece by piece. "It's all about pulling threads on jumpers until the whole thing falls apart," she said. She has made a career of pulling threads. For instance, after the claim was made in *Shakespeare Beyond Doubt* that the plays use Warwickshire dialect, she went through digitized databases to show that not a single one of the two dozen words and phrases that were cited were local Warwickshire words. Many were commonly used at the time, such as "mazzard" (a type of cherry), and appeared in the works of other playwrights who didn't come from Warwickshire. Other words were listed in *The English Dialect Dictionary* as Warwickshire dialect only because Shakespeare used them—and Shakespeare was thought to come from Warwickshire. It was a circular argument. When she published her research in the *Journal of Early Modern Studies*, Barber noted that Shakespeare's use—or nonuse—of Warwickshire dialect wasn't particularly important in itself, but that it illustrated the effect of the authorship question remaining taboo. Errors of etymology and reasoning had persisted because scholars couldn't safely challenge the orthodox position without risking their professional reputations. As it turned out, challenging assumptions about the authorship could actually lead to a better understanding of Shakespeare's language. "They can't resort to the Warwickshire dialect argument now," she said. "They can't. I mean, they have still tried. But they can't really."

Politely overturn enough of their claims, she believes, and the Stratfordians will have no arguments left. "All sides are calling each other 'idiots,'" she went on. "But it's not idiocy. It's just the way human brains are wired. If you allow yourself to be convinced of something, you will always be able to find evidence to support it . . . and that's why I argue for the importance of remaining uncertain and embracing uncertainty."

"Uncomfortable for most people," I suggested.

"You get used to it." She smiled.

"You don't want to get out of your uncertainty."

"No," she protested, "I would *love* some hard evidence."

"Do you think there are things to be found still?"

She nodded. "We've been looking in the wrong places. All the research money, the funding, the really gifted scholars, the people who can read Latin and secretary hand, have been looking in the wrong archives based on the orthodox story. A new document about Marlowe was found only in the 2000s!"

⁂

Barber loves Marlowe, the brilliant son of a shoemaker who raised himself up through the sheer force of his intellect, who pioneered new forms of English drama, who was slandered by enemies as atheist and queer, whose dangerous work in the intelligence services led to his premature demise, who has gone down in history—unjustly, she argues—as a violent hothead with a knife in his eye. "It's sexy, of course it is. He's a bad boy," she said. But he's not a thug, he's "a trusted government agent, he's an intellectual, he's a questioner, he's super, super intelligent." We were walking back along the promenade, past the piers and the cafes, toward her house. Barber was giving me the case for Marlowe—*her* case for Marlowe.

"People think his death is a bit of an inconvenience, but I actually think quite the opposite. I think his death—the timing of his death and when the name 'Shakespeare' appears—is absolutely a strength." *Venus and Adonis* was registered in London on April 18, 1593, but registered anonymously, under no name. Marlowe supposedly died a month later, on May 30. The poem then came out in June. (The first recorded purchase was in London on June 12 by a court official who worked for Lord Burghley.) "The timing is perfect," said Barber. "I write in a noted weed"—in familiar clothing—"so every word almost tells my name," she paraphrased the sonnet line. "It's basically saying, 'I can't change my style.'" Late Marlowe and early Shakespeare are "very hard to tell apart stylistically," she added. "Scholars have always seen the links between them. Computer programs have really struggled to tell them apart, unless you really distort the algorithm." If Marlowe was to keep writing, he needed not just a pseudonym, which would look suspicious if investigated, but a proper front, an actual person's name. "He has a better reason to hide his identity than anyone. We're not talking about 'It might ruin my reputation.' It's that or death!"

She was getting more and more passionate as she went on. As much as Barber champions the virtues of uncertainty, she, too, cannot help evolving her theory of the past. To her credit, she is clear-eyed about her Marlovian bias. "He came out of nothing. I identify with him," she admitted. "I kind of come out of nothing. My mum was a teacher at secondary school. My dad's dad was working class. I was sent to an Essex comprehensive. I didn't have Latin. I didn't have the connections." There it was again: class. How much was Barber's authorship view—her preference for Marlowe, her rejection of Oxford—colored by her own background? When I asked Waugh why he thought she didn't support the Oxfordian theory, he said, "It's class." Barber is "very left-wing. I mean, it's unfair for me to guess what she thinks, but if I were to guess, I'd say she's one of those people who's absolutely allergic to the idea of Shakespeare, who she loves, being an English toff earl."

Barber showed me in through a plain door set back slightly from the street in an alley where, she lamented, drunk beachgoers had a tendency to relieve themselves. Inside, the house was a sort of secret jewel box, the walls richly painted in garnet and gold and emerald green—a poet's house. We walked up to the top floor and out onto the terrace, lined with potted plants and flowers. Barber began pulling down laundry from a clothesline as she ran through the Marlovian theory, playing out the motivations and rationales of all the players involved. The archbishop of Canterbury and his allies would have wanted Marlowe dead, as an example to atheists; Burghley and his allies would have wanted their spy alive. "Marlowe's exile would have been a compromise," said Barber.

"Why was he absolutely facing death?" I asked.

"The blasphemies in the Baines note," she said, referencing the note that listed blasphemous things Marlowe had supposedly said. "It's enough to kill him, just like that. John Penry was killed for less." Penry, a Protestant preacher, was imprisoned and charged with sedition for an unpublished petition he wrote to the Queen. He was executed the day before Marlowe reportedly died.

If the charges were so serious, I wondered, then why was he let out after his arrest?

"Exactly!" Barber exclaimed. "It's really hard to understand, given the seriousness of these charges, why he isn't just slung into prison. Anyone else would have been just slung into prison. But no, if you're a key agent for the Crown, and you've got into this trouble because of your work for the Crown—they're working something out," she went on. "The only person that can sign off on him being sent into exile is the Queen. 'I'm going to make it seem like he's dead so people can say that was a punishment from God because he was a blasphemer, but at the same time, he can still be useful to you, Burghley.'" The coroner who conducted the inquest was not the local coroner but the Queen's coroner, Barber reminded me. "It means the Queen has got control over what's happening at that inquest. The Queen's fingers are on this."

To Barber, Elizabeth I's involvement answers the perplexing question of why Marlowe was allowed to roam free after his arrest: he had to be in order to stage his death. And it explains why he passed the day in a tavern in Deptford, of all places. Eleanor Bull—owner of the house in which the death reportedly occurred—was not just a random barkeep. She was cousin to the Queen's close confidante and attendant Blanche Parry, chief gentlewoman of the Privy Chamber, who worked closely with another cousin of hers, Lord Burghley. Some have suggested that Eleanor Bull's lodging house in Deptford was used as a government safe house. "Mrs. Bull was a widow of good family lineage, whose likely discretion would have suited secret agents," writes one scholar. Right on the Thames, the house may have been a stopping-off point for people going to and from the Continent.

"Why's he in an all-day meeting?" Barber continued. "It's an eight-hour meeting!" In *The Marlowe Papers*, Marlowe and his fellow dissemblers are planning—and waiting. They wait first for Poley to turn up. (The "expert dissembler" had been in the Netherlands and suddenly returned to join the little party at Deptford.) Then they have to procure a body to dress as Marlowe's. They use John Penry's body. The Protestant preacher, who had been imprisoned since March, was suddenly hanged on May 29 in South London—not far from Deptford. There is no record of what happened to his body. The men in Deptford wait for Penry's body to be delivered, and when it arrives, they take it upstairs and dress it in Marlowe's clothes. Then they stab the dead body in the eye—a sure way to guarantee that no one looks too closely. "Death's a great disguiser, and you may add to it," Barber said, quoting from Shakespeare's *Measure for Measure*, in which the characters perform a body substitution trick. Angelo demands Claudio's head, but they execute another prisoner instead, shaving his head and trimming his beard to "add" to the disguise of death. "Dead bodies do look different from live people," said Barber. "Then you get a jury of people who don't know Marlowe. They don't know what he looks like anyway. The jury is yeomen. They're not going to think three gentlemen are lying to them. This is the class system at work."

Next, they wait for the tide to go out. "Who serves the Queen / must travel with the currents, like the tide / is pulled by the moon," Poley tells Marlowe. "Rob Poley smiles / that noose of a smile he saves for lethal words. / 'This is good-bye.'" The pair make their escape. Poley was carrying letters from the Netherlands for the Queen but did not deliver them to her for another two weeks. When he did, it was recorded that he had been in the Queen's service the whole time. What was he doing? "Nothing in either of the orthodox stories explains Poley's absence," said Barber. Under torture, Thomas Kyd reported that Marlowe was planning to go "unto the King of Scots," although "Poley's gone for long enough that it might have been a Channel crossing rather than Scotland," Barber mused.

"Were other people exiled this way?"

"Well, obviously, successful ones won't be found out," she said. "It's not actually difficult to fake a death in this era. But we do know people fake their deaths because some get found out." The spy Gilbert Gifford, who worked for Francis Walsingham, apparently died in a prison in Paris in 1590, only to reappear in Marlowe's company in 1592 under the name Gifford Gilbert. Deaths in the world of espionage can be blinds for disappearances, she emphasized.

The biggest hole in the Marlovian theory is that there is no evidence of Marlowe's continued existence; if his death was faked, it was faked successfully. Marlovians retort that there is no evidence William of Stratford attended grammar school, either, yet scholars assume he did because it's necessary to create a plausible narrative for his authorship.

"Why not assassination?" I asked. Marlowe clearly had enemies.

"The problem is that no one has been able to make a good case for killing him. He was already going down! And if you're going to have him killed, why not just stab him in an alley in the dark and throw him in the Thames? It's quite easy, especially in that day and age. But if you want to fake someone's death, you make it good and documented. You go, 'Look, here's an inquest document by the Queen's own coroner showing he's dead. Here's some witnesses who say he's dead. He's definitely dead.' "

But then what about the rest of the logistics? "Could he really have written plays from abroad all those years and sent them back to London?"

"Yeah, why not? What about the on-the-ground evidence for the author being in Italy?"

"You would need to have someone who could take things back," I noted.

"Stuff gets sent back and forth all the time," said Barber. "You have the diplomatic service. You have traveling troupes of players. I think much more likely it goes through intelligence channels." She laid out a scenario in which Marlowe, exiled to the Continent, continued to work as an agent, providing intelligence as the Crown's eyes and ears in Italy, which was effectively enemy territory. The pope had issued a papal bull in 1570 declaring the Queen a heretic and excommunicating her. A spy exiled to Italy could be useful for gathering information on Catholic plots against the Crown. Themes of exile, banishment, disgrace, and lost identity run through the Shakespeare canon, Barber emphasized, and scholars acknowledge as much.

"Banishment is both the action which defines the canon and the reason for its existence," writes the scholar Jane Kingsley-Smith. "Again and again in his plays, an unforeseen catastrophe . . . suddenly turns what had seemed like happy progress, prosperity, smooth sailing into disaster, terror, and loss," writes Stephen Greenblatt. "The loss is obviously and immediately material, but it is also, and more crushingly, a loss of identity. To wind up on an unknown shore, without one's friends, habitual associates, familiar network—this catastrophe is often epitomized by the deliberate alteration or disappearance of the name and, with it, the alteration or disappearance of social status." The plays are obsessed with resurrecting characters believed wrongly to be dead, Barber added. Across the canon, thirty-three characters are presumed dead, seven of whom deliberately fake their deaths. In the Marlovian narrative, the obsession with resurrection starts to look like wish fulfillment: the author's desire to be restored to his former life. Marlowe may have hoped to return when the regime changed, Barber suggested. She cited the letter Francis Bacon wrote requesting that the new king "be good to concealed poets."

"If Marlowe was alive, why couldn't he have come back then?"

"Because I think you can't really resurrect someone," she said. "It causes too many problems. The people who were involved in disappearing him were still alive."

The idea of Shakespeare as an exiled spy is inescapably romantic, but it also captures something elemental about writers. All writers function a bit like spies. They are watchers, observing the people around them, studying character types, becoming flies on the wall for the sake of their art. They are obsessed with the gap between interior and exterior worlds, between what people think and what they say. "Everything is useful to a writer," Graham Greene insisted. "Every scrap, even the longest and most boring of luncheon parties." Greene was an agent for MI6, Britain's Secret Intelligence Service. He was a novelist before he became a spy, so writing was his cover for spying, but then spying also provided material for his writing. A surprising number of writers have been spies. Ian Fleming, who oversaw Operation Goldeneye—an Allied plan during World War II to keep Spain from joining the Axis powers—later drew on the agents he met during his time in the Naval Intelligence Division to create James Bond.

David Cornwell published his novels under the pseudonym John le Carré because active agents were forbidden to publish under their own names. Peter Matthiessen worked for the CIA and cofounded the *Paris Review*, the prestigious literary magazine, as a cover for his intelligence activities in France. Writers devise plots; spies unravel them. The playwright Anthony Munday, who worked for Oxford, was described as "our best plotter." In his earlier years, he traveled in Italy, probably as a spy infiltrating Catholic conspiracies.

The overlap between writing and spying obviously has to do with language, too. Poetic language is a language of encoded meanings. In the Renaissance, writers took this to an extreme, using what can only be called espionage techniques (anagrams, acrostics, palindromes, riddles) to communicate with readers. But all figurative language operates as a kind of code to be deciphered. Shakespeare, who observed human nature so closely, devised plots so brilliantly, and encoded meaning so cleverly, had all the qualities of a spy. But, of course, that doesn't mean he was one.

"Where *is* Deptford?" I asked. I was struggling to place it in my mental map of London.

"It's where I work," said Barber, referring to Goldsmiths. "I teach seminars in Deptford Town Hall." The surprise must have registered on my face because she laughed. "It's hilarious, isn't it? It was always meant to be."

Barber has a sense of fatedness about Marlowe—about her relationship to Marlowe. It's not just that she happens to teach at the site of his disappearance some four hundred years ago or that Marlowe came from a humble background like she did. It's also her name—Rosalind, after Shakespeare's heroine in *As You Like It.* In the play, Rosalind flees after Orlando, who has been exiled from court. Disguised as a boy, she searches for him in the forest, reading lines of love poems he has posted to trees. "That's what I'm doing!" Barber exclaimed. "I'm Rosalind going through the forest, looking at the poems pinned to trees!" One character even quotes from Marlowe's poem *Hero and Leander*: "Dead Shepherd," she says, referring to Marlowe, "now I find thy saw [saying] of might, 'Who ever lov'd that lov'd not at first sight?' " Another alludes to Marlowe's supposed death: "When a man's verses cannot be understood . . . it strikes a man more dead than a great reckoning in a little room." That word: *reckoning.* Scholars agree that the passage refers to the fight over the reckoning at Deptford. Shakespeare, whoever Shakespeare was, was familiar with the official account of Marlowe's death.

"*The* play with the Marlowe references, *the* person I'm named after, doing symbolically what I'm doing. Yeah, I believe in strange forces." She quoted *Hamlet*: " 'There are more things in heaven and earth, Horatio, than are dreamt of in your philosophy.' " "I resisted my fate for so long, but in the end, it got me," she said. "I was born to do this, fine."

⁂

Barber keeps pulling threads. In 2009 she published "Shakespeare Authorship Doubt in 1593," unraveling the belief that there were no doubts until the nineteenth century. In 2013 she began developing *Shakespeare: The Evidence*, a reference book that catalogues, point by point, all the evidence used on both sides of the debate, including the allusions omitted from orthodox texts. The book grew out of the event she did in Stratford with Stanley Wells and Paul Edmondson. "They don't even know this stuff exists," she said. "They don't put it in front of each other. It's not in their books. It's not in their journals." Barber's book does not argue for any candidate. It is blessedly, refreshingly dry, stripped of all speculation and narrative: just the facts.

In 2018 she launched the first MOOC (massive open online course) on the authorship question on Coursera in partnership with the University of London. The course, Introduction to Who Wrote Shakespeare, was rapidly flooded by Shakespeare's online warriors, who dominated the forums, attacking Barber and laying into every unknowing participant in the course. "It was kind of horrific, the amount of nasty attention I was getting and how difficult it was to manage what was going on in the forums while I was also trying to teach," she said. "It was like being bathed in a vat of acid every time." Unable to shut down the discussion forums, Barber started deleting insulting comments. Then the Shakespeare defenders complained that she was suppressing free speech. "I said, 'I'll leave up any argument you can make that doesn't involve insulting someone.' They attempted to flood it with 1-star reviews, but it still has a rating of 4.7 out 5 stars. Some thirteen thousand students have enrolled in the course, which continues to run, but for her own mental health, Barber no longer participates. One Stratfordian contacted her complaining that she wasn't active on the forums anymore, apparently missing the opportunity to attack her. "I said, 'I don't know if you've noticed, it's an online distance-learning course. There's videos. It just runs itself.'"

When the scholars behind *The New Oxford Shakespeare* used computational stylistics to identify specific hands in Shakespeare's plays—implying that Shakespeare's hand could be differentiated from, say, Marlowe's hand—Barber put her programming hat back on to show that their methods were mathematically unsound. If you applied the data set size that the scholars used to define Marlowe to Shakespeare, it could not find *Hamlet* to be Shakespeare's. Marlowe's known canon consists of only six plays. "The fact is that you haven't got a data set for Marlowe or nearly all other authors of the period that are large enough to do the analysis they're trying to do," she explained. "I came from IT. Garbage in, garbage out, they taught us. . . . And yet they're producing an expensive volume on the basis of this garbage."

The Marlovian theory needs Marlowe to be indistinguishable from early Shakespeare—to be, effectively, ur-Shakespeare. Naysayers contest that Marlowe and Shakespeare are very different: that *Tamburlaine*, for instance, is not on par with *Hamlet*. "It's just lazy thinking," Barber protested. "As if a writer doesn't develop their style. . . . It's not right to connect something written when someone's forty to something written when one's twenty-four." She sees a smooth development of style from Marlowe into early Shakespeare and late Shakespeare. "Late Shakespeare has as little to do with early Shakespeare as it has to do with Marlowe," she insisted.

Barber may have her own Marlovian reasons for contesting the findings of *The New Oxford Shakespeare*, but other scholars have raised similar critiques. The literary brawl was punctuated in 2019 by the intervention of a mathematician and programmer, Pervez Rizvi, who published a series of articles arguing that "much of the so-called cutting-edge research is pseudoscience." *The New Oxford Shakespeare* "uses mathematical models . . . but without the mathematical understanding that was needed to use them soundly," Rizvi wrote. "It was taken seriously by many because other Shakespeare scholars lacked the mathematical knowledge and the confidence to say that the emperor has no clothes."

Barber's goal is to do all the debunking of the incumbent that she can in her lifetime to make way for the rightful author. The real discoveries won't be found, she suspects, until after she's gone. But the "right" places to look depend on who you think is the right author. Barber mused about looking for traces of Marlowe in Italy.

We wandered back into the house. "What's really key is, do we not need to understand where genius comes from?" she said. "Because we've been sold an absolute pup, which is that this guy was just randomly born into being brilliant. Therefore, it's not accessible to the rest of us." To Barber, the so-called miracle of Shakespeare's genius obscured the truth of how his genius actually developed. It was dishonest. It made genius the product of divine chance rather than talent nurtured by a privileged education. "The thing that gets me about it is, the author is clearly an extremely educated person. I'm an educator. An education was absolutely vital for me, as it was for Marlowe, to get him out of the cobbler's shop, broadening his mind." Even if William went to the Stratford grammar school for a few years, he didn't go to university, she emphasized, and that's where the real education happened. "It's an argument for education," she insisted. "I think the real Shakespeare story is, Shakespeare was an educated person. I don't care which of the candidates it is. If they haven't read a hell of a lot of books, they're not Shakespeare."

How long would it be before the real story—whatever it was—triumphed? Mark Twain didn't think the Stratford man would vacate his pedestal for three centuries at least. That was in 1909. If Twain was right, we still had two centuries to go.

A cat crawled up on the sofa, seeking attention. "I do think in the end, it will win," said Barber, petting the cat. "I don't have any doubt about doubt."

It was nearly dark by the time I left. I felt like I was emerging from a haze. On the train back to London, I pulled up one of Barber's papers, published in a rather postmodern journal called *Rethinking History*, in which she read Shakespeare's sonnets through a Marlovian lens. She was able to get away with it because she framed the whole thing as a thought experiment demonstrating her point about history being an interpretation of the available data. If you look for Marlowe's story in the sonnets, you can find it. In fact, she argued, the sonnets can be interpreted to support the Marlovian narrative more easily than the Stratfordian one. The sonnets of separation, in which the poet pines for the young man, can be read as sonnets of exile: Marlowe's exile from England. "How heavy do I journey on the way," he writes in Sonnet 50. "My grief lies onwards and my joy behind." Finding himself in "limits far remote," he laments the loss of familiar things: "th' expense of many a vanished sight" (30). The "large length of miles" between himself and his friend has become an "injurious distance." There was something dizzying in rereading these lines through a Marlovian lens. Guided by Barber, I fell into another alternate history. "Let us divided live" (39), the poet writes. In Sonnet 44, he wishes flesh could travel like thought. Then "although my foot did stand / Upon the farthest earth removed from thee," he could still be with his beloved, for "nimble thought can jump both sea and land / As soon as think the place where he would be."

In *The Marlowe Papers,* Barber imagines that the friend is Henry Wriothesley, the 3rd Earl of Southampton. Lord Burghley is running a spy network out of his house. Marlowe shows up to report to him and meets his ward, the young Earl of Southampton, to whom he later addresses his poems and sonnets.

I continued reading Barber's paper. Through the Marlovian lens, the poet's disgraced name came into focus as Marlowe's slandered reputation. "Thence it comes my name receives brand." *Atheist, blasphemer, sodomite.* His "outcast state" was transformed in Sonnet 29 into Marlowe's literal state of exile:

When in disgrace with fortune and men's eyes
I all alone beweep my outcast state,
And trouble deaf heav'n with my bootless cries,
And look upon myself, and curse my fate.

The poet wishes to be restored to his former life—"Pity me, then, and wish I were renewed" (111)—but the man he once was has become the "prey of worms, my body being dead / The coward conquest of a wretch's knife" (74). The knife! Officially, Marlowe is dead, stabbed by a wretch's knife. He lives on only through his writing and his friend: "You are my all-the-world, and I must strive / To know my shames and praises from your tongue; / None else to me, nor I to none, alive" (112). But he urges his friend to avoid association with him: "Do not so much as my poor name rehearse" (71). The name of Christopher Marlowe must be forgotten: "My name be buried where my body is, / And live no more to shame nor me, nor you" (72).

I was struck all over again by the enigmatic perfection of the sonnets. They could be read as the literary exercises of "Will." Turn them over, and they were Oxford's autobiographical confessions. Shift the light again, and they become Marlowe's. I had read interpretations of them as Mary Sidney's poems: a woman writing to a young man. And still others that saw a little clique of poets exchanging sonnets back and forth, in conversation with one another. If Marlowe is assumed to be the author, Barber argued, the apparent mysteries and inconsistencies of the sonnets are clarified. Ambiguities vanish; paradoxes resolve; biographical events underlying strong emotions are easily identified. Above all, the Marlovian narrative provides a rationale for why the poet claims to have been silenced while he is still writing. In Sonnet 73, she notes, he compares his life to a dying fire—"consumed with that which it was nourish'd by"—echoing the Latin motto on Christopher Marlowe's putative portrait: *Quod me nutrit me destruit* (That which nourishes me destroys me).

I pulled up the portrait. It was discovered in the 1950s at Corpus Christi College, Cambridge—Marlowe's college. According to one account, it had been hidden behind a wall of paneling in a student's room, just above the room that had been assigned to Marlowe 370 years earlier. When a new heater was installed, the paneling and damaged portrait were discarded in a dumpster, where a student discovered it and took it to the college librarian. According to another account, a passerby noticed it in a pile of damp rubble during renovations to the master's lodge. I was frustrated at first that I couldn't even find a definitive account of the portrait's recovery seventy years ago. It was exhausting, this constant clawing for firm footing, for one fixed and reliable fact. But then I submitted to the uncertainty and felt much lighter.

The young man in the portrait is brown-eyed, a bit effeminate, wearing a dark velvet doublet with gold buttons. He crosses his arms and gazes at the viewer with a defiant expression. In the upper corner, an inscription gives the year, 1585, and the age of the man, twenty-one. Though he cannot be identified with any certainty, the date and location have led scholars to suspect he might be Christopher Marlowe, who would have been twenty-one years old in 1585. Marlovians will tell you that he bears an uncanny resemblance to a man in another portrait—a portrait rumored to depict Shakespeare. This man is older, balding, and heavyset, with a dark, vaguely Mediterranean complexion. He wears an earring and loose shirt ties. An eighteenth-century antiquarian claimed it was Shakespeare, but there is no name, date, or identifying motto. In 1856, the National Portrait Gallery in London acquired the portrait and called it the Chandos portrait after its former owner, the Duke of Chandos. It is probably the most famous work in the gallery's collection, but viewers have never warmed to it. "One cannot readily imagine our essentially English Shakespeare to have been a dark, heavy man, with a foreign expression, of decidedly Jewish physiognomy, thin, curly hair, a somewhat lubricious mouth, red-edged eyes, wanton lips, with a course expression and his ears tricked out with earrings," wrote a Victorian critic. While the gallery says that it "probably" depicts Shakespeare, it also acknowledges that the authenticity cannot be proven. The early history of the portrait is, in the words of the gallery's former curator, a jumble of "hearsay, half-remembered facts, and assumptions."

The Corpus Christi portrait is *maybe* Marlowe. The Chandos portrait is *maybe* Shakespeare. You can't build anything on a heap of maybes. It is interesting, however, that the Shakespeare Birthplace Trust doesn't use the Chandos portrait of Shakespeare—perhaps because it looks too much like the Corpus Christi portrait of Marlowe. They prefer the portrait that's more likely of Thomas Overbury, calling that "Shakespeare" instead. I pulled the Chandos portrait up next to the Corpus Christi portrait, remembering something that Barber had said: "To most people who haven't got skin in the game, it looks like the same person, twenty years later."

The Corpus Christi portrait, 1585

The Chandos portrait, ca. 1600–1610

ELEVEN

Negative Capability

THERE IS A PHRASE FOR the ability to dwell in the space of not knowing. It was coined not by a psychologist but by a poet. In 1817 John Keats wrote to his brothers, George and Thomas, describing a conversation he'd had with his friend the writer Charles Wentworth Dilke: "[S]everal things dove-tailed in my mind, and at once it struck me what quality went to form a Man of Achievement, especially in Literature, and which Shakespeare possessed so enormously—I mean Negative Capability, that is, when a man is capable of being in uncertainties, mysteries, doubts, without any irritable reaching after fact and reason."

What formed a great poet, a poet like Shakespeare, was—at least in Keats's view—his ability to resist advocating a singular vision of truth, to live with mystery and unanswered questions, to explore and articulate various points of view, not to reach for an absolute philosophy. And it was by dwelling in a state of openness—by rejecting the limitations of certainty—that he could achieve a greater artistic vision. As the critic Li Ou explains, "To be negatively capable is to be open to the actual vastness and complexity of experience, and one cannot possess this openness unless one can abandon the comfortable enclosure of doctrinaire knowledge."

The twentieth-century psychoanalyst Wilfred Bion saw that Keats's concept of negative capability had applications to psychology as well as poetry. Cultivating negative capability, Bion suggested, could help us tolerate the pain and discomfort of not knowing. Instead of rushing to impose false certainty on an ambiguous situation, we might learn to accept doubt, fragmentation, and uncertainty—and what then? If, for Keats, negative capability held the promise of artistic growth, for Bion it held the promise of psychic growth.

What might be gained from letting go of our certainty about Shakespeare? If scholars were no longer constrained by the Stratfordian paradigm—if the taboo was lifted—what might grow? Ros Barber's research on Shakespeare's nonuse of Warwickshire dialect offered a tiny glimpse into the ways in which the taboo inhibited inquiry. What other errors persisted? What questions weren't being asked? What avenues of research weren't being pursued? And then what riches lay on the other side of uncertainty? We might gain a deeper understanding of the plays and poems; of Renaissance history; of the nature of genius; of the relationship between life and art. But negative capability doesn't sit easily with history. How do you hold the desire to know the past—that "irritable reaching after fact and reason"—alongside a willingness to not know? To not reach? In writing a history, you implicitly close down alternate versions of that history. In asserting an alternate history, you close down others yet again.

"The certainty with which people kind of declare that this and that happened seems to me always to deserve a little bit of humility," Stephen Greenblatt told me one morning over Zoom.

After I returned to the States, I had been trying for some months to get hold of Greenblatt, America's preeminent Shakespearean, a charismatic Harvard professor, and author of the best-selling biography *Will in the World: How Shakespeare Became Shakespeare.* Mark Rylance introduced us over email. Greenblatt and Rylance—the Stratfordian and the anti-Stratfordian—are friends, which is a testament to the characters of both. Greenblatt responded warmly, agreeing to speak with me, but then I could never quite pin him down. He was in Greece and Italy for June and July, then Vermont for August. When I was back in the United States that fall, he was on sabbatical in England. I thought I might catch him in Boston in the new year, but then he was off to Vermont again, and then Italy once more for the remainder of his sabbatical. He was always unfailingly polite, but I couldn't quite shake the feeling that he was avoiding me. I almost flew to Rome, but that seemed a bit stalkerish. He hadn't invited me and, besides, he was being fuzzy about dates. I suspected I might arrive to discover he'd gone off to Florence for the week. So I suggested the only thing I thought he couldn't slip out of: a Zoom call.

Greenblatt is an academic rock star. As a young professor at Berkeley in the 1980s and 1990s, his lectures were said to be standing room only. He is considered one of the founders of New Historicism, a school of interpretation that seeks to understand literature in its historical context—in the times and circumstances of its author. In 2000 Greenblatt left Berkeley for Harvard. He received a million-dollar advance to write *Will in the World*, which showed, in the words of one reviewer, "small understanding of how to weigh historical evidence." One of his next books, which won the Pulitzer Prize, was described alternately as "brilliant" and plagued by historiographical errors that represent "an abuse of power." Though Greenblatt is now in his late seventies, he hasn't retired. He has small, dark eyes and a sharp, serious face. On Zoom, he had blurred out his background, so I couldn't gather anything of his Italian environs. His head floated on the screen, detached from physical space, like God appearing in the clouds.

I began by asking him about an article that appeared in *Harvard* magazine in 2004, shortly after the publication of his Shakespeare biography. "I set out to solve a mystery," Greenblatt said in the article, gesturing to the disconnect between the man's life and the works. But the process of writing the book "has made me respect that preposterous fantasy"—of an alternative author—"rather more than when I began," he said, "because I have now taken several years of hard work and forty years of serious academic training to grapple with the difficulty of making the connections meaningful and compelling between the life of this writer and the works that he produced." What impelled him to say that he found it "difficult" to make meaningful connections between the man and his works?

"We don't know that much about what our grandparents did, so when we go back a few generations, the amount of information we have is limited," he said.

The observation was perfectly true and perfectly silly, as though

Shakespeare—hailed as "immortal" in his own lifetime—could be compared to your average grandpa. When I asked him if it were possible to say, "I know Shakespeare wrote the works," or only possible to say, "I *believe* Shakespeare wrote the works," he didn't answer.

"It's an epistemological question," he said. "It's a question about anything we think we know from the past." Later, he brushed aside the issue by suggesting he wasn't qualified to answer: "These epistemological questions are above my pay grade." As we discussed the authorship question, his statements were, by turns, superficial and evasive. He was "reasonably confident" that Shakespeare wrote the plays attributed to him, though not every word, he admitted. "We know that the theater is a medium in which there are many hands involved." What did he think of the findings of *The New Oxford Shakespeare*? He was "interested," he said, but he was "burned years ago" when he edited the *Norton Shakespeare* and accepted Stanley Wells's and Gary Taylor's attribution of an anonymous poem, "Shall I Die?," as being by Shakespeare—an attribution that was later roundly rejected (including by Wells and Taylor). "There is about all such things, not just in literary attribution; in law, for example, always room for doubt," he said.

I wondered if he cared about the authorship. Maybe he was one of those people who thought it didn't matter, that only the plays mattered. "I do care," he insisted, "in the way that it would change things to discover that my grandparents actually came from Zimbabwe and not Lithuania. I would have to rethink things I thought I understood." I was intrigued by this recurring comparison to grandparents—as though Shakespeare were his grandfather, and if Shakespeare turned out to have been someone else, he would have to rethink not only Shakespeare but himself, too.

We talked about his Shakespeare biography, *Will in the World*, which had the unusual distinction of being both panned as "biographical fiction" and selected as a finalist for the Pulitzer Prize. The book had been an attempt "to fill in the blanks with what you can't know but you can try to speculate about," he said. "The speculation by itself doesn't seem to me all that interesting. What you can make of the speculation, if something really interesting comes of the speculation, then it's worth thinking through.

This is what I've come to feel about Mark Rylance or Derek Jacobi, that if it's somehow liberating for them to take what I believe is not the case and run with it, if it gets them somewhere . . ." Mark Rylance, he emphasized, is one of the best Shakespeare actors in the world. "If he's a better actor for believing that the words he's speaking were not written by William Shakespeare of Stratford, what do I care?"

He started talking about parallels in the sciences: a controversial book by one of his colleagues in Harvard's Physics Department laying out a theory that our solar system has been visited by intelligent life. The book had received an "unbelievable amount of blowback," Greenblatt said, but it was a "fantastically interesting book about not ruling out things that seem very, very unlikely."

Did he think then that alternative authorship theories shouldn't be ruled out?

I tried to bring us back from aliens to Shakespeare. In *Will in the World*, I'd noticed that he was selective about which sonnets he included, I said. He didn't discuss the sonnets that suggested the author intended his identity to be forgotten. He wrote beautiful passages about the fair youth and the dark lady, but nothing about "my name be buried where my body is," or "every word doth almost tell my name," or "I, once gone, to all the world must die." Why did he leave them out?

"You pick and choose in any story you're going to tell what actually works for you," he said.

Those sonnets were not part of the story he was telling. They didn't work in a Stratfordian biography.

"What do you make of them?" I pushed him.

"Now that you ask, I imagine that, on the whole, William Shakespeare of Stratford-upon-Avon, son of a glover, without a university education, thought that his name wasn't going to survive."

"Oh, he knows his verse will survive, though. It will outlast the gilded monuments of princes," I said, paraphrasing Sonnet 55. ("Not marble nor the gilded monuments / Of princes shall outlive this powerful rhyme.")

"That's true, that's true," he said.

Suddenly a phone rang. Greenblatt muted our call to take the incoming one. When he came back on, he said, "That was my wife, and I'm going to have to get off."

We'd been speaking for only twenty minutes. I had many more questions. How did he think Shakespeare learned French and Italian? His biography never attempted to explain Shakespeare's knowledge of those languages. Where did he think Shakespeare acquired his legal expertise? What about Shakespeare's knowledge of Italian cities? Did he think it was all inaccurate or did he agree with the Italian scholars that it showed an intimate acquaintance with the country? Why did he find it "striking" that Shakespeare's women are often reading? I wanted to see if confronted, Greenblatt would open himself up to negative capability—or twist himself into the usual Stratfordian contortions. I hoped we could pick up the conversation when he was back in Boston, but when he returned that spring, he slithered out of reach again. He was too busy, he explained, finishing his next book.

⁂

As I contemplated my next move, my thoughts turned to James Shapiro. It seemed fitting, after all the conversations I'd had since the *Atlantic* debacle, to return to him—to the beginning. In his article, he had invited me to come see a play at Shakespeare in the Park, but I knew that Shapiro was exceedingly unlikely to meet with me. Though the authorship question interested him enough to write an entire book on it, he avoided discussing it with anyone who might challenge him. In recent years, he had granted only one notable exception to his rule—his exchange with John Paul Stevens.

Since the mock trial in 1987, several more justices had joined Stevens in his dissent from orthodoxy. "It might well have been someone other than our Stratford man," Sandra Day O'Connor told the *Wall Street Journal*. Antonin Scalia, who once played Macbeth and had a penchant for citing Shakespeare in his court opinions, was openly Oxfordian. Ruth Bader Ginsburg wasn't sure who wrote Shakespeare, but she indulged her love of the plays by presiding over several fan-fictional Shakespeare trials, including the divorce proceedings of Claudio and Hero, Shylock's appeal, and Hamlet's insanity plea—a hearing determining his competency to stand trial for the murder of Polonius. ("My judgment was, yes, he was [competent]. But not only Polonius," she explained. "The grand jury should consider whether he should be indicted for Ophelia's death.") When Stevens died in 2019, Ginsburg delivered a eulogy, closing with Shakespeare. "Justice Stevens much appreciated the writings of the literary genius known by the name William Shakespeare," she said, taking care with her choice of words, "so I will end with a line from the Bard fitting the prince of a man Justice Stevens was: 'Take him for all in all, we shall not look upon his like again.' "

As I planned my interview with Shapiro, I read back over the copies I had made of his correspondence with Justice Stevens.

Stevens initiated the exchange, addressing a letter to Shapiro on Supreme Court letterhead. It was dated August 25, 2011. He wanted to know if Shapiro had "considered the possibility of collaboration" between Shakespeare and the Earl of Oxford. By way of evidence for Oxford, he cited a book from 1622 by Henry Peacham, *The Compleat Gentleman*, which listed the best Elizabethan poets for gentlemen to read. Peacham put Oxford first and, bizarrely, failed to mention Shakespeare.* As Stevens noted, Oxfordians take this list as yet another piece of evidence that "suggests that Oxford rather than Shakespeare was the principal author of plays attributed to him." Having read Shapiro's *Contested Will*, Stevens observed that "you omit comment on the Oxfordians' claim." It was true. Shapiro dismissed Oxfordian arguments as conspiracy theories without

*"In the time of our late Queen *Elizabeth*, which was truly a golden Age . . . above others, who honoured Poesie with their pennes and practise (to omit her Majestie, who had a singular gift herein) were *Edward* Earle of *Oxford*, the Lord *Buckhurst*, *Henry* Lord *Paget*; our *Phoenix*, the noble Sir *Philip Sidney*, M. *Edward Dyer*, M. *Edmund Spencer*, M. *Samuel Daniel*, with sundry others."

actually addressing the various pieces of evidence that make up the Oxfordian case. Now Stevens was challenging him to address one.

Shapiro responded rather fanboyishly, clearly tickled to be in correspondence with a Supreme Court justice. "It is a great honor to receive a letter from you. You are one of my heroes, someone who has long helped steer this country in the right direction and improved the lives of many Americans." He was happy to answer Stevens's questions and would be grateful if Stevens, in return, could answer a few of his. "[S]cholars are only beginning to turn their full attention to the subject of Shakespeare's collaborations," he wrote. But he dismissed the idea of collaboration between Oxford and Shakespeare, finding it "impossible to conceive of an aristocrat engaged in the back-and-forth of theatrical collaboration." In *Hamlet*, though, Shakespeare shows an aristocrat doing just that. When the traveling players come to court, the prince of Denmark hails one player as, "O my old friend," discusses dramatic composition with him, writes a speech to add into the play, and instructs the player at length on how to perform it. The scholar Oscar Campbell, one of Shapiro's predecessors at Columbia, considered this scene a "realistic picture" of Elizabethan life, arguing that such intimacy between an aristocrat and a player was not unlikely. But Shapiro couldn't "conceive" of it. Was history limited by what James Shapiro could imagine?

Shapiro did not respond to the issue of Henry Peacham's text listing Oxford as a great poet and omitting Shakespeare. Instead, he directed his own questions at the justice. "After reading the history of the Oxfordian movement (whose founder, J. T. Looney, despised the democratic values you have spent much of your life protecting, and who hit on a substitute author who embodied these antidemocratic, reactionary values), are you untroubled about subscribing to and in recent years playing a highly visible and legitimising role in this movement?" he asked.

I wasn't sure what Stevens knew of Looney, apart from what he had read in Shapiro's book, but he cut right through the noise: "The fact that Looney may have despised democracy seems to me to be irrelevant to the validity of any arguments he may have made either casting doubt on Shakespeare's authorship or supporting the hypothesis that Oxford played a role in writing the plays," he wrote. "I am not at all troubled by my encouragement of further study."

Shapiro's second question was about the issue of evidence. "How could someone so well versed in interpreting evidence reject the extensive documentary evidence linking William Shakespeare of Stratford to the plays?" he asked Stevens, explaining that "as deeply as I honor and respect your extraordinary accomplishments on the highest court in the land, I am profoundly disappointed in your anti-Stratfordian position." Stevens responded by emphasizing what he saw as the absence of evidence. "My response to your question about the weight of the evidence is based largely on attaching significance to the absence of evidence that I would have expected to be readily available," he wrote. "If he was the most famous and successful author of his time, is it not strange that there was no eulogy or other public comment at the time of his death?"

Stratfordians like to retort that absence of evidence is not evidence of absence—that the lack of evidence that the Stratford man owned books or was mourned at his death does not mean he didn't write the works. But it's the same argument used to defend the existence of God. Law books and legal briefs often note that "a reasonable doubt may arise not only from the evidence produced but also from a lack of evidence." To Stevens, the absence of evidence for the Stratford man gave rise to a reasonable doubt.

Stevens closed by following up on Peacham. "Do you attach any significance to Meachum's [*sic*] mention of Oxford and failure to mention Shakespeare?"

More than a month passed before Shapiro responded. When he did, he tried to argue that the absence of evidence for Shakespeare was not unusual. "You would be shocked how little writing survives—besides political and real estate and legal records—from late 16th and early 17th century England," he wrote, disregarding the letters, diaries, and journals that do survive (for instance, the diaries of Edward Alleyn, Philip Henslowe, Shakespeare's son-in-law, and the town clerk who once stayed at his house). "We know next to nothing about most of the dramatists of his day," Shapiro went on, again ignoring the letters, manuscripts, education records, and so forth that other dramatists left attesting to their literary careers. "But the major problem with your claim has to do with assumptions about 'most famous and successful,'" Shapiro admonished. "He was certainly not the most famous writer of his day. Jonson, a self-crowned laureate, was more famous. Donne too. Bacon as well. Perhaps even Nashe. And successful? Financially? In terms of literary accomplishment? That literary judgment was only rendered a century or so later. . . . So you need to think of Shakespeare as contemporaries saw him, as a major writer, one of perhaps a half dozen or so."

Stevens swiftly smacked down this argument by citing Shapiro's own evidence against him. "It seems to me that that characterization [of Shakespeare's fame] is supported by your comment on page 223 of your book that the 'sheer number of inexpensive copies of Shakespeare's work that filled London's bookshops after 1594 was staggering and unprecedented. No other poet or playwright came close to seeing seventy or so editions in print.'" Besides Shapiro's own words, Stevens could also have cited the praise of Shakespeare's contemporaries, such as poet Richard Barnfield, who wrote that Shakespeare would live "in fames immortal book," or Ben Jonson, who said he was "not of an age, but for all time." But how do you argue with a scholar who is ignoring the evidence in which he is supposed to be an expert?

"You did not comment on Meachum's [*sic*] mention of Oxford while failing to mention Shakespeare," Stevens added. He was not going to let Shapiro off the hook.

Shapiro did not respond for two months. He had been busy in London filming a BBC documentary on Shakespeare, he explained. Then he announced that he would be cutting off their correspondence. "This will probably be my last letter to you on the authorship question," he wrote, reiterating that Shakespeare wrote Shakespeare—as though repetition of the statement alone would convince a Supreme Court justice—and emphasizing again his disappointment. "You are a brilliant man, a great American, and one of my heroes. It will remain a source of profound disappointment, that someone as intelligent as you can continue to believe . . . that Shakespeare didn't write the plays. All I can say, one last time, is that he did."

I had the sense of Shapiro pounding his fists on the table, peeved that he had failed to persuade one of his great "heroes." He had grown emotional, repeated tired arguments, distorted the evidence, failed to answer Stevens's questions about Peacham (despite several reminders), and scolded the justice for his unbelief.

Stevens sent one last response, maintaining an unflummoxed graciousness.

"[I]t seems odd to me that a presumably knowledgeable critic like Henry Peacham would include Oxford and omit Shakespeare from his list of favorites . . . the *possibility* that the critic knew that Oxford had used a pseudonym or was a collaborator with Shakespeare does not seem to me to be 'unthinkable.' After all, evidence that Shakespeare did more collaborating than had originally been assumed does suggest that none of us can be absolutely certain about what was going on five centuries ago."

I set the letters aside, thinking about Stevens's remark that none of us can be certain about what happened in the Renaissance. The justice erred on the side of skepticism, of recognizing that our knowledge of the past is incomplete and imperfect. While Shapiro insisted on certainty, Stevens suggested humility—negative capability.

Opening my laptop, I wrote an email to Shapiro requesting an interview. A response landed in my inbox five minutes later. Shapiro refused to meet. The invitation he had issued in the *Atlantic* was just for show.

⁂

By the end of the summer, Queen Elizabeth II had died. I turned on the news to see guards in elaborate red-and-gold Tudor uniforms marching about London carrying swords and halberds. From a balcony of St. James's Palace, the Garter King of Arms—holding a scepter and wearing an ostrich-feathered velvet cap—read out the official proclamation declaring that "by the death of our late sovereign of happy memory," Prince Charles had become "our only lawful and rightful Liege Lord, Charles the Third." Trumpets sounded. Onlookers solemnly held their iPhones aloft. At the Tower of London the King's Guard, in their scarlet tunics and bushy black bearskin hats, fired a sixty-two-gun salute.

For the ten days of national mourning between the Queen's death and her funeral, Britain appeared to live in a Shakespeare play. It was a spectacular, immersive drama. No theater production could rival the costumes, props, and pageantry. In his first remarks as king, Charles III gave poetic shape to public emotions by quoting Shakespeare—twice. First, *Hamlet*: "May flights of Angels sing thee to thy rest," he said, paying tribute to his late mother in a television address. Then, *Henry VIII*: "As Shakespeare says of the earlier Queen Elizabeth, she was 'a pattern to all princes living,' " he observed in a speech to parliament. On the day of the Queen's funeral, I watched the procession: the royal family, the Household Cavalry, and members of the Royal Navy escorting the coffin—draped in the imperial standard and bearing the imperial state crown on a purple velvet pillow—through London to Westminster Abbey where it was carried down the long aisle, past Poets' Corner and the Shakespeare statue. In Stratford-upon-Avon the Royal Shakespeare Company screened the funeral as though it were, indeed, one of the plays in its repertoire.

On Twitter, the Shakespeare professor Jonathan Bate, Alexander Waugh's erstwhile combatant, was tweeting about the funeral. ("Very Prospero, that Lord Chamberlain wand-breaking moment," he noted, when the Lord Chamberlain broke his wand of office over the Queen's coffin.) Having left the University of Oxford, Bate had taken up a professorship at Arizona State University. In the arid American desert, he seemed vaguely nostalgic for England. I sent him an email requesting an interview and began drawing up questions. Among Bate's many books is one called *Shakespeare and Ovid*, devoted entirely to analyzing Ovid's influence on Shakespeare. (Bate calls him Shakespeare's "favorite author.") What would Professor Bate make of the reference in 1605 to "the late *English* quick-spirited, cleare-sighted *Ovid*"? Who could it be if not Shakespeare? And why was he "late" in 1605? Did Bate really think denying Shakespeare was like denying the Holocaust, as he once claimed? ("You deny the reality of Shakespeare one moment, you deny the reality of the Holocaust the next.") I liked the idea of discussing Shakespeare amid cactuses, beneath Arizona's wide blue skies. But Professor Bate never responded to my request, and I was drawn ineluctably back to England.

⁂

By the time I returned that fall, Boris Johnson, having resigned, had resumed writing his Shakespeare biography, the lettuce had outlasted Liz Truss, and Rishi Sunak, Britain's first prime minister of Indian origin, was installed at 10 Downing Street. At Audley End, a country house just north of London, Roger Stritmatter was analyzing three books that he claimed contained annotations in Oxford's handwriting pertaining to *Julius Caesar* and *Antony and Cleopatra.* They would deliver, he assured me, "a coup de grâce to the orthodox belief." Meanwhile, Mark Rylance was preparing to perform *I Am Shakespeare* at the Old Vic Theatre. In Paris, the Théâtre de l'Épée de Bois had concluded a short run of *Mary Sidney, Alias Shakespeare*, and in Melbourne *Emilia* was gearing up for its Australian premiere.

On a rainy Tuesday, I took the tube to Hampstead, in the north of London, to talk to Marjorie Garber. Garber is the Harvard scholar who writes suggestive things like, " 'Shakespeare' is present as an absence—which is to say, as a ghost." And: "A great deal seems invested in not finding the answer." She is one of the most powerful women in the academic world. Her first book, drawing heavily on Freud, explored Shakespeare's use of dream. In 1981, she became the first woman in Harvard's English Department to receive tenure. (Yale had denied her.) She has written some twenty books—mostly on Shakespeare but also on such varied subjects as cross-dressing, bisexuality, and real estate. When I was writing my undergraduate thesis at Princeton, I discovered *Shakespeare After All*, her magisterial, nine-hundred-page tour through the entire canon of plays. It was incisive, sweeping, brilliant. I came away feeling that there was nothing one could think about Shakespeare that Marjorie Garber hadn't already thought. Her mastery was absolute.

Garber has steered conspicuously clear of one area of Shakespeare study, however. Unlike Stanley Wells, Stephen Greenblatt, James Shapiro, or Jonathan Bate, she has never written a biography of Shakespeare. She dwells instead in analysis of the plays and of Shakespeare as a cultural phenomenon, reading through the lens of theory. Freud or Michel Foucault or Jacques Derrida. Her writing is full of typically postmodern constructions like, "Shakespeare is a concept—and a construct—rather than an author," and "There is no ground of Shakespeare that is not already cross-dressed." She nods to the "repudiation of the fiction of historical accuracy or 'objectivity,' the self-delusive and far from benign assumption that the past can be recaptured without contamination from the present." She likes undecidability, uncertainty, deconstruction—all of which might seem to align her with anti-Stratfordian sensibilities. But she hasn't repudiated the biographical Shakespeare. She hasn't really embraced him, either. If the quadrumvirate of Wells-Greenblatt-Shapiro-Bate represent one aspect of Shakespeare scholarship, she represents the other, more modern approach: ignoring the author, or treating him as a "construct" rather than a biographical person.

I walked past the boutiques and pubs of Hampstead and rang the doorbell of a handsome brick house on a quiet street. Garber showed me in and began making tea. She has dark hair cropped closely around her face and a serious, direct manner. Having retired from Harvard the previous year, she had settled here in England. The house was bright and modern, with sleek, geometric furniture and decorative objects positioned with an air of careful curation. Black-and-white prints of *Othello* by Leonard Baskin hung on the walls. Identical, interesting-looking vases lined the bookshelves. A few coffee-table books were displayed tastefully on a side table. The space was studied and spotless, like a Soho art gallery. Toward the back, it opened into a glass-enclosed sunroom facing the garden. Plants pressed in on the windows and raindrops slid down the glass overhead. Garber appeared carrying mugs of tea from the kitchen and gestured toward a dining table where she had laid out a bowl of strawberries and a plate of madeleines. She was talking about a book she had just finished writing. She had plans for another soon to follow.

We hadn't been talking long when she delivered what she described as her "position" on the authorship. "I'm interested in the plays. I teach the plays," she said. "I'm interested in the characters. I'm interested in the reception of the plays. I'm interested in how they've been interpreted over time. I'm interested in actors and how they've made us feel about Shakespeare's characters. I'm interested in the language."

She was interested, in short, in everything to do with the plays except who wrote them.

"Should I understand that you don't think there's any reason to doubt the authorship?" I asked.

"No, I'm not saying that. I'm saying that's not where my attention as a Shakespeare scholar goes. I'm not a biographical scholar and I don't make biographical claims. I don't make claims that, as a resident of Stratford, he would have heard about this or that bird. I don't make claims about how he would have walked down a certain street and seen something. That's not what I do."

Between us on the table lay a copy of a recent *New Yorker* cartoon, which Garber had printed out to show me. It depicted two schoolyard bullies approaching a nerdy-looking boy wearing glasses and a sweater vest. The caption read: "Word around school is you've been attributing Shakespeare's works to Edward de Vere." The bullies were implicitly Stratfordian; their victim was Oxfordian. It was a commentary on the discourse of the authorship question. Was it accusing Stratfordians of being thugs? Or suggesting that Oxfordians view themselves as victims?

"I think what's fabulous about this is the lay reader will recognize this as a concept," said Garber. "This is not a niche topic." Her posture toward the authorship question seemed to be one of detached amusement. She distanced herself from her colleagues. ("People invested in writing biographies about Shakespeare are invested in their subject and in their claims.") She dismissed the comparison to Holocaust denial as "frankly irresponsible . . . a category mistake." As we discussed the passions on all sides of the authorship question, Garber wondered aloud, "Is it possible to be agnostic on this question?"

"Are you agnostic?" I asked.

"I wouldn't make any claims at all about it. I wouldn't position myself with regard to this," she said. "As I say, I'm committed to the plays."

"You don't consider yourself a Stratfordian, then?" I asked.

"I'm a Shakespearean," she insisted. "That's what I am. I'm interested in the plays."

We went in circles like this for four hours. Every time I tried to pin her down on what she thought about the authorship of the plays to which she had devoted her career, she would say that she wasn't interested in the authorship. She was interested in the plays. She seemed to have staked out some territory beyond authorship, where she could talk about the plays without ever talking about the author. This position was entirely consistent with her postmodern approach to literature generally—the irrelevance of the author, the supremacy of the text. But as we went around and around, it began to feel slightly absurd.

"If it came out that the author was someone else, you wouldn't feel you have to rethink your interpretation of the plays in any way?" I asked.

"I rethink my interpretation of the plays every day," she said.

"It wouldn't make you go back and look at them differently knowing they came from a different person?"

"I don't think of them as coming from a person," she said. "I think of them as a text."

"Right, but the text doesn't just appear out of thin air," I pushed back.

"Sometimes it does, actually." She referenced anonymous texts like the Rosetta stone and medieval morality plays—texts that *seem* to appear out of thin air because their authors are unknown to us. She treated the plays like anonymous texts, I realized, like they didn't have an author.

"Do you think there are reasonable grounds to doubt the authorship?" I tried again.

"I've no idea," she said.

"You don't know?"

"It's not my research. I keep telling you that."

"But that's so crazy!" I blurted out. "You're a Shakespearean. You've spent your whole life studying Shakespeare. Would an Austen scholar say, 'I don't know' about Austen?"

"But we know a lot about Austen," she said.

It was as though, in her carefully studied way, she had put on blinders. She would look at the plays—brilliantly, with unparalleled insight and intelligence. She would look at their reception among readers over the years, their performance by actors, their interpretation by scholars. But she wouldn't look at their author. When I asked if she followed anti-Stratfordian research, she said, "I do not." I was a little surprised that she didn't want to know more at least about the Oxfordian theory given the important role Freud has played in her work. Freud is one of Garber's major intellectual influences. She calls him a "master." We were sitting, in fact, only a mile from Freud's house—now the Freud Museum—where he spent the last year of his life after fleeing Nazi-occupied Vienna. (Had the Freudian aura drawn her to Hampstead?) Garber explained that she would read Oxfordian arguments if they were published in scholarly, peer-reviewed journals, but as they hadn't been, she hadn't read them. A reasonable answer, though Freud read them regardless of where they were published.

"I don't dismiss anything out-of-hand," she added. "I want to know what the data is." She asked me for some of the data that Oxfordians cite, so I mentioned the 1589 reference to the "crew of Courtly makers . . . who have written excellently well as it would appear if their doings could be found out and made public with the rest, of which number is first that noble Gentleman Edward Earle of Oxford."

"Really?" she exclaimed.

Oxford was also listed among the "best" for comedy in 1598, I added.

"Really?" she exclaimed again. "That's very interesting." She seemed to teeter on the brink of being interested in the authorship before she caught herself. "I don't think it would affect the plays," she said.

Maybe it wouldn't. But wasn't she just a little bit curious? Didn't she want to know the origin of the plays about which she clearly cared so deeply? I was baffled. We talked and talked and got nowhere. The sun set. We hadn't touched the strawberries or the madeleines.

"Write me down as a Shakespearean," she said again as I got up to leave.

On the tube ride home, I wrote it all down. The studied living room with everything in its correct place. The black-and-white prints of *Othello*. The rows of identical vases on the bookshelves. The atmosphere of disciplined, almost clinical precision. And the famous Shakespeare scholar sitting at her dining table saying, over and over, that she wasn't interested in the author as the rain slid down the glass roof overhead. As though if I could get the images down, I might crack the mystery—not of belief but of indifference.

Epilogue

When Hermia defies her father in *A Midsummer Night's Dream,* he invokes an ancient Athenian law: a woman must marry the suitor chosen by her father or else face death. Hermia flees into the forest. The problem of the play is the problem of "authority gone archaic." The law requiring a daughter to obey her father or die is outdated.

This symbolic structure—the authority of the father, the disobedience of the daughter—kept coming back to me over the course of my journey through the forest of the authorship question. Questioning Shakespeare felt like transgressing some ancient, outdated law. And the problem was one of "authority gone archaic." The law no longer made sense; the world had outgrown it. It had outgrown it, in fact, some time ago. After George Greenwood published *The Shakespeare Problem Restated* back in 1908, the *Sunday Times* concluded that the traditional story was an "almost inconceivable hypothesis." The *Bristol Times* agreed that the verdict "of all unprejudiced persons must be . . . that the claimant [Shakespeare of Stratford] was not, and could not possibly have been, the poet." "That fellow Greenwood has finally settled the business!" Henry James exclaimed.

It was unsettling to discover these articles and realize I was traversing the same ground that had been covered over a century before. But every time the question flared up, the hammer of the law came down again to crush it.

There was the 1950 article in the *New Yorker*, praising Looney's book. The PBS documentary in 1989. The *Harper's* and *Atlantic* cover stories in the 1990s. The cycle of disobedience and punishment kept repeating. Scholars held fast to their authority. Meanwhile, journalists faced a crisis of authority. Were they meant to hold scholars accountable, in the way they hold politicians or business leaders accountable? Or were they meant to defer to the scholars, accepting their assertions unquestioningly? When my article was published in the *Atlantic*, the British journalist Oliver Kamm took me to task for not deferring. Journalists are "duty bound to check with real experts in [the] field," he scolded me on Twitter. But I had checked. And like other journalists before me, I had found a host of problems.

Shakespeare is the pinnacle of Western culture, according to scholars, but they see nothing in his plays that a grammar school education couldn't provide. His knowledge of Italy is all wrong—or else it's right, but he got it from "a few choice conversations." His mastery of the law surpasses that of his fellow writers, but it can be chalked up to his genius. In fact, his genius covers all of the gaps, explains away everything that they cannot explain—for instance, why he sometimes sounds like Aeschylus, though Aeschylus hadn't yet been translated into English. He radically expanded the English language, introducing words and ideas from Greek, French, and Italian—but he only wrote the plays to make money and didn't care a smidge about them, which is why he didn't mention them in his will. It is snobbery to suggest the author was a courtier—yet scholars insist a portrait of the courtier Thomas Overbury is Shakespeare to make their author more courtly. He was famous—contemporaries lavished praise upon him—but if anyone mentions that there was no notice of his passing, well, he wasn't *that* famous. His sonnets are among the most profound, impassioned poems in English, but as their story is a complete mismatch with the man, he must only have written them as "literary exercises." In fact, nothing about his life corresponds to his works. The glass slipper does not fit.

"A scholar's business is to add to what is known. That is all," observes a scholar in Tom Stoppard's play *The Invention of Love* (1997). "But it is capable of giving the very greatest satisfaction, because knowledge is good. It does not have to look good or sound good or even do good. It is good just by being knowledge. And the only thing that makes it knowledge is that it is true." The scholar is fed-up with the state of scholarship in his field—literary criticism. "The fudge and flim-flam, the hocuspocus and plain dishonesty that parade as scholarship in the journals would excite the professional admiration of a hawker of patent medicines," he opines.

I don't know if Stoppard had Shakespeare scholars in mind when he wrote that passage, but there may be no better description of the field: *the fudge and film-flam, the hocuspocus and plain dishonesty* . . .

Still, the law stands. The penalty for transgression is as severe as ever. How does this play end?

It is instructive to look to the comedies: the heroines "urge throughout the play values which, with their help, will triumph in the more enlightened society of the end." Hermia is allowed to marry the suitor of her choice. But only because another authority intercedes. The Duke of Athens overrides the will of her father and the ancient law. The society evolves. Archaic authority is supplanted by enlightened authority.

Remember, this is a love story. *The course of true love never did run smooth.*

Acknowledgments

My first thanks go to Molly Friedrich and Lucy Carson at the Friedrich Agency for prodding me to write this book. They have been indefatigable cheerleaders, and I'm grateful for their support and guidance throughout this process.

There is still a lot of fear around the authorship question in many corners of the literary world, so I feel fortunate to have found kindred subversive spirits at Simon & Schuster. I'm indebted to everyone who contributed to this book, but above all to my wonderful editors, Priscilla Painton and Megan Hogan, for their enthusiasm, deft editing, wise counsel, and moral support over these many months.

I'm grateful to production editor Samantha Hoback for her tremendous patience and calm in converting this evolving manuscript into a book. For their various contributions, I would also like to thank Alison Forner in the art department, Christine Calella in publicity, and Elizabeth Venere in marketing. Finally, thank you to Jonathan Karp for supporting this project.

This book benefitted from conversations with many scholars beyond those who are quoted in these pages, and I'm grateful to them for sharing their insights. I would also like to thank my early readers. I shared versions of these chapters with Idrees Kahloon, Gina Luria Walker, Don Rubin, Julia Cleave, and Ken Feinstein. I'm indebted to them for their perceptive feedback. I would also like to thank Gerit Quealy for sharing her research on Penelope Rich, Frank Lawler for his translation of Abel

Lefranc's *Sous le Masque de William Shakespeare*, and Dan Law for his insights on *A Room of One's Own.*

I'm grateful to Philip Bashe for copyediting this manuscript with such care. It was fact-checked by the tireless Kristina Rebelo, a queen of precision and good humor (to whom I'm additionally indebted for her angelic assistance with the endnotes).

Jamie Keenan designed the beautiful cover, and I'm grateful for his clever eye.

Writing is a privilege, and I suspect I wouldn't be writing if not for the encouragement of my wonderful English teachers and professors at Stone Ridge, Princeton, and Stanford. I also owe so much to the brilliant editors who have taken me under their wing and made me better, especially Chris Carduff at the *Wall Street Journal.*

I couldn't have written this book without the support of friends and family. Preanka, Claire, Chelsea, Marjorie, Amy, Laila, Anna, and Caitlin, meeting you at Stone Ridge all those years ago was one of the luckiest strokes of my life. Thank you for your friendship, laughter, and keeping me in line.

Jenny, thank you for being the funniest woman in DC.

I'm grateful for the support of my enthusiastic aunts, uncles, and cousins. My romps in London were made possible by Philip and Elena Fletcher. Thank you for your endless generosity and hospitality.

I would like to remember my grandfather, Professor Othmar Winkler, who did not live to see this book published but whose spirit of questioning runs through its pages.

Caroline, Luke, Julia: I'm at a loss for words. You've lifted me up, kept me going, believed in me when I didn't. I'm not sure I deserve such siblings. Thank you.

My greatest debt is to my parents, Tom and Lauren Winkler—for their love, sacrifices, and unflagging support. "Thank you" will always be pathetically insufficient. In truth, you have made all of my words possible.

Credits

52: Thompson, Edward Maunde, *Shakespeare's Handwriting: A Study* (Oxford: Clarendon Press, 1916). Licensed via Wikimedia Commons; 52: Drake, Nathan, *Shakespeare and His Times: Including the Biography of the Poet*, vol. 1 (1817), p. xiv. Licensed via Wikimedia Commons PD-US-expired; 53: Walter Wilson Greg, *English Literary Autographs, 1550–1650*; 83: Folger Shakespeare Library, licensed under a Creative Commons Attribution-Share Alike 4.0 International License (CC BY-SA 4.0); 84: Image taken from First Folio, *Mr. William Shakespeare's Comedies, Histories & Tragedies*. Originally published/produced in London: Isaac Iaggard and Edward Blount, 1623. Held and digitized by the British Library, and uploaded to Flickr Commons. Licensed under the Creative Commons CCO 1.0 Universal Public Domain Dedication; 132: William James Linton, *The Illustrated London News* via Wikimedia Commons PD-US-expired; 132: Library of Congress Prints and Photographs Division, reproduction number: LC-DIG-ppmsc-08872 via Wikimedia Commons PD-US-expired; 141: Licensed from Sicinius under the Creative Commons Attribute-Share Alike 4.0 International license; 142: William Dugdale via Wikimedia Commons PD-US-expired; 154, 196, 265: Wikimedia Commons/Public Domain; 212, 317: Wikimedia Commons.

Notes

PROLOGUE

ix *It involved a squabble*: In re Hopkins' Will Trusts. Naish and Another v. Francis Bacon Society Inc. and Others, July 8, 1964. *The Law Reports* (Chancery Division) [1965] Ch 669, Ch D.

ONE The Question That Does Not Exist

2 "*He was at home*": Hugh Trevor-Roper, "What's in a Name?" *Réalités*, November 1962, 41–43.

2 "*the extent and loudness*": Blair Worden, "Shakespeare in Life and Art: Biography and Richard II," in *Shakespeare, Marlowe, Jonson: New Directions in Biography*, ed. Takashi Kozuka and J. R. Mulryne (Burlington, VT: Ashgate, 2006), 24.

2 "*That would shut the buggers up!*": Stanley Wells, quoted in Robert Gore Langton, "The Campaign to Prove Shakespeare Didn't Exist," *Newsweek* online, last modified December 29, 2014, https://www.newsweek.com/2014/12/26/campaign-prove-shakespeare-didnt-exist-293243.html.

2 "*The relationship between an artist's biography and his writing*": Blair Worden, "Shakespeare and Politics," in *Shakespeare Survey* (Cambridge: Cambridge University Press, 1992), 1–15.

2 "*painfully formed signature*": E. Maunde Thompson, *Shakespeare's England*, vol. 1 (London: Oxford University Press, 1916), 294.

3 "*all or the greatest part of the nobility then in town*": Quoted in Ian Donaldson, *Ben Jonson: A Life* (Oxford: Oxford University Press, 2011), 428.

3 "*It is exasperating and almost incredible*": Trevor-Roper, "What's in a Name?", 41–43.

4 *After the Bible, the works of Shakespeare*: *The Literary Encyclopedia. Vol. 1.2.1.03: English Writing and Culture: Renaissance, 1485–1625*, ed. William M. Hamlin et al.

4 *"Shakespeare one gets acquainted with without knowing how"*: Jane Austen, *Mansfield Park* (London: Thomas Egerton, 1814), 241.

4 *"Since England bore thee, master of human song"*: Robert Bridges, *October and Other Poems with Occasional Verses on the War* (eBook #55031 July 2, 2017), 24.

5 *Today children in India study Shakespeare's plays*: Jyotsna Singh and Modhumita Roy interview with Barbara Bogaev, Folger Shakespeare Library, *Shakespeare Unlimited* podcast audio, January 27, 2016.

5 *China's authoritarian leader*: "Books Recommended by President Xi Inspire Netizens," Society, *Global Times* (China) online, last modified April 23, 2020, https://www.globaltimes.cn/content/1186551.shtml.

5 Macbeth *was adapted to Zulu*: Richard Eder, "Theater: 'Umabatha,' ZuluFolklore 'Macbeth,' " *New York Times*, April 10, 1979, C10.

5 Love's Labour's Lost *staged in Kabul*: William C. Carroll, "*Love's Labour's Lost* in Afghanistan," *Shakespeare Bulletin* 28, no. 4 (winter 2010): 443–58(c).

5 *A dozen replicas of the Globe Theatre*: Michelle Manning, "Globe-al Dominance: The Rise in Reconstructed Globe Theatres," *Shakespeare in the World* (blog), Shakespeare & Beyond online, last modified March 27, 2018, https://shakespeareandbeyond.folger.edu/2018/03/27/rise-in-reconstructed-globe-theatres/.

5 *a poll commissioned by the think tank Demos*: "Shakespeare Tops List of Symbols Giving Britons Pride," *BBC News* online, last modified November 20, 2011, https://www.bbc.com/news/uk-15811246.

5 *Volodymyr Zelensky appealed to the UK Parliament for aid*: Maureen Dowd, "Zelensky Answers Hamlet," Opinion, *New York Times*, March 12, 2022, https://www.nytimes.com/2022/03/12/opinion/zelensky-ukraine-russia-biden.html.

5 *"fell upon the ground and kissed it"*: Quoted in Barbara A. Mowat, "The Founders and the Bard," *Yale Review* 97, no. 4 (October 2009): 1.

5 *sliced a "relic" from the armchair*: Ibid.

5 *In 1787 George Washington escaped*: Alden Vaughan and Virginia Mason Vaughan, *Shakespeare in America* (Oxford: Oxford University Press, 2012), 7.

5 *"There is hardly a pioneer's hut"*: Alexis de Tocqueville, quoted in ibid., 76.

5 *Abraham Lincoln kept three tomes*: Robert Berkelman, "Lincoln's Interest in Shakespeare," *Shakespeare Quarterly* 2, no. 4 (October 1951): 304.

6 *"But alas!" he wrote in a letter*: Quoted in Edward Steers Jr., *Lincoln's Assassination* (Carbondale: Southern Illinois University Press, 2014), 43.

6 *"The hold which Shakespeare"*: James Russell Lowell, *Literary Essays* (Boston: Houghton, Mifflin, 1890), 19, 25.

6 *Great Texas Fair of 1936*: Graham Holderness, "Bardolatry: or, The Cultural Materialist's Guide to Stratford-upon-Avon," in *The Shakespeare Myth*, ed. Graham Holderness (Manchester, UK: Manchester University Press, 1988), xviii.

7 *"Shakespeare's knowledge of classics and philosophy"*: E. K. Chambers, *Pelican Record*, no. 2 (December 1891): 56.

7 *The plays merely* "looked *learned*": Alfred Harbage, *Shakespeare Without Words and Other Essays* (Cambridge, MA: Harvard University Press, 1972), 50.

7 "*Shakespeare was superhuman*": Samuel Schoenbaum quoted in Al Austin, "The Shakespeare Mystery," WGBH Educational Foundation online, last modified April 1989, https://www.pbs.org/wgbh/pages/frontline/shakespeare/debates/austinarticle.html.

8 *"How this particular man"*: "Shakespeare's Life," in William Shakespeare, *The Tragedy of Macbeth* (Folger Shakespeare Library), ed. Barbara A. Mowat and Paul Werstine (New York: Simon & Schuster, 2013), p. xxxvi.

8 *"It is a great comfort"*: Charles Dickens, *Complete Writings*, vol. 37, 206, 11.

8 "*Others abide our question*": Matthew Arnold, "Shakespeare," *Poetry Foundation*, 2022, https://www.poetryfoundation.org/poems/43603/shake speare-56d2225fc8ead.

8 "*in this age of sound and fury*": Henry James, "Introduction to *The Tempest*," in *The Complete Works of William Shakespeare*, ed. Sidney Lee (New York: Harper & Brothers, 1907), xxiv–xxv.

9 *"So desiring you to be good to concealed poets"*: Francis Bacon, *The Works of Francis Bacon*, vol. 10, *The Letters and the Life*, vol. 3, ed. James Spedding, Robert Leslie Ellis, and Douglas Denon Heath (London: Longmans Green, Reader, and Dyer, 1868), 65.

9 *"busied only in penning comedies for the common players"*: Discovery first published by James Greenstreet, "A Hitherto Unknown Noble Writer of Elizabethan Comedies," *Genealogist*, New Series 7 (1891): 205–8.

9 "*paradise for poets*": *The Collected Works of Mary Sidney Herbert, Countess of Pembroke*, ed. Margaret Hannay, Noel Kinnamon, and Michael Brennan (Oxford: Clarendon Press, 1998), 13.

10 *it was "madhouse chatter"*: Sidney Lee, letter to the editor, the *Times*, December 20, 1901, in George Greenwood, *The Shakespeare Problem Restated* (London: John Lane, 1908), vii.

10 *"like asking the College of Cardinals to honestly research the Resurrection"*: Robin Fox, quoted in *Shakespeare Beyond Doubt? Exposing an Industry in Denial*, ed. John Shahan and Alexander Waugh (Tamarac, FL: Llumina Press, 2013), inside front cover.

10 "*Was Shakespeare a Woman?*" Elizabeth Winkler, *Atlantic*, June 2019, 86–95.

13 *Shakespeare's drama "deserves the name feminist"*: Juliet Dusinberre, *Shakespeare and the Nature of Women* (New York: St. Martin's Press, 1975), xx.

13 *"Shakespeare's sympathy with and almost uncanny understanding of women characters"*: Anne Barton, "The Taming of the Shrew," in *The Riverside Shakespeare*, ed. G. Blakemore Evans et al. (Boston: Houghton Mifflin, 1972), 107.

13 *"I—and others—shed blood"*: Dusinberre, *Shakespeare and Nature of Women*, xi.

13 "*still immersed in preconceptions*": Ibid., 305.

13 *"In the simplest terms"*: Ibid., xi.

14 *"It is striking how many of Shakespeare's women are shown reading"*: Stephen Greenblatt et al., eds., *The Norton Shakespeare* (New York: W. W. Norton, 1997), 11.

15 *accused me of "conspiracism"*: Oliver Kamm, "Conspiracism at the Atlantic," *Quillette,* last modified May 16, 2019, https://quillette.com/2019/05/16/con spiracism-at-the-atlantic/.

15 *"Shakespeare derangement syndrome"*: "Shakespeare Derangement Syndrome," *Shakespeare Magazine*, last modified May 16, 2019, http://www.shakespeare magazine.com/2019/05/an-american-magazine-has-published-an-article -titled-was-shakespeare-a-woman-in-response-we-have-written-an-article -titled-shake speare-derangement-syndrome/.

15 *in the grip of "neurotic fantasies"*: Noah Millman, "What If Shakespeare Was a Woman?," *Week*, last modified May 19, 2019, https://theweek.com/arti cles/841609/what-shakespeare-shakespeare.

16 *"Of course he was"*: Dominic Green, "Was Shakespeare a Woman?," *Spectator*, last modified May 13, 2019, https://spectatorworld.com/book-and-art/shake speare-woman-atlantic/.

16 *a "crazy-sounding" conspiracy theory*: David Marcus, "No, Shakespeare Was Not a Jewish Woman, He Was Just a Genius," *Federalist*, last modified May 13, 2019, https://thefederalist.com/2019/05/13/no-shakespeare-not-jewish-woman -just-genius/.

16 *"I'm absolutely certain that women had a hand"*: Phyllis Rackin, "The Hidden Women Writers of the Elizabethan Theater," *Atlantic* online, last modified June 8, 2019, https://www.theatlantic.com/entertainment/archive/2019/06 /shakespeares-female-contemporaries/590392/.

16 *it was "not impossible" that Bassano had worked with him*: David Scott Kastan, "Shakespeare Didn't Write Alone," *Atlantic* online, last modified June 8, 2019, https://www.theatlantic.com/entertainment/archive/2019/06/shakespeares -plays-had-other-authors-too/590389/.

16 *"Shakespeare's women far surpass"*: Mark Rylance, "Keep Questioning Shakespeare's Identity," *Atlantic* online, last modified June 8, 2019, https://www .theatlantic.com/entertainment/archive/2019/06/mark-rylance-keep-ques tioning-shakespeares-identity/590395/.

16 *"To speculate about the authorship of Shakespeare's plays"*: James Shapiro, "Shakespeare Wrote Insightfully About Women. That Doesn't Mean He Was One," *Atlantic* online, last modified June 8, 2019, https://www.theatlantic.com/enter tainment/archive/2019/06/shakespeare-was-not-woman/590794/.

18 *"It is immoral to question history"*: " 'Anonymous'—Professor Carol Rutter and Professor Stanley Wells Discuss the Shakespeare Authorship Question,"

YouTube, 25:18, University of Warwick, November 2, 2011, https://www.youtube.com/watch?v=YfJ45tT6pV0.

19 *("He plays fast and loose with discovered 'facts' ")*: William B. Long, "Shapiro's Shakespeare Redivivus," review of *The Year of Lear: Shakespeare in 1606,* by James Shapiro, *Medieval and Renaissance Drama in England* 30 (2017): 188.

19 "*It is to be hoped*": Simon Callow, "How Leir Became Lear," *Wall Street Journal,* October 2, 2015.

19 *"walled off from serious study by Shakespeare scholars"*: James Shapiro, *Contested Will: Who Wrote Shakespeare?* (New York: Simon & Schuster, 2010), 5.

19 *the forgery had been unmasked by an anti-Stratfordian*: William Niederkorn, "Absolute Will," *Brooklyn Rail*, April 7, 2010.

19 *"Why, after two centuries, did so many people"*: Shapiro, *Contested Will*, 9.

19 *"I happen to believe"*: Ibid., 8.

20 *"turned against Shakespeare"*: Ibid., 156.

20 "*a mechanism of exclusion*": Michael Q. Dudley, "With Swinish Phrase Soiling Their Addition: Epistemic Injustice, Academic Freedom, and the Shakespeare Authorship Question," in *Teaching and Learning Practices for Academic Freedom,* ed. Ednakshi Sengupta and Patrick Blessinger (Bingley, UK: Emerald, 2021), 139.

21 *the N*ew York Times *found that 17 percent of Shakespeare professors*: "Did He or Didn't He? That Is the Question" (survey), *New York Times* online, April 22, 2007, https://www.nytimes.com/2007/04/22/education/edlife/22shakespeare-survey.html?searchResultPosition=1.

21 *"If we knew a little more of Shakespeare's self and circumstance"*: D. H. Lawrence, *The Complete Poems of D. H. Lawrence* (Ware, UK: Wordsworth Editions, 1994), v.

22 " *'Shakespeare' is present as"*: Marjorie Garber, *Shakespeare's Ghost Writers: Literature as Uncanny Causality* (New York: Methuen, 1987), 26.

22 *Since the 1998 film* Shakespeare in Love: Kevin Gilvary, *Fictional Lives of Shakespeare* (New York: Routledge, 2018), 1.

22 *"The death of the author"*: Roland Barthes, "The Death of the Author," *Aspen*, nos. 5/6 (1967).

22 *a psychiatrist named Richard Waugaman*: Richard M. Waugaman, "Friendly Fire: Shakespeare's Accidental Enemies, A Review of the Shakespeare Authorship Controversy," *International Journal of Applied Psychoanalytic Studies* 17, no. 4 (December 2020): 345–60.

24 *("The man from Stratford")*: Sigmund Freud and Arnold Zweig, *The Letters of Sigmund Freud and Arnold Zweig* (London: Hogarth P. [for] the Institute of Psycho-Analysis, 1970), 140.

24 *("Freud is essentially prosified Shakespeare")*: Harold Bloom, "Freud: A

Shakespearean Reading," in *The Western Canon: The Books and School of the Ages* (New York: Harcourt Brace, 1994), 24.

25 *"Too often absurdities in the traditional attribution"*: Dean Keith Simonton, quoted in Waugh, eds., *Shakespeare Beyond Doubt?*, inside front cover.

27 *"Nothing,* nothing, *generates consensus among Shakespeareans"*: Paul Menzer, "The Firing Squad: A Comment upon 'Friendly Fire,' " *International Journal of Applied Psychoanalytic Studies* 17, no. 4 (December 2020): 362–64.

28 *"involved in a system of belief "*: William Leahy, "Shakinomics; or, the Shakespeare Authorship Question and the Undermining of Traditional Authority," in *Shakespeare and His Authors: Critical Perspectives on the Authorship Question,* ed. William Leahy (London: Continuum, 2010), 118.

30 *"Who wrote Shakespeare? I don't care"*: Gregory Doran, quoted in Mark Brown, "I Don't Care Who Wrote Shakespeare, Says RSC Artistic Director," *Guardian* (US edition) online, last modified February 4, 2020, https://www.theguardian.com/stage/2020/feb/04/i-dont-care-who-wrote-shakespeare-says-rsc-artistic-director#:~:text=%E2%80%9CWho%20wrote%20Shakespeare%3F,who%20could%20have%20written%20them.

30 *"Although Shakespeare is so elusive"*: F. E. Halliday, *The Cult of Shakespeare*, (New York: Gerald Duckworth, 1957).

31 *"When we feel ourselves"*: Kathryn Schulz, *Being Wrong: Adventures in the Margin of Error* (New York: HarperCollins, 2010), 179.

TWO Biographical Fiction

33 "*Let us imagine*": Stephen Greenblatt, *Will in the World: How Shakespeare Became Shakespeare* (New York: W. W. Norton, 2004), 23.

34 *He signed documents only with a mark*: E. Maunde Thompson, "Neither of the poet's parents appear to have been able to write at all; they simply made their marks in execution of deeds," *Shakespeare's England*, vol. 1 (London: Oxford University Press, 1916), 294; J. O. Halliwell-Phillipps *Outlines of the Life of Shakespeare* (London: Longmans, Green, 1881), 34.

34 "*Most plain-dealing men in early modern England used marks*": David Cressy, *Literacy and the Social Order: Reading and Writing in Tudor and Stuart England* (Cambridge: Cambridge University Press, 1980), 59.

34 *Of the nineteen elected officials in Stratford*: Charles Knight, *Shakespeare: A Biography*, 15–17, cited in Diana Price, *Shakespeare's Unorthodox Biography: New Evidence of an Authorship Problem* (Westport, CT: Greenwood, 2001), 14.

34 *could not write her name, either*: Greenblatt, *Will in the World,* 24.

35 *deplored the quality of the provincial grammar schools*: Roger Ascham, *The Scholemaster* (London, 1570), 187–88, 239, 243; Henry Peacham, *The Compleat Gentleman* (London, 1634).

35 *"scarce and expensive"*: Virgil Whitaker, *Shakespeare's Use of Learning: An Inquiry into the Growth of his Mind and Art* (San Marino, CA: Huntington Library, 1964), 37.

35 *was censured by a colleague . . . as "biographical fiction"*: Colin Burrow, "Who Wouldn't Buy It?," review of *Will in the World: How Shakespeare Became Shakespeare*, by Stephen Greenblatt, *London Review of Books* 27, no. 2 (January 2005): 9–11. The idea that Shakespeare biographies are fiction is also explored in Kevin Gilvary, *The Fictional Lives of Shakespeare* (New York: Routledge, 2018), and in David Ellis, *The Truth About William Shakespeare: Fact, Fiction, and Modern Biographies* (Edinburgh: Edinburgh University Press, 2012), which laments that all these speculations come at the risk of "a general lowering of intellectual standards and the degradation of the art of biography."

36 *"deep narratives"*: George Lakoff, *The Political Mind: A Cognitive Scientists's Guide to Your Brain and Its Politics* (New York: Penguin Books, 2009).

36 *("What matters is not the true story")*: Gary Taylor, "Stephen, Will and Gary Too," *The Guardian*, October 8, 2004.

36 *convened a conference called Shakespeare and the Problem of Biography*: Brian Cummings, "Shakespeare, Biography, and Anti-Biography," delivered as the opening lecture at a conference at the Folger Institute's "Shakespeare and the Problem of Biography," April 3, 2014.

37 *"To survive, the Shakespeare family business"*: David Fallow, "His Father John Shakespeare," in *The Shakespeare Circle: An Alternative Biography*, ed. Paul Edmondson and Stanley Wells (Cambridge: Cambridge University Press, 2015), 32, 38.

37 *"I have been told by some anciently conversant"*: Edward Ravenscroft quoted in Halliwell-Phillips, *Outlines of the Life of Shakespeare*, vol. 2, 262.

38 *an "upstart crow"*: Peter Bull, "Tired with a Peacock's Tail: All Eyes on the Upstart Crow," *English Studies* 101, no. 3 (2020): 284–311.

38 *The pamphlet, published as*: *Greenes Groats-worth of Wit* (London: William Wright, 1592).

41 *Many actors were tradesmen*: David Kathman, "Grocers, Goldsmiths, and Drapers: Freemen and Apprentices in the Elizabethan Theater," *Shakespeare Quarterly* 55, no. 1 (Spring 2004): 1–49.

41 *"the coincidence of the names"*: Greenblatt, *Will in the World*, 311.

42 *"Shakespeare among the English"*: Francis Meres, *Palladis Tamia* (London: Cuthbert Burbie, 1598).

42 *("For much of his life, he was investing in property")*: Stanley Wells, quoted in Annie Maccoby Berglof, "Why Shakespeare Was Also a Savvy Property Investor and Developer," *Financial Times*, April 18, 2014.

44 *"If Shakespeare was indifferent"*: Samuel Schoenbaum, *William Shakespeare: A Compact Documentary Life* (New York: Oxford University Press, 1987), 220.

45 *wrote a letter about his "sundrie royall Cantos"*: Price, *Shakespeare's Unorthodox Biography*, 117.

45 *"Spenser, our principal poet"*: Ibid.

45 *"hath made diverse plays and written other books"*: Ibid., 118.

45 *"write prayers instead of plays"*: Ibid., 124.

45 *"writing for the stage and for the press"*: Ibid.

45 *"making the stage the speaker of my lines"*: Ibid., 123–24.

45 *"those services of his wit and pen"*: Ibid., 115.

45 *"our great Poet, Ben Jonson"*: Ibid.

45 *"Perhaps we should despair"*: Samuel Schoenbaum, *Shakespeare's Lives* (Oxford: Clarendon Press, 1970), 568.

45 *"my cosen Shakspeare"*: Tara Hamling, "His 'Cousin': Thomas Greene," in *The Shakespeare Circle*, 135–44.

45 *referring at one point to the "excellent poet" Michael Drayton*: Price, *Shakespeare's Unorthodox Biography*, 118.

45 *"small market-town . . . all its consequences"*: William Camden, *Remains Concerning Britain* (1605; Toronto: University of Toronto Press, 1984), 445.

46 *("Camden, most reverend head")*: Epigrams, XIV, "To William Camden," Ben Jonson and William Gifford, *The Works of Ben Jonson* (Boston: Phillips, Sampson, and Company, 1853), 786.

46 *"Shakespeare was nurtured by Nature"*: Richard Farmer, "An Essay on the Learning of Shakespeare," 1776.

46 *"He was Nature's own child"*: Henry Mercer Graves, *An Essay on the Genius of Shakespeare* (London: Ibotson and Palmer, 1826).

47 "gouts *of blood"* and *"Shakespeare grafts on his own English speech"*: Sidney Lee, *The French Renaissance in England: An Account of the Literary Relations of England and France in the Sixteenth Century* (New York: Charles Scribner's Sons, 1910), 244.

47 *"Frequently we find whole lines"*: Ernesto Grillo, *Shakespeare and Italy* (Glasgow: University of Glasgow Press, 1949), 125. See also Sidney Lee, "Shakespeare and the Italian Renaissance," Annual Shakespeare Lecture, *Proceedings of the British Academy* 7 (1915–1916).

47 *Petruchio and Hortensio greet each other in perfect Italian*: Grillo, *Shakespeare and Italy*, 125.

47 *"[W]hat can we say when we find"*: Gilbert Highet, *The Classical Tradition: Greek and Roman Influence on Western Literature* (New York: Oxford University Press, 2015), 201.

47 *Others, too, have admitted "unmistakable" commonalities*: Michael Silk, "Shakespeare and Greek Tragedy: Strange Relationship" in *Shakespeare and the Classics*, ed. Charles Martindale and A. B. Taylor, (Cambridge: Cambridge University Press, 2004), 241.

47 *The echoes are "strong" . . . ("try not to hold that against him")*: Stanley Wells, "Shakespeare: Man of the European Renaissance," in *Renaissance Shakespeare/ Shakespeare Renaissances: Proceedings of the Ninth World Shakespeare Congress*, ed. Martin Procházka et al. (Newark: University of Delaware Press, 2014), 5.

47 *French, Italian, Latin, and "intermediate Greek"*: George Etheridge, "An Encomium on Henry VIII and Elizabeth I by George Etheridge" (British Library Royal, MS 16 C X, 1566).

48 *"fidelity to the most minute details"*: Emilie Montegut, *Oeuvres de Wm. Shakespeare*, vol. 2 (Paris: Hachette, 1867), 340.

48 *"virtually impeccable and absolutely amazing"*: Abel Lefranc "Les Eléments français de 'Peines d'amour perdues' de Shakespeare," *Revue Historique* 178 (1936): 411–12, 414–15.

48 *the author "adverts to incidents of current social and political life"*: Oscar Campbell "Love's Labour's Lost Restudied," in *Love's Labour's Lost: Critical Essays*, ed. Felicia Hardison Londré (New York: Garland Publishing, 1997), 84.

48 "*It is Shakespeare's genius*": Hugh Richmond, *Puritans and Liberties: Anglo-French Literary Relations in the Reformation* (Berkeley: University of California Press, 1981), 338.

48 *"To credit this amazing piece of virtuosity"*: J. Dover Wilson, *The Essential Shakespeare: A Biographical Adventure* (Cambridge: Cambridge University Press, 1967), 41–42.

48 *It is "the most natural"*: William Shakespeare, *The Pictorial Edition of the Works of Shakespeare*, vol. 1, ed. Charles Knight (Peter Fenelon Collier, 1839), 433.

49 "*Nothing can uproot my belief*": Charles Armitage Brown, *Shakespeare's Autobiographical Poems: Being His Sonnets Clearly Developed, with His Character Drawn Chiefly from His Works* (London: J. Bohn, 1838), 100.

49 "*The milieu of the time and place with regard to Italy*": E. K. Chambers, *William Shakespeare: A Study of Facts and Problems*, vol. 1 (London: Oxford University Press, 1930), 61.

49 *network of canals and rivers*: Noemi Magri, *Such Fruits Out of Italy: The Italian Renaissance in Shakespeare's Plays and Poems* (Buchholz, Germany: Verlag Laugwitz, 2017), 87–109.

49 "*These lines make no sense*": Scott McCrea, *The Case for Shakespeare: The End of the Authorship Question* (Westport, CT: Praeger, 2005), 75–76.

49 *going "by water to Padua"*: Sir Richard Guylforde, quoted in Alexander Waugh, "Keeping Shakespeare Out of Italy," in *Shakespeare Beyond Doubt? Exposing an Industry in Denial*, ed. John Shahan and Alexander Waugh (Tamarac, FL: Llumina Press, 2013), 76.

49 "*one can, if one wishes, go by coach*": "*De Lizafousina on peutallersi on veut par carrosse à Padouë. Toutefois le coursde'eauest plus plaisant à cause des beaux palais*

qui sont edifies à ses rives." Cited in Violet Jeffrey, "Shakespeare's Venice," *Modern Language Review* 27, no. 1 (January 1932): 32.

50 *"We crossed the river Naviglio"*: Michel de Montaigne, quoted in Sir Edward Sullivan, "Shakespeare and the Waterways of North Italy," *Nineteenth Century and After* (February 1908): 215–32.

50 *topographical knowledge of Florence*: Richard Paul Roe, *The Shakespeare Guide to Italy: Retracing the Bard's Unknown Travels* (New York: Harper Perennial, 2011), 206–11.

50 Othello *refers to the "Saggitary"*: Magri, *Such Fruits Out of Italy*, 173–82.

50 *Surely there was no synagogue in . . . Venice?*: Benedikt Hottemann, "Surely There Was No Synagogue in Venice," *Shakespeare and Italy* (Vienna, Austria: Lit Verlag, 2011), 260; however, Roe, *Shakespeare Guide to Italy*, 28–33, finds five synagogues built in Venice between 1529 and 1584.

50 *confessed himself "surprised"*: Murray Levith, *Shakespeare's Italian Settings and Plays* (New York: Palgrave Macmillan, 1989), 62.

50 *"displays such an intimate"*: Grillo, *Shakespeare and Italy*, 136.

51 *Shakespeare's "detailed knowledge" of an obscure fresco*: Roger Prior, "Shakespeare's Visit to Italy," *Journal of Anglo-Italian Studies* 9 (2008): 1–31.

51 *"A curious Shakespeare could have learned"*: James Shapiro, *Contested Will: Who Wrote Shakespeare?* (New York: Simon & Schuster, 2010), 275.

51 *"the most complete mastery of the technical phrases"*: Richard Grant White, "William Shakespeare—Attorney at Law and Solicitor in Chancery," *Atlantic Monthly*, April 1859, 84–105.

51 *"no dramatist of the time"*: Richard Grant White, *Memoirs of the Life of Shakespeare* (Boston: Little, Brown, 1865), 373.

51 *"the wonder of his genius"*: Allardyce Nicholl, *Shakespeare* (London: Methuen, 1952), 68.

52 *"Just a mere glance"*: Unpublished letter from Mortimer Adler to Max Weismann, director, Center for the Study of the Great Ideas, November 7, 1997, in "Past Doubters," available at Shakespeare Authorship Coalition online, https://doubtaboutwill.org/past_doubters.

52 *"It is obvious at a glance"*: Jane Cox and David Thomas, *Shakespeare in the Public Records* (London: Her Majesty's Stationery Office Books, 1985), 33.

52 *In a letter to the* Times: Jane Cox to the *Times,* quoted in John Michell, *Who Wrote Shakespeare?* (London: Thames and Hudson, 1996), 97–101.

53 *they "cannot get outside of him"*: Harold Bloom, *The Anxiety of Influence: A Theory of Poetry*, 2nd ed. (New York: Oxford University Press, 1997), xxvii.

53 Walt Whitman, quoted in Horace Traubel, *With Walt Whitman in Camden*, vol. 1 (Boston: Small, Maynard & Company, 1906), 136, and in Warren Hope and Kim Holston, *The Shakespeare Controversy: An Analysis of the Authorship Theories*, 2nd ed. (Jefferson, NC: McFarland, 2009), 49.

54 *"I am 'sort of' haunted"*: Henry James to Violet Hunt, August 26, 1903, in *The Letters of Henry James,* vol. 1 (New York: Charles Scribner's Sons, 1920), 424.

54 *"that strangest of all fallacies"*: Henry James, "Introduction to *The Tempest*," xxvi–xxvii.

54 *"So far as anybody actually knows"*: Mark Twain, *Is Shakespeare Dead?* (New York: Harper & Brothers, 1909), 35.

THREE Crafty Cuttle

56 *Some were signed "Ignoto" (Latin for "Unknown")*: Marcy North, *The Anonymous Renaissance: Cultures of Discretion in Tudor-Stuart England* (Chicago: University of Chicago Press, 2003), 87.

56 *"By one that hath no name"*: Ibid., 79, 89.

56 *Some authors' names appeared only as initials*: North, *The Anonymous Renaissance,* 87.

56 *Nicholas Breton also appeared as "Salohcin Treboun"*: Ibid., 86.

56 *"Let no man ask my name"*: Fulke Greville, "Caelica LXXXIII," in *The Selected Poems of Fulke Greville,* ed. Thom Gunn (Chicago: University of Chicago Press, 1968), 117.

56 *"Die er thowe let his name be known"*: Quoted in Marcy North, "Anonymity's Revelations in 'The Arte of English Poesie,' " *Studies in Literature, 1500–1900* 39 (199): 181.

57 *"Democritus," the latter of whom*: Ibid., 19.

57 *A religious critic like "Martin Marprelate"*: Ibid., 99.

57 *hyphenated names such as "Simon Smell-knave" and "Thomas Tell-troth"*: Ibid., 39.

57 *female pseudonyms like "Jane Anger"*: Ibid., 5.

57 *and "Constantia Munda"*: Ibid., 39.

57 *took on the name "Ester Sowernam"*: Ibid.

57 *so did the reasons for employing it*: Ibid., 16.

57 *Lord Burghley . . . used anonymity to print surreptitious propaganda*: Ibid., 281.

57 *"loath to be known of their skill"*: George Puttenham, *The Arte of English Poesie* (London: Alex, Murray & Son, 1869), 5.

58 *"It is ridiculous"*: John Selden, *Table-Talk, Being Discourses of John Selden* (London: Jacob Tonson, 1689), 42.

58 *(publisher printed it criminally by "fraud and force")*: Thomas Sackville and Thomas Norton, "The P. to the Reader," *The Tragedie of Ferrex and Porrex* (London: John Day, 1570).

58 *"a paradoxical link"*: Marcy North, "Anonymity's Revelations in 'The Arte of English Poesie,' " *Studies in English Literature, 1500–1900* 39 (1999): 1–18.

58 *Between 1475 and 1640, more than eight hundred authors . . . published anonymously*: North, *The Anonymous Renaissance,* 3.

58 *"The flexibility of anonymity"*: Ibid., 26.

58 *"popular and marketable"*: Ibid., 27.

58 *this practice, which he called "underhand brokery"*: Robert Greene, "Greenes Farewell to Folly" in *The Life and Complete Works in Prose and Verse of Robert Greene,* vol. 8, ed. A. B. Grosart (printed privately, 1881–83), 232–33.

58 *In 1596 the Earl of Essex . . . "but it skills not"*: Susan Doran, *Elizabeth I and Her Circle* (Oxford: Oxford University Press, 2015), 179.

59 *"extant among other honorable personages writings"*: John Bodenham, *Belvedere, or the Garden of the Muses* (London, 1600), xxv.

59 *"argued that Hayward was pretending"*: Sidney Lee, "Hayward, Sir John," in *Dictionary of National Biography*, vol. 9, *Harris–Hovenden,* ed. Leslie Stephen and Sidney Lee (New York: Macmillan, 1908), 311–13.

60 *"The younger sort takes much delight"*: Gabriel Harvey, *Gabriel Harvey's Marginalia,* ed. G. C. Moore Smith (Stratford-upon-Avon, UK: Shakespeare Head Press, 1913), 232.

61 *"No youth there present was more beautiful"*: Quoted in Charlotte Carmichael Stopes, *The Life of Henry, Third Earl of Southampton, Shakespeare's Patron* (Cambridge: Cambridge University Press, 1922).

62 *Southampton was still a minor . . . literary amusements*: Kevin Gilvary, *The Fictional Lives of Shakespeare* (New York: Routledge, 2018), 167, 176.

62 *"No one in Shakespeare's lifetime"*: Jonathan Bate, *The Genius of Shakespeare* (Oxford: Oxford University Press, 1998), 73.

62 *For more than two hundred years*: James Shapiro, *Contested Will: Who Wrote Shakespeare?* (New York, Simon & Schuster, 2010), book jacket.

63 *No one expressed doubt*: Stanley Wells and Paul Edmondson, eds., *Shakespeare Beyond Doubt: Evidence, Argument, Controversy* (Cambridge: Cambridge University Press, 2013), 87.

63 *"I could here dismaske"*: Gabriel Harvey, *Pierce's Supererogation* (London: John Wolfe, 1593), 106.

63 *described in* The Homeric Hymns: Anonymous, *Hesiod: The Homeric Hymns,* trans. Hugh G. Evelyn-White (Cambridge, MA: Harvard University Press, 1914), 455.

63 *Pallas-Minerva "is said to be a brandisher goddess"*: Thomas Cooper, *Thesauras Linguae Romane & Britannicae* (London: Henry Denham, 1573).

63 *"For Pallas first, whose filed flowing skill"*: George Gascoigne, *A Hundred Sundrie Flowres* (London: Federick Etchaells and Hugh Macdonald, 1926), 63.

63 *"Go where Minerva's men"*: Jasper Heywood, *Thyestes* in *The Oxford Anthology of Tudor Drama*, ed. Greg Walker (Oxford: Oxford University Press, 2014), 248.

64 *"conflicts radically with a belief "*: Rosalind Barber, "Shakespeare Authorship Doubt in 1593," *Critical Survey* 21, no. 2 (2009), 83–110.

64 *"shameless" imitation*: J. Denham Parsons, "Earliest Critical Notice of

Shakespeare," *Notes & Queries*, CLVII (July 29, 1929); see also Joseph Quincy Adams, ed. *Oenone and Paris by T. H.* (Washington, DC: Folger Shakespeare Library, 1943).

64 *"Maiden head of my Pen"*: Adams, ed., *Oenone and Paris by T. H.*, 3.

65 *"Yet Tarquyne pluckt his glistering grape"*: *Willobie His Avisa* (London: John Lane The Bodley Head Ltd, 1594), 19.

66 *"probably the most famous of Elizabethan poetic riddles"*: "B. N. de Luna, *The Queen Declined: An Interpretation of Willobie His Avisa, with the Text of the Original Edition* (Oxford: Clarendon Press, 1970), 1.

66 *"deafly masking thro"*: Thomas Edwards, "L'Envoy to Narcissus," in *Cephalus and Procris* (London, 1595).

66 *"on to anothers name"*: Joseph Hall, *Virgidemiarum*: *Satires* (London: William Pickering, 1825), 50.

67 *Certain scenes in* The Rape of Lucrece: Lynn Enterline, *The Rhetoric of the Body from Ovid to Shakespeare* (Cambridge: Cambridge University Press, 2006), 171–74.

68 *"So* Labeo *did complaine"*: John Marston, *The Metamorphosis of Pygmalion's Image and Certain Satires* (London: James Roberts, 1598), 25.

68 *"We may agree that Hall"*: H. N. Gibson, *The Shakespeare Claimants*: *A Critical Survey of the Four Principal Theories Concerning the Authorship of the Shakespearean Plays* (New York: Routledge, 1962), 63.

68 *"whip and scourge, my chiefest meaning"*: John Weever, *Epigrammes in the Oldest Cut and Newest Fashion* (London: Sidgwick & Jackson, 1911), 12.

69 *"O sweet Shakspeare!"*: William Dun Macray, *The Pilgrimate to Parnassus with The Two Parts of the Return from Parnassus* (Oxford: Clarendon Press, 1886), 58, 138, 140.

70 *"fine, imprisonment, loss of ears"*: William Hudson, "A Treatise on the Court of Star Chamber," in *Collectanea Juridica, Consisting of Tracts Relative to the Law and Constitution of England*, vol. 2, ed. Francis Hargrave (London: E. and R.Brooke, 1792), 224.

70 *"functional ambiguity"*: Annabel Patterson, *Censorship and Interpretation*: *The Conditions of Writing and Reading in Early Modern England* (Madison: University of Wisconsin Press, 1984), 18.

70 *riddles, anagrams, acrostics, logogriphs, palindromes, eteostiches, telestichs*: See Jonson's "An Execration Upon Vulcan" in C. H. Herford et al., eds., *Ben Jonson* vol. 8 (Oxford: Clarendon Press, 1947), 204.

71 "*A Certain man was to a Judge complaining*": John Harrington, *The Most Elegant and Witty Epigrams of Sir John Harrington, Knight* (Epigram 18) (London: John Budge, 1618).

71 "*To Our English Terence Mr. Will: Shake-speare*": *The Complete Works of John Davies of Hereford*, ed. A. B. Grosart (Edinburgh: Edinburgh University Press, 1878), 26.

71 *"It is well-known"*: Roger Ascham, *The Scholemaster* (1570), quoted in G. Gregory Smith, ed., *Elizabethan Critical Essays,* vol. 1 (Oxford: Clarendon Press, 1904; London: Oxford University Press, 1971), 28.

71 *"resign the credit of their comedies"*: Michel de Montaigne, *Essays,* 199.

72 *"there is none . . . that explicitly"*: Wells, "Allusions to Shakespeare to 1642," *Shakespeare Beyond Doubt*, 81.

72 *"that well-known poet"*: Thomas Vicars, *Xeirogogia*: *manductio ad Artem Rhetoricam* (London: Joannis Haviland, 1628), 70.

74 *"It is better to read the sonnets"*: C. L. Barber, *Elizabethan Poetry: Modern Essays in Criticism*, vol. 10, ed. Paul Alpers (Oxford: Oxford University Press, 1967), 300.

74 *"With this key, Shakespeare unlocked his heart"*: William Wordsworth, "Scorn not the Sonnet," *The Sonnets of William Wordsworth* (London: Edward Moxon, 1838), 54.

74 *"so odd a story"*: C. S. Lewis, *English Literature in the Sixteenth Century: Excluding Drama* (Oxford: Oxford University Press, 1973), 503.

75 *"it is not unreasonable to look in them"*: Paul Edmondson and Stanley Wells, "The History and Emergence of the Sonnet as a Literary Form," in *Shakespeare's Sonnets*, ed. Peter Holland and Stanley Wells (Oxford: Oxford University Press, 2004), 21.

75 *"without an equal mixture of disgust and indignation"*: George Steevens, quoted in *New Variorum Shakespeare*, vol. 25, *The Sonnets*, 2 vols., ed. Hyder Edward Rollins (Philadelphia: J. B. Lippincott, 1944), 55.

75 *"casts a slur on the dignity"*: James Schiffer, "Reading New Life into Shakespeare's Sonnets: A Survey of Criticism," in *Shakespeare's Sonnets*: *Critical Essays*, ed. James Schiffer (Oxfordshire, UK: Taylor & Francis, 2013).

75 *"the strongest act of Parliament"*: George Steevens, quoted in "Sketch of the Life of Shakespeare," Alexander Chalmers, *The Works of William Shakespeare* (Philadelphia: Lippincott, 1868), 12.

75 *"The story Shakespeare recounts"*: Logan Pearsall Smith, in *Shakespeare's Sonnets*: *Critical Essays*, ed. James Schiffer (New York: Garland, 2000), 30.

75 *"No capable poet, much less a Shakespeare"*: A. C. Bradley, *Oxford Lectures on Poetry* (Bloomington: Indiana University Press, 1961).

75 *"Shakespeare's sonnets are an island"*: Douglas Bush, ed., *Shakespeare's Sonnets* (New York: Penguin, 1963).

77 *"I think the evidence that"*: Jess Bravin, "Justice Stevens Renders an Opinion on Who Wrote Shakespeare's Plays," *Wall Street Journal*, April 18, 2009.

77 *"I hope it may be of value to others"*: James Shapiro, "An Unexpected Letter from John Paul Stevens, Shakespeare Skeptic," *New Yorker,* August 6, 2019.

FOUR Seeliest Ignorance

79 *Henry Folger referred to his books as "the boys"*: Stephen Grant, *Collecting Shakespeare: The Story of Henry and Emily Folger* (Baltimore: Johns Hopkins University Press, 2014), x.

79 "*The poet is one of our best sources*": Emily Folger, quoted in ibid., 33.

79 *Shakespeare's history plays heralded the "inauguration of modern democracy"*: Walt Whitman, "What Lurks Behind Shakespeare's Historical Plays?, *November Boughs* (London: Paisley and Paternoster, Row 1889), 53–54.

79 "*His comedies are a revel*": Emily Folger, *Vassar Quarterly* 86, no. 2 (March 1, 1990): 18.

80 *"The Folger Shakespeare Library fittingly takes"*: *Evening Star* (Washington, DC), April 23, 1932, 6.

80 "*The cornerstone of cultural discipline*": Robert Sawyer, *Shakespeare Between the World Wars: The Anglo-American Sphere* (New York: Palgrave Macmillan, 2019), 10.

80 *Henry Folger was a founding member*: Grant, *Collecting Shakespeare,* 78.

81 *Henry Folger acquired an annotated 1570 Geneva Bible*: Mays, *Millionaire and the Bard*, 222.

81 "*coming towards the end*": Grant, *Collecting Shakespeare,* 78.

81 *"The plays show no evidence of profound book learning"*: Louis Wright, *The Folger Library: Two Decades of Growth, An Informal Account* (Charlottesville: University Press of Virginia, 1968), 156.

81 *deemed anti-Stratfordian ideas "pernicious"*: Gail Kern Paster, "The Ghost of Shakespeare," *Harper's,* April 1999, 38.

81 "*While we at the Folger will remember Justice Stevens*": Gail Kern Paster, "By Any Other Name," letter to the editor, *New Yorker,* August 19, 2019, https://www.newyorker.com/magazine/2019/08/26/letters-from-the-august-26-2019-issue.

81 *"The Folger has been a major location"*: "Shakespeare FAQ," Folger Shakespeare Library online, accessed May 6, 2019, https://www.folger.edu/shakespeare-faq#:~:text=The%20Folger%20has%20been%20a,one%20of%20the%20great%20mysteries.

82 *Henry and Emily Folger*: For general background on the Folgers, see Andrea Mays, *The Millionaire and the Bard*: *Henry Folger's Obsessive Hunt for Shakespeare's First Folio* (New York: Simon & Schuster, 2016), 173.

83 *a fashionable gentleman named Sir Edward Dering*: For more on Dering and discoveries of First Folios, see Emma Smith, *Shakespeare's First Folio*: *Four Centuries of an Iconic Book* (Oxford: Oxford University Press, 2016).

84 "*much too big for the body*": Leah Marcus, *Puzzling Shakespeare: Local Reading and Its Discontents* (Berkeley: University of California Press, 1990), 20.

84 *"horrible hydrocephalus development"*: Quoted in ibid., 2.

84 *"pudding faced"*: J. Dover Wilson, *The Essential Shakespeare: A Biographical Adventure* (Cambridge: Cambridge University Press, 1967), 6.

84 *"grotesquely large and vilely drawn"*: Marion Harry Spielmann, *The Title Page of the First Folio of Shakespeare's Plays: A Comparative Study of the Droeshout Portrait and the Stratford Bust* (London: H. Milford, 1924), 32.

84 *"is so strangely illustrated"*: Anonymous, "A Problem for the Trade," *The Gentleman's Tailor* 46, April 1911, 93.

84 *makes Shakespeare "look like an idiot"*: Northrop Frye, *The Educated Imagination* (Bloomington: Indiana University Press, 1964), 73.

85 *"Writing with the left hand"*: Artemidorus Daldianus, *The Third Booke of Artemidorus His Exposition of Dreames*, 124.

85 *which some skeptics see as an indication that the face is a mask*: For an anti-Stratfordian analysis of the Droeshout portrait, see John Rollett, "Shakespeare's Impossible Doublet," in *Shakespeare Beyond Doubt? Exposing an Industry in Denial,* ed. John Shahan and Alexander Waugh (Tamarac, FL: Llumina Press, 2013), 113–25.

85 *"Droeshout's deficiencies are, alas, only too gross"*: Schoenbaum, *William Shakespeare: A Compact Documentary Life*, 315.

85 *"Shakespeare's plays are printed"*: William Prynne, quoted in Gerald Eades Bentley, *Profession of Dramatist in Shakespeare's Time, 1590–1642* (Princeton, NJ: Princeton University Press, 2015), 57.

86 *"The poem undermines the visual power"*: Marcus, *Puzzling Shakespeare,* 18–19.

87 *"the supreme tactician"*: Richard Dutton, *Ben Jonson* (Cambridge: Cambridge University Press, 1983), 4.

87 *"this most complex of authors"*: Patterson, *Censorship and Interpretation*, 62.

87 *"the very common device"*: Quintilian, *The Orator's Education*, vol. 4, bks. 9–10, trans. Donald A. Russell (Cambridge MA: Harvard University Press, 2001).

87 *"the multitude commend Writers"*: Ben Jonson, *Timber or Discoveries* 1641, in *Ben Jonson,* eds. C. H. Herford et al. (Oxford: Clarendon Press, 1947), 583.

88 *"the most crucial single document"*: Samuel Schoenbaum, *Internal Evidence and Elizabethan Dramatic Authorship: An Essay in Literary History and Method* (Evanston, IL: Northwestern University Press, 1996), 167.

88 *"wholly unused to composition"*: George Steevens, quoted in *The Plays and Poems of William Shakspeare* [*sic*]: Edmond Malone. Vol. 2. London: 1821, 6.

88 *"every word of the first half"*: Steevens, quoted in ibid., 674.

88 *(The letter "so strongly echoes")*: Marcus, *Puzzling Shakespeare*, 22.

89 *"The First Folio's omissions, errors"*: Bruce Danner, "The Anonymous Shakespeare: Heresy, Authorship, and the Anxiety of Orthodoxy," in *Anonymity in Early Modern England: What's in a Name?*, ed. Janet Wright Starner and Barbara Howard Traister (Burlington, VT: Ashgate, 2011), 147.

90 *We default to truth*: Timothy R. Levine, "Truth-Default Theory (TDT): A

Theory of Human Deception and Deception Detection," *Journal of Language and Social Psychology* 33, no. 4 (September 2014): 378–92.

90 *"a deception practiced for"*: *Oxford English Dictionary.*

92 *a poet . . . "not of an age but for all time!"*: Ben Jonson, "To the Memory of My Beloved, the Author Mr William Shakespeare, and What He Hath Left Us," *Poetry Foundation.*

93 *"though thou hadst" is in the subjunctive voice*: C. Mansfield Ingleby, *Shakespeare's Centurie of Prayse* (London: Trübner, 1874), 172.

94 *("These dramas, the most treasured jewels of our literary heritage")*: Richard Levin, "Shakespeare's Second Globe," in *TLS* (*Times Literary Supplement*) *Shakespeare*, ed. Michael Caines (January 1974), 81.

94 *grandest court theater*: See E. K. Chambers, *The Elizabethan Stage*, vol. 4 (Oxford: Clarendon Press, 1923), 77–128.

94 *"painting of seven cities"*: Ernest Law, *A Short History of Hampton Court,* 2nd ed. (London: George Bell and Sons, 1906), 153–54, 164; and Alexander Waugh, "Waugh on Jonson's 'Sweet Swan of Avon,' " *Oxfordian* 16 (2014): 97–103.

94 *"A Stately place for rare and glorious shew"*: John Leland, *Genethliacon* (1543), quoted in William Camden, *Camden's Britannia* (London: 1610), 420.

95 *"Avondunum"*: *Kykneion asma–Cygnea cantio* (1545), 108.

95 *"we now pronounce Hampton for Avondune"*: Raphael Hollinshed, *The First and Second Volumes of Chronicles*, augmented by John Hooker (1586), 101.

95 *Hampton Court is "corruptly called Hampton for Avondun or Avon"*: This quotation is found beneath "Hampton" in Lambarde's *Topographical and Historical Dictionary of England,* written in the 1590s but unpublished until 1730.

95 *"Swan Song"*: John Leland (1545), lines 110–11.

95 *"Jonson was allowing, and probably expecting"*: Waugh, "Waugh on Jonson's 'Sweet Swan,' " 97–103.

96 "*If, Passenger, thou canst but read: Stay*": Ben Jonson, "An Epitaph on Henry Lord La-Ware," in *The Works of Ben Jonson* (Boston: Philips, Sampson, 1853), 836.

97 *("At last we shall dissolve this Riddle")*: *The Works of Beaumont and Fletcher*, vol. 2, ed. George Darley (London: Routledge, 1866), 151.

97 *"This Shadow is renowned Shakespear's?"*: *Poems*: *written by Wil. Shake-speare, Gent.* (London, 1640), https://www.bl.uk/collection-items/shakespeares-collected-poems-1640.

98 *"Is the apparent author the real author?"*: Garber, *Shakespeare's Ghost Writers*, 11.

99 *The Shakespearean preoccupation with deception and illusion is Platonic*: For Shakespeare's Platonism, see Colin McGinn, *Shakespeare's Philosophy*: *Discovering the Meaning Behind Shakespeare's Plays* (New York: HarperCollins, 2006);

and A. D. Nuttall, *Shakespeare the Thinker* (New Haven: Yale University Press, 2007).

FIVE Bardolatry

103 *"Spectacles of pleasure"*: Quoted in Gary Taylor, *Reinventing Shakespeare: A Cultural History from the Restoration to the Present* (Oxford: Oxford University Press, 1989), 7.

103 *"had he but studied Scripture"*: Ibid., 9.

104 *"whole subsequent history of Shakespearian criticism"*: Ibid., 12.

104 *a woman with "the very best legs that ever I saw"*: Ibid., 18.

104 *"piece of Shakespeare's"*: Ibid., 46.

105 *"Shakespear's pow'r is sacred as a King's"*: Ibid., 30.

105 *"We all well know that the immortal Shakespears Playes"*: Ibid., 28.

105 *Shakespeare "is rarely called anything but 'divine' in England"*: Voltaire, quoted in Shapiro, *Contested Will*, 30.

105 *"With us islanders"*: Ibid.

105 *"One would think he has been Metamorphosed"*: *CCXI Sociable Letters Written by the Thrice Noble, Illustrious, and Excellent Princess, the Lady Marchioness of Newcastle* (London: 1664).

106 "to the Fair Supporters of Wit and Sense": Fiona Ritchie, Women and Shakespeare in the Eighteenth Century (Cambridge: Cambridge University Press, 2014), 147.

106 *"I have heard that Mr. Shakspeare"*: *Diary of the Reverend John Ward, A.M., Vicar of Stratford-upon-Avon* (London: Henry Colburn, 1839), 183.

106 *"His father was a Butcher"*: John Aubrey, *Brief Lives*, vol. 2 (Oxford: Clarendon Press, 1898), 963.

106 *"knowledge of an Author"*: Nicholas Rowe, "Some Account of the Life of Mr. William Shakespear," in *The Works of Mr. William Shakespear* (London: 1709).

106 *entrenching a Shakespearean mythos*: For seventeenth- and eighteenth-century attempts to construct Shakespeare's life, see Gilvary, *The Fictional Lives of Shakespeare*, 54–73.

108 *Schoenbaum dubbed Shakespeare the "Deerslayer"*: Schoenbaum, *William Shakespeare: A Compact Documentary Life*, 97.

108 *"appears to me so dull"*: Quoted in Katy Mair, "An Archival and Material Reading of Shakespeare's Will," in *Shakespeare on the Record: Researching an Early Modern Life*, ed. Hannah Leah Crummé (London: Bloomsbury, 2019), 179.

108 *"a rich assemblage of Shakespeare papers"*: Quoted in Shapiro, *Contested Will*, 19.

109 *"Who wrote Shakespeare?"*: James Townley, *High Life Below Stairs: A Farce in Two Acts* (London: 1759).

109 *"The passage cannot, however, be taken as accidental"*: R. C. Churchill, *Shakespeare and His Betters* (London: Max Reinhardt, 1925), 30.

109 *"a person belonging to the playhouse"*: Herbert Lawrence, *The Life and Adventures of Common Sense: An Historical Allegory* (1769), 147–48.

109 *The "learned pig" recounting his previous human incarnations*: *The Story of the Learned Pig, By an Officer of the Royal Navy* (London: R. Jameson, 1786), 38.

109 *They were particularly drawn to the mulberry tree*: Gilvary, *Fictional Lives of Shakespeare*, 68.

110 *"The Immortal Shakespeare was born in this house"*: Julia Thomas, *Shakespeare's Shrine: The Bard's Birthplace and the Invention of Stratford-upon-Avon* (Philadelphia: University of Pennsylvania Press, 2012), 9.

110 *"And thou like him immortal be!"*: Ibid., 16.

110 *"Untouched and sacred be thy shrine"*: Ibid., 17.

111 *"a part of the kingdom's riches"*: Taylor, *Reinventing Shakespeare*, 121.

111 *"England may justly boast the honour"*: Ibid.

111 "scandalous Behaviour of ": Johanne M. Stochholm, Garrick's Folly: The Shakespeare Jubilee of 1769 at Stratford and Drury Lane (London: Methuen, 1964), 112.

111 *"[L]et your streets be well pav'd & kept clean"*: Thomas, *Shakespeare's Shrine*, 17.

111 *"the point at which Shakespeare"*: Christian Deelman, *The Great Shakespeare Jubilee* (New York: Viking Press, 1964), 7.

112 *"Yet steals a sigh"*: Thomas, *Shakespeare's Shrine,* 19.

112 *"Glory of the British Nation" and the "Prince of Dramatic Poets"*: Quoted in Gilvary, *Fictional Lives of Shakespeare,* 68.

112 *"Driven to the last necessity"*: Robert Shiells, *The Lives of the Poets of Great Britain and Ireland: to the Time of Dean Swift. Compiled from Ample Materials Scattered in a Variety of Books, . . . by Mr. Cibber* (London: 1753), 130; quoted also in Gilvary, *Fictional Lives of Shakespeare,* 67.

112 *"meagre and imperfect narrative"*: Gilvary, *Fictional Lives of Shakespeare*, 65.

112 *"a dupe to every wag"*: Ibid., 58.

113 *"An Attempt to Ascertain"*: Ibid., 75.

113 *"to weave the whole into one uniform and connected narrative"*: Ibid., 84.

113 *"Despite the most diligent inquiries"*: Ibid.

113 *"the French Revolution only tended"*: Taylor, *Reinventing Shakespeare,* 148.

113 *The defense of British culture*: Taylor, *Reinventing Shakespeare*, 147–61.

114 *("I do esteem much my play")*: Jeffrey Kahan, *Reforging Shakespeare: The Story of a Theatrical Scandal* (Bethlehem, PA: Lehigh University Press, 1998), 64.

114 *a prefatory note from Shakespeare to his "gentle readers"*: Shapiro, *Contested Will*, 24.

114 *"so much gratification to the literary world"*: Kahan, *Reforging Shakespeare*, 67.
114 *"How happy am I"*: Ibid., 83.
114 *"an acute and penetrating judgement"*: Shapiro, *Contested Will*, 22.
115 *"these papers can be"*: Ibid., 25.
115 *Shakespeare's "brief account of his life"*: Ibid., 26.
115 *"All sensible persons"*: Kahan, *Reforging Shakespeare*, 175.
115 *not even good forgeries*: Shapiro, *Contested Will*, 32–33.
115 *"When this solemn mockery is o'er"*: Ibid., 246.
116 *"in some of the most important parts"*: Arthur Sherbo, in "James Boswell's Editing of, and Contributions to, the 1821 Boswell-Malone Shakespeare," *Papers of the Bibliographical Society of America* 99, no. 1 (March 2005): 71–111.
116 *"he could never be prevailed on to begin it"*: Gilvary, *Fictional Lives of Shakespeare*, 69.
116 *a "curious journal of Shakespeare"*: Shapiro, *Contested Will*, 63.
117 *"On looking back to the life of Shakespeare"*: Gilvary, *Fictional Lives of Shakespeare*, 93.
117 *"be good to the poor players"*: Shapiro, *Contested Will*, 64.
117 *"This information is now hardly"*: Gilvary, *Fictional Lives of Shakespeare*, 101.
118 *Thomas Carlyle declared that it was "impiety"*: Thomas Carlyle, *On Heroes, Hero-Worship, and the Heroic in History* (London: Fraser, 1841).
119 *Hegel called "the infinite breadth"*: Taylor, *Reinventing Shakespeare*, 167.
119 *"Deutschland ist Hamlet"*: Ibid.
119 *"one of the masterpieces of "*: Ibid., 168.
119 *Shakespeare was "the artist who has created most"*: Ibid.
119 *"Shakespeare was declared to rule world literature"*: Michael Dobson, *The Making of the National Poet: Shakespeare, Adaptation, and Authorship, 1660–1769* (Oxford: Clarendon Press, 1992), 7.
119 *the "immortal house"*: Thomas, *Shakespeare's Shrine*, 138.
119 *"as a pilgrim would"*: Ibid., 18.
119 *"tabernacled in the flesh"*: Ibid., 14.
119 *George Bernard Shaw, "bardolatry"*: See Gilvary, *Fictional Lives of Shakespeare*, 106; see also Robert B. Pierce, "Bernard Shaw as Shakespeare Critic," *Shaw: The Annual of Bernard Shaw Studies* 31, no. 1 (2011): 118–32.
119 The Pilgrim of Avon: Thomas, *Shakespeare's Shrine*, 20.
120 *a "descriptive reverie"*: Gilvary, *Fictional Lives of Shakespeare*, 100.
120 *"From the obscurity in which his life is shrouded"*: Thomas, *Shakespeare's Shrine*, 21.
120 *"happy days of boyhood"*: Ibid., 22.
120 *"The mother is plying her distaff "*: Ibid.
121 *"something of his school progress"*: Ibid., ii.

121 *"hypothesis upon hypothesis"*: Gilvary, *Fictional Lives of Shakespeare,* 100.

121 *"confine his fancy within the bounds"*: Ibid.

121 *"Like most things written about Shakespeare"*: Thomas, *Shakespeare's Shrine,* 24.

122 *"to us Englishmen, the national, the domestic Poet"*: Ibid., 25.

122 *"Of no person"*: Ibid., 21.

122 *Shakespeare received the longest entry, later exceeded only by that of Queen Victoria*: Gilvary, *Fictional Lives of Shakespeare,* 102.

122 *("a credible tradition")*: Ibid., 103.

122 *"twisted by a master artificer"*: Ibid., 106.

122 *"it is all a record of external events"*: Ibid., 107.

123 *"psychological aberration"*: Stanley Wells's article on the "Authorship Debate" posted to the website of the Shakespeare Birthplace Trust, https://doubtaboutwill.org/letters_to_sbt_and_rsc/1.

123 *"sucking Shakespeare's blood"*: Paul Edmondson and Stanley Wells, "Sucking Shakespeare's Blood," in *Shakespeare Bites Back*: *Not So Anonymous* (e-book) (Stratford-upon-Avon, UK: Shakespeare Birthplace Trust, 2011), 26, available for free online at https://bloggingshakespeare.com/wp-content/uploads/2011/10/Shakespeare_Bites_Back_Book.x43452.pdf.

123 *"Bard Blood at the Palace"*: Chris Hastings, "Bard Blood at the Palace as Princes Split over Shakespeare: Philip and Charles at Odds over Playwright's Authenticity," *Daily Mail* (London) online, last modified April 26, 2014, https://www.dailymail.co.uk/news/article-2614113/Bard-blood-Palace-Princes-split-Shakespeare-Philip-Charles-odds-playwrights-authenticity.html.

124 *The* Independent *reported*: Andrew Woodcock, "Downing Street Denies Boris Johnson Missed Covid Meetings to Write Shakespeare Book," *Independent* online, last modified May 24, 2021, https://www.independent.co.uk/news/uk/politics/boris-johnson-dominic-cummings-shakespeare-b1852830.html.

124 *Meanwhile, the* Daily Mirror: Pippa Crerar and Dan Bloom, "Questions for Boris Johnson over Mystery of Shakespeare Book and '£98k' Advance," *Daily Mirror* (UK) online, last modified May 24, 2021, https://www.mirror.co.uk/news/politics/questions-boris-johnson-over-mystery-24176394.

124 *pay back his $500,000 advance*: Alison Flood, "Boris Johnson Offered to Pay for Help Writing Shakespeare Biography, Says Scholar," *Guardian* (US edition) online, last modified July 2, 2021, https://www.theguardian.com/books/2021/jul/02/boris-johnson-offered-to-pay-for-help-writing-shakespeare-biography-says-scholar.

125 *"clear evidence" of his authorship*: Wells and Edmondson, *Shakespeare Beyond Doubt*, 130.

125 *others were glossed over hurriedly as "cryptic"*: Ibid., 74, 79.

126 *"Shakespeare has enemies"*: Paul Edmondson, " 'The Shakespeare Establishment'

and the Shakespeare Authorship Discussion," in Stanley Wells and Paul Edmondson, eds., *Shakespeare Beyond Doubt: Evidence, Argument, Controversy* (Cambridge, Cambridge University Press, 2013), 225–35.

127 *"the most dirty, unseemly"*: Thomas, *Shakespeare's Shrine*, 141.

128 *"There is nothing like"*: Washington Irving, *The Works of Washington Irving*, vol. 2 (London: Bell & Daldy, 1866), 194.

128 *"the nobility and gentry"*: Thomas, *Shakespeare's Shrine*, 40.

128 *"What, Birthplace here?"*: Ibid., 102.

128 *"As long as this was confined"*: Ibid., 103.

129 *"one or two enthusiastic Jonathans"*: Ibid., 53.

129 *"rescue a property"*: Ibid., 39.

129 *"for the nation"*: Ibid., 43.

129 *"last and precious opportunity"*: Ibid., 44.

129 *"[T]he extraordinary sensation"*: Ibid., 103.

130 *the Birthplace was a "deception"*: Ibid., 92.

130 *"paltry hut"*: Ibid., 94.

130 *"Here we may safely trust to tradition"*: Ibid., 97.

130 *"It is the easiest thing"*: Ibid., 100.

130 *"The want of absolute certainty"*: Ibid., 99.

130 *"Let not our poetical sympathies"*: Ibid., 100.

131 *"The people of Stratford are as dirty as ever"*: Ibid., 141.

131 *make the building a more "attractive site"*: Ibid., 72.

131 *"a murky cloud of misunderstanding"*: Ibid., 87.

131 *"seems to have grown mysteriously"*: Ibid., 73.

131 *"There can be little doubt"*: Ibid.

133 *"a brilliant token"*: Ibid., 51.

133 *While 65 editions of Shakespeare's works*: Ibid., 157.

133 *"Bible of Humanity"*: Charles Laporte, *The Victorian Cult of Shakespeare* (Cambridge: Cambridge University Press, 2020), 5, 32, 103.

133 *"I was not prepared"*: Thomas, *Shakespeare's Shrine,* 80.

134 *"If you cannot understand"*: Bernard Levin, "On Quoting Shakespeare," *Enthusiasms* (London: J. Cape, 1983).

134 *"Stratford permits—indeed encourages—one of the biggest frauds"*: Bernard Levin, "The Stratford Frauds," *Daily Mail* (London), February 18 and November 30, 1966.

134 *"Anne Hathaway's Cottage"*: Thomas, *Shakespeare's Shrine*, 4, 132.

134 *"Shakespeare Courting Chair"*: "Shakespeare's Courting Chair," Shakespeare Birthplace Trust online, last modified July 11, 2010, https://www.shakespeare.org.uk/explore-shakespeare/blogs/shakespeares-courting-chair/.

135 *"had not held our office"*: Ian Ousby, *The Englishman's England: Taste, Travel and the Rise of Tourism* (London: Pimlico, 2002), 55.

135 *The legends were an "abomination"*: Hope and Holston, *The Shakespeare Controversy*, 49.

135 *Stanley Wells claimed it as a portrait of Shakespeare*: Stanley Wells, ed., *Shakespeare Found! A Life Portrait at Last: Portraits, Poet, Patron, Poems* (Stratford-upon-Avon, UK: Cobbe Foundation and the Shakespeare Birthplace Trust, 2009).

135 *called Wells's claim "codswallop"*: Vanessa Thorpe, "A Portrait of William Shakespeare? 'Codswallop,' Says Expert," *Observer* online, last modified April 18, 2009, https://www.theguardian.com/culture/2009/apr/19/shakespeare-portrait-contested.

135 *Even other Shakespeare scholars agreed*: Charlotte Higgins, "A True Shakespeare 'Portrait'? Surely Not . . ." *Guardian* (US edition) online, last modified March 10, 2009, https://www.theguardian.com/culture/charlottehigginsblog/2009/mar/10/art-classics; Katherine Duncan-Jones, "Shakespeare Unfound(ed)? The Real Identity of the Sitter for the New 'Shakespeare' Portrait," *Times Literary Supplement*, March 18, 2009.

136 *"absolute extermination and obliteration"*: *The Letters of William James*, vol. 2 (Boston: Atlantic Monthly Press, 1920), 166.

136 *"Say they end by denying Shakespeare"*: Hope and Holston, *Shakespeare Controversy*, 50.

136 *published in 1903 as "The Birthplace"*: Henry James, *The Better Sort* (London: Methuen, 1903).

137 *"felt no emotion whatever in Shakespeare's house"*: Quoted in Bryan Homer, *An American Liaison: Leamington Spa and the Hawthornes, 1855–1864* (Madison, NJ: Farleigh Dickinson University Press, 1998), 52–53.

137 *"If I were to allude to Stratford"*: Henry James, *Portraits of Places* (Leipzig: Bernhard Tauchnitz, 1884), 259.

138 *"Modern progress is"*: Thomas, *Shakespeare's Shrine*, 88.

139 *In 1756 the owner, Reverend Francis Gastrell*: Denise Winterman, "The Man Who Demolished Shakespeare's House," *BBC News Magazine* online, last modified March 7, 2013, https://www.bbc.com/news/magazine-21587468.

140 *he "could see neither coffin nor bones"*: Washington Irving, *The Sketch Book of Geoffrey Crayon, Gent.* (New York: Putnam, 1819).

140 *But in 2016 a team of archaeologists*: "*Shakespeare's Tomb*—2016 British Documentary," YouTube, 54:35, All Things British, https://www.youtube.com/watch?v=SoRrdZgnyRw.

141 *"heavy unintellectual expression"*: Sidney Lee, *A Life of William Shakespeare* (London: Smith, Elder, 1899), 287.

141 *"self-satisfied pork-butcher"*: J. Dover Wilson, quoted in Graham Holderness, *Cultural Shakespeare: Essays in the Shakespeare Myth* (Hatfield, UK: University of Hertfordshire Press, 2001), 152.

141 *"preserve those Monuments from that fate"*: Sir William Dugdale, *Antiquities of Warwickshire* (1656), quoted in Alexander Waugh, " 'Thy Stratford Moniment'—Revisited," *de Vere Society Newsletter,* October 2014, available at Shakespeare Oxford Fellowship online, last modified March 18, 2015, https://shake speareoxfordfellowship.org/thy-stratford-moniment-revisited/. For further anti-Stratfordian analysis, see Richard F. Whalen, "The Stratford Bust: A Monumental Fraud," in *Shakespeare Beyond Doubt? Exposing an Industry in Denial*, ed. John Shahan and Alexander Waugh (Tamarac, FL: Llumina Press, 2013), 136–51.

142 *Shakespeare Birthday Celebrations*: https://www.shakespearescelebrations.com.

143 *Parish records show alterations*: Waugh, " 'Thy Stratford Moniment'—Revisited," 1.

143 *("The skilfullest Anatomist")*: Sir Aston Cokayne, in *The Life, Diary, and Correspondence of Sir William Dugdale*, ed. William Hamper (London: Harding, Leopard, 1827), 482.

143 *"somewhat cryptically calls on the passerby"*: Stanley Wells, *Shakespeare for All Time* (Oxford: Oxford University Press, 2002), 46.

143 *Alexander Waugh, the latest to venture an explanation*: Waugh, " 'Thy Stratford Moniment'—Revisited," 6–8.

144 *"Judicious Beaumont"*: Gerard Langbaine, *An Account of the English Dramatic Poets* (1691), 208, 217.

144 *"the heavenly mind of prudent Socrates"*: Francis Thynne, "Upon the picture of Chaucer," in Gordon Braden and Jackson Campbell Boswell, eds., *Petrarch's English Laurens, 1475–1700* (Farmham: Ashgate, 2012), 203.

144 *"the genius of Socrates"*: Latin epitaph commissioned from Stephanus Surigonius for the *Works of Geoffrey Chaucer*, 1542. The epitaph (translated) reads: "There is nothing in which this man [Chaucer] was not distinguished, whose illustrious works are embellished with the excellent modes of expression, with the genius of Socrates [*Socratis ingenium*], the springs of philosophy, with all the secrets which holy doctrine contains and all the worthy arts you could wish for: all here buried with this most worthy poet in this small grave."

144 *"Virgil of England," an* "imitator" *of Virgil who sang "in full Virgilian voice," and "our modern Maro"*: Quoted in David Scott Wilson-Okamura, *Spenser's International Style* (Cambridge: Cambridge University Press, 2013), 24.

144 *"where Shakespear, Spenser, Camden, and the rest"*: Samuel Speed, *Fragmenta Carceris* (London: James Cottrell, 1674).

144 *"amongst the Ancient Poets"*: John Denham, "*On Mr. Abraham Cowley: His Death and Burial Amongst the Ancient Poets*," *Poems and Translations* (London: John Macock for H. Herringman, 1668), 89–90. Denham writes of Cowley: "By *Shakespear, Johnson, Fletcher's* lines, / Our Stages lustre *Rome's* outshines: / These Poets neer our Princes sleep, / And in one Grave their Mansion keep."

144 "*Did Sir John really think?*": C. M. Ingleby, L. Toulmin-Smith, and F. J. Furnivall, *The Shakspere Allusion Book; A Collection of Allusions to Shakspere from 1591 to 1700*, vol. 2 (New York: Duffield, 1909), 159.

SIX Aberration and the Academy

147 "*If one were to provide*": Terry Eagleton, "The Rise of English," in *Literary Theory: An Introduction* (Minneapolis: University of Minnesota Press, 1983), 20.

147 "*to emancipate us*": F. D. Maurice, quoted in Peter Barry, *Beginning Theory: An Introduction to Literary and Cultural Theory* (Manchester, UK: Manchester University Press, 2002), 13.

147 "*It seems as if few stocks*": Matthew Arnold, *The Letters of Matthew Arnold, 1848–1888*, vol. 1, ed. G. W. E. Russell (London: Macmillan, 1895), 115.

148 "*into intellectual sympathy with the educated*": Matthew Arnold, ed., *Reports on Elementary Schools, 1852–1882,* ed. Francis Sandford (London: Macmillan, 1889), 20.

148 "*If these [middle] classes*": "The Popular Education in France" in Matthew Arnold, *Democratic Education*, ed. R. H. Super (Ann Arbor: University of Michigan Press, 1962), 22.

148 "*The future of poetry is immense*": Matthew Arnold, introduction, in *The English Poets*, vol. 1, *Chaucer to Donne*, ed. T. H. Ward (London: Macmillan, 1880), xvii.

148 "*intellectual leaders of our race*": Chris Baldick, *The Social Mission of English Criticism, 1848–1932* (Oxford: Clarendon Press, 1987), 66.

149 *English helps to "promote sympathy"*: Ibid., 62.

149 "*The main purpose is not to educate the masses*": Ibid., 64.

149 "*The wondrous knowledge of the heart*": Ibid., 66.

149 "*liable to dangerous explosions of political feeling*": Ibid., 65.

150 *a "convenient sort of nonsubject"*: Eagleton, "Rise of English," 24.

150 "*Of all the 'solid' subjects*": Baldick, *The Social Mission of English Criticism*, 68.

150 "*In America, some are maintaining*": Ibid.

150 "*foremost among these*": Ibid., 70.

151 "*taste for pleasures not sensual*": Ibid.

151 "*the supreme figure of our literature*": Martin Blocksidge, "Shakespeare: Iconic or Relevant?," in *Shakespeare in Education*, ed. Martin Blocksidge, (London: Continuum, 2005), 3.

151 "*an effect of Shakespeare's having*": Nancy Glazener, "Print Culture as an Archive of Dissent: Or, Delia Bacon and the Case of the Missing Hamlet," *American Literary History* 19, no. 2 (Summer 2007): 329–49.

152 "*seemed to saturate herself with the plays*": Vivian Hopkins, *Prodigal Puritan: A Life of Delia Bacon* (Cambridge, MA: Harvard University Press, 1959), 69.

152 *"she looked and spoke"*: Theodore Bacon, *Delia Bacon: A Biographical Sketch* (Boston: Houghton, Mifflin, 1888), 25.

153 *"mere* factotum *of the theatre"*: Joseph C. Hart, *The Romance of Yachting: Voyage the First* (New York: Harper & Brothers, 1848), 241.

153 *"vulgar and unlettered man"*: Ibid., 237.

153 *"Is it more difficult to suppose"*: Anonymous, "Who Wrote Shakespeare?," *Chambers' Edinburgh Journal* 18, no. 449 (August 7, 1852): 87–89.

153 *"little clique of disappointed and defeated politicians"*: Delia Bacon, "William Shakespeare and His Plays; An Enquiry Concerning Them," *Putnam's Monthly* 7, no. 37 (January 1856), reprinted in *Americans on Shakespeare, 1776–1914*, ed. Peter Rawlings (Aldershot, UK: Ashgate, 1999), 209.

153 *"Lear is the "impersonation of absolutism"*: Delia Bacon, *The Philosophy of the Plays of Shakspere Unfolded* (London: Groombridge and Sons, 1857).

153 *"Condemned to refer the origin of these works"*: Delia Bacon, "William Shakespeare and His Plays," 189.

154 *("If one could but paint his mind")*: Nicholas Hillard, portrait of Francis Bacon at age eighteen, National Portrait Gallery online, accessed October 9, 2020, https://www.npg.org.uk/collections/search/portrait/mw115306/Francis-Bacon-1st-Viscount-St-Alban.

154 *Shakespeare's "knowledge of legal terms"*: George Greenwood, *The Shakespeare Problem Restated* (London: John Lane, 1908), 373.

154 *"proofs of something like"*: William Shakespeare, *The Works of William Shakespeare*, vol. 1, with the various readings, notes, a life of the poet, and a history of the early English stage by J. Payne Collier (London: Whittaker, 1844), lxxxiv.

155 *"I have taken all knowledge"*: Jürgen Klein and Guido Giglioni, "Francis Bacon," in the Stanford Encyclopedia of Philosophy (online), ed. Edward N. Zalta (Fall 2020 ed.), accessed October 9, 2020, https://plato.stanford.edu/cgi-bin/encyclopedia/archinfo.cgi?entry=francis-bacon.

155 *"So did philosophy"*: William Rawley, ed., "32 Elegies Written on the Death of Francis Bacon by his Colleagues of Cambridge and Oxford," *The Manes Verulamiani*, trans. Willard Parker (New York: Bacon Society, 1927).

155 *"some good pens which forsake me not"*: Francis Bacon to Sir Tobie Mathew, 1623: "My labours are now most set to have those works, which I had formerly published, well translated into Latin by the help of some good pens which forsake me not." Quoted in Basil Montagu, *The Works of Francis Bacon,* vol. 3 (Philadelphia: Parry & McMillan, 1859), 151.

155 *"though in modern states"*: Francis Bacon, *De Augmentis Scientiarum, The Philosophical Works of Francis Bacon*, vol. 4, ed. James Spedding (London: Longmans, 1861), 316.

156 *"Let us proceed then to ciphers"*: John Robertson, ed., *The Philosophical Works*

of Francis Bacon, reprinted from the texts and translations, with the notes and prefaces, of Ellis & Spedding (New York: Routledge, 1905), 527.

156 *"was a jovial actor and manager"*: Ralph Waldo Emerson, *Representative Men: Seven Lectures* (London: Routledge, 1850), 135.

156 *"Her discovery, if it really be one"*: Quoted in Shapiro, *Contested Will*, 100.

156 *"I have seen nothing in America"*: Helen Deese, "Two Unpublished Emerson Letters: To George P. Putnam on Delia Bacon and to George B. Loring," *Essex Historical Collections* (1986), 122.

157 *"Mr. Carlyle came down on me with such a volley"*: Bacon, *A Biographical Sketch*, 62.

157 *London's publishers similarly received the theory with "terror"*: Hopkins, *Prodigal Puritan,* 194.

157 *"How can we undertake"* Delia Bacon, "William Shakespeare and His Plays," 169.

157 *"its own laws and intuitions"*: Ibid., 173.

158 *"that dirty, doggish group of players"*: Ibid., 190.

158 *"learned and eloquent scholar"*: Ibid., 169.

158 *"Oh, stupidity past finding out!"*: Ibid., 180.

158 *"the revolt of the layman"*: Taylor, *Reinventing Shakespeare*, 220.

158 *"solely that he might"*: Richard Grant White, *Memoirs of the Life of William Shakespeare* (Boston: Little, Brown, 1865), 111.

158 *"[A]s the writer was plainly"*: Richard Grant White, "The Bacon-Shakespeare Craze," *Atlantic Monthly* 51 (April 1883), 521.

159 *"The professionalization of Shakespearian editing and criticism"*: Glazener, "Print Culture as an Archive of Dissent," 329–49.

159 *A "degree of disgrace"*: William Henry Smith, *Was Lord Bacon the Author of Shakespeare's Plays?: A Letter to Lord Ellesmere* (London: William Skeffington, 1856), 8.

159 *"merely to initiate inquiry"*: Ibid., 14.

160 *The publication brought "the whole literary pack down on her"*: Horace Traubel, *With Walt Whitman in Camden,* vol. 5 (Carbondale: Southern Illinois University Press, 1964), 337.

160 *the Baconian theory went global*: Reginald Charles Churchill, *Shakespeare and His Betters* (Bloomington: Indiana University Press, 1959), 60–61.

160 *"an idolater of Shakespeare"*: Mark Twain, *Is Shakespeare Dead?* (New York: Harper & Brothers, 1909), 5.

160 *"very excited and unsatisfactory state"*: Local physician, quoted in Theodore Bacon, *Delia Bacon,* 308.

161 *"eccentric American spinster"*: Samuel Schoenbaum, *Shakespeare's Lives* (Oxford: Clarendon Press, 1970), 385, 391.

161 *the "mother" of all anti-Stratfordians*: Jonathan Bate, *The Genius of Shakespeare* (Oxford: Oxford University Press, 1989), 96.

161 *"responsible for triggering"*: James Shapiro, *Contested Will: Who Wrote Shakespeare?* (New York: Simon & Schuster, 2010), 87.

161 *in the nineteenth century, the list of reasons women could be institutionalized included*: http://www.mass-gov-courts.org/transallegheny-lunatic-asylum.html.

161 *"Delia Bacon's claim"*: Shapiro, *Contested Will*, 97.

162 *Shakespeare "suffered collateral damage"*: Ibid., 75.

162 *"We all know how much* mythus*"*: Whitman, "What Lurks Behind Shakespeare's Historical Plays?," 52.

162 *" 'Gentle' is the epithet often applied to him"*: Walt Whitman, *The Complete Prose Works of Walt Whitman*, vol. 7 (New York: Putnam's, 1902), 74.

162 *In 1867 a mysterious, fire-damaged manuscript*: *Northumberland Manuscript* (1598), DNP MS 525, fol. 46, The Northumberland Collection and Archive (Alnwick, UK). For a discussion of the Baconian theory and the Northumberland manuscript, see John Mitchell, *Who Wrote Shakespeare?* (London: Thames and Hudson, 1996), 113–60.

163 *Bacon was probably gay*: The first Baconian to assert openly that Bacon was gay was Walter Begley in *Is it Shakespeare?* (London: John Murray), 1903.

163 *"that bloody Perez," Lady Bacon wrote*: Michell, *Who Wrote Shakespeare?*, 117.

164 *"At every turn and point"*: James Plaisted Wilde Penzance, *Lord Penzance on the Bacon-Shakespeare Controversy: A Judicial Summing-Up* (London: S. Low, Marston, 1902), 85.

164 *"No young man could have been at work"*: Ibid., 87.

164 "*blown to pieces*": Richard Grant White, "The Anatomizing of William Shakespeare," *Atlantic*, June 1884.

164 *"Had the plays come down to us anonymously"*: Horace Howard Furness, quoted in Appleton Morgan, *The Shakespearean Myth*: *William Shakespeare and Circumstantial Evidence* (Cincinnati: Robert Clarke, 1881), 201.

165 *the cipher hunters*: See Michell, *Who Wrote Shakespeare?*," 134–60; see also Churchill, *Shakespeare and His Betters*, 37–69; "*The Goal in Sight*": *Baconiana*, 7, 3rd ser. (1909), 145–49.

165 *"You will only reap disappointment"*: Schoenbaum, *Shakespeare's Lives*, 415.

165 *William and Elizebeth Friedman*: The Friedmans are discussed in Michell, *Who Wrote Shakespeare?*, 144–60. See also William F. Friedman and Elizebeth S. Friedman, *The Shakespearean Ciphers Examined* (Cambridge: Cambridge University Press, 1957).

166 *Sir Sidney Lee assailed the Baconian theory*: Sidney Lee, letter to the London *Times*, December 20, 1901, quoted in Greenwood, *The Shakespeare Problem Restated*, vii.

166 *"Why so warm, Sir Fretful?"*: Ibid.

166 *"There are the wild Baconians"*: George Greenwood, introduction, in E. W. Smithson, *Baconian Essays* (London: Cecil Palmer, 1922), 25–26.

166 *"that petulant spirit"*: Greenwood, *Shakespeare Problem Restated*, ix.

167 *"And we, who see the absurdity"*: Greenwood, introduction, in Smithson, *Baconian Essays*, 15.

167 *"an extremely erudite, fair, and discriminating piece of work"*: Henry James, quoted in George Greenwood, *Lee, Shakespeare and a Tertium Quid* (London: Cecil Palmer, 1923), 20.

167 *"Mr. Greenwood's masterly exposition"*: Helen Keller, quoted in Shapiro, *Contested Will*, 117.

168 *an article in* Oxford *magazine argued*: see Baldick, *The Social Mission of English Criticism*, 61.

168 *he began his lectures with "Gentlemen . . ."*: Arthur Quiller-Couch, quoted in Eagleton, *Literary Theory*, 24.

168 *"They have studied him for a hundred years"*: Walter Raleigh, quoted in Robert Sawyer, *Shakespeare Between the World Wars: The Anglo-American Sphere* (New York: Macmillan, 2019), 32.

168 *"If only by the structure"*: Quoted in Baldick, *The Social Mission of English Criticism*, 88.

168 *"capture by the enemy"*: Ibid., 92.

168 *"Do we lay it aside?"*: Ibid., 91.

169 *"arch" of national education around the "keystone"*: Ibid., 94.

169 *"would form a new element of national unity"*: Ibid., 95.

169 *"antagonistic to, and contemptuous of, literature"*: Ibid., 96.

169 *"what is wrong with our industry"*: Ibid., 100.

169 *"A humane education"*: Ibid., 101–2.

170 *"The Professor of Literature"*: Ibid., 97.

170 *"What the teacher has to consider"*: Ibid., 100–101.

170 *"England is sick"*: Ibid., 105.

171 *"the forces of immigration became a menace"*: Joseph Quincy Adams, "Shakespeare and American Culture" (Dedication Speech for the Folger Library, April 23, 1932), in *Shakespeare in America: An Anthology from the Revolution to Now*, ed. James Shapiro (New York: Library of America, 2014), 432–33, 438.

171 *"narrated reality"*: Michel de Certeau, *The Practice of Everyday Life*, vol. 1, 3rd ed. (Berkeley: University of California Press, 2011), 186.

177 *"the finest and most searching Lear I have ever seen"*: Charles Spencer, "King Lear, Donmar Warehouse, Review," *Daily Telegraph* (UK), December 8, 2010.

177 *"among the near-complete Hamlets"*: Benedict Nightingale, London *Times*, February 18, 2008.

177 *"Mark Rylance speaks Shakespeare"*: Al Pacino, quoted in Cynthia Zarin, "After Hamlet," *New Yorker*, May 5, 2008.

SEVEN Wolfish Earls

181 *"The verbal texture of Shakespeare"*: Brian Boyd, introduction in Samuel Schuman, *Nabokov's Shakespeare* (New York: Bloomsbury Academic, 2014), x.

181 *Nabokov began to doubt*: Philip Howerton, Jr., "Vladimir Nabokov and William Shakespeare," *Shakespeare Oxford Society Newsletter*, 1990.

181 *"Shakespeare"*: Vladimir Nabokov, *Selected Poems*, ed. Thomas Karshan (New York: Alfred A. Knopf, 2012), 11–12.

182 *"instincts of a born courtier"*: Northrope Frye, *Northrope Frye on Shakespeare*, ed. Robert Sandler (New Haven: Yale University Press, 1986), 10, 59.

182 *Some Europeans singled out Roger Manners, the 5th Earl of Rutland*: For the Rutlandite theory, see Michell, *Who Wrote Shakespeare?*, 211–22.

183 *In 1918 a new heresy emerged*: Abel Lefranc, *Sous Le Masque de 'William Shakespeare': William Stanley, Vie Comte de Derby* (Paris: Péyot, 1918–1919). trans. by Frank Lawler (Veritas Publications, 2022). The Derbyite theory is also summarized in Michell, *Who Wrote Shakespeare?*, 190–226.

185 *John Thomas Looney published* "Shakespeare" Identified: J. Thomas Looney, *"Shakespeare" Identified* (London: Cecil Palmer, 1920). For Looney's background, see Hope and Holston, *The Shakespeare Controversy*, 69–87, and Michell, *Who Wrote Shakespeare?*, 161–89.

185 *a "strongly evangelical environment"*: J. T. Looney to Charles Wisner Barrell, June 6, 1937, in *Shakespeare Fellowship Quarterly* 5, no. 2 (April 1944): 20.

185 *positivism, a philosophical movement*: For more on positivism, see Terence Wright, *The Religion of Humanity: The Impact of Comtean Positivism on Victorian Britain* (Cambridge: Cambridge University Press, 1986).

186 *"[I]t taught me to apply"*: Looney to Barrell, June 6, 1937.

186 *"a misleading method of enquiry"*: Looney, *"Shakespeare" Identified*, 78.

186 *"more or less unconscious indications of himself"*: Ibid., 73.

186 *"touched with scepticism"*: For Looney's list of characteristics, see ibid., 103.

186 *"circumventing a scheme of self-concealment"*: Ibid., 73.

187 *"Puttenham and Meres reckon him among the best"*: Sidney Lee, "Vere, Edward de," in *Dictionary of National Biography*, vol. 56 (London: Smith, Elder, 1885–1900), 228.

187 *"in a kindred key"*: Lee, *The French Renaissance in England*, 227.

187 *"Personally, I find it utterly impossible"*: Looney, *"Shakespeare" Identified*, 158.

187 *"fit in exactly with the theory"*: Ibid., 127.

188 *"so amazingly strange and wholly unique"*: John Thomas Looney, *Shakespeare Pictorial*, November 1935.

188 *"no cipher, cryptography, or hidden message"*: Shapiro, *Contested Will*, 195.

189 *"an unlifted shadow somehow lies across"*: Alexander Balloch Grosart, ed., *The Fuller Worthies' Library*, vol. 4 (London: Robson and Sons, 1872).

189 *the dramatist John Bale . . .* King Johan *. . . a source for Shakespeare's* King John: "Bale's heading to the catalog of fourteen plays in the *Anglorum Heliades* (1536) states that he composed them especially for Master John Vere, the Earl of Oxford." Jesse Harris, "John Bale: A Study of the Minor Literature of the Reformation," *Illinois Studies in Language and Literature* 25, no. 4 (1940): 68.

189 *Scholars have wondered how Shakespeare came into possession of Bale's old, unpublished manuscript*: James Moray, "The Death of King John in Shakespeare and Bale," *Shakespeare Quarterly* 45, no. 3 (Fall 1994): 327–31.

189 *rebuked by the bishop of Winchester as "lewd fellows"*: Alan H. Nelson, *Monstrous Adversary: The Life of Edward de Vere, 17th Earl of Oxford* (Liverpool, UK: Liverpool University Press, 2003), 13.

190 *"with seven score horse all in black"*: Ibid., 34.

190 *Lady Anne "was brought to his bed"*: Francis Osborne, *Traditional Memoirs of the Reigns of Queen Elizabeth & King James* (1658). A similar anecdote about the "bed trick" was recorded by Thomas Wright, *The History and Topography of Essex* (1836).

190 *(Golding praised his pupil's zeal)*: In a dedicatory letter to Oxford from *Trogus Pompeius* (1564), Arthur Golding wrote, "I have had experience therof myself, howe earnest a desire your honor hath naturally graffed in you, to read, peruse, and communicate with others, as well the Histories of auncienttyme, and thynges done long ago, as also of the present estate of thinges in ouredayes, and that not withoute a certaynpregnancie of witte and rypenesse of vnderstandyng."

191 *"The play which furnishes"*: John Thomas Looney, introduction, in *The Poems of Edward de Vere* (1921), which he edited; republished by the Shakespeare Oxford Fellowship online, last modified May 2, 2007, https://shakespeareoxford fellowship.org/intro-to-poems-of-de-vere/.

191 *"Dr. Caius," like the Cambridge professor*: Mark Anderson, *"Shakespeare" by Another Name: The Life of Edward De Vere, Earl of Oxford, the Man Who Was Shakespeare* (San Francisco: Untreed Reads, 2011), 9.

191 *"Our scholarly Shakespeareans have written much"*: J. Thomas Looney, "Correspondence. *The Shakespeare Controversy*. To the Editor of *The Bookman's Journal*," 1, no. 26 (April 23, 1920): 484; reprinted in the *Oxfordian* 20 (2018): 147.

191 *had "more followers and was the object"*: Nelson, *Monstrous Adversary*, 120.

191 *"It is clear that"*: G. B. Harrison quoted in "*Sergeant* Shakespeare?," *Parameters: Journal of the US Army War College* 17, no. 1 (Spring 1987): 129.

Other works on Shakespeare's military knowledge include Paul Jorgensen, *Shakespeare's Military World* (Berkeley: University of California Press, 1956); and Duff Cooper, *Sergeant Shakespeare* (New York: Viking, 1950).

191 *He took "singular delight"*: Thomas Twynne, dedication to *Breviary of Britayne* Humphrey Llwd (London: Abraham Ortelius, 1573), in ibid., 237.

192 *"too much addicted that way"*: Ibid.

192 *"by right" of his "excellent virtue and rare learning"*: John Brooke, *The Staffe of Christian Faith* (London: John Daye, 1577), AIII.

192 *"seems to be the book"*: Joseph Hunter, *New Illustrations of the Life, Studies, and Writing of Shakespeare*, vol. 2 (London: J. B. Nichols and Son, 1845), 243–44.

193 *Oxford had "an addell heade"*: Nelson, *Monstrous Adversary*, 2.

193 *his son-in-law's "determined mischief "*: Ibid., 95 (given as "determyned myschefe").

193 *("In some of these")*: George Russell French, *Shakspeareana Genealogica* (London: Macmillan, 1869), 303.

193 *a bill to make fish eating compulsory*: "Arguments to Prove That It Is Necessary for the Restoring of the Navy of England to Have More Fish Eaten and Therefore One Day More in the Week Ordained to Be a Fish Day, and That to Be Wednesday Rather Than Any Other," in M.A.P., "Cecil, Sir William (1520 or 1521–98), of Little Burghley, Northants., Stamford, Lincs., Wimbledon, Surr., Westminster, Mdx. and London," in the History of Parliament online, accessed May 2, 2021, www.historyofparliamentonline.org/volume/1558-1603/member/cecil-sir-william-1521-98.

193 *"Can Polonius have resembled some nickname"*: E. K. Chambers, *William Shakespeare*, 418.

194 *"Long may you live in joy and health"*: George Coryat, oration delivered at New College Oxford (September 1566); published in *Coriates Crudities* (1611); also in *Progresses and Public Processions of Queen Elizabeth*, vol. 1, ed. John Nichols (New York: AMS Press, 1823), 231–36.

194 *"singularly amusing" to a sixteen-year-old*: Alexander Waugh, "My Shakespeare, Rise!," in *My Shakespeare: The Authorship Controversy*, ed. William Leahy (Brighton, UK: Edward Everett Root, 2018), 49.

194 *She "delighteth more in his personage"*: Quoted in B. M. Ward, *The Seventeenth Earl of Oxford, 1550–1604* (London: John Murray, 1928), 78.

194 *"not in the usual way"*: Quoted in Waugh, "My Shakespeare, Rise!," 51.

194 *probably through Rousillon*: Anderson, *"Shakespeare" by Another Name*, 106–108.

194 *Portia's estate in* The Merchant of Venice: Magri, *Such Fruits Out of Italy*, 110–31.

194 *a sixteenth-century fresco of Portia*: Antonio Foscari, *Frescos within Palladio's Architecture* (Zurich: Lars Mueller, 2013), 106–113; Shakespeare Authorship Roundable: "Did Many Hands Make Light Work?"

194 *uses imagery from a painting of the tale by Titian*: Magri, *Such Fruits Out of Italy*, 17–26.

194 commedia dell'arte: Kathleen Lea, *Italian Popular Comedy: A Study in the*

Commedia dell' arte, 1560–1620 with Special Reference to the English Stage (Oxford: Oxford University Press, 1934); Allardyce Nicholl, *The World of Harlequin* (Cambridge: Cambridge University Press, 1963).

195 *on the Italian model*: Frances A. Yates, *Theatre of the World* (London: Routledge and K. Paul, 1969), connects the Theatre, built in London in 1576, with the design of the Roman theater expounded by the classical architect Vitruvius in his book *de Architectura.*

195 *"It is said that a great Lord"*: L. Grenade, *Singularities of London*, 1578 (London Topographical Society, 2014).

195 *("Naked we landed out of Italy")*: Nathaniel Baxter, "To the Right Noble, and Honorable Lady *Susan Vera* Monlgomriana" *Sir Philip Sidney's Ourania, That Is, Endimion's Song and Tragedie*: *Containing all Philosophie* (London: Edward White, 1606).

195 *"fable of the world"*: Nelson, *Monstrous Adversary*, 146.

196 *"Bring in the child"*: Ibid., 177.

196 *"could not rule her brother's tongue"*: Ibid., 172.

196 *(he reportedly called the poet a "puppy")*: Ibid., 196.

196 *"would not give pleasure to Frenchmen"*: Ibid., 181.

196 *"womanish" works*: Gabriel Harvey, "Speculum Tuscanisimi," in *Three Proper, and Wittie, Familiar Letters*, Edmund Spenser (London: H. Bynneman, 1580), 36.

197 *an unnamed, ostentatiously dressed man looking "very womanly"*: Nelson, *Monstrous Adversary*, 228.

197 *He was "a fellow peerless in England"*: Harvey, "Speculum Tuscanisimi," 36.

197 *"of spirit passing great"*: George Chapman, *The Revenge of Bussy D'Amois* (London, 1613), ed. Frederick Boas (Boston: D.C. Heath, 1905), 237.

197 *"For who marketh better than he"*: John Soowthern, "To the right honourable the Earle of Oxenford," *Pandora* (London: Thomas Hackette, 1584).

198 "*Of French and Italian muses*:" Gabriel Harvey, "Apostrophe ad eundum," in *Gratulationis Valdinensis* (Londini: Henrici Binnemani, 1578), trans. Thomas Hugh Jameson (New Haven: Yale University Press, 1938), 125–47.

198 *("In comedy Lyly is")*: R. W. Bond, *The Complete Works of John Lyly*, vol. 2 (Oxford: Clarendon Press, 1902), 243.

198 *"in the rare devices of poetry"*: William Webbe, *Discourse on English Poetrie* (1586), ed. Sonia Hernández-Santano (Cambridge: Modern Humanities Research Association, 2016), 81.

198 *"youth, time, and fortune spent in her Court"*: AMS Hatfield MSS, Cal. XI.27; Nelson, *Monstrous Adversary*, 397 ("yowth, tyme & fortune spent in her Courte").

199 "une belle comedie qui se conclust": H. R. Woudhuysen, *Leicester's Literary Patronage* (Oxford: University of Oxford Press, 1981), 309–10.

199 *"a brave and comely ship"*: Anthony Munday, *Zelauto* (London: John Charlewood, 1580), 35.
199 *"a pleasant conceit of* Vere*"*: Listed in Francis Peck, *Desiderata Curiosa or a Collection of divers Scarce and Curious Pieces relating chiefly to matters of Enligh History*, vol. 1 (London: Thomas Evans, 1732).
199 *"for Comedie and Enterlude"*: Puttenham, *The Arte of English Poesie*, 77.
199 *Francis Meres listed him among the "best"*: Francis Meres, *Palladis Tamia* (London: Cuthbert Burbie, 1598), 283.
199 *"in her Majesties time"*: Puttenham, *Arte of English Poesie*, 79.
200 *"monstrous adversary . . . who would drink my blood rather than wine"*: Nelson, *Monstrous Adversary*, 214.
200 *"I cannot particularly charge my Lord"*: Francis Southwell, note, to Lord Henry Howard, National Archives SP 12/151/57, ff. 118–19. See also Nelson, *Monstrous Adversary*, 214.
200 *references to the "Jews of Italy"*: Nelson, *Monstrous Adversary,* 213.
200 *"This lie is very rife with him"*: National Archives SP 12/151/er, ff.100-2, quoted in Anderson, *Shakespeare by Another Name*, 171.
200 *"flowed with that facility"*: Ben Jonson, *Timber; or Discoveries* (London: Cassell, 1892).
201 *"I fear thou are so much wedded"*: Nelson, *Monstrous Adversary*, 295.
201 *"a worthie favorer and fosterer of learning"*: Robert Greene, dedicatory letter to *Gwydonius; The Card of Fancy* (London: William Ponsonby, 1584).
201 *"It were infinite to speake of his infinite expense"*: Gervase Markham, *Honour in his Perfect* (London: Benjamin Fisher, 1624), 16.
201 *"over many greedy horse-leeches"*: Nelson, *Monstrous Adversary,* 326–27.
201 *privy seal warrant*: Bernard R. Ward, "Shakespeare and Elizabethan War Propaganda," *Royal Engineers Journal* (December 1928).
202 *"policy of plays"*: Thomas Nashe, *Pierce Penilesse* (1592) in *The Works of Thomas Nashe*, vol. 1, ed. Ron McKerrow (London: Sidgwick & Jackson, 1910), 211–13.
202 *Shakespeare "had an allowance so large"*: *Diary of the Reverend John Ward, A.M., Vicar of Stratford-Upon-Avon* (London: Henry Colburn, 1839), 183.
202 *According to the Oxfordian theory*: Magri, *Such Fruits out of Italy*, 17–26.
203 *"Thimperfections of her father"*: Nelson, *Monstrous Adversary*, 350.
203 *It was while Derby was staying at Castle Hedingham*: Lefranc, *Sous le Masque de William Stanley*, trans. Frank Lawler, 68.
203 *"I find comfort in this air"*: Ibid., 353.
203 *"I cannot but find a great grief "*: Anderson, *Shakespeare by Another Name*, 351.
204 *"Of him I will only speak"*: College of Arms Archive, Vincent MS 445. According to the librarian at Westminster Abbey, records of bodies removed from other

places to be reburied at Westminster Abbey were not entered into the Abbey registers (Waugh, "My Shakespeare, Rise!," 77).

204 *"the picture of a great soul, misunderstood"*: Looney, *"Shakespeare" Identified*, 368.

204 *"one of those composite productions"*: J. T. Looney, letter to George Greenwood, March 14, 1922, Folger Shakespeare Library.

205 *"one of the strongest links"*: Ibid., 307.

205 *"the deceased, but ever-living Author . . . Fletcher"*: See "To the Memory of the Deceased but Ever-Living Author, in These His Poems, Mr. John Fletcher," *The Dramatic Works of Beaumont and Fletcher*, vol. 1 (London: John Stockdale, 1811), lxxxii.

206 *The dedication "has been telling us"*: Looney, *"Shakespeare" Identified*, 355.

206 *"A few coincidences we may treat"*: Ibid., 80.

206 *It was a "long overdue act"*: Ibid., 3.

206 *"a sad waste of print and paper"*: Alfred Pollard, "Another 'Identification' of Shakespeare," *Times Literary Supplement*, March 4, 1920, 149.

207 *"it has been impossible to do"*: J. T. Looney, letter to the *Times Literary Supplement*, March 25, 1920, 201.

207 *"a hypothesis which . . . is consistent"*: E. K. Chambers, "Shakespeare," in *The Encylopaedia Britannica*: *A Dictionary of Arts, Sciences, Literature and General Information*, 11th ed., vol. 24 (New York: Encyclopaedia Britannica, 1911), 777.

207 *Scholars see jokes about "equivocation" in* Macbeth: Many scholars have seen links between references to "equivocation" and the trials of the Gunpowder plotters, especially that of the Jesuit Henry Garnet in 1606, who admitted his use of the word. However, "equivocation" was in use long before 1606. The Jesuit priest Edmund Campion (executed in 1581) was accused of using "verbal equivocation," as reported by Anthony Munday in *A Discoverie of Edmund Campion, and His Confederates.* The Jesuit priest Robert Southwell also used "equivocation" at his trial in 1595, after which a pamphlet circulated, entitled *A Treatise of Equivocation* (1598).

207 *There is no evidence to contradict 1606"*: William Shakespeare, *Macbeth—The Oxford Shakespeare*, ed. Nicholas Brooke (Oxford: Oxford University Press, 1990), 59. Wells and Taylor write that the play was "composed probably in 1606" (*Complete Works,* 975); A. R. Braunmuller dates it to 1603 (*Macbeth* [Cambridge: Cambridge University Press, 1994], 6); and J. Dover Wilson proposes 1601 or 1602 (*Macbeth* [Cambridge: Cambridge University Press], 1951).

207 *many accounts of shipwrecks*: Kenneth Muir, *The Sources of Shakespeare's Plays* (London: Routledge, 1978), 280, accepts that Shakespeare might have composed

The Tempest without the Strachey letter: "The extent of the verbal echoes of [the Bermuda] pamphlets has, I think, been exaggerated. There is hardly a shipwreck in history or fiction which does not mention splitting, in which the ship is not lightened of its cargo, in which the passengers do not give themselves up for lost, in which north winds are not sharp, and in which no one gets to shore by clinging to wreckage." David Lindley, editor of *The Tempest* in the New Cambridge Shakespeare series, 1st ed. (Cambridge: Cambridge University Press, 2002), 31, agrees: "There is virtually nothing in these texts [the Bermuda pamphlets] which manifests the kind of unambiguous close verbal affinity we have seen in other sources [Virgil, Ovid, and Montaigne] so far considered."

207 *based on* Decades of the New World: Roger Stritmatter and Lynne Kositsky, "Shakespeare and the Voyagers Revisited," *Review of English Studies* 58 (2007): 447–72; " 'O Brave New World': 'The Tempest' and Peter Martyr's 'De Orbe Novo,' " *Critical Survey* 21, no. 2 (2009): 7–42; *On the Date, Sources, and Design of Shakespeare's* The Tempest (Jefferson, NC: McFarland, 2013).

208 *"This is a remarkable book"*: "A New Mask for Shakespeare," *Bookman's Journal* 1, no. 2 (March 19, 1920): 408.

208 *Looney "makes a far stronger case for Oxford"*: "The Real Shakespeare," *Halifax* (NS) *Evening Courier*, March 4, 1920, 4.

208 *"a case deserving of serious consideration"*: C.R., "Shakespeare: Was he Edward de Vere, Lord Oxford?" *Nottingham Journal and Express* (UK), April 22, 1920, 4.

208 *"almost proves that Shakespeare's works were written by Edward de Vere"*: *Hull Daily Mail* (UK), March 4, 1920, 4. The notice is untitled.

208 *"the best detective story I've ever read"*: John Galsworthy, quoted in Schoenbaum, *Shakespeare's Lives*, 602.

208 *The Oxfordian theory apparently stayed with Joyce*: For an Oxfordian reading of James Joyce, see Gary Goldstein, "Who Was James Joyce's Shakespeare?," *Oxfordian* 19 (2017): 173–79.

208 *"I must confess, I am very impressed"*: Sigmund Freud and Ernest Jones, *The Complete Correspondence of Sigmund Freud and Ernest Jones, 1908–1939*, ed. R. Andrew Paskauskas (Cambridge, MA: Harvard University Press, 1993).

209 *Lear could only be understood psychologically*: Richard Waugaman, "An Unpublished Letter by Sigmund Freud on the Shakespeare Authorship Question," *Scandinavian Psychoanalytic Review* 39, no. 1 (2016): 148–51.

209 *"the figure of the father"*: Ernest Jones, *The Life and Work of Sigmund Freud*, vol. 3 (New York: Basic Books, 1953), 458; see also Richard Waugaman, "An Unpublished Letter by Sigmund Freud on the Shakespeare Authorship Question," *Scandinavian Psychoanalytic Review* 39, no. 1 (2016): 148–51.

209 *"nobly born and highly cultivated"*: Sigmund Freud, "Address Delivered in the Goethe House at Frankfurt," *The Standard Edition of the Complete Psychological*

Works of Sigmund Freud, vol. 21, trans. James Strachey (London: Hogarth Press, 1966), 208–12.

210 *Pollard tried to argue*: Alfred Pollard, *Shakespeare's Hand in* The Play of Sir Thomas More (Cambridge: Cambridge University Press, 1923), 1–40.

210 *"too small a sample size"*: "Shakespeare's handwriting: Hand D in the Booke of Sir Thomas More," Folger Shakespeare Library online, accessed March 13, 2021, https://shakespearedocumented.folger.edu/resource/document/shakespeares-handwriting-hand-d-booke-sir-thomas-more. For further arguments refuting "Hand D," see Michael Hays, "Shakespeare Hand in Sir Thomas More: Some Aspects of the Paleographic Argument," *Shakespeare Studies* 8 (1975): 241–53.

210 *"a very successful resistance movement"*: Paul Werstine, "Shakespeare More or Less: A. W. Pollard and Twentieth-Century Shakespeare Editing," *Florilegium* 16 (1999): 125.

210 *They suspected . . . that certain passages*: For the history of efforts to identify Shakespeare's coauthors, see Gabriel Egan, "A History of Shakespearean Authorship Attribution," in *The New Oxford Shakespeare Authorship Companion,* ed. Gary Taylor and Gabriel Egan (Oxford: Oxford University Press, 2017), 27–47.

210 *this "disintegration" of Shakespeare*: E. K. Chambers, "The Disintegration of Shakespeare," *Annual Shakespeare Lecture of the British Academy* (London: Oxford University Press for the British Academy, 1924).

211 *"many pens and one Master Mind"*: George Greenwood, *Is There a Shakespeare Problem?* (London: John Lane, 1916), 454.

211 *An American woman named Eva Turner Clark*: Eva Turner Clark, *The Man Who Was Shakespeare* (New York: Richard Smith, 1937).

212 *Allen's "extravagant & improbable" hypothesis*: J. T. Looney, letter to Christopher Paul, published in the *Shakespeare Oxford Newsletter* 43, no. 3 (Summer 2007): 8–9.

212 *"a solution to the mystery"*: "The Extraordinary General Meeting," *Shakespeare Fellowship Newsletter,* March 1946, 1.

213 *"This is where our interest in Shakespeare"*: J. T. Looney to Eva Turner Clark, November 10, 1939, *Shakespeare Fellowship Quarterly* 5, no. 2 (April 1944): 22–23.

214 *"I will never again believe"*: Hamilton Basso, "The Big Who-Done-It," *New Yorker*, April 8, 1950, 113.

214 *an article in the* American Bar Association Journal: Richard Bentley, "Elizabethan Whodunit: Who Was William Shake-Speare?," *American Bar Association Journal* 45, no. 2 (February 1959): 143–46, 204–8.

214 *"We are talking to each other"*: Richard Horne, *Shakespeare Oxford Society Newsletter*, February 28, 1969.

214 *The "sheer volume of heretical publication appalls"*: Schoenbaum, *Shakespeare's Lives*, 449.

214 *When Charlton Ogburn . . . published an article in* Harvard *magazine*: Charlton

Ogburn, "The Man Who Shakespeare Was Not . . . and Who He Was," *Harvard*, November 1974.

215 *Ogburn had "embarrassed those of us"*: Walter Kaiser, letter to the editor, *Harvard,* quoted in Charlton Ogburn, *The Mysterious William Shakespeare: The Myth and the Reality* (New York: Dodd, Mead, 1984), 177.

215 *"English faculties, abetted by a generally subservient press"*: Charlton Ogburn, "President's Message," *Shakespeare Oxford Society Newsletter*, Fall 1976, 1–3.

215 *"What I was saying"*: James Lardner, "The Authorship Question," *New Yorker*, April 3, 1988, 89.

215 *"This brilliant, powerful book is a major event"*: David McCullough, foreword, in Ogburn, *Mysterious William Shakespeare*, x; Richmond Crinkley, "New Perspectives on the Authorship Question," *Shakespeare Quarterly* 36, no. 4 (Winter 1985): 515–22.

216 *Shakespeare was put "on trial"*: For an account of the 1987 mock trial, see Lardner, "Authorship Question," 87–106.

216 *"in my early years after law school"*: Ibid., 100.

216 *"You didn't clear that with the rest of us"*: Ibid.

218 *"The Oxfordians have presented"*: Harry Blackmun, letter to Charlton Ogburn, 1987, quoted in Ogburn, *Mysterious William Shakespeare*, vi.

218 *In 1992, he published an article*: John Paul Stevens, "The Shakespeare Canon of Statutory Construction," *University of Pennsylvania Law Review* 140, no. 4 (April 1992), 1373–87.

218 *"I have never thought"*: Lewis Powell, letter to Charlton Ogburn, 1987, quoted in Ogburn, *Mysterious William Shakespeare*, vi.

218 *found the Oxfordian theory "congenial"*: Lewis H. Lapham, "Full Fathom Five," *Harper's*, April 1999, 12.

219 *"Academics err in failing to acknowledge the mystery"*: Mortimer Adler to Max Weissman, director, Center for the Study of Great Ideas, November 7, 1997, in "Past Doubters," available at Shakespeare Coalition online, https://doubtaboutwill.org/past_doubters.

219 *(The news was splashed in the* New York Times*)*: William S. Niederkorn, "A Historic Whodunit: If Shakespeare Didn't, Who Did?," Theater, *New York Times*, February 10, 2002, 7.

219 *"sometimes fabulously constricted"*: Roger Stritmatter, "The Marginalia of Edward de Vere's Bible: Providential Discovery, Literary Reasoning, and Historical Consequence" (doctoral dissertation, University of Massachusetts, Amherst, 2001), 7–8.

220 *Oxford marked only 13 percent of verses*: Richard Waugaman, "The Pseudonymous Author of Shakespeare's Work," *Princeton Alumni Weekly*, March 2008, https://www.princeton.edu/~paw/web_exclusives/plus/plus_031908wegeman.html.

220 *"99 and 44/100 percent certain"*: In a personal communication to Roger Stritmatter during an online discussion forum on June 3, 1995, Alan Nelson wrote: "I am 99 and 44/100 percent certain that the annotating hand is Oxford's; I am 100 percent sure (if it's possible to be that) that the Bible is Oxford's," quoted in "Edward de Vere Geneva Bible FAQ," Shake-Speare's Bible.com, accessed June 9, 2021, https://shake-speares-bible.com/bible-faq/. Nelson is also quoted as saying, "The hand is simply not the same hand that wrote [the] letters. The people who claim this is clearly Oxford's hand just don't know their paleography," in Scott Heller, "In a Centuries-Old Debate, Shakespeare Doubters Point to New Evidence," *Chronicle of Higher Education*, June 4, 1999, A22.

221 *"In time, more and more traditional scholars"*: John Paul Stevens, unpublished letter to Roger Stritmatter, August 3, 2001.

EIGHT Purple Robes Distained

224 *came across him on YouTube*: "Who Wrote Shakespeare?—Sir Jonathan Bate & Alexander Waugh," YouTube, 1:24.26, How to Academy Mindset, filmed September 21, 2017, Emmanuel Centre, London, https://www.youtube.com/watch?v=HgImgdJ5L6o&ab_channel=HowToAcademyMindset.

224 *Waugh cited an article published in 2016*: Ros Barber, "Shakespeare and Warwickshire Dialect," *Journal of Early Modern Studies* 5 (2016): 91–118.

224 *Evelyn Waugh, Alexander's grandfather*: For the Waugh family, including Evelyn and Auberon Waugh, see Alexander Waugh, *Fathers and Sons: The Autobiography of a Family* (New York: Broadway Books, 2004).

224 *"Nobody ever wrote a more unaffectedly elegant English"*: Clive James, "Waugh's Last Stand," *New York Review* online, last modified December 4, 1980, https://www.nybooks.com/articles/1980/12/04/waughs-last-stand/.

227 *News of Waugh's discovery*: Dalya Alberge, "Zounds! He's Cracked the de Vere Code," London *Sunday Times*, October 13, 2012.

228 *"Shakespeare was a nom de plume"*: Alexander Waugh, "Alexander Waugh's Diary: Shakespeare Was a Nom de plume—Get Over It," *Spectator*, November 2, 2013.

228 *"On Alexander Waugh"*: Jeffrey Burghauser, "On Alexander Waugh," *New English Review*, July 2021.

229 *"[S]ince it is openly acknowledged by orthodox scholars"*: Alexander Waugh and Roger Stritmatter, general introduction, in "The New Shakespeare Allusion Book," vol. 1 (unpublished manuscript, 2021), 9.

229 *"Scholars in the audience would have understood"*: Ibid., 384.

230 *"Virbius like"*: John Warren, "Of Master William Shakespeare" in *Shakespeare's Poems*, ed. John Benson (London: 1640).

231 *Stanley Wells, recognizing the problem*: Stanley Wells and Gary Taylor, eds., *The*

Oxford Shakespeare: The Complete Works (Oxford: Oxford University Press, 2005), lxxv.

231 *"To the learned and attentive reader"*: Ibid., vol. 2, 310.

232 *"I must acknowledge my lines not worthy"*: Thomas Heywood, "To my approved good Friend, Mr. Nicholas Okes," *An Apology for Actors* (London: 1612).

232 *Jaggard "reissued it in the knowledge"*: Waugh and Stritmatter, "New Shakespeare Allusion Book," vol. 1, 564.

232 *"explicitly raising the question"*: Ibid., vol. 1, 1320.

233 *"Apollo has cultivated thy mind in the arts"*: Gabriel Harvey, "Apostrophe ad eundum," in *Gratulationis Valdinensis* (Londini: Henrici Binnemani, 1548), trans. Thomas Hugh Jameson (New Haven: Yale University Press, 1938), 125.

233 *"liberal as the Sunne"*: George Chapman, *The Revenge of Bussy D'Amois* (London: 1613), ed. Frederick Boas (Boston: D. C. Heath & Co., 1905), 237.

233 *beloved of "th'Heliconian imps"*: Edmund Spenser, "To the right Honourable the Earle of Oxenford, Lord high Chamberlayne of England," *The Fairie Queene* (London, 1596).

233 *"repurified Poetrie from Arts"*: Thomas Nashe, *Have with You to Saffron-Walden* in *The Works of Thomas Nashe*, vol. 3, ed. Ronald McKerrow (London Sidgwick & Jackson, 1910), 77.

234 *"obscure lurking in basest corners"*: Gabriel Harvey, *Four Letters and Certain Sonnets* (London: 1592).

234 *"I lurke in no corners"*: Thomas Nashe, *Strange Newes* (1592) in McKerrow, ed., *Works of Thomas Nashe*, 329.

234 *"my Lord . . . whom I have servd"*: Thomas Kyd, letters to Sir John Puckering and Arthur Freeman, excerpted in *Thomas Kyd: Facts and Problems* (Oxford: Clarendon Press, 1976), 13–21.

234 *"the children of Phoebus"*: Thomas Dekker, *A Knight's Conjuring* (1607), ed. Edward Rimbault (London: C. Richards, 1842), 75.

235 *Scholars and readers have "an ethical obligation"*: Gary Taylor, "Artiginality: Authorship After Postmodernism," in *The New Oxford Shakespeare Authorship Companion*, ed. Gary Taylor and Gabriel Egan (Oxford: Oxford University Press, 2017), 25, 20.

236 *The findings of* The New Oxford Shakespeare: See, for example, Daniel Pollack-Pelzner, "The Radical Argument of the New Oxford Shakespeare," *New Yorker*, February 19, 2017.

236 *two geniuses working together*: "Christopher Marlowe Credited as Shakespeare's Co-writer," BBC News online, last modified October 24, 2016, https://www.bbc.com/news/entertainment-arts-37750558.

236 *"I am quite undone"*: Thomas Nashe, *Pierce Penniless* (1592) in McKerrow, ed., *Works of Thomas Nashe*, 158.

236 *George Peele was driven "to extreme shifts"*: *Greenes Groatsworth of Wit* (1592).

236 *"miserable example of misfortune"*: John Lyly, "Petition to Queen Elizabeth" (1595) and letter to Robert Cecil (December 22, 1597) in *The Complete Works of John Lyly*, vol. 1., ed. R. Warwick Bond (Oxford: Oxford University Press, 1902), 64–65, 68–69.

239 *"favorite poet"*: Jonathan Bate, *Shakespeare and Ovid* (Oxford: Oxford University Press, 1993), vii.

240 *"There is a prejudice against anagrams"*: Christopher Ricks, "The Anagram," in *Along Heroic Lines* (Oxford: Oxford University Press, 2021), 19–56.

242 *"the only Quintessence that hitherto"*: William Camden, "Anagrammes," in *Remaines Concerning Britain* (London: 1870), 182.

242 *a line in Sonnet 145 puns*: William Shakespeare, *All the Sonnets of Shakespeare*, ed. Paul Edmondson and Stanley Wells (Cambridge: Cambridge University Press, 2020), 49.

242 *"the flowers that stand about the Prince's Crown"*: Anonymous, The First Parte of Pasquils Apologie (London: J. Charlewood, 1590).

246 *despised democracy*: Shapiro, *Contested Will*, 181–82, 187–89.

246 *"between the human soul and elemental brute force"*: J. T. Looney letter to Flodden Heron, July 5, 1941, from "A Great Pioneer's Ideas on Intellectual Freedom," *SF Quarterly*, vol. VI/3 (July 1945): 33–34.

246 "shocked at the inhuman treatment": J. T. Looney letter to Sigmund Freud, July 15, 1938, from the collections of the Manuscript Division of the Library of Congress.

247 *("my monstrous adversary . . .")*: Nelson, *Monstrous Adversary*, 267.

247 *Oxford's youthful verse was "atrocious"*: Ibid., 160–61.

251 *"a great deal of work has gone into this volume"*: Oxford University Press reader's report on "The New Shakespeare Allusion Book."

252 "*spoke with great admiration*": Email from Luke Ingram to Alexander Waugh and Roger Stritmatter, March 19, 2019.

252 *"aristocracy has never produced genius"*: Email from Michael Fishwick to Sarah Chalfant, April 2, 2019.

252 *"Surely you have heard of Ronsard"*: Email from Alexander Waugh to Michael Fishwick, April 3, 2019.

NINE Some Heaven-Born Goddess

259 *a young Venetian widow named Christine de Pizan*: Rosalind Brown-Grant, introduction, in Christine de Pizan, *The Book of the City of Ladies*, trans. Rosalind Brown-Grant (London: Penguin Books, 1999); and Maureen Quilligan, *The Allegory of Female Authority: Christine de Pizan's* Cités des Dames (New York: Cornell University Press, 1991).

260 *Italian noblewoman Vittoria Colonna*: Ramie Targoff, *Renaissance Woman: The Life of Vittoria Colonna* (New York: Farrar, Straus and Giroux, 2018), 147.

260 *Anne Locke became the first person in England*: Michael R. G. Spiller, "A Literary 'First': The Sonnet Sequence of Anne Locke (1560)," *Renaissance Studies: Journal of the Society for Renaissance Studies* 11 (1997): 42.

260 *"relic of the sense of chastity"*: Virginia Woolf, *A Room of One's Own* (London: Harcourt Brace, 1929), 50.

261 *Harvey referred cryptically to an "excellent gentlewoman"*: Gabriel Harvey, *Pierce's Supererogation* (London: John Wolf, 1593), 153, 170.

261 *"all her conceits are illuminate"*: Gabriel Harvey, *A New Letter of Notable Contents* (London: 1593), 17.

261 *Mary Sidney was first proposed*: Gilbert Slater, *Seven Shakespeares: A Discussion of Various Theories with Regard to Shakespeare's Identity* (London: Cecil Palmer, 1931).

262 *The case for Mary Sidney*: Robin Williams, *Sweet Swan of Avon: Did a Woman Write Shakespeare?* (Berkeley, CA: Wilton Circle Press, 2006).

262 *She was "such a sister"*: Margaret P. Hannay, *Philip's Phoenix: Mary Sidney, Countess of Pembroke* (New York: Oxford University Press, 1990), 80.

262 *"We remember how much"*: John Buxton, *Sir Philip Sidney and the English Renaissance* (London: Macmillan, 1964), 31.

263 *"They first produced"*: Albert C. Baugh, *A Literary History of England,* vol. 2 (New York: Appleton-Century-Crofts, 1948), 472.

263 *The subject of his ardour was Penelope Rich*: Sally Varlow, *The Lady Penelope: The Lost Tale of Love and Politics in the Court of Elizabeth I* (London: Carlton, 2007).

263 *Despite these little clues*: Hoyt Hudson, "Penelope Devereux as Sidney's Stella," *Huntington Library Bulletin*, no. 7, April 1935, 89–129.

263 *Mary took up her brother's literary mantle*: "Mary Sidney, *The Tragedy of Antoine* (1595) (text)," in *Renaissance Drama by Women: Texts and Documents,* ed. S. P. Cerasano and Marion Wynne-Davies (London: Routledge, 1996), 13.

263 *"technical virtuosity in inventing verse forms"*: Mary Sidney Herbert, *The Collected Works of Mary Sidney Herbert, Countess of Pembroke*, eds. Margaret Hannah, Noel Kinnamon, and Michael Brennan (Oxford: Clarendon Press, 1998), 57.

263 *The Psalms constitute "a virtuoso performance"*: Theodore Steinberg, "The Sidneys and the Psalms," in *Ashgate Critical Essays on Women Writers in England, 1550–1700*, vol. 2, *Mary Sidney, Countess of Pembroke,* ed. Margaret Hannay (London: Routledge, 2009), 267.

263 *"it was more than a woman's skill"*: Ibid., 273–74.

264 *"a workshop for poetical experimentation"*: Garry Waller, *Mary Sidney, Countess of Pembroke: A Critical Study of Her Writings and Literary Milieu* (Salzburg, Germany: University of Salzburg Press, 1979), 45.

264 *"The complete body of her works"*: Hannay, Kinnamon, and Brennan, eds. *The Collected Works of Mary Sidney Herbert, Countess of Pembroke*, 54–55.

266 *"We would probably all want"*: "Joyce Carol Oates: By the Book," *New York Times Book Review*, September 6, 2012, 6.

267 *a "man-womanly mind," she called it*: Woolf, *Room of One's Own*, 99.

267 *"Shakespeare has no heroes"*: John Ruskin, quoted in Adrian Poole, *Shakespeare and the Victorians* (London: Bloomsbury Academic, 2004), 195.

267 *"Shakespeare was clearly"*: Orson Welles, *My Lunches with Orson: Conversations between Henry Jaglom and Orson Welles*, ed. Peter Biskind (New York: Henry Holt, 2013), 276.

268 *Women from the middle classes supported the day-to-day business*: Natasha Korda, "Labours Lost: Women's Work and Early Modern Theatrical Commerce," in *From Script to Stage in Early Modern England*, ed. Peter Holland and Stephen Orgel (New York: Palgrave Macmillan, 2004), 195.

268 *Some women performed as actors*: Pamela Allen Brown and Peter Parolin, eds., *Women Players in England, 1500–1660: Beyond the All-Male Stage* (Burlington, VT: Ashgate, 2005); Ann Thompson, "Women/'women' and the Stage," in *Women and Literature in Britain, 1500–1700*, ed. Helen Wilcox (Cambridge: Cambridge University Press, 1996).

268 *They wrote liturgical drama and royal entertainments*: Nancy Cotton, "Women Playwrights in England: Renaissance Noblewomen," in *Readings in Renaissance Women's Drama: Criticism, History, and Performance, 1594–1998*, ed. Susan Cerasano and Marion Wynne-Davies (London: Routledge, 1998).

268 *In Italy, women were writing plays*: Pamela Allen Brown, *The Diva's Gift to the Shakespearean Stage: Agency, Theatricality, and the Innamorata* (Oxford: Oxford University Press, 2021).

268 *it could have been staged at a private residence*: Alison Findlay, *Playing Spaces in Early Women's Drama* (Cambridge: Cambridge University Press, 2006), 35–36.

268 *The ideological constraints in which women operated*: Phyllis Rackin, "Anonymous Was a Woman," in *Shakespeare Without Boundaries*, ed. Christa Jansohn, Lena Cowen Orlin, and Stanley Wells (Newark: University of Delaware Press, 2010), 41.

269 *a "tripartite collaboration"*: William Plummer Fowler, *Shakespeare Revealed in Oxford's Letters* (Portsmouth, UK: Randall, 1986), 498.

271 *Penelope Rich was the first woman ever*: Gerald Massey, *The Secret Drama of Shakespeare's Sonnets* (London: Richard Clay, 1888).

271 *a "fair woman with a black soul"*: Quoted in Varlow, *The Lady Penelope*, 247.

272 *In 1973 a scholar named A. L. Rowse*: A. L. Rowse, *Shakespeare's Sonnets: The Problems Solved* (New York: Palgrave Macmillan, 1973).

272 *The Bassanos were musicians and instrument makers*: David Lasocki and Roger Prior, *The Bassanos: Venetian Musicians and Instrument Makers in England, 1531–1665* (Aldershot, UK: Scolar Press, 1995).

272 *When Emilia was seven*: Susanne Woods, *Lanyer: A Renaissance Woman Poet* (Oxford: Oxford University Press, 1999), 3, 14.

274 *variants of her family name crop up*: John Hudson, *Shakespeare's Dark Lady: Amelia Bassano Lanier: The Woman Behind Shakespeare's Plays?* (Stroud, UK: Amberley, 2014).

275 *"Shakespeare's co-author"*: Mark Bradbeer, *Aemilia Lanyer as Shakespeare's Co-Author* (London: Routledge, 2022).

278 *"middlebrows"*: Virginia Woolf, "Middlebrow," in *The Death of the Moth, and Other Essays* (London: Hogarth Press, 1947), 115.

279 *"So now, for me, however the works of Shakespeare were created"*: Mark Rylance, "Keep Questioning Shakespeare's Identity," *Atlantic* online, last modified June 8, 2019, https://www.theatlantic.com/entertainment/archive/2019/06/mark-rylance-keep-questioning-shakespeares-identity/590395/.

280 *"I do not wish to be associated"*: Matthew Taylor, "Mark Rylance Resigns from RSC over BP Sponsorship," *Guardian* (US edition) online, last modified June 21, 2019, https://www.theguardian.com/stage/2019/jun/21/mark-rylance-resigns-from-royal-shakespeare-company-rsc-over-bp-sponsorship.

284 *"This is an old and proper wrong"*: Mark Rylance, "Did Shakespeare Write His Own Plays? That Is the Question," London *Sunday Times,* February 3, 2019.

290 *"How should we regard the 'missing matter'?"*: Robert Proctor and Londa Schiebinger, eds., *Agnotology: The Making and Unmaking of Ignorance* (Stanford, CA: Stanford University Press, 2008), 7.

TEN The Reckoning

291 *Wilbur Zeigler published*: Wilbur Gleason Zeigler, *It Was Marlowe: A Story of the Secret of Three Centuries* (Chicago: Donohuge, Henneberry, 1895).

292 *"had done her Majesty good service"*: PRO Privy Council Registers PC2/14/381. Government documents relating to Marlowe are transcribed in Constance Brown Kuriyama, *Christopher Marlowe: A Renaissance Life* (Ithaca, NY: Cornell University Press, 2002).

292 *Marlowe "haunts Shakespeare's expression"*: Peter Ackroyd, *Shakespeare: The Biography* (London: Chatto & Windus, 2005), 140.

292 *What "Marlowe had begun . . . Shakespeare would complete"*: Patrick Cheney, *Shakespeare's Literary Authorship* (Cambridge: Cambridge University Press, 2008), 25.

292 *"curiously difficult for the young Shakespeare"*: Harold Bloom, *Christopher Marlowe,* Bloom's Major Dramatists, 2nd ed. (New York: Chelsea House, 2002), 10.

292 *Shakespeare "only became Shakespeare"*: Jonathan Bate, *The Genius of Shakespeare* (Oxford: Oxford University Press, 1998), 105.

293 *"containing the opinion of one Christopher Marly"*: B. L. Harley, British Library, Catalogue of English Literary Manuscripts 1450–1700, MS 6848 ff, 185–86.

295 *rippled through the group*: Dr. T. C. Mendenhall, "A Mechanical Solution of a Literary Problem," *Popular Science Monthly* 60 (December 1901): 97–105.

295 *had "concocted a lying account of Marlowe's behaviour"*: J. Leslie Hotson, *The Death of Christopher Marlowe* (London: Nonesuch Press, 1925), 40.

296 *Some take the report at its word*: Paul E. J. Hammer, "A Reckoning Reframed: The 'Murder' of Christopher Marlowe Revisited," *English Literary Renaissance* 26, no. 2 (Spring 1996): 225–42.

296 "*profoundly slippery trio*": Charles Nicholl, *The Reckoning: The Murder of Christopher Marlowe* (London: Jonathan Cape, 1992), 34.

304 her *case for Marlowe*: Rosalind Barber, "My Shakespeare—Christopher Marlowe," in *My Shakespeare: The Authorship Controversy*, ed. William Leahy (Brighton, UK: Edward Everett Root, 2018), 85–112.

306 *"Mrs. Bull was a widow"*: Park Honan, *Christopher Marlowe: Poet and Spy* (Oxford: Oxford University Press, 2005), 344.

308 *Deaths in the world of espionage*: Roy Kendall, *Christopher Marlowe and Richard Baines: Journeys Through the Elizabethan Underground* (Madison, NJ: Farleigh Dickinson University Press, 2003), 149.

308 "*Banishment is both*": Jane Kingsley-Smith, *Shakespeare's Drama of Exile* (New York: Palgrave Macmillan, 2003), 1.

309 *"Again and again in his plays"*: Greenblatt, *Will in the World*, 85.

311 *"Shakespeare Authorship Doubt in 1593"*: Rosalind Barber, "Shakespeare Authorship Doubt in 1593," *Critical Survey* 21, no. 2 (June 2009): 83–110.

312 *put her programming hat back on*: Rosalind Barber, "Big Data or Not Enough? Zeta Test Reliability and the Attribution of Henry VI," *Digital Scholarship in the Humanities* 36, no. 3 (September 2021): 542–64.

312 *"much of the so-called cutting-edge research"*: Pervez Rivzi, shakespearestext.com/nos.htm. For his papers, see Perez Rivzi, "The Interpretation of Zeta Test Results," *Digital Scholarship in the Humanities* 34, no. 2 (June 2019), 401–18. Pervez Rivzi, "The Problem of Microattribution," *Digital Scholarship in the Humanities* 34, no. 3 (September 2019), 605-615. Perez Rivzi, "The Use of t-test in Shakespeare Scholarship," *Digital Scholarship in the Humanities* 36, no. 3 (September 2021), 712–18.

314 journal called Rethinking History: Rosalind Barber, "Exploring Biographical Fictions: The Role of Imagination in Writing and Reading Narrative," Rethinking History: The Journal of Theory and Practice 14, no. 2 (2010): 165–87.

316 *"hearsay, half-remembered facts, and assumptions"*: Tarnya Cooper, *Searching for Shakespeare* (New Haven: Yale University Press, 2006), 54.

ELEVEN Negative Capability

318 *"[S]everal things dove-tailed"*: Walter Jackson Bate, *John Keats* (Cambridge, MA: Harvard University Press, 2009), 249.

318 *"To be negatively capable"*: Li Ou, *Keats and Negative Capability* (London: Continuum International, 2009), 2; Brian Rejack and Michael Theune, eds., *Keats's Negative Capability: New Origins and Afterlives* (Liverpool, UK: Liverpool University Press, 2019), 2.

318 *Wilfred Bion saw that Keats's concept of negative capability*: Joan Symington and Neville Symington, *The Clinical Thinking of Wilfred Bion* (New York: Routledge, 1996).

320 *was described alternately as "brilliant"*: Maureen Corrigan, " 'The Swerve': The Ideas That Rooted the Renaissance," review of *The Swerve: How the World Became Modern*, by Stephen Greenblatt, *Fresh Air,* September 20, 2011, available online at https://www.npr.org/programs/fresh-air/2011/09/20/140625860/.

320 *"represent an abuse of power"*: Laura Saetveit Miles, "Stephen Greenblatt's *The Swerve* Racked Up Prizes—and Completely Misled You About the Middle Ages," Vox, last modified July 20, 2016, https://www.vox.com/2016/7/20/12216712/harvard-professor-the-swerve-greenblatt-middle-ages-false.

320 *"I set out to solve a mystery"*: Jonathan Shaw, "The Mysterious Mr. Shakespeare," *Harvard* online, September/October 2004, https://www.harvardmagazine.com/2004/09/the-mysterious-mr-shakes.html.

323 *"It might well have been"*: Ashby Jones, "The Court, Led by Stevens, (Mostly) Rules Against Shakespeare," *Wall Street Journal*, April 20, 2009.

324 *"Justice Stevens much appreciated"*: Tyler Foggatt, "Justice Stevens's Dissenting Shakespeare Theory," *New Yorker,* July 29, 2019.

324 *"considered the possibility of collaboration"*: Correspondence between John Paul Stevens and James Shapiro, August 25, 2011, to January 31, 2012, Folger Institute, Folger Shakespeare Library, Washington, DC.

324 *Peacham put Oxford first*: Henry Peacham, "Of Poetry," *The Compleat Gentleman* (London: F. Constable, 1622).

325 *"realistic picture" of Elizabethan life*: Oscar Campbell, "*Love's Labour's Lost* Restudied," in *Love's Labour's Lost: Critical Essays*, ed. Felicia Hardison Londré (New York: Garland Publishing, 1997), 89.

330 *"Shakespeare is a concept"*: Garber, *Shakespeare's Ghost Writers*, 236.

331 *"There is no ground of Shakespeare that is not already cross-dressed"*: Marjorie Garber, *Vested Interests: Cross-Dressing and Cultural Anxiety* (New York: Routledge, 1992), 40.

331 *"repudiation of the fiction of historical accuracy"*: Garber, *Shakespeare's Ghost Writers*, 62.

Epilogue

335 *"authority gone archaic"*: Leonard Tennenhouse, *Power on Display: The Politics of Shakespeare's Genres* (New York: Routledge Library Editions: Shakespeare, 1986), 73.

335 *"almost inconceivable hypothesis"*: *Sunday Times* review quoted in James Warren, *Shakespeare Revolutionized: The First Hundred Years of J. Thomas Looney's "Shakespeare" Identified* (Cary, North Carolina: Veritas Publications, 2021), 13.

335 *the verdict "of all unprejudiced persons"*: *The Bristol Times* review quoted in Warren, *Shakespeare Revolutionized*, 14.

335 *"That fellow Greenwood"*: Henry James quoted in Col Montagu Douglas, "Editorial," *Shakespeare Fellowship News-Letter*, no. 1 (January 1937), 1.

336 *"duty bound to check with real experts"*: Oliver Kamm, Twitter Post, May 12, 2019, 4:52 a.m., https://twitter.com/OliverKamm?s=20&t=L518aFq3hfktB2L10yx0Xg.

336 *"A scholar's business"*: Tom Stoppard, *The Invention of Love* (New York: Grove Press, 1998), 37–38.

337 *"urge throughout the play"*: Barton, "The Taming of the Shrew" in *The Riverside Shakespeare*, 107.

Selected Bibliography

Anderson, Mark. *"Shakespeare" by Another Name: The Life of Edward De Vere, Earl of Oxford, the Man Who Was Shakespeare*. San Francisco: Untreed Reads, 2011.

Bacon, Theodore. *Delia Bacon: A Biographical Sketch*. Boston: Houghton, Mifflin, 1888.

Baldick, Chris. *The Social Mission of English Criticism, 1848–1932*. Oxford: Clarendon Press, 1987.

Barber, Rosalind. "Big Data or Not Enough? Zeta Test Reliability and the Attribution of Henry VI," *Digital Scholarship in the Humanities* 36, no. 3 (September 2021): 542–64.

Barber, Rosalind. "Exploring Biographical Fictions: The Role of Imagination in Writing and Reading Narrative," *Rethinking History: The Journal of Theory and Practice* 14, no. 2 (2010): 165–87.

Barber, Rosalind. "Shakespeare Authorship Doubt in 1593," *Critical Survey* 21, no. 2 (2009), 83–110.

Bate, Jonathan. *Shakespeare and Ovid*. Oxford: Oxford University Press, 1993.

Bate, Jonathan. *The Genius of Shakespeare*. Oxford: Oxford University Press, 1998.

Bloom, Harold. *Christopher Marlowe,* Bloom's Major Dramatists, 2nd ed. New York: Chelsea House, 2002.

Bloom, Harold. "Freud: A Shakespearean Reading," in *The Western Canon: The Books and School of the Ages.* New York: Harcourt Brace, 1994.

Bradbeer, Mark. *Aemilia Lanyer as Shakespeare's Co-Author*. London: Routledge, 2022.

Brown, Pamela Allen and Peter Parolin, eds. *Women Players in England, 1500–1660: Beyond the All-Male Stage.* Burlington, VT: Ashgate, 2005.

Campbell, Oscar. "*Love's Labour's Lost* Restudied," in *Love's Labour's Lost: Critical Essays*. Edited by Felicia Hardison Londré. New York: Garland Publishing, 1997.

Carlyle, Thomas. *On Heroes, Hero-Worship, and the Heroic in History*. London: Fraser, 1841.

Chambers, E. K. "The Disintegration of Shakespeare," *Annual Shakespeare Lecture of the British Academy*. London: Oxford University Press for the British Academy, 1924.

Chambers, E. K. *William Shakespeare: A Study of Facts and Problems*, vol. 1. London: Oxford University Press, 1930.

Churchill, R. C. *Shakespeare and His Betters*. London: Max Reinhardt, 1925.

Clark, Eva Turner. *The Man Who Was Shakespeare*. New York: Richard Smith, 1937.

Cooper, Tarnya. *Searching for Shakespeare*. New Haven: Yale University Press, 2006.

Cotton, Nancy. "Women Playwrights in England: Renaissance Noblewomen," in *Readings in Renaissance Women's Drama: Criticism, History, and Performance, 1594–1998*. Edited by Susan Cerasano and Marion Wynne-Davies. London: Routledge, 1998.

Cox, Jane and David Thomas. *Shakespeare in the Public Records*. London: Her Majesty's Stationery Office Books, 1985.

Cressy, David. *Literacy and the Social Order: Reading and Writing in Tudor and Stuart England*. Cambridge: Cambridge University Press, 1980.

Deelman, Christian. *The Great Shakespeare Jubilee*. New York: Viking Press, 1964.

Dobson, Michael. *The Making of the National Poet: Shakespeare, Adaptation, and Authorship, 1660–1769*. Oxford: Clarendon Press, 1992.

Dudley, Michael. "With Swinish Phrase Soiling Their Addition: Epistemic Injustice, Academic Freedom, and the Shakespeare Authorship Question," in *Teaching and Learning Practices for Academic Freedom*. Edited by Ednakshi Sengupta and Patrick Blessinger. Bingley, UK: Emerald, 2021.

Dusinberre, Juliet. *Shakespeare and the Nature of Women*. New York: St. Martin's Press, 1975.

Ellis, David. *The Truth About William Shakespeare: Fact, Fiction, and Modern Biographies*. Edinburgh: Edinburgh University Press, 2012.

Emerson, Ralph Waldo. *Representative Men: Seven Lectures*. London: Routledge, 1850.

Findlay, Alison. *Playing Spaces in Early Women's Drama*. Cambridge: Cambridge University Press, 2006.

Fowler, William Plummer. *Shakespeare Revealed in Oxford's Letters*. Portsmouth, UK: Randall, 1986.

Friedman, William F. and Elizebeth S. Friedman, *The Shakespearean Ciphers Examined*. Cambridge: Cambridge University Press, 1957.

Garber, Marjorie. *Shakespeare's Ghost Writers: Literature as Uncanny Causality*. New York: Methuen, 1987.

Gilvary, Kevin. *The Fictional Lives of Shakespeare*. New York: Routledge, 2018.

Grant, Stephen. *Collecting Shakespeare: The Story of Henry and Emily Folger*. Baltimore: Johns Hopkins University Press, 2014.

Greenblatt, Stephen. *Will in the World: How Shakespeare Became Shakespeare*. New York: W. W. Norton, 2004.

Greenwood, George. *Is There a Shakespeare Problem?* London: John Lane, 1916.

Greenwood, George. *The Shakespeare Problem Restated*. London: John Lane, 1908.

Grillo, Ernesto. *Shakespeare and Italy*. Glasgow: University of Glasgow Press, 1949.

Halliwell-Phillipps, J. O. *Outlines of the Life of Shakespeare*. London: Longmans, Green, 1881.

Hannay, Margaret P. *Philip's Phoenix: Mary Sidney, Countess of Pembroke*. New York: Oxford University Press, 1990.

Holderness, Graham, ed. *The Shakespeare Myth*. Manchester: Manchester University Press, 1988.

Honan, Park. *Christopher Marlowe: Poet and Spy*. Oxford: Oxford University Press, 2005.

Hope, Warren and Kim Holston. *The Shakespeare Controversy: An Analysis of the Authorship Theories*, 2nd ed. Jefferson, NC: McFarland, 2009.

Hopkins, Vivian. *Prodigal Puritan: A Life of Delia Bacon*. Cambridge, MA: Harvard University Press, 1959.

Hotson, J. Leslie. *The Death of Christopher Marlowe*. London: Nonesuch Press, 1925.

Hudson, John. *Shakespeare's Dark Lady*: *Amelia Bassano Lanier*: *The Woman Behind Shakespeare's Plays?* Stroud, UK: Amberley, 2014.

James, Henry. "The Birthplace," *The Better Sort*. London: Methuen, 1903.

James, Henry. "Introduction to *The Tempest*," in *The Complete Works of William Shakespeare*. Edited by Sidney Lee. New York: Harper & Brothers, 1907.

Kendall, Roy. *Christopher Marlowe and Richard Baines: Journeys Through the Elizabethan Underground*. Madison, NJ: Farleigh Dickinson University Press, 2003.

Kingsley-Smith, Jane. *Shakespeare's Drama of Exile*. New York: Palgrave Macmillan, 2003.

Lasocki, David and Roger Prior. *The Bassanos: Venetian Musicians and Instrument Makers in England, 1531–1665*. Aldershot, UK: Scolar Press, 1995.

Leahy, William ed. *My Shakespeare: The Authorship Controversy*. Brighton, UK: Edward Everett Root, 2018.

Leahy, William ed. *Shakespeare and His Authors: Critical Perspectives on the Authorship Question*. London: Continuum, 2010.

Lee, Sidney. *A Life of William Shakespeare*. London: Smith, Elder, 1899.

Lefranc, Abel. *Sous Le Masque de 'William Shakespeare': William Stanley, Vie Comte de Derby* (Paris: Péyot, 1918–1919). trans. by Frank Lawler. Cary, NC: Veritas Publications, 2022.

Looney, J. Thomas. *"Shakespeare" Identified*. London: Cecil Palmer, 1920.

Magri, Noemi. *Such Fruits Out of Italy: The Italian Renaissance in Shakespeare's Plays and Poems*. Buchholz, Germany: Verlag Laugwitz, 2017.

Marcus, Leah. *Puzzling Shakespeare: Local Reading and Its Discontents*. Berkeley: University of California Press, 1990.

Massey, Gerald. *The Secret Drama of Shakespeare's Sonnets*. London: Richard Clay, 1888.

Mays, Andrea. *The Millionaire and the Bard: Henry Folger's Obsessive Hunt for Shakespeare's First Folio*. New York: Simon & Schuster, 2016.

Michell, John. *Who Wrote Shakespeare?* London: Thames and Hudson, 1996.

Nelson, Alan H. *Monstrous Adversary: The Life of Edward de Vere, 17th Earl of Oxford*. Liverpool, UK: Liverpool University Press, 2003.

Nicholl, Charles. *The Reckoning: The Murder of Christopher Marlowe*. London: Jonathan Cape, 1992.

North, Marcy. *The Anonymous Renaissance: Cultures of Discretion in Tudor-Stuart England*. Chicago: University of Chicago Press, 2003.

Nuttall, A. D. *Shakespeare the Thinker*. New Haven: Yale University Press, 2007.

Ogburn, Charlton. *The Mysterious William Shakespeare: The Myth and the Reality*. New York: Dodd, Mead, 1984.

Patterson, Annabel. *Censorship and Interpretation: The Conditions of Writing and Reading in Early Modern England*. Madison: University of Wisconsin Press, 1984.

Price, Diana. *Shakespeare's Unorthodox Biography: New Evidence of an Authorship Problem*. Westport, CT: Greenwood, 2001.

Prior, Roger. "Shakespeare's Visit to Italy," *Journal of Anglo-Italian Studies* 9 (2008), 1–31.

Rackin, Phyllis. "Anonymous Was a Woman," in *Shakespeare Without Boundaries*. Edited by Christa Jansohn, Lena Cowen Orlin, and Stanley Wells. Newark: University of Delaware Press, 2010.

Richmond, Hugh. *Puritans and Liberties: Anglo-French Literary Relations in the Reformation*. Berkeley: University of California Press, 1981.

Ricks, Christopher. "The Anagram," in *Along Heroic Lines*. Oxford: Oxford University Press, 2021.

Ritchie, Fiona. *Women and Shakespeare in the Eighteenth Century*. Cambridge: Cambridge University Press, 2014.

Roe, Richard Paul. *The Shakespeare Guide to Italy: Retracing the Bard's Unknown Travels*. New York: Harper Perennial, 2011.

Rowse, A. L. *Shakespeare's Sonnets: The Problems Solved*. New York: Palgrave Macmillan, 1973.

Sawyer, Robert. *Shakespeare Between the World Wars: The Anglo-American Sphere*. New York: Macmillan, 2019.

Schoenbaum, Samuel. *Shakespeare's Lives*. Oxford: Clarendon Press, 1970.

Schoenbaum, Samuel. *William Shakespeare: A Compact Documentary Life*. New York: Oxford University Press, 1987.

Shahan, John and Alexander Waugh, ed. *Shakespeare Beyond Doubt? Exposing an Industry in Denial*. Tamarac, FL: Llumina Press, 2013.

Shapiro, James. *Contested Will: Who Wrote Shakespeare?* New York: Simon & Schuster, 2010.

Slater, Gilbert. *Seven Shakespeares: A Discussion of Various Theories with Regard to Shakespeare's Identity*. London: Cecil Palmer, 1931.

Smith, Emma. *Shakespeare's First Folio: Four Centuries of an Iconic Book*. Oxford: Oxford University Press, 2016.

Stevens, John Paul. "The Shakespeare Canon of Statutory Construction," *University of Pennsylvania Law Review* 140, no. 4 (April 1992), 1373–87.

Stritmatter, Roger. "The Marginalia of Edward de Vere's Bible: Providential Discovery, Literary Reasoning, and Historical Consequence," PhD diss. University of Massachusetts, Amherst, 2001.

Stritmatter, Roger and Lynne Kositsky, *On the Date, Sources, and Design of Shakespeare's* The Tempest. Jefferson, NC: McFarland, 2013.

Taylor, Gary. *Reinventing Shakespeare: A Cultural History from the Restoration to the Present*. Oxford: Oxford University Press, 1989.

Taylor, Gary and Gabriel Egan. *The New Oxford Shakespeare Authorship Companion*. Oxford: Oxford University Press, 2017.

Thomas, Julia. *Shakespeare's Shrine: The Bard's Birthplace and the Invention of Stratford-upon-Avon*. Philadelphia: University of Pennsylvania Press, 2012.

Traubel, Horace. *With Walt Whitman in Camden*, vol. 1. Boston: Small, Maynard & Company, 1906.

Trevor-Roper, Hugh. "What's in a Name?" *Réalités* (1962), 41–43.

Twain, Mark. *Is Shakespeare Dead?* New York: Harper & Brothers, 1909.

Varlow, Sally. *The Lady Penelope: The Lost Tale of Love and Politics in the Court of Elizabeth I*. London: Carlton, 2007.

Waller, Garry. *Mary Sidney, Countess of Pembroke: A Critical Study of Her Writings and Literary Milieu*. Salzburg, Germany: University of Salzburg Press, 1979.

Warren, James. *Shakespeare Revolutionized: The First Hundred Years of J. Thomas Looney's "Shakespeare" Identified*. Cary, NC: Veritas Publications, 2021.

Waugh, Alexander. *Fathers and Sons: The Autobiography of a Family*. New York: Broadway Books, 2004.

Wells, Stanley. *Shakespeare for All Time*. Oxford: Oxford University Press, 2002.

Wells, Stanley and Gary Taylor, eds. *The Oxford Shakespeare: The Complete Works*. Oxford: Oxford University Press, 2005.

Wells, Stanley and Paul Edmondson, eds., *Shakespeare Beyond Doubt: Evidence, Argument, Controversy*. Cambridge: Cambridge University Press, 2013.

Whitman, Walt. "What Lurks Behind Shakespeare's Historical Plays?", *November Boughs*. London: Paisley and Paternoster, Row 1889.

Williams, Robin. *Sweet Swan of Avon: Did a Woman Write Shakespeare?* Berkeley, CA: Wilton Circle Press, 2006.

Wilson, J. Dover. *The Essential Shakespeare: A Biographical Adventure*. Cambridge: Cambridge University Press, 1967.

Woods, Susanne. *Lanyer: A Renaissance Woman Poet*. Oxford: Oxford University Press, 1999.

Woolf, Virginia. *A Room of One's Own*. London: Harcourt Brace, 1929.

Woolf, Virginia. "Middlebrow," in *The Death of the Moth, and Other Essays*. London: Hogarth Press, 1947.

Index

About the Author

Elizabeth Winkler is a journalist and book critic whose work has appeared in *The Wall Street Journal*, *The New Yorker*, *The New Republic*, *The Times Literary Supplement*, and the *Economist*, among other publications. She received her undergraduate degree from Princeton University and her master's in English literature from Stanford University. Her essay "Was Shakespeare a Woman?," first published in *The Atlantic*, was selected for *The Best American Essays 2020*. She lives in Washington, DC.